the daily READER

FRED WHITE

----

366 selections of great prose
and poetry to inspire
a productive and meaningful
writing life

WRITER'S DIGEST BOOKS
Cincinnati, Ohio
www.writersdigest.com

For more resources for writers, visit www.writersdigest.com/books.

To receive a free weekly e-mail newsletter delivering tips and updates about writing and about Writer's Digest products, register directly at http://newsletters.fwpublications.com.

13 12 11 10 09   5 4 3 2 1

Distributed in Canada by Fraser Direct
100 Armstrong Avenue
Georgetown, Ontario, Canada L7G 5S4
Tel: (905) 877-4411

Distributed in the U.K. and Europe by David & Charles
Brunel House, Newton Abbot, Devon, TQ12 4PU, England
Tel: (+44) 1626-323200, Fax: (+44) 1626-323319
E-mail: postmaster@davidandcharles.co.uk

Distributed in Australia by Capricorn Link
P.O. Box 704, Windsor, NSW 2756 Australia
Tel: (02) 4577-3555

Library of Congress Cataloging-in-Publication Data
White, Fred D., 1943-
  The daily reader : 366 selections of great prose and poetry to inspire a productive and meaningful writing life / by Fred White.
     p. cm.
  ISBN 978-1-58297-589-4 (pbk. : alk. paper)
  1. College readers. 2. English language--Rhetoric--Problems, exercises, etc. 3. English language--Composition and exercises. I. Title.
  PE1417.W443 2009
  808'.0427--dc22   2009015125

Edited by Melissa Hill
Designed by Terri Woesner
Illustrations by Kate Quinby, Croak & Hum
Production Coordinated by Mark Griffin

This, too, for Therese ...
A Passionate Reader

introduction

In his *Life of Samuel Johnson* (1791), James Boswell noted, with little exaggeration, that a writer "will turn over half a library in order to make one book." To put this nugget of wisdom another way, the act of writing is the act of entering the formal (in the sense of leaving a permanent record), never-ending conversation of humankind. As is true of informal, oral conversation, the more familiar you are with what has already been discussed, the likelier your own contributions will be substantive and valued, and stimulate further conversation.

Writers, then, must be readers. They must be constant readers, passionate not only about the subjects they're interested in (which should be many), but about the act of reading itself. Reading enlarges the mind and the possibilities of language and thought. Reading takes us beyond our limited range of physical experience—enables us to journey through space and time to discover the best of what has been achieved in the arts and sciences, in history, law, politics, and commerce.

How does one even begin to choose from the millions of books that have been published since Homer first picked up a stylus or dictated to a scribe nearly three thousand years ago? You might begin by asking yourself which subjects fascinate you the most, or make your imagination soar, or help you to better cope with a complex world. These will be the subjects that will help you grow as a writer.

As a writer, you must also be an absolute sponge—a glutton—for a great many subjects, not just the ones that fascinate you the most. All knowledge is interconnected. If you want to write psychological thrillers, you should read deeply in psychology, medicine and health, anthropology, all sorts of literature (after all, literature is about the human condition, and psychology is central to human behavior), and of course, mystery and thriller fiction, if only to learn how the pros do it.

The books and occasional shorter works from which I've selected passages for your writerly reflection inevitably represent a personal choice; but I hasten to add that I am an educator, so I took pains to select works that are considered classics in their respective genres and/or disciplines. The selections are short enough to serve as a teaser—to get you to read the work in its entirety—and are just long enough for you to learn something from, whether it be a single concept from a philosophical work or a suspenseful moment from one of many suspenseful moments in a mystery or science fiction novel. Most importantly: I've selected passages that should make any writer—veteran or newbie—want to start writing. And just in case the selections themselves don't get the words gushing from your pen, I've added a reflection on the passage together with a writing prompt after each selection.

There are at least two ways to use this book: One, use it to sustain a daily writing regimen. The most important step you can take toward becoming a successful author is to cultivate the habit of writing every day. Spend three weeks with *The Daily Reader*, writing in response to three weeks' worth of prompts, and you will very likely have that precious writing habit established once and for all.

Two, flip through the book and more-or-less randomly select an entry that piques your curiosity. Read it, reflect on it, and use it as a springboard for one or two hours' worth of intensive writing. Before too long, something will start to congeal: a premise for a novel or a play, a theme for a sequence of poems. I suggest you write your exercises on loose-leaf paper and keep them organized with index tabs in a binder. Arrange and rearrange the writings as you see fit. And, just as importantly, revise them on a regular basis. Remember: Reading begets writing and writing begets even more writing, and more reading.

JANUARY 1
Male and Female:
A Study of Sexes in a Changing World
by Margaret Mead

In discussing men and women, I shall be concerned with the primary differences between them, the difference in their reproductive roles. Out of the bodies fashioned for complementary roles in perpetuating the race, what differences in functioning, in capacities, in sensitivities, in vulnerabilities arise? How is it what men can do related to the fact that their reproductive role is over in a single act, what women can do related to the fact that their reproductive role takes nine months of gestation, and until recently many months of breast feeding? What is the contribution of each sex, seen as itself, not as a mere imperfect version of the other?

FOR FURTHER REFLECTION

What can we learn about humanity through the lens of anthropology? Through her astute observation of other cultures, Margaret Mead, one of the twentieth century's greatest anthropologists, gives us a better sense of the connection between biology and destiny. In our modern technological society, for example, Mead writes, "it is easy to lose sight of the immediacy of the human body plan." In so-called primitive societies, where men, women, and children wear very little clothing, primary bodily experiences are not displaced the way they are in modern societies.

. . . . TRY THIS . . . .

Write an essay in which you speculate on the attitudes in modern urban society toward nakedness—for example, that it is shameful or prurient. Why do you suppose these attitudes are nonexistent in non-technological societies? Why do you suppose some modern people reject this attitude and join nudist colonies? After completing a draft of your essay, read more of Margaret Mead's work and then revise your essay accordingly.

"Of Water, as Painted by Turner"

by John Ruskin

from *Modern Painters*

The noblest sea that Turner has ever painted … is that of the Slave Ship, the chief Academy picture of the Exhibition of 1840. It is a sunset on the Atlantic after prolonged storm, but the storm is partially lulled, and the torn and streaming rainclouds are moving in scarlet lines to lose themselves in the hollow of the night. The whole surface of sea included in the picture is divided into two ridges of enormous swell, not high, nor local, but a low, broad heaving of the whole ocean, like the lifting of its bosom by deep-drawn breath after the torture of the storm. Between these two ridges, the fire of the sunset falls along the trough of the sea, dyeing it with an awful but glorious light, the intense and lurid splendor which burns like gold and bathes like blood. Along this fiery path and valley, the tossing waves by which the swell of the sea is restlessly divided, lift themselves in dark, indefinite, fantastic forms, each casting a faint and ghastly shadow behind it along the illumined foam. They do not rise everywhere, but three or four together in wild groups, fitfully and furiously, as the under strength of the swell compels … them, leaving between them treacherous spaces of level and whirling water, now lighted with green and lamp-like fire, now flashing back the gold of the declining sun. … Purple and blue, the lurid shadows of the hollow breakers are cast upon the mist of the night, which gathers cold and low, advancing like the shadow of death upon the guilty [slave] ship as it labours amidst the lightning of the sea, its thin masts written upon the sky in lines of blood, girded with condemnation in that fearful hue which signs the sky with horror, and mixes its flaming flood with the sunlight. …

FOR FURTHER REFLECTION

John Ruskin, the great Victorian critic of art and architecture, as well as social reformer, championed the paintings of J.M.W. Turner in his first book, *Modern Painters*, for their moral aesthetic power. Unsurpassed in his ability to translate attributes of a work of art into majestic prose, Ruskin became one of England's most influential voices in shaping aesthetic taste.

...................................TRY THIS....................................

Describe one of your favorite paintings, sculptures, or architectural structures, using minute, sensory details. Call attention to the moral as well as the aesthetic vision conveyed by the work as you perceive it.

JANUARY 3

The Dream of Spaceflight: Essays on the Near Edge of Infinity
by Wyn Wachhorst

Wriggling from his orbiting capsule for man's first walk in space, cosmonaut Alexei Leonov was born into the starry deep, floating at the end of his umbilical. All about him was a blackness so intense it seemed he could reach out and touch its texture, a darkness so deep that the hair rose on his neck and the flesh crawled on his back. Before him lay the vast curvilinear presence of planet Earth—soft, glowing, haloed against the black abyss. Leonov tumbled slowly in the windless, orderless void, hearing only the rhythms of his body, severed from the mothering Earth—who seemed at long last to have borne a space creature like herself.

FOR FURTHER REFLECTION

From the very onset of the space age—which began on October 4, 1957, when the Soviet Union launched Sputnik I, the first artificial satellite to orbit the earth—space exploration has been largely observed through the lens of international politics, which overshadows the adventure and the romance of space flight. Generally, it has been up to the science fiction visionaries to rhapsodize on the latter; but in his eloquent little book, Wyn Wachhorst, a historian, revisits the accomplishments of the space age, now over half a century old, to refocus the impact of space exploration on the human spirit.

..................................TRY THIS....................................

Imagine that you're an astronaut on a mission in earth orbit, or on a lunar or Martian expedition. In a couple of pages, describe your emotional reaction to walking on the surface of another world, or seeing the Earth from orbit or from the moon.

"The Forces of Evolution"

by Edward O. Wilson

from *The Diversity of Life*

The fundamental evolutionary event is a change in the frequency of genes and chromosome configurations in a population. If a population of butterflies shifts through time from 40 percent blue individuals to 60 percent blue individuals, and if the color blue is hereditary, evolution of a simple kind has occurred. Larger transformations are accomplished by a great many such statistical changes in combination. Shifts can occur purely in the genes, with no effect on wing color or any other outward trait. But whatever their nature or magnitude, the changes in progress are always expressed in percentages of individuals within or among populations. Evolution is absolutely a phenomenon of populations. Individuals and their immediate descendants do not evolve.

FOR FURTHER REFLECTION

Biological evolution is frequently misunderstood by the public; but in the above passage, E.O. Wilson, one the world's most distinguished environmental biologists (he is most famous for his studies of ants and the vital role they play in nature), elucidates it by locating its essential meaning in the distribution (within a given population) of a particular trait. Evolution, in other words, occurs when the distribution of a particular trait or set of physical traits (like wing color or design, or beak size or shape) changes in a statistically important way within a given species. These traits can be manipulated artificially to produce short-term evolution (better known as breeding), or long-term evolution, covering many thousands or millions of years.

...................................TRY THIS....................................

Write a dialogue scene between an evolutionary biologist and a skeptic who doesn't understand evolution or denies that it exists. The challenge here will be to present the principles of evolution so clearly, and backed with such compelling evidence, that the skeptic will come to understand.

The Library at Night
by Alberto Manguel

The power of readers lies not in their ability to gather information, in their ordering and cataloguing capability, but in their gift to interpret, associate and transform their reading. For the Talmudic schools, as for those of Islam, a scholar can turn religious faith into an active power through the craft of reading, since the knowledge acquired through books is a gift from God. According to an early *hadith*, or Islamic tradition, one scholar is more powerful against the Devil than a thousand worshippers. For these cultures of the Book, knowledge lies not in the accumulation of texts or information, nor in the object of the book itself, but in the experience rescued from the page and transformed again into experience, in the words reflected both in the outside world and in the reader's own being.

FOR FURTHER REFLECTION

To read is to exercise a very special kind of power: the power to harness understanding and thereby triumph over ignorance and superstition. There is no greater emblem of the power of reading than the library, as Alberto Manguel makes vividly clear in his book. In the Internet age, when it is all too tempting merely to access information, we must never lose sight of what it means to read deeply and well.

.................................TRY THIS...................................

Spend a few hours in your local public or college library and do two things: (1) Conduct in-depth research on a historical figure or event that interests you greatly; and (2) spend an hour or so simply browsing. Bring a notebook with you and jot down everything you discover along the way. Browsing, like directed research, is an excellent way to discover ideas for stories and essays.

Oranges
by John McPhee

The color of an orange has no absolute correlation with the maturity of the flesh and juice inside. An orange can be as sweet and ripe as it will ever be and still glisten like an emerald in the tree. Cold—coolness, rather—is what makes an orange orange. In some parts of the world, the weather never gets cold enough to change the color; in Thailand, for example, an orange is a green fruit, and traveling Thais often blink with wonder at the sight of oranges the color of flame. The ideal night-time temperature in an orange grove is forty degrees. Some of the most beautiful oranges in the world are grown in Bermuda, where the temperature, night after night, falls consistently to that level. Andrew Marvell's poem wherein the "remote Bermudas ride in the ocean's bosom unespied" was written in the sixteen fifties, and contains a description, from hearsay, of Bermuda's remarkable oranges, set against their dark foliage like "golden lamps in a green night."

FOR FURTHER REFLECTION

Who would have guessed that an entire book could be written just about oranges? McPhee, who is truly an artist of the factual, fascinates us with the culinary, agricultural, historical, as well as folkloric and mythological, aspects of the fruit, transforming what would otherwise be a totally commonplace, virtually nondescript foodstuff into an object of endless fascination.

. . . . TRY THIS . . . .

Take a "John McPhee" approach to a fruit or vegetable and find out as much about its history and lore as you can; then write an essay in which you call attention to some of these tidbits of information. Remember to include the human element.

JANUARY 7

"The Alligator on the Beach"

by Roger Osborne

from *The Floating Egg: Episodes in the Making of Geology*

In 1758 a strange event took place at Whitby. Two friends, Captain William Chapman and Mr Wooler (whose forename is lost to history) discovered some fossil bones embedded in the rock at the beach at Saltwick. They removed the bones and were able to identify them as the fossilised remains of the skeleton of an alligator. Remarkable though this was, the peculiarity of the event did not lie in the discovery itself—fossil bones must have been found on this coast for as long as the area was inhabited. But what happened next signified a change in the relations of the human mind to the natural world. Whereas previously the two men might have kept some bones as souvenirs and perhaps showed them to a few friends, now they did something else. They each wrote a formal report of their find … with the intention … that these should be published in the *Philosophical Transactions* of the Royal Society. This monthly journal published a form for the exchange of information and ideas on all aspects of natural history. It was the original scientific journal and without it science would simply never have been able to develop in the way that it has.

FOR FURTHER REFLECTION

We sometimes overlook the fact that science consists not only of discovery and experimentation, but of writing—reporting and interpreting one's findings. As the British science writer Roger Osborne makes clear, writing can actually bring a discipline into its own, as was the case with paleontology.

. . . . TRY THIS . . . .

Write an article in which you discuss the role that good writing plays in conveying ideas in geology or paleontology. Possible points to consider: how science writers generate fascination about dinosaurs; best approaches to communicating concepts of geological time; the process of fossilization.

Alexandria: City of the Western Mind
by Theodore Vrettos

Within a century after Alexandria was built [in the fourth century B.C.E.], it was larger than Carthage and growing so swiftly that it acknowledged no superior, even Rome. It had already become the center not only of Hellenism, but also of Judaism. Its Mouseion was the leading university of its time—the finest teachers, philosophers, and scientists flourished within its walls. Here ancient scholars produced the Septuagint (Greek translation of the Hebrew Old Testament), and on these streets Julius Caesar would stroll with Cleopatra to the wild cheers of the populace. ...

By the early part of the first century [B.C.E.], the city had grown so rapidly that travelers and historians overwhelmingly agreed she was the greatest city of the civilized world and surpassed all others in size, elegance, and luxury.

FOR FURTHER REFLECTION

One of the greatest pleasures of reading is to be able to vicariously experience what life was like in a long-ago and faraway place. Works of history may offer a few sensory impressions of the places they describe, but their job is mainly to paint the big picture, the causes and effects. Re-creating the sensory impressions associated with daily life, however, is the job of the historical novelist, extrapolating from the details provided by the historian. After reading Vrettos's history of Alexandria, you will have acquired a keen understanding of what took place there over the centuries, how the city was organized, and the people who lived and worked there—basic preparation for writing a story that takes place in this marvelous city.

......................................TRY THIS....................................

Describe a scene based on Vrettos's reference to Julius Caesar strolling with Cleopatra through the streets of Alexandria. Bring the scene to life by describing the citizens lining the streets to catch a glimpse of these legendary leaders. Try to capture as many sensory impressions as possible to give your readers the sensation of being there.

JANUARY 9
"Madame Eglentyne"
by Eileen Power
from *Medieval People*

Let us see what light the [bishops'] registers will throw upon Madame Eglentyne, before Chaucer observed her mounting her horse outside the Tabard Inn. Doubtless she first came to the nunnery when she was quite a little girl, because girls counted as grown up when they were fifteen in the Middle Ages; they could be married out of hand at twelve, and they could become nuns for ever at fourteen. Probably Eglentyne's father had three other daughters to marry, each with a dowry, and a gay young spark of a son, who spent a lot of money on fashionable suits. ... So he thought he had better settle the youngest at once, and he got together a dowry (it was rarely possible to get into a nunnery without one, though Church law really forbade anything except voluntary offerings), and, taking Eglentyne by the hand one summer day, he popped her into a nunnery a few miles off, which had been founded by his ancestors. ... Eglentyne would have to remain a novice for some years, until she was old enough to take the vows. So she would stay in the convent and be taught how to sing and to read, and to talk French ... with the other novices. ... The great purpose for which the nunneries existed ... was the praise of God. Eglentyne spent a great deal of her time singing and praying in the convent church.

FOR FURTHER REFLECTION
People are what bring a historical period to life. As Emerson wrote, "There is properly no history; only biography." By consulting such documents as bishops' registers, letters, and diaries, Eileen Power enables us to envision Chaucer's vivacious prioress in clearer historical context.

...................................TRY THIS....................................

Write a short story in which Madame Eglentyne is a central character. You may first want to read Chaucer's portrait of her in the General Prologue to the *Canterbury Tales*, as well as read more about women's lives in the Middle Ages.

JANUARY 10

"Theodore Roosevelt and the Panama Canal"
by Paul Johnson

from *A History of the American People*

Theodore Roosevelt's most notable achievement, in some ways, was to push through the Panama Canal. That meant softening up with cash the corrupt and venal government of Colombia, which owned the Panama Isthmus. Under the Hay-Herran Treaty of 1903, America was to build the canal and pay Colombia $10 million down and an annual rental of $250,000. The Colombian government, to the fury of TR, upped its demand to $25 million. Unwilling to be hornswoggled by what he called ... 'the foolish and homicidal corruptionists of Bogata,' TR connived at a local conspiracy to set up a separate state of Panama, recognized by his government in November 1903. A new treaty was put through immediately with the Panamanian government, on the same financial terms, but which extended the width of the Canal Zone from 6 to 10 miles and gave the United States 'in perpetuity, the use, occupation and control' of it.

FOR FURTHER REFLECTION

History might be thought of as a lens that brings events into sharp focus, and the sharper the focus, the messier the events become. What in, say, an almanac might be described as a simple event about the Panama Canal—that it began in 1903 and took thirty-five years to complete—becomes a complicated political intrigue when historians like Paul Johnson examine the event in minute detail.

.... TRY THIS ....

Think of a well-known event in world history—e.g., the building of the Great Wall of China, the trial of Socrates, the English Civil War, the battle of Little Big Horn, the Teapot Dome Scandal—and write an essay that emphasizes the little-known behind-the-scenes events that bring to light the big picture.

JANUARY 11
"Apollo and Daphne" by Ovid

from *Metamorphoses*, Bk. I. Translated by Horace Gregory

So did Apollo's heart break into flames,
The sterile fires that feed on empty hopes.
And while he gazed at Daphne's floating hair
That fell in tendrils at her throat and
forehead
He thought, "What if that fair head wore
a crown?"
He looked into her eyes and saw the stars.
Though staring does not satisfy desire,
His eyes praised all they saw—her lips,
her fingers,
Her hands, her naked arms from wrist
to shoulder;
And what they did not see he thought
the best.
Yet she ran from him swifter than light air
That turns to nothingness as we pursue it,
Nor did she stop to hear Apollo calling:
"O daughter of the deep green-shadowed
River,
Who follows you is not your enemy.
...
The god by grace of hope, the girl, despair,
Still kept their increasing pace until
his lips

Breathed at her shoulder; and almost spent,
The girl saw waves of a familiar river,
Her father's home, and in a trembling voice
Called, "Father, if your waters still hold
charms
To save your daughter, cover with green
earth
The body I wear too well," and as she spoke
A soaring drowsiness possessed her;
growing
In earth she stood, white thighs embraced
by climbing
Bark, her white arms branches, her fair
head swaying
In a cloud of leaves; all that was Daphne
bowed
In the stirring of the wind, the glittering
green
Leaf twined within her hair and she
was laurel.
Even now Phoebus embraced the
lovely tree
Whose heart he felt still beating in its side;
He stroked its branches, kissed the
sprouting bark.

FOR FURTHER REFLECTION

Ovid was one of the most popular and controversial Roman poets. Emperor Augustus accused Ovid of corrupting youth, sending him into permanent exile and burning his manuscripts. Ovid's great poem retells the Greek myths. In the story of how Apollo strove to subdue Daphne, Ovid captures the intensity of the sun god's love of the mortal girl, whose beauty rivaled nature—indeed, who literally is transformed into a tree in order to escape the god's sexual advances.

.....................................TRY THIS.....................................

Write your own prose or poetic rendering of the Apollo-Daphne story. For example, you might make Apollo a prince and Daphne a peasant girl possessing magical powers.

JANUARY 12

"General Prologue" by Geoffrey Chaucer

from *The Canterbury Tales*

[Original Middle English]	[Modern English version by Fred White]
Ye goon to Caunterbury—God yow speede	You're on your way to Canterbury—
The blissful martir quite yow youre meede!	God speed!
And wel I woot, as ye goon by the weye,	May the blessed martyr reward you!
Ye shapen yow to talen and to playe;	And well I know, as you make your
For trewely, confort ne myrthe is noon	way there,
To ride by the waye doumb as a stoon;	You'll tell stories and have a good time;
And therefore wol I maken yow disport,	For truly, there can be no comfort or mirth
As I seyde erst, and doon yow som confort.	To ride along dumb as a stone;
...	And therefore I'll make for you a pastime,
This is the point, to speken short and pleyn,	As I said before, to give you some comfort.
That ech of yow, to shorte with oure weye,	...
In this viage shall tell tales tweye	This is the point, to speak concisely
To Caunterbury-ward, I mene it so,	and plainly,
And homeward he shall tellen othere two,	So each of you, to make the way
Of aventures that whilom han bifalle.	seem shorter,
And which of yow that bereth	Shall tell each tell two stories, one
hym best of alle,	On the way to Canterbury—I mean it—
That is to seyn, that telleth in this caas	And the other two on the way home,
Tales of best sentence and moost solaas,	Of adventures that have befallen him.
Shal have a soper at our aller cost ...	And whoever tells his story best of all,
	That is to say, whoever tells in this case
	Tales that are the wisest and
	most entertaining,
	Shall be given a dinner at our cost ...

FOR FURTHER REFLECTION

The Canterbury Tales is a high-spirited (in all senses of *spirited*!) celebration of life in all of its guises. As the pilgrims make their way from London to Canterbury to pay homage to Thomas Becket, each tells a story that is at once entertaining and morally instructive. So well do these tales achieve their dual purpose that the work seems to be celebrating the power of storytelling itself, and the role that storytelling plays in actually shaping and defining our lives, not merely serving as a diversion or entertainments.

...................................TRY THIS....................................

Write a frame story in which you bring several persons (the more diverse the better!) together for a common purpose—to make a modern-day pilgrimage.

"An Essay on Criticism" by Alexander Pope

Of all the causes which conspire to blind
Man's erring judgment, and
      misguide the mind,
What the weak head with
      strongest bias rules
Is pride, the never-failing vice of fools.
Whatever Nature has in worth deny'd,
She gives in large recruits of needful pride;
For as in bodies, thus in souls, we find
What wants in blood and spir-
      its, swell'd with wind:
Pride, where wit fails, steps
      in to our defence,
And fills up all the mighty void of sense.
If once right reason drives that cloud away,
Truth breaks upon us with resistless day.
Trust not yourself; but your defects to know,
Make use of ev'ry friend—and ev'ry foe.
A little learning is a dang'rous thing;
Drink deep, or taste not the Pierian spring:
There shallow draughts in-
      toxicate the brain,
And drinking largely sobers us again.
Fir'd at first sight with what
      the Muse imparts,

In fearless youth we tempt
      the heights of arts,
While from the bounded level of our mind,
Short views we take, nor see
      the lengths behind;
But more advanc'd, behold
      with strange surprise
New distant scenes of endless science rise!
So please'd at first the tow'ring Alps we try,
Mount o'er the vales, and seem
      to tread the sky;
Th' eternal snows appear already past,
And the first clouds and moun-
      tains seem the last;
But, those attain'd, we tremble to survey
The growing labours of the lengthen'd way,
Th' increasing prospect tires
      our wand'ring eyes,
Hills peep o'er hills, and
      Alps on Alps arise!
A perfect judge will read each work of wit
With the same spirit that its author writ:
Survey the whole, nor seek
      slight faults to find
Where nature moves, and rapture
      warms the mind.

FOR FURTHER REFLECTION

The Age of Enlightenment witnessed the rise of modern science, of democratic rule, and the re-evaluation of humanity's relationship to nature. The arts were regarded as vehicles for transmitting Enlightenment ideas most effectively. Alexander Pope brilliantly captures these ideals while at the same time lampooning misguided views. We call his poetry didactic: It conveys insightful truths about human nature, but in a manner (e.g., the poetic form known as heroic couplets, adapted from ancient Greek epic poetry) that delights us with its cleverness and satiric bite.

. . . . TRY THIS. . . . .

Take an adage such as "Two wrongs don't make a right," and develop the adage into a poetic meditation, making use of imaginative analogies and concrete examples.

A Connecticut Yankee in King Arthur's Court

by Mark Twain

Mainly the Round Table talk was monologues—narrative accounts of the adventures in which ... prisoners were captured and their friends and backers killed and stripped of their steeds and armor. As a general thing—as far as I could make out—these murderous adventures were not forays undertaken to avenge injuries, nor to settle old disputes or sudden fallings out; no, as a rule they were simply duels between strangers—duels between people who had never even been introduced to each other, and between whom existed no cause of offense whatsoever. Many a time I had seen a couple of boys, strangers, meet by chance, and say simultaneously, "I can lick you," and go at it on the spot; but I had always imagined until now, that that sort of thing belonged to children only, and was a sign and mark of childhood; but here were these big boobies sticking to it and taking pride in it clear up into full age and beyond. Yet there was something very engaging about these great simple-hearted creatures, something attractive and lovable. There did not seem to be brains enough in the entire nursery, so to speak, to bait a fish-hook with, but you didn't seem to mind that, after a little, because you soon saw that brains were not needed in a society like that, and, indeed would have marred it, hindered it, spoiled its symmetry—perhaps rendered its existence impossible.

FOR FURTHER REFLECTION

By placing his no-nonsense protagonist, Hank Morgan, in sixth-century England, Mark Twain gave himself the ideal opportunity to poke fun not only at medieval-minded ideas (like monarchy, superstition, and ostentation), but (a little less obviously) on modern-day (i.e., nineteenth-century) progressivism and industrialism as well. Along the way, readers have great fun enjoying the juxtaposition of two very different world views thirteen centuries apart, and the comic mayhem Morgan causes when he imposes his pragmatic ideals on a society swayed by pageantry, magic, and the divine right of kings.

......................................TRY THIS....................................

Write a story in which individuals from two vastly different cultures or time-periods come together. You might present it as a time-travel story similar to Twain's, or you might simply draw from history—the Spanish Conquistadors' confrontation with the Aztecs, for example.

"The Sound of Trees"
by Robert Frost

from *Mountain Interval* and *The Poetry of Robert Frost*

I wonder about the trees.
Why do we wish to bear
Forever the noise of these
More than another noise
So close to our dwelling place?
We suffer them by the day
Till we lose all measure of pace,
And fixity in our joys,
And acquire a listening air.
They are that that talks of going
But never gets away;
And that talks no less for knowing,
As it grows wiser and older,

That now it means to stay.
My feet tug at the floor
And my head sways to my shoulder
Sometimes when I watch trees sway,
From the window or the door.
I shall set forth for somewhere,
I shall make the reckless choice
Some day when they are in voice
And tossing so as to scare
The white clouds over them on.
I shall have less to say,
But I shall be gone.

FOR FURTHER REFLECTION

One of the best loved of modern poets, Robert Frost (1874–1963) is sometimes thought of as a poet of nature—which is true, but not in the romantic sense of the word. For Frost, nature holds profound and often disturbing mysteries of which we can only catch fleeting glimpses. The result, as with "The Sound of Trees," is a poetry that poses questions without clear answers; a poetry that tends to leave us more in the dark than before. Like us, trees grow old; but unlike us, they are more clearly rooted in nature and a part of the forces of nature. As we pass into oblivion, they remain.

. . . . TRY THIS . . . .

Try your hand at a poem that describes an object of nature such as a tree, a flower, a mountain, a river, or a waterfall—and use it as a springboard for contemplating the mysteries of being that it conjures up for you.

"The Surgeon as Priest"

by Richard Selzer

from *Mortal Lessons: Notes on the Art of Surgery*

One enters the body in surgery, as in love, as though one were an exile returning at last to his hearth, daring uncharted darkness in order to reach home. Turn sideways, if you will, and slip with me into the cleft I have made. Do not fear the yellow meadows of fat, the red that sweats and trickles where you step. Here, give me your hand. Lower between the beefy cliffs. Now rest a bit upon the peritoneum. All at once, gleaming, the membrane parts ... and you are *in*.

It is the stillest place that ever was. As though suddenly you are struck deaf. ... This is no silence of the vacant stratosphere, but the awful quiet of ruins, of rainbows, full of expectation and holy dread. Soon you shall know surgery as a Mass served with Body and Blood, wherein disease is assailed as though it were sin.

Touch the great artery. Feel it bound like a deer in the might of its lightness, and know the thunderless boil of the blood. Lean for a bit against this bone. It is the only memento you will leave to the earth.

FOR FURTHER REFLECTION

A retired surgeon and professor of surgery with the Yale School of Medicine, Richard Selzer has also distinguished himself as an essayist who initiates the reader into the operating room and the physician's daily routines. What enables laypersons to comprehend a practice that would otherwise be too technical or arcane are the startling metaphors—the uncharted darkness of the body's interior; the yellow meadows of fat, and so forth. Metaphorical language enables us to understand and appreciate those specialized areas of human endeavor that would otherwise be lost to us.

.................................TRY THIS....................................

All of us have acquired a certain degree of medical knowledge, if only through our regular visits with our physicians, our illnesses, our medications. Write an essay about one such medical experience, engaging the reader with metaphorical language where appropriate.

Hunger of Memory:
The Education of Richard Rodriguez
by Richard Rodriguez

The bilingualists insist that a student should be reminded of his differences from others in mass society, his heritage. But they equate mere separateness with individuality. The fact is that only in private—with intimates—is separateness from the crowd a prerequisite for individuality. ... In public, by contrast, full individuality is achieved, paradoxically, by those who are able to consider themselves members of the crowd. Thus it happened for me: Only when I was able to think of myself as an American, no longer an alien in *gringo* society, could I seek the rights and opportunities necessary for full public individuality.

FOR FURTHER REFLECTION

One of the most debated topics in American education today is over the manner of teaching English as a second language: Should teachers take a bilingual approach or an English-only (immersion) approach? Is it possible to have both at once (bilingual *and* immersion)? The arguments are compelling for each model.

. . . . TRY THIS . . . .

1. Write a story in which your protagonist is an adolescent or young adult whose native language is not English, who does not know a word of English, and whose most promising job prospect requires that he be proficient (if not completely fluent) in English.

2. What approach to teaching English as a second language do you advocate? Defend your approach in a persuasive essay.

A Thief of Time

by Tony Hillerman

The moon lit only part of the [canyon] wall, and the slanting light made it difficult to see, but she [anthropologist Dr. Eleanor Friedman-Bernal] stopped to inspect it. In this light, the tapered, huge-shouldered shape of the mystic Anasazi shaman lost its color and became merely a dark form. Above it a clutter of shapes danced, stick figures, abstractions: the inevitable Kokopelli, his humped shape bent, his flute pointed almost at the ground … the zigzag band of pigment representing a snake. Then she noticed the horse. … A Navajo addition, obviously, since the Anasazi had vanished three hundred years before the Spanish came on their steeds. It was a stylized horse, with a barrel body and straight legs. … The rider seemed to be a Kokopelli—Watersprinkler, the Navajos called him. At least the rider seemed to be blowing a flute. Had this addition been there before? She couldn't remember. Such Navajo additions weren't uncommon. But this one puzzled her. Then she noticed, at each of the three feet of the animal, a tiny prone figure. Three. Each with the little circle representing the head separated from the body. Each with one leg cut away.

Sick. And they hadn't been here four years ago. These she would have remembered.

For the first time [she] became aware of the darkness, the silence, her total isolation. She had dropped her backpack while she rested. Now she picked it up, put an arm through the carry strap, changed her mind. She unzipped a side pocket and extracted the pistol.

FOR FURTHER REFLECTION

Some of the most enjoyable mysteries published are set in a specific historical-cultural context, be it ancient Rome during the time of Julius Caesar, England during the reign of Henry VIII, or—in the case of a Tony Hillerman novel—the American Southwest of the present day. Readers not only become absorbed in a baffling murder mystery, they also learn a great deal about the period, as in this case, American Indian archaeology, spirituality, and folklore.

. . . . .TRY THIS. . . . .

Your first step for writing a mystery with a historical setting is to write a two-page detailed description of the setting in which your story will unfold, drawing from your own experiences. Let your descriptions evoke the mood and more than one of the senses—not just sights.

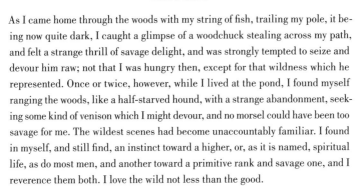

JANUARY 19
"Higher Laws"
by Henry David Thoreau
from *Walden*

As I came home through the woods with my string of fish, trailing my pole, it being now quite dark, I caught a glimpse of a woodchuck stealing across my path, and felt a strange thrill of savage delight, and was strongly tempted to seize and devour him raw; not that I was hungry then, except for that wildness which he represented. Once or twice, however, while I lived at the pond, I found myself ranging the woods, like a half-starved hound, with a strange abandonment, seeking some kind of venison which I might devour, and no morsel could have been too savage for me. The wildest scenes had become unaccountably familiar. I found in myself, and still find, an instinct toward a higher, or, as it is named, spiritual life, as do most men, and another toward a primitive rank and savage one, and I reverence them both. I love the wild not less than the good.

FOR FURTHER REFLECTION

Walden is not just a nature book or memoir or philosophical treatise, but an endlessly fascinating synthesis of all three. After sharing his ideas of simplicity, of living "deliberately as nature," and explaining why he thinks "the mass of men lead lives of quiet desperation," Thoreau surveys his own (and by extension our own) psychic landscape, where morality and instinct collide. Human civilization, we learn from Freud, endures as a result of the struggle between the desire to satisfy basic human needs, including the gratification of various appetites, and the need to live rational, principled, organized lives.

..................................TRY THIS...................................

In a short story, dramatize a situation in which your protagonist must find a way to reconcile his or her need to fulfill basic desires and the need to find moral centeredness. Give your story either a rural or urban setting—past, present, or future.

Symposium
by Plato

from *Great Dialogues of Plato*. Translated by W.H.D. Rouse

[Socrates conveying Diotima's notions of love]

"The right way to approach the things of love, or to be led there by another, is this: beginning from these beautiful things, to mount for that beauty's sake ever upwards, as by a flight of steps, from one to two, and from two to all beautiful bodies, and from beautiful bodies to beautiful pursuits and practices, and from practices to beautiful learnings, so that from learnings he may come at last to that perfect learning which is the learning solely of that beauty itself, and may know at last that which is the perfection of beauty. 'There in life and there alone, my dear Socrates,' said the inspired woman, 'is life worth living for man, while he contemplates Beauty itself.'"

FOR FURTHER REFLECTION

It is often thought that Platonic love means idealized love, free of bodily pleasures, but that is not quite true. For Plato (conveying the ideas of his mentor Socrates), physical love—Eros—was just as important as ideal love in the pursuit of beauty and wisdom, in that one could not progress toward the ideal without it. It is a way of saying that unless we have bodies, we cannot engage in intellectual and spiritual pursuits.

..............................TRY THIS..................................

Create a dialogue among three or more individuals, each of whom possesses a different view of love. For example, one person might insist that sexual desire must be unrestrained for society to be healthy, while another person insists that society is healthiest when sexual desire is successfully rechanneled, say into athletics or game-playing.

The Universe and Dr. Einstein[*]
by Lincoln Barnett

Since the mass of a moving body increases as its motion increases, and since motion is a form of energy (kinetic energy), then the increased mass of a moving body comes from its increased energy. In short, energy has mass! ... This extraordinary relationship becomes more vivid when its terms are translated into concrete values: i.e., one kilogram of coal (about two pounds), if converted entirely into energy, would yield 25 billion kilowatt hours of electricity, or as much as all the power plants in the U.S. could generate by running steadily for two months.

$E = mc^2$ provides the answer to many of the long-standing mysteries of physics. It explains how radioactive substances like radium and uranium are able to eject particles at enormous velocities and go on doing so for millions of years. It explains how the sun and all the stars can go on radiating light and heat for billions of years; for if our sun were being consumed by ordinary processes of combustion, the earth would have died in frozen darkness eons ago.

FOR FURTHER REFLECTION

Einstein's 1905 paper describing the relationship between matter and energy— of demonstrating how matter and energy are manifestations of each other relative to a particular frame of reference plotted in four dimensions (the fourth being that of time)—revolutionized physics and our understanding of the basic forces of nature. It also showed that states of movement or rest were relative to a given frame of reference (e.g., you may be sitting still relative to the Earth; but relative to, say, the moon, you're rotating with the earth at 1,000 mph; and relative to the sun, you (along with the Earth and the moon) are revolving around the sun at 66,000 mph.

................................TRY THIS....................................

Write an explanation of Einstein's Theory of Relativity that a fifth-grade child could understand. What metaphors or analogies can you produce that would help young people in this age group comprehend this somewhat counter-intuitive concept?

---

[*] For another entry on Einstein, see the entry for April 17.

The Age of American Unreason
by Susan Jacoby

Free inquiry and the diffusion of knowledge—inevitably involving more education for more people—have always been the secular rays of hope in every vision of America's future, but they will not suffice in an era when, despite the steady rise in the formal educational level of the population, so many Americans seem to know less and less. Science—how deep a faith it inspired in the Enlightenment rationalists of America's founding generation and their freethinking later nineteenth-century heirs!—can by itself provide no remedy for those who, out of ignorance or in servitude to an anti-rational form of faith, know little and care less about the basic principles that constitute the scientific method. Technology, our servant, has also become our master, as the information highway—potentially the greatest tool for the diffusion of learning ever devised—has, for too many, become a highway to the far-flung regions of junk thought.

FOR FURTHER REFLECTION

Building upon Richard Hofstadter's study, *Anti-Intellectualism in American Life* (1963), Susan Jacoby examines the climate of learning in the United States today, and is disturbed not only by the way in which new technologies emphasize rapid information access at the expense of more time-consuming deep learning, but by the way in which "junk thought" (ideas bred by people's unwillingness to separate fact from opinion, or by their insistence that all opinions have equal validity) takes precedence over in-depth empirical investigation—a legacy of intellectual pursuit upon which America was founded.

.................................TRY THIS....................................

Write an essay in which you reflect on the influence of digital information access upon people's reading and thinking habits. Does accessing information through the Internet, for example, help or hinder deep learning? Why?

JANUARY 23
The Interpretation of Dreams
by Sigmund Freud
Translated by James Strachey

In the pages that follow I shall bring forward proof that there is a psychological technique which makes it possible to interpret dreams, and that, if the procedure is employed, every dream reveals itself as a psychical structure which has a meaning and which can be inserted at an assignable point in the mental activities of waking life. I shall further endeavour to elucidate the processes to which the strangeness and obscurity of dreams are due and to deduce from those processes the nature of the psychical forces by whose concurrent or mutually opposing action dreams are generated.

FOR FURTHER REFLECTION

Dreams have always played an important role; in the ancient world, soothsayers regarded dreams as portents and made predictions based on what they seemed to signify, in a way not unlike that of astrologers preparing horoscopes. But it wasn't until the dawn of the twentieth century that Sigmund Freud demonstrated, in his monumental work, *The Interpretation of Dreams*, that dreams were the surface manifestation of deep subconscious anxieties and yearnings. What seemed like gibberish on the surface proved to be a kind of psychic code, a set of disguised, symbolic images and actions that played out forbidden desires and fears in a way that the mind's censorious superego could tolerate.

....TRY THIS....................................

Write a story in which your central character is haunted by a recurring dream. Show him or her struggling to make sense of the dream (perhaps with a psychiatrist's help) in order to get to the root of a deep psychological affliction. You might want to see Alfred Hitchcock's 1945 masterpiece, *Spellbound* (Gregory Peck and Ingrid Bergman), to get an idea of how one such scenario is played out.

JANUARY 24
Blue Highways: A Journey Into America
by William Least Heat Moon

Highway 89 wound among the volcanic dumpings from Lassen that blasted Hat Creek valley about three hundred times between 1914 and 1917. Scrub covered the ash, cinders, and lava as the wasteland renewed itself; yet even still it looked terribly crippled. Off the valley floor, California 299 climbed to ride the rim of the Pit River gorge. I ate a sandwich at the edge of a deep rift that opened like jaws to expose rocks so far below they were several hundred million years older than the ones I sat on. From the high edge I looked down on the glossy backs of swallows as they glided a thousand feet, closed their wings like folded fans, and plummeted into the abyss. It was a wild, mad, silent, spectacular descent of green iridescence that left me woozy.

Again on the road, I drove up a lumpy, dry plateau, all the while thinking of the errors that had led me to Hat Creek. The word error comes from a Middle English word, *erren*, which means "to wander about," as in the knight errant. The word evolved to mean "going astray" and that evolved to mean "mistake." ... Yesterday, I had been mistaken and in error, taking one wrong road after another. As a result, I had come to a place of clear beauty.

FOR FURTHER REFLECTION
The title of William Least Heat Moon's travel memoir refers to the two-lane highways that are represented as thin blue lines on road maps; they are the back roads of America, overshadowed by the freeways and interstate highways. To travel these blue roads, though, is to rediscover many of the natural wonders of America, as well as the charm and "true grit" of American culture that refuses to modernize, to be influenced by new technologies and fads.

......................................TRY THIS....................................

Take a blue-highway trip in your state and keep detailed journal notes of what you encounter—forgotten landmarks, farms, small-town shops and activities. Later, consider working some of your notes into a travel essay.

The Art of Pilgrimage: The Seeker's Guide to Making Travel Sacred

by Phil Cousineau

The pilgrim's motives have always been manifold: to pay homage, to fulfill a vow or obligation, to do penance, to be rejuvenated spiritually, or to feel the release of catharsis. The journeys all begin in a restive state, in deep disturbance. Something vital was missing in life: Vitality itself may be lurking on the road or at the heart of a distant sanctuary.

The ritual act of pilgrimage attempts to fill that emptiness. It can happen halfway around the world ... [or] just down the road. ... Participation can be communal ... or it may be solitary. ... What unites the different forms of pilgrimage is intensity of intention, the soul's desire to return to the center, whether it portends ecstasy or agony.

FOR FURTHER REFLECTION

The need for spiritual fulfillment is a basic need for most of us, and one especially effective way of replenishing the spirit is to take a journey to a sacred place—a city, a monument, a cathedral, a mountain or valley. As the title of Cousineau's book indicates, pilgrimage is an *art*, requiring thoughtful preparation, such as reading deeply about the site to be visited.

.... TRY THIS ....

Here is a four-part writing task. First, write a journal entry in which you describe the sacred place you wish to visit on pilgrimage. Include your reasons for wanting to visit there. Next, maintain a detailed pilgrimage journal, making sure you record your thoughts and observations en route. Third, describe the sacred site as you experience it directly. Finally, when you return, write an essay on the spiritual fulfillment you derived from your pilgrimage.

Gulliver's Travels
by Jonathan Swift

I was alarmed at midnight with the cries of many hundred people [Lilliputians] at my door; by which, suddenly awaked, I was in some kind of terror. ... Several of the Emperor's court making their way through the crowd, intreated me to come immediately to the palace, where her Imperial Majesty's apartment was on fire, by the carelessness of a maid of honour, who fell asleep while she was reading a romance. I got up in an instant; and orders being given to clear the way before me, and it being likewise a moonshine night, I made a shift to get to the palace without trampling on any of the people. I found they had already applied ladders to the walls of the apartment, and were well provided with buckets, but the water was at some distance. These buckets were about the size of a large thimble, and the poor people supplied me with them as fast as they could; but the flame was so violent that they did little good. I might easily have stifled it with my coat, which I unfortunately left behind me for haste, and came away only in my leathern jerkin. The case seemed wholly desperate and deplorable, and this magnificent palace would have infallibly been burnt down to the ground, if, by a presence of mind, unusual to me, I had not suddenly thought of an expedient. I had the evening before drank plentifully of a most delicious wine. ... By the luckiest chance in the world, I had not discharged myself of any part of it.

FOR FURTHER REFLECTION

A master satirist, Swift is able to lampoon his target by employing formal deadpan diction (as if the events he narrates make the most logical sense—and they do, actually, once we are able to suspend disbelief and accept the circumstances at hand), in this case Lemuel Gulliver's visit to a land (called Lilliput) whose inhabitants are human in every way except for their size: They're only six inches tall. By reducing people to such minuscule proportions, the pomp and circumstance of monarchy, the folly of war, pride and arrogance and such are given a startling new perspective.

...................................TRY THIS...................................

Try your hand at satire by writing a story in which you call attention to some human folly by approaching it from an unusual perspective. For example, write about a wine-tasting event by exaggerating the way in which the tasters describe the different varieties of wines.

2001: A Space Odyssey
by Arthur C. Clarke

[Moon-Watcher] sat up in the fetid darkness of the cave, straining his senses out into the night, and fear crept slowly into his soul. Never in his life—already twice as long as most members of his species could expect—had he heard a sound like this. The great cats approached in silence, and the only thing that betrayed them was a rare slide of earth, or the occasional crackling of a twig. Yet this was a continuous crunching noise that grew steadily louder. It seemed that some enormous beast was moving through the night, making no attempt at concealment, and ignoring all obstacles. Once Moon-Watcher heard the unmistakable sound of a bush being uprooted; the elephants and dinotheria did this often enough, but otherwise they moved as silently as the cats.

And then there came a sound which Moon-Watcher could not possibly have identified, for it had never been heard before in the history of the world. It was the clunk of metal upon stone.

FOR FURTHER REFLECTION

In his novel *2001: A Space Odyssey* (written while collaborating with Stanley Kubrick on the screenplay for the film—a work that many consider the crowning achievement of a distinguished career in science fiction), Arthur C. Clarke (1917–2008) envisions alien beings, unimaginably more advanced than us, influencing human evolution at crucial junctures. The first juncture occurs when a prehominid species begins to show signs of abstract thinking and the capacity for tool-making—and Moon-Watcher is among the most promising individuals; it is because of his signs of promise that the aliens, via the mysterious monolith, give him just the right nudge to take him and his fellow man-apes to the next stage: learning to use animal bones as both tools and weapons—the birth of human reason as well as of technology.

............................TRY THIS....................

1. Work out a plotline for a story in which alien beings come to earth and masquerade as human schoolteachers. What kind of influence would they exert on their students? What would be the consequence of that influence?

2. What would intelligent life be like elsewhere in the universe? Describe your vision in a speculative essay.

JANUARY 28

"The Fall of the House of Usher"
by Edgar Allan Poe

from *Tales* and *The Selected Poetry and Prose of Edgar Allan Poe*

[Roderick Usher] was enchained by certain superstitious impressions in regard to the dwelling which he tenanted, and whence, for many years, he had never ventured forth ... an effect which the *physique* of the gray walls and turrets, and of the dim tarn into which they all looked down, had, at length, brought about upon the *morale* of his existence.

He admitted, however, although with hesitation, that much of the peculiar gloom which thus afflicted him could be traced to a more natural and far more palpable origin—to the severe and long-continued illness—indeed to the evidently approaching dissolution—of a tenderly beloved sister—his sole companion for long years—his last and only relative on earth. ... While he spoke, the lady Madeline (for so was she called) passed slowly through a remote portion of the apartment, and, without having noticed my presence, disappeared. I regarded her with an utter astonishment not unmingled with dread. ... A sensation of stupor oppressed me, as my eyes followed her retreating steps.

FOR FURTHER REFLECTION

Poe's genius lay in his ability not only to quickly immerse the reader in Gothic gloom and unsettling strangeness, but to make it all seem real; for Poe was a master of what he called tales of ratiocination, in which exposition and precise descriptive detail are combined, as in a scientific treatise. "The Fall of the House of Usher" is a marvelous example of such a tale: We become so immersed in the gloom and foreboding of Roderick Usher's house that we are convinced of its authenticity. In such a milieu, characters, no matter how grotesque, feel like real people.

.....................................TRY THIS.....................................

Work up a mood-inspiring description of a setting for one of your stories in progress. Decide beforehand what specific kind of mood you want to evoke. A gauzy, dreamy mood for a romance? A dark, oppressive mood for a ghost story or psychological thriller?

JANUARY 29

Labyrinths of Iron: Subways in History, Myth, Art, Technology & War
by Benson Bobrick

One afternoon in the fall of 1816, a French émigré engineer, Marc Isambard Brunel, was at work installing a sawmill at Chatham dockyard in England when he came upon a fragment of keel timber deeply pierced with holes. Worm-eaten timber was a common dockyard sight. ... Nevertheless, he paused and picked it up. Within he could see the notorious shipworm, *teredo navalis*—*calamitas patrium*, Linnaeus had called it, because of all the vessels it had sunk—still indefatigably at work. Admiringly, he noted the shell-shielded structure of the head, with its two serrated edges like files, grinding casually through the hard oak, while the soft transparent body smoothly lined the surrounding passageway with a shell-like secretion of lime. For a moment he stood as if transfixed, as an idea began to take shape in his mind that would revolutionize the history of tunneling and prepare the way for the subways of the modern world.

FOR FURTHER REFLECTION
The history of science and technology is filled with the type of creative thinking exemplified by Brunel's insight (triggered by his close observation of a shipworm) into industrial tunneling. Combined with mechanical savvy—how does one go about building a *machine* that can cut through miles of subterranean rock?—the human imagination has the power to transform the world.

. . . . TRY THIS . . . .

Write a feature article about Marc Brunel that is slanted for juvenile readers. Call special attention to how the inventor proceeded from his initial flash of insight (observing the shipworm) to planning a subway tunneling machine.

Stanley Kubrick, Director

by Alexander Walker

Kubrick spoke of how he became struck by people's virtually listless acquiescence in the possibility—in fact, in the increasing probability—of nuclear war, by either design or accident. *Dr. Strangelove* was undertaken with the conscious aim of sounding an alert that would startle people into a response and even resistance to such a fate. And laughter, not for the first time, was the device selected to penetrate the soundproofing of the paralyzed will. The largely unimaginable prospect of the extinction of the human race is turned into the satirical embodiment of its leaders' collective madness.

FOR FURTHER REFLECTION

Kubrick is at heart an ironist and satirist. The irony and satire can be comical—as with memorable lines like "No fighting in the War Room!" from *Dr. Strangelove*—or heart-rending, as when Spartacus's fellow captured slaves all stand up at once to proclaim to the conquering general Crassus, "I am Spartacus!" thereby subjecting themselves to the agony of crucifixion.

..................................TRY THIS....................................

Write an essay on the Stanley Kubrick film that you consider his masterpiece. Before you begin the essay, watch several Kubrick films and jot down your observations regarding his directing technique for each of them.

On Writing: A Memoir of the Craft
by Stephen King

Once I start work on a project, I don't stop and I don't slow down unless I absolutely have to. If I don't write every day, the characters begin to stale off in my mind—they begin to seem like characters instead of real people. The tale's narrative cutting edge starts to rust and I begin to lose my hold on the story's plot and pace. Worst of all, the excitement of spinning something new begins to fade. The work starts to *feel* like work, and for most writers that is the smooch of death. Writing is at its best—always, always, always—when it is a kind of inspired play for the writer. I can write in cold blood if I have to, but I like it best when it's fresh and almost too hot to handle.

FOR FURTHER REFLECTION

We writers are perpetually hungry for insights into how to succeed at our enormously demanding yet enormously soul-satisfying profession; naturally, when a mega-successful author like Stephen King writes a book on writing, we sit up and pay close attention. *"Once I start work on a project, I don't stop."* Just that one blunt sentence from King is enough to send us with new resolve back to our keyboards.

. . . . TRY THIS . . . .

Begin a new writing project with iron-willed resolve: "Once I start this I will not stop." That is to say, do not fail to work on the project every day without fail until a draft is completed.

FEBRUARY 1

"Language and Modern Human Origins"
by Roger Lewin
from *The Origin of Modern Humans*

In all mammals apart from humans, the larynx is high in the neck, a position with two consequences. First, it allows the larynx to lock into the nasopharynx—the air space near the "back door" of the nasal cavity—[that] permits the animal to breathe and drink at the same time. Second, because the pharyngeal cavity—the sound box—is necessarily small as a result of the high larynx, the range of sounds the animal can make is quite limited. For typical mammals, vocalization therefore depends principally on the shape of the oral cavity and lips, which modify the sounds produced in the larynx.

In humans, the larynx is much lower in the neck, with the consequence that humans cannot drink and breathe simultaneously; they constantly risk choking on food or liquid as it is swallowed. With a hazard of this magnitude, some great benefit must be conferred by the low position of the larynx. The most obvious is a much larger pharyngeal space above the vocal cords, allowing a greater range of sound modification.

FOR FURTHER REFLECTION

Roger Lewin (the first recipient of the Lewis Thomas Award for Excellence in Communicating Life Sciences[*]) calls attention to the biological basis for speech, and to the fact that evolution, like just about everything else in life, is a process of give and take. A given animal species possesses exactly the kind of vocal range it needs to survive; humans require a much greater range to accommodate their ability to sing and yell, but most importantly to produce the complex vocalizations necessary to create language—that exclusively human attribute without which civilization could not have been possible.

. . . . TRY THIS . . . .

Write a journal entry or essay in which you reflect upon the interplay between human biology and human behavior. You might also reflect on the value (if any) derived from an understanding of that interplay. What debt do we owe to the biological sciences in understanding and appreciating human nature?

---

[*] The entry for March 16 features a passage from a work by Lewis Thomas.

Leonardo: The Artist and the Man
by Serge Bramly
Translated by Sian Reynolds

The *Mona Lisa* fits well with [the] sense of falling light, of a damp and misty atmosphere, at the very end of the day, when shapes emerge miraculously from a "darkening shadow." One feels that the daylight is fading, in a moment night will have swallowed up the gentle scene—and yet this woman is smiling. Vasari [in *Lives of the Artists*] tells us that Leonardo obtained the *Mona Lisa*'s smile by having the sitter surrounded by musicians, singers, and clowns. It is a fleeting smile, nothing to do with happiness. Nor is there any question of seduction. One thinks: This woman is smiling, yet the rest of the picture speaks of annihilation—the absent sun, the desolate and grandiose landscape threatened by darkness, the dark clothes, the black veil around the woman's hair, which might be a sign of mourning. ... She is no longer young, by the standards of the time. Her smile is that of the wife, the eternal mother, who has experienced all pleasure and all pain, and who even in affliction remains all-knowing, full of compassion. A womanly equivalent of Christ, she sits with hands quietly folded, peacefully defying time, the "consumer of all things."

FOR FURTHER REFLECTION

The greatness of a work of art, we might say, can be described in terms of the thoughts and feelings it can generate. Serge Bramly, a French author and winner of the 1983 Booksellers' Prize for *La Danse du Loup* (*Dance of the Wolf*), manages to find just the right language to capture the bewitching character of Leonardo's masterpiece.

. . . . TRY THIS . . . .

1. Write your own description of Leonardo's *Mona Lisa*, one of the world's most famous paintings. Describe the painting's compositional elements, the style, the colors; also describe the feelings it arouses.
2. Write an essay about the woman herself, and why Leonardo painted her portrait.

FEBRUARY 3

A Briefer History of Time
by Stephen Hawking, with Leonard Mlodinow

Today we know that stars visible to the naked eye make up only a minute fraction of all the stars. We can see about five thousand stars, only about .0001 percent of all the stars in just our own galaxy, the Milky Way. The Milky Way itself is but one of more than a hundred billion galaxies that can be seen using modern telescopes— and each galaxy contains on average some one hundred billion stars. If a star were a grain of salt, you could fit all the stars visible to the naked eye on a teaspoon, but all the stars in the universe would fill a ball more than eight miles wide.

Stars are so far away that they appear to us to be just pinpoints of light. We cannot see their size or shape. But, as [Edwin] Hubble noticed, there are many different types of stars, and we can tell them apart by the color of their light. ... The relative intensities of the various colors emitted by a given source of light are called its spectrum. By focusing a telescope on an individual star or galaxy, one can observe the spectrum of the light from that star or galaxy.

FOR FURTHER REFLECTION

When we contemplate the vastness and splendor of the heavens, our spiritual, aesthetic, and intellectual perceptions fuse together. Cosmologists like Stephen Hawking, Carl Sagan (see the entry for April 3), and others are able to explain astronomical phenomena in a way that enhances our understanding. When these explanations are coupled with the breathtaking images from the Hubble space telescope, our sense of wonder regarding the nature of the universe is likewise enhanced. The many different kinds of stars and galaxies; the unimaginable distances involved; the brain-numbing realization that the farther away something is from us in space, the farther away it is in time as well—such revelations are what bring enchantment to the study of astronomy.

..................................TRY THIS....................................

Choose one of your favorite topics in astronomy—one of the planets in our solar system, comets like Halley's or the comet that crashed into Jupiter's atmosphere in 1994, asteroids and the potential threat they may hold for Earth, supergiant stars, distant galaxies—and write an article about it aimed at children or teenagers. Make sure you define technical terms, and that your explanations are both clear and engaging.

FEBRUARY 4

The Double Helix: A Personal Account of the Discovery of the Structure of DNA
by James D. Watson

The key to [Linus Pauling's] success was his reliance on the simple laws of structural chemistry. The a-helix had not been found by only staring at X-ray pictures; the essential trick, instead, was to ask which atoms like to sit next to each other. In place of pencil and paper, the main working tools were a set of molecular models superficially resembling the toys of preschool children.

We could thus see no reason why we should not solve DNA in the same way. All we had to do was to construct a set of molecular models and begin to play—with luck, the structure would be a helix. Any other type of configuration would be much more complicated.

FOR FURTHER REFLECTION

It is refreshing to learn that a Nobel Prize–winning biologist—the co-discoverer, with Francis Crick, of the structure of DNA—engaged in metaphoric thinking, not just the hard-line, deductive reasoning typically associated with scientific work. "Which atoms like to sit next to each other?" does not seem like a scientific question, but on a deep level it really is: Being able to imagine (i.e., create images in the mind's eye) situations that have not (yet) been observed in real life is, we might say, a prerequisite for scientists and artists alike.

...............................TRY THIS...................................

1. Write a biographical profile of one of your favorite scientists, focusing on his or her methods of research and/or on one of that person's eureka moments.

2. Scientists are seldom portrayed as heroes outside of science fiction. Write a short story in which your central character is an ethically minded scientist (biologist, anthropologist, physicist, chemist, or environmentalist) who confronts an opponent who is antiscience.

Proust and the Squid:
The Story and Science of the Reading Brain
by Maryanne Wolf

We were never born to read. Human beings invented reading only a few thousand years ago. And with this invention, we rearranged the very organization of our brain, which in turn expanded the ways we were able to think, which altered the intellectual evolution of our species. Reading is one of the single most remarkable inventions in history; the ability to record history is one of its consequences. Our ancestors' invention could come about only because of the human brain's extraordinary ability to make new connections among its existing structures, a process made possible by the brain's ability to be shaped by experience. This plasticity at the heart of the brain's design forms the basis for much of who we are, and who we might become.

FOR FURTHER REFLECTION

One of the fascinating things about human evolution is that it seems to transcend its biological aspects. Our brains, in other words, have evolved to the point where they can modify their own nature. Such appears to be the case with reading. Maryanne Wolf, a professor of child development and director of the Center for Reading and Language Research, examines the phenomenon of reading and the light it sheds upon the miraculous workings of the human brain, especially the brains of children.

....................................TRY THIS....................................

If you haven't been keeping a reading journal, begin one now. After completing a stint of reading for the day, write a paragraph or so about your impressions of the book, story, essay, or whatever. You don't need to finish the work before responding to it. In fact, your changing impressions of a work from day to day will likely prove to be a valuable record of both your own reading processes and the complexity of the work itself.

"Coffee"

by Reay Tannahill

from *Food in History*

Coffee originated in Ethiopia, and there are as many myths about who first discovered that it was edible, and then drinkable, as there are about the origins of wine. In fact, the word "coffee" comes, via the Turkish *kahveh*, from Arabic *qahwah*, which originally meant "wine." Coffee became the wine of the Muslims, to whom real wine was forbidden.

Cultivation of the wild *coffea arabica* bush may have begun as early as the sixth century, although the first written reference is attributed to a tenth-century Arab physician. To begin with, the berries seem to have been chewed whole or else crushed to a paste with fat (presumably mutton fat). Later, the entire fruit was infused to make a kind of tisane [medicinal beverage], but it was only when in the thirteenth century the beans were cleaned and roasted before infusing that modern coffee was invented. It is said to have achieved its first real popularity among Muslims with the religious sect known as dervishes, whose devotions included chanting and whirling continuously until they were reduced to a state of catalepsy. The effect of the caffeine would presumably be to extend the pre-cataleptic period and thus the length of the devotions.

FOR FURTHER REFLECTION

Like everything else, food and drink have their histories, and learning these histories enriches our appreciation of world cultures as well as our culinary experiences. Reay Tannahill's book makes it clear that food, like art, religion, politics, and technology, has been instrumental in shaping civilization.

.................................TRY THIS....................................

Do some research into the earliest uses of one of your favorite foods or beverages. Use your research to write a feature on "The Earliest Uses of …," slanting the piece for a culinary magazine or the food section of your local newspaper.

FEBRUARY 7

All the Strange Hours:
The Excavation of a Life
by Loren C. Eiseley

Always, standing above excavations, my own or others upon which I labored, I have been both excited about what the shovel would reveal and disconsolate and stricken at the sacrilege done to the dead. Once, high on the side of a sullen mountain bastion in Texas, our little scouting party had unearthed in a cavern a child's skeleton tenderly wrapped in a rabbit-skin blanket and laid on a little frame of sticks in the dry, insulating dust. An assemblage of bone needles and a "killed" rabbit stick broken to accompany the dead had been tucked away with the child. I stood silent and was not happy. Something told me that the child and its accouterments should have been left where the parents intended before they departed, left to the endless circling of the stars beyond the cavern mouth and the entering shaft of sun by day. This for all eternity. Yet I knew also the valley population was growing. Vandals and pothunters would inevitably discover the child's resting place. Eventually all would be crushed, broken, or sold for antiques. … Here, perhaps, an institution might at least rescue what would otherwise be destroyed or dispersed.

FOR FURTHER REFLECTION

It is often assumed that science is soulless, reductive, attentive only to the interaction of natural forces and the laws governing their behavior. But through his eloquent writings, the great anthropologist Loren Eiseley (1907–1977) repeatedly shows us how scientific understanding can lead to and even embrace a spiritual experience, as was the case in excavating a child's ancient grave. Life and death, time and eternity, are sacred mysteries that scientific scrutiny can actually enhance rather than negate.

...................................TRY THIS....................................

Write a journal entry in which you reflect on the interplay of rational inquiry and spiritual experience when, say, experiencing a particular natural phenomenon such as an earthquake, a waterfall, an eclipse, a rainbow, or a phenomenon that would be less likely to arouse spiritual feelings, such as a spider in its web or a mosquito extracting blood from your arm.

The Roman Way

by Edith Hamilton

However fierce the urge of [Roman] nature was, the feeling for law and order was deeper, the deepest thing in them. Their outbreaks were terrible; civil wars, ... dealings with conquered enemies which are a fearful page in history. Nevertheless, the outstanding fact about Rome is her unwavering adherence to the idea of a controlled life, subject not to this or that individual, but to a system embodying the principles of justice and fair dealing.

How savage the Roman nature was which the Roman law controlled is seen written large in Rome's favorite amusements ...: wild beast hunts—so-called, the hunting place was the arena; naval battles for which the circus was flooded by means of hidden canals; and, most usual and best loved by the people, the gladiators when the great amphitheatre was packed close tier upon tier, all Rome there to see human beings by the tens and hundreds killing each other, to give the victor in a contest the signal for death and eagerly watch the upraised dagger plunge into the helpless body and the blood spurt forth.

FOR FURTHER REFLECTION

The dividing line between barbarity and civilization, law and lawlessness, is often more difficult to discern than we care to admit; and nowhere is this more evident than in ancient Roman society. We speak casually of "the grandeur that was Rome"—and indeed there was much grandeur in arts, technology, and civic life; but sharpen focus a bit and the grandeur is tarnished by such Roman practices as crucifixion and arena entertainments like butchering human beings for sport.

..................................TRY THIS..................................

Write a short story about a Roman gladiator who is preparing for the day he must fight a fellow gladiator to the death. As an alternative, make your protagonist a member of the Roman Senate who attempts to put a stop to such blood sports in the arena.

"The Rise of Renaissance Humanism"

by William Manchester

from *A World Lit Only by Fire: The Medieval Mind and
the Renaissance*

In 1497, the Holy Roman emperor Maximilian I served as humanism's midwife by appointing Conradus Celtis, a Latin lyrical poet, to the most prestigious academic chair in Vienna. Celtis used his new post to establish the Sodalitas Danubia, a center for humanistic studies, thereby winning immortality among intellectual historians as *Der Erzhumaniste* (the Archhumanist).

Within a year his first manuscripts were at hand. Aldus Manutius, the great Italian printer and inventor of italic type (for an edition of Virgil), had been toiling for twenty years on the Aldine Press to produce a series of Greek classics. His *editio princips*, a five-volume folio Aristotle edited by Aldus himself, was in proof and ready for scholars by late 1498. During the next fourteen years it was followed by the works of all the Hellenic giants: Theocritis, Aristophanes, Thucydides, Sophocles, Herodotus, Euripides, Homer, and Plato.

All this ferment led to that rarest of cultural phenomena, an intellectual movement which alters the course of both learning and civilization.

FOR FURTHER REFLECTION

The great flowering of humanistic learning that occurred in fifteenth-century Italy, birthplace of the Renaissance, was due not only to the rediscovery and translation into the vernacular languages of great works of literature, history, science, and so forth, but to the technology of printing and book production—a technology that disseminated learning throughout the civilized world to a degree that manuscript copying never could.

......................................TRY THIS....................................

Explore the life of a notable figure from the Renaissance—either well-known (like Leonardo da Vinci) or little known (like Conradus Celtis or Aldus Manutius) and make him or her the protagonist of a short story set in the fifteenth or sixteenth century.

FEBRUARY 10

"The Flapper"

by Nathan Miller

from *New World Coming: The 1920s and
the Making of Modern America*

Pretty and impudent, the flapper was the symbol of the sexual revolution associated with the postwar era. She challenged prevailing notions about gender roles and defied the double standard. In essence, she demanded the same social freedoms for herself that men enjoyed. Flappers flouted conventionality, drank in speakeasies and the new nightclubs, doubled the nation's consumption of cigarettes by reaching "for a Lucky instead of a sweet," and flirted openly. Scott Fitzgerald described her as "lovely and expensive and about nineteen."

The flapper bobbed her peroxided or hennaed hair, wore bright red lipstick, and painted two circles of rouge on her face. She adorned her androgynous figure with flimsy dresses and short skirts, and wore a tight-fitting cloche hat, long strings of beads, flesh-colored hose rolled below her rouged knees, numerous bangles on her arms, and unbuckled galoshes. Sleeves disappeared and in summer the flapper sometimes dispensed with stockings.

FOR FURTHER REFLECTION

It was during the Roaring Twenties—that wild and revolutionary decade between the end of World War I and the stock market crash of 1929—that Victorian values were washed away with bathtub gin and drowned out with jazz. No one chronicled the behavior or perpetuated the allure of this period more effectively than F. Scott and Zelda Fitzgerald—he through his novels and stories, she through her feature articles, and both of them through their own high-society living. In F. Scott Fitzgerald's short stories—read by millions in the *Saturday Evening Post* and other magazines—the flapper became an icon for the age.

......................................TRY THIS....................................

Read a few of Fitzgerald's short stories, such as "Bernice Bobs Her Hair," "The Jelly Bean," and "The Ice Palace," and then write a short story of your own set in the 1920s, a time of prohibition and increased sexual freedom. You might consider dramatizing, for example, your viewpoint character's struggle between wanting to lead an upright life as represented by his or her parents, and craving the risqué adventures of the flapper.

Odyssey (Book 11) by Homer

Translated by Robert Fagles

"O my son [Odysseus]—what brings
  you down to the world
of death and darkness? You are still alive!
It's hard for the living to catch
  a glimpse of this.
Great rivers flow between
  us, terrible waters,
the Ocean first of all—no
  one could ever ford
that stream on foot, only aboard
  some sturdy craft.
Have you just come from Try,
  wandering long years
with your men and ship? Not
  yet returned to Ithaca?
You've still not seen your wife
  inside your halls?"

    "Mother,"
I replied, "I had to venture down
  to the House of Death,

to consult the shade of
  Tiresias, seer of Thebes.
Never yet have I neared
  Achaea, never once
set foot on native ground,
always wandering—endless
  hardship from that day
I first set sail with King Agamemnon
  bound for Troy,
the stallion-land, to fight the Trojans there.
  . . .
Please tell me about my wife,
  her turn of mind,
her thoughts . . . still standing fast beside our son,
still guarding our great
  estates, secure as ever now?
Or has she wed some other
  countryman at last,
the finest prince among them?"

FOR FURTHER REFLECTION

Homer's *Odyssey* has given us the word for any epic, transformative journey—
inward as well as outward. After fighting heroically to defeat the Trojans, Odysseus embarks on a treacherous ten-year journey back home. The goddess
Circe, who had turned his men into swine and kept Odysseus captive for a year,
agreed to release him provided he visit the seer Tiresias in the Underworld
in order to learn his (Odysseus's) fate. Here, then, Odysseus's great journey
through life is extended to an experience of the afterlife as well.

. . . . TRY THIS . . . .

Write an episode for a modern odyssey that takes place in a smaller or larger
place and time frame. Think of James Joyce's *Ulysses*, which takes place in a
single day in early twentieth-century Dublin; or of Arthur C. Clarke and Stanley
Kubrick's *2001: A Space Odyssey*, which takes place over a period of four million years or longer, across interstellar space.

FEBRUARY 12

"Holy Sonnet #14"
by John Donne

Batter my heart, three person'd God; for you
As yet but knock, breathe, shine, and seek to mend;
That I may rise, and stand, o'erthrow me, and make me new.
I, like an usurpt town, to another due,
Labour to admit you, but Oh, to no end,
Reason your viceroy in me, me should defend,
But is captive'd, and proves weak or untrue.
Yet dearly I love you, and would be loved faine,
But am betroth'd unto your enemy:
Divorce me, untie, or break that knot again,
Take me to you, imprison me, for I
Except you enthrall me, never shall be free,
Nor ever chaste, except you ravish me.

FOR FURTHER REFLECTION

One of the first reactions most readers have to this sonnet, one of the best
known from Donne's sequences of holy sonnets, is that its imagery does not
seem all that holy. But one of the characteristics of Donne's poetic genius is
that he brilliantly fuses the sacred with the profane. The speaker in the above
poem hungers so intensely to feel God's presence in his heart that he implores
God to *batter* his heart, to *usurp* his life, even to *imprison* and *ravish* him. Does
that not seem rather extreme? Perhaps not if, let us say, the speaker has begun
to have doubts about his religious convictions; or if he wants his spiritual
experience to be equal to the most extreme physical experiences.

..................................TRY THIS....................................

Write a poem or story in which you use physical, sensual images to describe a
spiritual experience. Perhaps you'll want your speaker or narrator to be suffering
from a loss of faith as a result of a traumatic incident.

FEBRUARY 13

Paradise Lost (Book I)

by John Milton

Farewell happy Fields
Where joy for ever dwells: Hail horrors, hail
Infernal world, and thou profoundest Hell
Receive thy new Possessor: One who brings
A mind not to be chang'd by Place or Time.
The mind is its own place, and in itself
Can make a Heav'n of Hell, a Hell of Heav'n.
What matter where, if I be still the same,
And what I should be, all but less than he
Whom Thunder hath made greater? Here at least
We shall be free; th'Almighty hath not built
Here for his envy, will not drive us hence:
Here we may reign secure, and in my choice
To reign is worth ambition though in Hell:
Better to reign in Hell than serve in Heav'n.

FOR FURTHER REFLECTION

One of the most curious ironies of literature is that the villains are often much more fascinating and memorable than the heroes. Nowhere is this more apparent than in Milton's portrayal of Satan in what is generally regarded as the greatest epic poem in English. How easily we can identify with Satan's thirst for vengeance after he (as the angel Lucifer) is catapulted from Heaven, knowing full well the terrible price of his rebelliousness.

...................................TRY THIS....................................

Plan a story set in the modern world in which your protagonist exhibits Satan-like characteristics and a Satan-like turn of fate (e.g., because of some transgression, he has been ousted from a high-status job).

"Sonnet 14"

by Elizabeth Barrett Browning

from *Sonnets from the Portuguese*

If thou must love me, let it be for nought
Except for love's sake only. Do not say
"I love her for her smile—her look—her way
Of speaking gently,—for a trick of thought
That falls in well with mine, and certes brought
A sense of pleasant ease on such a day"—
For these things in themselves, Beloved, may
Be changed, or change for thee,—and love, so wrought,
May be unwrought so. Neither love me for
Thine own dear pity's wiping my cheeks dry,—
A creature might forget to weep, who bore
Thy comfort long, and lose thy love thereby!
But love me for love's sake, that evermore
Thou mayst love on, through love's eternity.

FOR FURTHER REFLECTION

The 43 sonnets that comprise *Sonnets from the Portuguese* constitute one of the most cherished sonnet cycles in the language, along with the sonnet cycles of Spenser, Donne, and Shakespeare. The speakers in Barrett Browning's sonnets alternate from male to female, so that the cycle becomes a staging of the lovers' profoundest mutual sentiments. The most famous sonnet in the cycle, of course, is "How do I love thee? / Let me count the ways" (Sonnet 43).

.................................TRY THIS....................................

On this Valentine's Day, compose a love poem for the man or woman in your life. It need not be a sonnet; it need not rhyme; but aim for sincerity, specific details, and try to speak in your own voice instead of some contrived "poetic" voice.

FEBRUARY 15

Slaughterhouse-Five
by Kurt Vonnegut, Jr.

The man assigned to the [hospital] bed next to Billy's was a former infantry captain named Eliot Rosewater. Rosewater was sick and tired of being drunk all the time.

It was Rosewater who introduced Billy to science fiction, and in particular to the writings of Kilgore Trout. Rosewater had a tremendous collection of science-fiction paperbacks under his bed. He had brought them to the hospital in a steamer trunk. ...

Kilgore Trout became Billy's favorite living author, and science fiction the only sort of tales he could read.

Rosewater was twice as smart as Billy, but he and Billy were dealing with similar crises in similar ways. They had both found life meaningless, partly because of what they had seen in war. Rosewater, for instance, had shot a fourteen-year-old fireman, mistaking him for a German soldier. So it goes. And Billy had seen the greatest massacre in European history, which was the fire-bombing of Dresden. So it goes.

So they were trying to re-invent themselves and their universe. Science fiction was a big help.

FOR FURTHER REFLECTION

Kurt Vonnegut, Jr. (1922–2007) is a master satirist, a late twentieth-century Mark Twain, who captured the absurdity of warfare, of technology run amuck, of clinging to false ideals. By examining his life through the four-dimensional perspective of an alien race (the Tralfamadorians), Billy Pilgrim gains unusual insight into the human condition.

..................................TRY THIS..................................

Dramatize a scene for your novel-in progress in which the absurdity, futility, or tragic happenstance of war is made apparent. For example, you might set the scene in a prisoner-of-war camp, on the battlefield, or even inside a war room (as in Stanley Kubrick's satirical film, *Dr. Strangelove*).

FEBRUARY 16

Complications: A Surgeon's Notes on an Imperfect Science
by Atul Gawande

Surgeons, as a group, adhere to a curious egalitarianism. They believe in practice, not talent. People often assume that you have to have great hands to become a surgeon, but it's not true. When I interviewed to get into surgery programs, no one made me sew or take a dexterity test or checked if my hands were steady. You do not even need all ten fingers to be accepted. To be sure, talent helps. Professors say every two or three years they'll see someone truly gifted come through a program—someone who picks up complex manual skills unusually quickly, sees the operative field as a whole, notices trouble before it happens. Nonetheless, attending surgeons say that what's most important to them is finding people who are conscientious, industrious, and boneheaded enough to stick at practicing the one difficult thing day and night for years on end.

FOR FURTHER REFLECTION

Surgery is both an art and a science. After years of training and hands-on apprenticeship, surgeons are thoroughly trained and are therefore licensed to practice; but the deepest learning comes through years of repeated application of those skills in the OR. Every patient presents a new challenge, just as—in the arts—every project (painting, architectural project, literary work) presents its own set of complex and unique challenges. Greatness in surgery is achieved through confronting and triumphing over these never-ending challenges.

.....................................TRY THIS.....................................

Ask your physician or surgeon to explain one or two of his or her greatest post-residency challenges, and what was learned from the experience. Interview one or two other physicians, asking the same questions. Use the information you obtain to write an essay about a physician-surgeon's day-to-day challenges.

FEBRUARY 17

The Los Angeles Diaries: A Memoir
by James Brown

Through a window in the waiting room on the tenth floor of the Black Tower [at Universal Studios] I look out over the green rolling hills of Forest Lawn where my brother is buried. He was twenty-seven and alcoholic when he ended his life, and at this moment, in this place and time, I see myself in him, sitting here, waiting to meet with [a motion picture studio] executive. I imagine he once occupied this same space, if not this exact office then another in the building, and I imagine he felt as I do now. Anxious. In need of a drink. Maybe, like me, he questioned why he was here, if this was what he really wanted. If he belonged. Maybe, like me, he was both repelled and attracted to a business that is at least in part responsible for his destruction.

FOR FURTHER REFLECTION

Writing for the movie industry is probably the most difficult writing there is. The competition is ferocious, especially for those trying to break in; and while the financial rewards can be substantial, the need to meet high commercial standards can break a screenwriter's morale. James Brown, who has written for film and television in addition to publishing several novels, understands all too well the psychological demands of the screenwriting craft.

. . . . TRY THIS. . . . .

After reading works about Hollywood writers—for example Budd Schulberg's *What Makes Sammy Run?* and F. Scott Fitzgerald's *The Pat Hobby Stories*, write a story about a modern-day Hollywood writer who either makes it big or fails miserably.

FEBRUARY 18

Murder at the Gardner
by Jane Langton

It was time to explain to [detective] Homer Kelly the ticklish troubles afflicting the [Isabella Gardner] museum. Shackleton Bowditch began it. Shackleton was a Harvard Fellow, an acquaintance of Homer's from the old days of the bombing at Memorial Hall. "You see, Homer," said Shackleton, "it's these strange things that have been happening. That's why we called you in." …

"The frogs in the courtyard pool," said Catherine. … "Someone put pollywogs in the pool, and they turned into frogs, and pretty soon they were hopping all over the floor."

Homer scribbled Frogs on his agenda sheet. "What else?" …

"The pictures have been shifted," whispered Preston Carver [a Trustee], arching his eyebrows, leaning forward and speaking in a whisper.

"Shifted?" said Homer. "You mean, moved around from place to place?"

"They change places in the night," said Titus Moon. "The Crivelli and the portrait of Count Inghirami in the Raphael Room. The Botticelli and the School of Botticelli hanging across from it in the Long Gallery. The Rubens—" Titus gestured at the portrait of Thomas Howard on the wall—"was hanging upside down. And someone pasted a mustache on van Kyck's *Lady with a Rose*."

FOR FURTHER REFLECTION

In a Jane Langton mystery, a criminal investigation—in this case, master-pieces of Renaissance painting were stolen from the Isabella Stewart Gardner museum in Boston (based loosely on an actual crime)—is laced with wit. We find ourselves laughing even as we find ourselves steeped in suspense. We also learn a great deal about the literary or artistic background in question. Langton's other mysteries involve the New England transcendentalist writers (*God in Concord*), Emily Dickinson (*Emily Dickinson Is Dead*), M.C. Escher (*The Escher Twist*), and Thomas Jefferson (*Murder at Monticello*).

...................................TRY THIS....................................

Work up an outline of a mystery story in which your private eye or detective protagonist is an expert in some craft or science. Make this subject a part of the story background.

Silent Spring

by Rachel Carson

In Greek mythology the sorceress Medea, enraged at being supplanted by a rival for the affections of her husband Jason, presented the new bride with a robe possessing magic properties. The wearer of the robe immediately suffered a violent death. This death-by-indirection now finds its counterpart in what are known as "systemic insecticides." These are chemicals with extraordinary properties which are used to convert plants or animals into a sort of Medea's robe by making them actually poisonous. This is done with the purpose of killing insects that may come in contact with them, especially by sucking their juices or blood.

FOR FURTHER REFLECTION

Rachel Carson's *Silent Spring*, more than any other single work, awakened America to the harsh reality that human beings, through indiscriminate use of pesticides like DDT, and through wanton disregard for the preservation of natural resources, were responsible for widespread environmental destruction. What makes *Silent Spring* so memorable is Carson's ability to convey key scientific concepts, like chlorinated hydrocarbons (molecules in which atoms vital to life, such as carbon and oxygen, bond with chlorine, a poisonous gas), through memorable analogies drawn from literature and mythology.

.................................TRY THIS...................................

Take a concept from a specialized field of study—one that you're familiar with—and explain it to lay readers. For example, explain the cause of earthquakes by using, as an analogy, two rubber blocks moving in opposite directions but being forced to slide against each other.

Zen and the Art of Motorcycle Maintenance
by Robert Pirsig

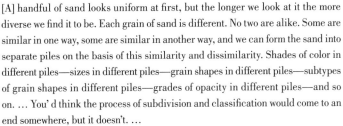

[A] handful of sand looks uniform at first, but the longer we look at it the more diverse we find it to be. Each grain of sand is different. No two are alike. Some are similar in one way, some are similar in another way, and we can form the sand into separate piles on the basis of this similarity and dissimilarity. Shades of color in different piles—sizes in different piles—grain shapes in different piles—subtypes of grain shapes in different piles—grades of opacity in different piles—and so on. ... You' d think the process of subdivision and classification would come to an end somewhere, but it doesn't. ...

Classical understanding is concerned with the piles and the basis for sorting and interrelating them. Romantic understanding is directed toward the handful of sand before the sorting begins. Both are valid ways of looking at the world. ... What has become an urgent necessity is a way of looking at the world that does violence to neither of these two kinds of understanding and unites them into one. Such an understanding will not reject sand-sorting or contemplation of unsorted sand for its own sake.

FOR FURTHER REFLECTION

Phaedrus, the narrator of Robert Pirsig's book, undertakes a pilgrimage to reunify the "classical" and "romantic" ways of perceiving reality (i.e., the scientific/analytic and the artistic/synthetic), convinced that their segregation is unhealthy for civilization as well as for oneself. Phaedrus, who represents Pirsig's fragmented self as the result of a nervous breakdown, embarks on a motorcycle journey across the United Sates in an effort to reintegrate his divided self.

..................................TRY THIS....................................

Work up a story idea in which your logical, methodical protagonist struggles to find common ground with his or her artistic, intuitive, unmethodical spouse, child, or boss.

Mathematics and the Imagination
by Edward Kasner and James Newman

Most of us learned that a straight line is the shortest distance between two points. If this statement is supposed to apply to the earth on which we live, it is both useless and untrue. ... The nineteenth-century mathematicians Riemann and Lobachevsky knew that the statement, if true at all, applied only to special surfaces. It does not apply to a spherical surface on which the shortest distance between two points is the arc of a great circle. Since the shape of the earth approximates a sphere, the shortest distance between two points anywhere on the surface of the earth is *never* a straight line, but is a portion of the arc of a great circle.

Yet for all *practical* purposes, even on the surface of the earth, the shortest distance between two points is given by a straight line. That is to say, in measuring ordinary distances with a steel tape or a yardstick, the principle is substantially correct. However, for distances beyond even a few hundred feet, allowance must be made for the curvature of the earth. When a steel rod over 600 feet in length was ... constructed in a large Detroit automobile factory, it was found that the exact measurement of its length was impossible without allowing for the earth's curvature.

FOR FURTHER REFLECTION

In mathematics, common sense often collides with the exotic and seemingly irrational. Relativity is a good example. It can be shown mathematically that time slows down the faster one travels—but only in relation to the person at rest; the moving person's own time frame has not changed. Practical applications, like taking measurements for construction, can apply the everyday principles of plane geometry—but, as Kasner and Newman make clear, very large measurements must take into account the fact that, on the surface of the earth, the shortest distance between two points is not a straight line.

...................................TRY THIS...................................

Write a journal entry about a mathematical or geometrical property that has fascinated you. Perhaps you have been bemused by Zeno's paradox of motion, or the fact that adding the numbers in a sum attained by multiplying any given number by 9 will always equal 9 (234 x 9 = 2106; 2 + 1 + 0 + 6 = 9). If you're mathematically savvy, give a rational explanation of the seeming mystery.

FEBRUARY 22

It Takes a Village, and Other Lessons Children Teach Us
by Hillary Rodham Clinton

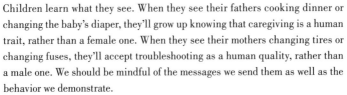

Children learn what they see. When they see their fathers cooking dinner or changing the baby's diaper, they'll grow up knowing that caregiving is a human trait, rather than a female one. When they see their mothers changing tires or changing fuses, they'll accept troubleshooting as a human quality, rather than a male one. We should be mindful of the messages we send them as well as the behavior we demonstrate.

Differences in adults' treatment of girls and boys begin well before they reach their first birthdays, as has been demonstrated by studies in which infants in diapers or snowsuits are left in the care of adults who think they know the child's sex because of the names they are told. The same baby is treated differently depending on whether the adult thinks it is a boy or a girl. For example, an adult might identify and respond to the same infant's cry as anger in a "boy" and fear in a "girl."

FOR FURTHER REFLECTION

Hillary Clinton suggests that it is a mistake to associate certain tasks as "male" or "female." For one thing, it belies actual experience. Women *are* perfectly capable of changing tires (or overhauling engines, for that matter); there is no reason why men should be reluctant to cook (are not the great majority of chefs male?). Shouldn't caring and compassion transcend gender?

...................................TRY THIS....................................

Write an essay on gender roles as you've experienced them. Do you find traditional gender roles (e.g., parental roles) valid or harmful, and if so, why? Refer to specific cases to illustrate your assertions.

Beyond Freedom & Dignity
by B.F. Skinner

Any evidence that a person's behavior may be attributed to external circumstances seems to threaten his dignity or worth. We are not inclined to give a person credit for achievements which are in fact due to forces over which he has no control. We tolerate a certain amount of such evidence, as we accept without alarm some evidence that a man is not free. No one is greatly disturbed when important details of works of art and literature, political careers, and scientific discoveries are attributed to "influences" in the lives of artists, writers, statesmen, and scientists respectively. But as an analysis of behavior adds further evidence, the achievements for which a person himself is to be given credit seems to approach zero, and both the evidence and the science which produces it are then challenged.

FOR FURTHER REFLECTION

B.F. Skinner (1904–1990) is one of the pioneers of behavioral psychology—the branch of psychology that approaches human behavior as the product of external, identifiable forces or stimuli. Hence, giving money to a homeless person may appear to be an act of pure benevolence, of free will; but a behavioral psychologist would argue that the behavior is prompted by specific forces (e.g., religious obligations; dread of retribution, divine or otherwise, for not exhibiting Christian charity; superstitious reprisal; and so on).

...................................TRY THIS...................................

After reading Skinner's *Beyond Freedom & Dignity* in its entirety, write an essay in which you support or refute the premises of behavioral psychology. Draw from your own experiences for examples that illustrate free will or the lack of it.

Dinner With Persephone
by Patricia Storace

Today is the Feast of the Metamorphosis, known to us as the Transfiguration, when Christ allowed his disciples to glimpse the radiant divinity he had previously withheld from his face. This shimmering alteration is a part of all miraculous tales, even present in one as familiar as Cinderella, in the changing of the pumpkin into a coach and the metamorphosis of an abused, miserable, dirty child into a glowingly beautiful and lovable woman. In Greece, it is one of the commonest subjects for icons, Christ's face like the sun surrounded with golden rays, and disciples dropping awed to their knees before him, while the word "Metamorphosis" sparkles somewhere in the painted scene, here in this country of the double nature, where even the language has a double nature, divine and mortal.

FOR FURTHER REFLECTION

It sometimes takes a poet like Patricia Storace (who has received an American Academy of Arts and Letters prize for poetry) to capture the spirit of a mystical place like Greece, steeped as it is in history. The Feast of the Metamorphosis is particularly relevant for Grecian culture because of its Christian as well as mythological significance.

. . . . TRY THIS . . . .

Where, in all your travels, have you felt most connected spiritually? Write a poem, short story, or essay that captures this spiritual experience. At the same time, try to capture the particular character and sensory impressions of the city or village you're writing about.

Confessions

by St. Augustine

from Book XI. Translated by R.S. Pine-Coffin

My answer to those who ask "What was God doing before he made heaven and earth?" is not "He was preparing Hell for people who pry into mysteries." This frivolous retort has been made before now, so we are told, in order to evade the point of the question. But it is one thing to make fun of the questioner and another to find the answer. So I shall refrain from giving this reply. For in matters of which I am ignorant I would rather admit the fact than gain credit by giving the wrong answer and making a laughing-stock of a man who asks a serious question. ...

[Eternity] is supreme over time because it is a never-ending present. ... For what is now the future, once it comes, will become the past, whereas you are unchanging, your years can never fail. Your years neither go nor come, but our years pass and others come after them, so that they all may come in their turn. Your years are completely present to you all at once. ... Your today is eternity.

FOR FURTHER REFLECTION

Augustine's late-fourth-century masterwork consists not only of confessions of sins, but of his deepest thoughts about God, spirituality, and human destiny; and of his meditations on Christianity, to which he converted from paganism. One of the most vexing issues for him was the relationship between time and eternity. Was God outside of time? The illusion of mortal humans? Such questions are the subject of intense discussion to this day.

..................................TRY THIS...................................

Here's a topic that will keep you busy for quite some time. In your own way, drawing from your own experiences, try answering the question "What is time?"

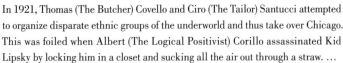

FEBRUARY 26

"A Short Look at Organized Crime"
by Woody Allen

from *Getting Even*

In 1921, Thomas (The Butcher) Covello and Ciro (The Tailor) Santucci attempted to organize disparate ethnic groups of the underworld and thus take over Chicago. This was foiled when Albert (The Logical Positivist) Corillo assassinated Kid Lipsky by locking him in a closet and sucking all the air out through a straw. …

Dominick (The Herpetologist) Mione shot Lucky Lorenzo (so nicknamed when a bomb that went off in his hat failed to kill him) outside a bar in Chicago. In return, Corillo and his men traced Mione to Newark and made his head into a wind instrument.

FOR FURTHER REFLECTION

Mario Puzo's bestselling novel, *The Godfather*, and especially the string of Godfather films it spawned, resulted in a heavily romanticized view of Mafia-based organized crime in America that belied its terrorist-like brutality and its multi-billion-dollar destructiveness upon commerce across eight decades. Woody Allen's strategy for deromanticizing the Mafia is to make their operatives seem like cartoon characters.

·····························TRY THIS····························

1. Think of a movement or organization (political, criminal, or otherwise) that in your opinion needs to be dropped down a few notches in stature. Write a humorous piece that makes the individuals involved seem comical.
2. Write a serious short story about a member of an organized crime family who struggles to redeem himself.

The Definitive Time Machine: A Critical Edition of H.G. Wells's Scientific Romance
by H.G. Wells

Plainly, this second species of Man was subterranean. ... At first, proceeding from the problems of our own age, it seemed clear as daylight to me that the gradual widening of the present merely temporary and social difference between the Capitalist and the Labourer, was the key to the whole position. ... There is a tendency to utilise underground space for the less ornamental purposes of civilization; there is the Metropolitan Railway in London, for instance, there are new electric railways, there are subways, there are underground workrooms and restaurants, and they increase and multiply. ...

The great triumph of Humanity I had dreamed of took a different shape in my mind. It had been no such triumph of moral education and general cooperation as I had imagined. Instead, I saw a real aristocracy, armed with a perfected science and working to a logical conclusion the industrial system of today. Its triumph had not been simply a triumph over Nature, but a triumph over Nature and the fellow man. This, I must warn you, was my theory at the time. ... But even on this supposition the balanced civilization that was at last attained must have long since passed its zenith, and was now far fallen into decay. The too-perfect security of the Upperworlders had led them to a slow movement of degeneration, to a general dwindling in size, strength, and intelligence.

FOR FURTHER REFLECTION

H.G. Wells's role as a writer of science fiction was to imagine how tendencies of the present day (in his case, the end of the nineteenth century) would play out in the future. What would happen to humanity if the leisure class became utterly dependent on the laborer class? The leisure class would achieve their utopian vision of freedom from work but would become too complacent to strive for self-betterment; the laborers would also degenerate—through the dehumanizing forces of the industry and technology they brought into being.

...................................TRY THIS...................................

Pay close attention to a social practice such as mass-media advertising or big-business athletic events, and so on—and imagine what that practice will be like fifty or a hundred years from now. Write a short story about, say, a world in which a person's every move can be tracked by ultrasophisticated GPS devices.

Frankenstein, or, The Modern Prometheus
by Mary Shelley

[While roaming through the mountains] I suddenly beheld the figure of a man, at some distance, advancing towards me with superhuman speed. He bounded for the crevices in the ice, among which I had walked with caution. ... I perceived, as the shape came nearer ... that it was the wretch whom I had created. I trembled with rage and horror, resolving to wait his approach and then close with him in mortal combat. He approached; his countenance bespoke bitter anguish, combined with disdain and malignity, while its unearthly ugliness rendered it almost too horrible for human eyes. ...

"Devil," I exclaimed, "do you dare approach me? And do you not fear the fierce vengeance of my arm wreaked on your miserable head? Begone, vile insect! Or rather, stay, that I may trample you to dust! And, oh! That I could, with the extinction of your miserable existence, restore those victims whom you have so diabolically murdered!"

"I expected this reception," said the demon. "All men hate the wretched; how, then, must I be hated, who am miserable beyond all living things! Yet you, my creator, detest and spurn me, thy creature, to whom thou are bound by ties only dissoluble by the annihilation of one of us. You propose to kill me. How dare you sport thus with life? Do your duty towards me, and I will do mine towards you and the rest of mankind.

FOR FURTHER REFLECTION

What are the moral obligations of a creator toward his creature, and how should the creature respond in turn? Mary Shelley (1797–1851) gave the ancient myth of Prometheus a modern interpretation. If one has the power to bring new life into the world, one must assume the moral responsibility of nurturing that new life, no matter what its defects. Failure to do so would have disastrous consequences for both creator and creature.

..................................TRY THIS....................................

Create a real-world scenario for the Frankenstein (or Prometheus) story. For example, write a story about a woman who learns that she will be giving birth to a severely defective child, and whose initial impulse is to abort it. What will cause her to change her mind?

FEBRUARY 29

American Genesis: A Century of Invention and Technological Enthusiasm, 1870–1970
by Thomas P. Hughes

Since 1870 inventors, scientists, and system builders have been engaged in creating the technological systems of the modern world. Today most of the industrial world lives in a made environment structured by these systems, not in the natural environment of past centuries. Charles Darwin helped explain the influences of nature; Sigmund Freud tried to comprehend the psychological forces crackling like electrical charges within and all around us; but as yet we reflect too little about the influences and patterns of a world organized into great technological systems. Usually we mistakenly associate modern technology not with systems but with objects as the electric light, radio and television, the airplane, the automobile, the computer, and nuclear missiles. To associate modern technology solely with individual machines and devices is to overlook deeper currents of modern technology that gathered strength and direction during the half-century after Thomas Edison established his invention factory at Menlo Park. ... Large systems—energy, production, communication, and transportation—compose the essence of modern technology.

FOR FURTHER REFLECTION

Thomas Hughes, a professor of the history and sociology of science at the University of Pennsylvania, makes an important distinction between technological *artifacts* like computers and automobiles, and technological *systems*, such as global electronic communication systems and transportation systems. Before a technological system can be managed, its intricate workings must be thoroughly understood.

...................................TRY THIS....................................

Which technological system, in your opinion, is in greatest need of reform? Write an essay in which you examine the problems, say, with the Internet or with mobile-phone communication. What can be done to improve the system? Think not only of the artifacts themselves that are involved, but in the way that systems are managed, promoted, and utilized.

The Spell of the Sensuous: Perception and Language in a More-Than-Human World
by David Abram

Nothing is more common to the diverse indigenous cultures of the earth than a recognition of the air, the wind, and the breath, as aspects of singularly sacred power. By virtue of its pervading presence, its utter invisibility, and its manifest influence on all manner of visible phenomena, the air, for oral peoples, is the archetype of all that is ineffable, unknowable, yet undeniably real and efficacious. Its obvious ties to speech—the sense that spoken words are structured breath (try speaking a word without exhaling at the same time), and indeed that spoken phrases take their communicative power from this invisible medium that moves between us—lends the air a deep association with linguistic meaning and with thought. Indeed, the ineffability of the air seems akin to the ineffability of awareness itself, and we should not be surprised that many indigenous peoples construe awareness, or "mind," not as a power that resides inside their heads, but rather as a quality that they themselves *are inside of*, along with the other animals and the plants, the mountains and the clouds.

FOR FURTHER REFLECTION

One of the liabilities of our modern technological culture is that we tend to lose our intimate connectedness to the natural world. Wind and rain become merely meteorological phenomena; the moon becomes nothing more than a dead, cratered sphere of rock. It would do us some good, perhaps, to turn to aboriginal peoples to help us rediscover the sacredness of nature, to once again become attuned to the spirits and life forces inhabiting the wind and soil, mountains and trees. We need to remind ourselves that we're more intimately a part of the natural world than science and technology would indicate.

. . . . TRY THIS . . . .

Take yourself to a quiet, scenic spot and spend an hour absorbing the surroundings, being attentive to the wind, the different species of trees and wildflowers, the animal and insect life. Let thoughts and feelings come to you gradually—and write them down. Later, sort through your notes and write an essay about whether you were able to find the spiritual connectedness you were seeking.

"The Silence of Vermeer"

by Sister Wendy Beckett

from *The Story of Painting*

There is something about the reverent awareness of the still life painter that reminds one of the great solitary of 17th century Holland, Jan Vermeer (1632–75). He was not literally solitary, having 11 children and a powerful family of in-laws, but none of the hubbub that must have filled his small house is ever evident in his miraculous paintings, far less any suggestion of family.

Vermeer does not need brightness in his paintings. *Woman Holding a Balance* [ca. 1664], for example, has the shutters almost closed, with light stealing obliquely around the edges. It catches the downy fur on the lady's jacket, the decorated linen that falls gracefully around her tilted head, the pearls gleaming on the shadowed table. It glances off a finger here and a necklace there, but it insists only on its silence. Silence "expresses" the purity of what exists; pure because it exists. This picture has some symbolism in that the lady is testing her empty balance, and the picture behind her shows the *Last Judgment*. But the meaning is equally in the "balance" that we experience in the actual painting: darkness and light are held in dynamic equilibrium, and in fact the picture as a whole displaces a variety of balances—warm human flesh against the silky and furry garment, the unstable human hand against the frozen certainties of metal.

FOR FURTHER REFLECTION

Wendy Beckett is one of America's most learned and entertaining authorities on the history of painting, as her thought-provoking commentary on the Dutch Master Vermeer demonstrates. Notice how skillfully she captures Vermeer's handling of light, the way it illuminates objects as well as the young woman. An art historian with the heart of a poet and spiritualist, Sister Beckett teaches us how to view great art with heightened perception and appreciation.

.................................TRY THIS.................................

Write a commentary of one or two pages on a painting that Sister Beckett discusses in her book—but finish it before you read hers. Follow this procedure with several other paintings until you feel that your powers of observation and appreciation for subtleties have improved.

Time Travel in Einstein's Universe: The Physical Possibilities of Travel Through Time

by J. Richard Gott

Do you want to visit Earth 1,000 years from now? Einstein showed how to do it. All you have to do is get in a spaceship, go to a star a bit less than 500 light-years away, and return, traveling both ways at 99.995 percent of the speed of light. When you come back, Earth will be 1,000 years older, but you will be only 10 years older. Such speed is possible—in our largest particle accelerators we bring protons to speeds higher than this (the best so far has been 99.999946 percent of the speed of light, at Fermilab). ... Protons don't weigh much, so accelerating them to high speed is relatively inexpensive. But since a human being weighs about 40 octillion times as much as a proton, in terms of energy alone, sending a person would be a great deal more expensive than sending a proton.

FOR FURTHER REFLECTION

There are aspects of theoretical physics that seem more like passages from *Alice in Wonderland*, none more so than what is known as the twin paradox. Imagine twin brothers, aged twenty. One of them travels to a nearby star at 99.9 percent the speed of light while the other remains on Earth. When the space-faring twin returns a year later by his onboard clock, he is shocked to find that his brother is now an old man in his nineties. Relativity equations show that the closer one's velocity approaches light speed (it can never attain it or exceed it), the more time (and space) compresses relative to a stationary observer. As Dr. Gott points out, we can accelerate protons to this velocity, but to do so with humans would take unimaginably greater energy than we could produce with existing technology. This does not stop science fiction writers from imagining stories of interstellar travel at light-speed or hyper-light-speed velocities.

......................................TRY THIS....................................

Try your hand at a science fiction story in which time travel by way of light-speed transport is a factor. For example, use Dr. Gott's scenario in which an expedition returns after ten years' ship time from an interstellar voyage to an Earth that has aged a thousand years.

"Keystone Species"

by Connie Barlow

from Green Space, Green Time: The Way of Science

A keystone species is one whose impact on its community or ecosystem is not only large but disproportionately large relative to its abundance or biomass. Like the keystone of an arch, removal of a keystone species jeopardizes the integrity of the whole. With the loss of a keystone species, a cascade of adjustments must take place.

The riparian forest that I tend is home to, and tremendously shaped by, a particular mammal that serves as a keystone. For several years this stretch of forest has been intensively managed by a family of beavers, *Castor canadensis*. Beavers are famous as America's foremost ecosystem engineers. Because they eat the living cambium of young trunks and branches of cottonwood and willow, beavers are voracious loggers. In this particular stretch of river, for example, they tend to wipe out the entire streamside forest in four or five years of occupancy. They then move on to greener pastures, returning a dozen years later to harvest the saplings that have since resprouted from the old cottonwood and willow roots. A ten-year-old cottonwood tree may thus be growing from a rootstock many decades old.

FOR FURTHER REFLECTION

We learn from environmentalists that species are interconnected, and that certain species play such a central role that their removal could cause an entire ecosystem to collapse. Because of the high stakes involved, we need writers like Connie Barlow, who are able to communicate these concepts clearly and forcefully.

. . . . TRY THIS . . . .

Barlow identifies other keystone species: a starfish of the Pacific Northwest responsible for maintaining a wide range of intertidal creatures; fruit bats in the South Pacific that are important pollinators of several flowering tree species; alligators, because they create troughs that track declining water tables, thereby providing other species with a steady water supply during dry seasons. Read about one of these species in-depth and write an article about its importance to the environment.

MARCH 5

A Splendor of Letters:
The Permanence of Books in an
Impermanent World
by Nicholas Basbanes

The contention that a book is measurably more than a gathering of paper stitched between two covers is not an argument that emerged full-blown in the computer age as a withering defense of print. In fact it is a creed that has been articulated passionately over the years by numerous observers, none more eloquently than the graceful essayist Charles Lamb (1775–1834), an insatiable consumer of literature who confessed in one of his Elia pieces that he dedicated "no inconsiderable portion" of his time to consuming other people's thoughts. ...

Robert Darnton, a professor of history at Princeton University ... is one of the world's leading practitioners of a discipline pioneered in France in the 1960s known as *l'histoire du livre*, the social aspect of the "history of the book," and in his writing an unwavering champion of print. "The notion that you are going to read everything from another sort of machine, a computer, is to misunderstand the nature of reading and the nature of books, the nature of book culture," he told me in an interview.

FOR FURTHER REFLECTION

In this digital age in which information of any kind can be retrieved in seconds from the Internet, in which books are being digitized and downloaded into handheld readers, we may find ourselves wondering about the continued value of print books. Nicholas Basbanes, one of our most erudite and outspoken defenders of the traditional book and the literary culture it has nurtured over the centuries, argues via numerous anecdotes and conversations with writers, librarians, private collectors and archivists that a book is more than the information it contains or the story it tells. It is an artifact whose physical properties must be factored into the reading experience.

.... TRY THIS ....

Write an essay in which you defend or refute the idea that physical books have outlived their usefulness. Be sure to represent both sides of the argument fairly.

"A Supper to Sleep On"
by M.F.K. Fisher
from *The Art of Eating*

Some insist that the oysters should be sizzled in the butter until they are curled, and then added to the hot milk. Others say they should be heated to boiling in their own juice, and that the boiling milk and the butter should be poured over them. …

The only stew I ever heard of made without either cream or milk was from three gentle sisters. … It was a strange stew, and could not have been as handsome as one made with cream, but it was even better, the sisters murmured with politeness but a kind of stubborn sensuality. It had a stronger, finer smell, they said … and it tasted purer, more completely oyster.

Their mother melted a good nubbin of fresh butter in a pan. In another pan she put the oysters, a dozen or so for everyone, with all their juices and about a cupful more of water for each dozen. She brought the water with the oysters in it just to the boil, so that the oysters began to think of curling without really getting at it, and then quickly skimmed them off and into a hot tureen. She brought the water to a boil again, and threw in pepper and salt. Then she poured the hot butter over the oysters, and the hot broth over all.

FOR FURTHER REFLECTION

A prolific writer for decades on subjects relating to food, dining, and social activities associated with food, M.F.K Fisher delightfully entwines culinary activities with the lives of those who do the cooking—not just skilled chefs, but people of all backgrounds who have exercised ingenuity and long experience in preparing their fine dishes.

. . . . .TRY THIS. . . . .

Spend some time describing the way you prepare your favorite dishes. What special spin (additional ingredients, methods of cooking) do you put on them? Once you have half a dozen or so entries completed, write an essay in which you write about yourself as a cook. You can take a humorous approach if you wish.

MARCH 7
"Ichthyosaurs"
by Stephen Jay Gould
from *Eight Little Piggies: Reflections in Natural History*

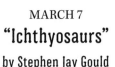

Ichthyosaurs are a group of marine reptiles with bodies so fishlike in external form that they have become the standard textbook example of "convergence"—evolved similarity from two very different starting points as independent adaptive responses to a common environment and mode of life (wings of birds and bats, eyes of squids and fishes). Ichthyosaurs are not closely related to dinosaurs, though they arose at about the same time and became extinct before the great wipeout that ended the dinosaurs' reign 65 million years ago.

In considering the convergence of ichthyosaur upon fish, we marvel most at the form and location of fins and paddles—the machinery of swimming and balancing. The fore and hind paddles are, perhaps, least remarkable. ... But the dorsal (back) and caudal (tail) fins are boggling in their precision of convergence with analogous structures in fishes.

FOR FURTHER REFLECTION

Biological evolution is much more intricate than most journalistic descriptions of it convey, which is why writers like Stephen Jay Gould (1941–2002)—who was one of the finest evolutionary biologists in the country—are so important for laypersons to turn to for information that is accurate without becoming highly technical. In the above excerpt from one of his numerous collections of essays on natural history, Dr. Gould lucidly explains the principle of evolutionary convergence—how two very different genuses (in this case reptiles and fish) can sometimes follow very similar evolutionary paths within a shared milieu (in this case the ocean), and as a result develop similar or even identical physiological characteristics.

.................................TRY THIS.................................

Children love to read about exotic creatures that inhabited the earth many millions of years ago. Learn all you can about ichthyosaurs, or another relatively little known creature (T. rex's have been written about too much!), and write about them for young audiences.

MARCH 8
"The Trojan Horse"
by Barbara W. Tuchman
from *The March of Folly: From Troy to Vietnam*

The question of whether a historical underpinning existed for the Wooden Horse was raised by Pausanias, a Latin traveler and geographer with a true historian's curiosity, who wrote a *Description of Greece* in the 2nd century A.D. He decided the Horse must have represented some kind of "war machine" or siege engine because, he argues, to take the legend at face value would be to impute "utter folly" to the Trojans. The question still provokes speculation in the 20th century. If the siege engine was a battering ram, why did not the Greeks use it as such? If it was the kind of housing that brought assaulters up to the walls, surely it would have been greater folly for the Trojans to take it in without breaking it open first. One can be lured this way down endless paths of the hypothetical. The fact is that although early Assyrian monuments depict such a device, there is no evidence that any kind of siege engine was used in Greek warfare in Mycenaean or Homeric times.

FOR FURTHER REFLECTION

Legends can be so fascinating that centuries or millennia later they become accepted as historical fact. Such is the case with the story of the Trojan horse that Homer immortalizes in the *Iliad*. Yes, historically, the Trojans, if they ever did fight a war with the Greeks, would most likely never have been so naïve as to allow such a giant artifact through their gates; but it certainly makes a splendid story and has served well as a moral metaphor: Always be suspicious of an enemy who offers you a gift, no matter what the reason.

······························TRY THIS····························

Work up a "Trojan horse" story set in the modern world—that is, imagine, let us say, that the ambassador to Country X wishes to attack Country Y and decides to use a peace offering as a decoy. How will the ambassador convince Country Y of his or her country's good intentions?

The Six Wives of Henry VIII
by Alison Weir

In an age of arranged marriages, a wife could not expect her husband to be faithful. Marriages were business arrangements, pleasure could be found elsewhere. Adultery in men was common, and Henry VIII is known to have strayed frequently during his first two marriages. Nor did he expect to be censured for it: he once brutally advised Anne Boleyn to shut her eyes as her betters had done when she dared to upbraid him for being unfaithful.

The medieval tradition of courtly love still flourished at the Tudor court. It was a code of behaviour by which the chivalrous knight paid court to the lady of his heart, who was usually older, married, and of higher rank—and thus conveniently unattainable. A man could refer to his "mistress" in the noblest sense, without implying that there was any sexual relationship, yet all too often the courtly ideal was merely an excuse for adultery.

FOR FURTHER REFLECTION

The double standard toward fidelity that men, especially monarchs, possessed in ages past (and perhaps even today) probably does not surprise us, but we sometimes shake our heads over the hypocrisy of it all. An unfaithful woman would be cast out and condemned as a whore, if not executed, whereas a man would enjoy even greater stature.

...................................TRY THIS...................................

Maintaining a double standard toward infidelity is an ideal target for satire. Write a satirical story in which a married man of relatively high social stature, who for one reason or another has fallen out of favor with people, decides to have an affair as a way of regaining admiration.

Africa in History: Themes and Outlines
by Basil Davidson

Gathering in Manchester in 1945, the members of the sixth Pan-African Congress, including Kwame Nkrumah, afterwards president of Ghana, Jomo Kenyatta, afterwards president of Kenya, and a representative of Nnamdi Azikiwe, afterwards president of Nigeria, still spoke ... of the Pan-African cause, but they struck a markedly new note. Unlike their predecessors, they demanded not only respect for Africans, but also autonomy and even independence.

New and more radical nationalist parties were soon formed in colonies such as the Gold Coast, Nigeria and French West Africa where the ruling power was prepared, if still with great reluctance, to allow them to exist. ...

Little by little, and then with gathering speed, the nationalist cause spread far outside the limits of the educated minority which had first proclaimed it, and assumed mass dimensions as it drew within its orbit ever larger numbers of townspeople and peasants. These movements soon thrust ahead of the few concessions which British or French colonial governors were ready to accept as necessary; and the dozen years after 1945 were accordingly full of violent clashes and upheavals, repressions, shootings and imprisonments.

FOR FURTHER REFLECTION

Before African colonies could achieve independence there had to be a paradigm shift in the attitude held by the imperial powers toward the native peoples under their rule—namely, that they possessed the right and the ability to govern themselves. It was not an easy task and took many years of creative diplomacy to raise the imperial governments' collective consciousness.

..................................TRY THIS....................................

Research one or two African colonies under French, British, or Portuguese rule during the mid-twentieth century and their struggle to achieve their independence; next, write an article chronicling each country's transition from colony to independent nation, emphasizing the setbacks and the breakthroughs. Remember to focus on individuals who were instrumental in the struggle for freedom.

MARCH 11

Medea

by Euripides

Translated by Rex Warner

Medea [to Jason]

... I think that the plausible speaker
Who is a villain deserves the greatest punishment.
Confident in his tongue's power to adorn evil,
He stops at nothing. Yet he is not really wise.
As in your case. There is no need to put on the airs
Of a clever speaker, for one word will lay you flat.
If you were not a coward, you would not have married
Behind my back, but discussed it with me first.

Jason

And you, no doubt, would have furthered the proposal,
If I had told you of it, you who even now
Are incapable of controlling your bitter temper.

FOR FURTHER REFLECTION

One of the greatest dramas of betrayal and revenge ever written, *Medea* still
rivets us 2,500 years after it was written. Much of the power in this play comes
from the keen intelligence and gravitas of both principal characters, the phi-
landering Jason and his cruelly vengeful wife, Medea; each understands all
too well the other's weaknesses, which in turn enables us to understand the
reasons for their respective downfalls.

. . . . TRY THIS . . . .

Write a dramatic confrontation, either for a play or a story, in which the combat-
ants (perhaps an overprotective parent and blindly rebellious child) point out
each other's flaws. If you wish, bring the confrontation to a climax in which one
or the other person breaks down or finds a way to reconcile their differences.

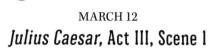

MARCH 12
Julius Caesar, Act III, Scene 1
by William Shakespeare

**[Mark Antony, encountering Brutus, Cassius, et al.,
Caesar's assassins; beholding the body of Caesar]**

O mighty Caesar! Dost thou lie so low?
Are all thy conquests, glories, triumphs, spoils,
Shrunk to this little measure? Fare thee well.
I know not, gentlemen, what you intend,
Who else must be let blood, who else is rank:
If I myself, there is no hour so fit
As Caesar's death's hour, nor no instrument
Of half that worth as those your swords, made rich
With the most noble blood of all this world.
I do beseech ye, if you bear me hard,
Now, whilst your purpled hands do reek and smoke,
Fulfill your pleasure. Live a thousand years,
I shall not find myself so apt to die:
No place will please me so, no mean of death,
As here, by Caesar, and by you cut off,
The choice and master spirits of this age.

FOR FURTHER REFLECTION

We hear of political assassinations occasionally, and with rare exceptions
we register it as mere "news"; the actual act of murder is abstracted. (Those
closer to home are exceptions like the Kennedy assassination. There our consciousness was further exacerbated by the Zapruder footage that allowed us
to witness the bloody horror.) In *Julius Caesar*, Shakespeare transforms his
audiences into eyewitnesses—first to the butchering and then to the assassins'
effort to rationalize it as a noble deed. Marc Antony, however, reminds us of the
assassins' savagery through his extraordinary apotheosis of Caesar's corpse.

......................................TRY THIS....................................

Find a news story about an accident, an act of terrorism, or an especially brutal
sports event (such as a boxing match) and transform it into an up close dramatic
incident in graphic detail.

A Journal of the Plague Year
by Daniel Defoe

from *Enlightened England: An Anthology of English Literature From Dryden to Blake*

People in the rage of the distemper, or in the torment of their swellings, which was indeed intolerable, ... throwing themselves out at their windows, shooting themselves, &c; mothers murdering their own children in their lunacy; some dying of mere grief as a passion, some of mere fright and surprise without any infection at all; others frighted into idiotism and foolish distractions, some into despair and lunacy, others into melancholy madness.

The pain of the swelling was in particular very violent, and to some intolerable; the physicians and surgeons may be said to have tortured many poor creatures even to death. The swellings in some grew hard, and they applied violent drawing plasters or poultices to break them; and if these did not do, they cut and scarified them in a terrible manner.

... It often pierced my very soul to hear the groans and cries of those who were thus tormented, but ... if these swellings could be brought to a head, and to break and run, or, as the surgeons call it, to digest, the patient generally recovered.

FOR FURTHER REFLECTION

It is one thing to be told that the bubonic plague decimated millions, quite another to read eyewitness accounts of the suffering. Writers' journals are invaluable tools for capturing the particulars of an event, thereby preserving, for future generations, a sense of what it was really like, to a degree that conventional historical accounts often overlook.

. . . . TRY THIS . . . .

Use your writer's journal to chronicle an important event over a substantial period— a month or two, or a year, depending on the complexity and significance of the event. Possible subjects include a relative's battle with a debilitating disease or accident; your child's progress through preschool and kindergarten (or some other pivotal period in his or her education); your own progress in developing an important skill, such as a foreign language or mastery of a complex piece of machinery.

"Song of Myself," Section 6
by Walt Whitman

A child said What is the grass? Fetching it to me with full hands;
How could I answer the child? I do not know what it is any more than he.
I guess it must be the flag of my disposition, out of hopeful green stuff woven.
Or I guess it is the handkerchief of the Lord,
A scented gift and remembrancer designedly dropt,
Bearing the owner's name someway in the corners, that we may see and remark,
    and say *Whose?*

Or I guess the grass is itself a child, the produced babe of the vegetation.

Or I guess it is a uniform hieroglyphic,
And it means, Sprouting alike in broad zones and narrow zones,
Growing among black folks as among white,
Kanuck, Tuckahoe, Congressman, Cuff, I give them the same, I receive them
    the same.

And now it seems to me the beautiful uncut hair of graves.

FOR FURTHER REFLECTION

With those almost intoxicatingly capacious free-verse lines that characterize
Leaves of Grass, one of the triumphs of American literature, Whitman beautifully captures the essence of American democracy; the saga of American life;
and the diverse, transcendent beauty of the American landscape. But *Leaves
of Grass*, especially "Song of Myself," is also a deeply spiritual meditation
on human nature in the context of the natural world. At the heart of even the
most commonplace facets of nature such as grass, God's handiwork can be
perceived—and that handiwork is rich in poetic mystery: grass as the offspring
of vegetation; grass as a set of hieroglyphic symbols for the pervasiveness and
tenacity of life; grass as *democratic*.

...................................TRY THIS....................................

Write a poem in the free verse celebratory manner of Whitman, in which you
meditate on a facet of nature—grass, flowers, trees, clouds, fog, stars, snow, or
rain. Try to capture the spiritual and/or symbolic character of this phenomenon.

To the Lighthouse
by Virginia Woolf

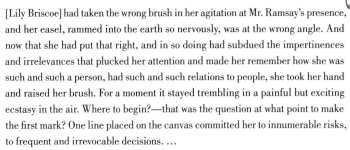

[Lily Briscoe] had taken the wrong brush in her agitation at Mr. Ramsay's presence, and her easel, rammed into the earth so nervously, was at the wrong angle. And now that she had put that right, and in so doing had subdued the impertinences and irrelevances that plucked her attention and made her remember how she was such and such a person, had such and such relations to people, she took her hand and raised her brush. For a moment it stayed trembling in a painful but exciting ecstasy in the air. Where to begin?—that was the question at what point to make the first mark? One line placed on the canvas committed her to innumerable risks, to frequent and irrevocable decisions. ...

With a curious physical sensation, as if she were urged forward and at the same time must hold herself back, she made her first quick decisive stroke. The brush descended. It flickered brown over the white canvas; it left a running mark. A second time she did it—a third time. And so pausing and so flickering, she attained a dancing rhythmical movement, as if the pauses were one part of the rhythm and the strokes another, and they were all related; and so, lightly and swiftly pausing, striking, she scored her canvas with brown running nervous lines which had no sooner settled there than they enclosed (she felt it looming out at her) a space.

FOR FURTHER REFLECTION

What is it like to be inside the head of an artist in the throes of creativity? As writers, we can all identify with Lily Briscoe's heightened state of mind as she struggles to determine the initial brushstrokes of a painting. Artistic creativity is filled with anxiety, but it is also filled with the excitement of discovery. Lily Briscoe is struggling to capture the essential personhood of Mrs. Ramsay in her painting of her friend, just as Virginia Woolf, through stream-of-consciousness narration, attempts to capture the relationship between the passage of time and the changes that occur in family relationships.

..................................TRY THIS....................................

Drawing from your own experience as a creative writer, develop a narrative in which you attempt to convey what an artist (not necessarily a writer) experiences during some stage of producing his or her work of art.

"The Odds on Normal Aging"
by Lewis Thomas
from *The Fragile Species*

Of all the things that can go wrong in aging, the loss of the mind is far and away the worst and most feared. And here, I believe, is the greatest of all opportunities for medical science in the improvement of the human condition. I think that most aging people would willingly put up with all the other inconveniences of age, the awkwardness, the enfeeblements, even the assorted pains and aches, in trade for the assurance of hanging onto their minds. I cannot think of a higher priority for biomedical science today, and I believe that most younger people, now at no threat from Alzheimer's disease or any other kind of dementia, would agree with the priority. ... We need more and better research on the aging brain, on the biochemical and structural changes associated with dementia, on strokes and their prevention, on the slow viruses, and on autoimmune mechanisms.

FOR FURTHER REFLECTION

A dedicated physician, biochemist, and cancer researcher as well as a National Book Award–winning essayist (for *The Lives of a Cell*, 1974), Lewis Thomas (1913–1993) has succeeded in communicating important insights about biology and medicine, especially with regard to holistic medicine—the complex interaction of bodily systems—such as the role of mental health on aging. Mind and body cannot be separated; what affects one affects the other.

......................................TRY THIS..................................

1. Write a short story in which your viewpoint character's physical health affects—positively or negatively or both—his or her mental health.
2. Research the latest findings on the role of mental health on aging and present them in a feature article for the general public. Highlight the contributions of individual doctors and scientists, and quote them where appropriate.

MARCH 17

I Know Why the Caged Bird Sings
by Maya Angelou

The lamplight in the Store gave a soft make-believe feeling to our world which made me want to whisper and walk about on tiptoe. The odors of onions and oranges and kerosene had been mixing all night and wouldn't be disturbed until the wooded slat was removed from the door and the early morning air forced its way in with the bodies of people who had walked miles to reach the pickup place. …

In those tender mornings the Store was full of laughing, joking, boasting and bragging. One man was going to pick two hundred pounds of cotton, and another three hundred. Even the children were promising to bring home fo' bits and six bits.

The champion picker of the day before was the hero of the dawn. If he prophesied that the cotton in today's field was going to be sparse and stick to the bolls like glue, every listener would grunt a hearty agreement.

The sound of the empty cotton sacks dragging over the floor and the murmurs of waking people were sliced by the cash register as we rang up the five-cent sales.

FOR FURTHER REFLECTION

What makes a memoir successful? In many cases it is an artful combination of startlingly candid realism, wit, and a poet's or novelist's ability to find thematic significance in many diverse incidents. In her memoir of growing up in rural Arkansas and elsewhere, Maya Angelou skillfully captures her and her brother Baily's interaction with colorful (and sometimes unsavory) characters, like the cotton farmers who frequent her grandparents' general merchandise store.

. . . . TRY THIS. . . . .

Narrate an incident from your childhood that involves one or two colorful or unsavory characters. Use dialogue and sensory descriptions to bring these individuals, and the setting, to life.

MARCH 18

A Mist of Prophecies:
A Novel of Ancient Rome
by Steven Saylor

[Cicero's sister-in-law Fabia to Goriadanus the Finder, regarding the recently murdered Cassandra, who, like her Trojan namesake, was rumored to possess the gift of prophecy]

"Our Cassandra's gift came to her mostly in the form of visions. What she saw, she didn't always understand and couldn't always put into words. She herself made no interpretation of her visions; she only related them as they occurred. Often she had no recollection of them afterward."

"I should think such a gift would be rather unreliable, producing more riddles than answers."

"Her visions required interpretation, if that's what you mean. ... But if a person listened to her closely, and if that person already possessed a genuine sympathy for the divine world—"

"A person like yourself," I said.

"Yes, I was able to make sense of Cassandra's visions. ..."

FOR FURTHER REFLECTION

Reading a Saylor novel, we find ourselves immersed in the world of ancient Rome as well as caught up in a baffling murder mystery. The murdered Cassandra possessed vital prophetic visions, but what they signified required an equally important gift: interpretation.

...................................TRY THIS....................................

Create a character with the ability to predict the future but who can only make those predictions in the form of riddles or strange metaphors. The principal intrigue in your story will be that of another character's efforts to translate those riddles and metaphors into conventional language.

"The Grandeur of the Yosemite Fall"

by John Muir

from *The Yosemite*

During the time of the spring floods the best near view of the fall is obtained from Fern Ledge on the east side above the blinding spray at a height of about 400 feet above the base of the fall. A climb of about 1400 feet from the Valley has to be made, and there is no trail, but to anyone fond of climbing this will make the ascent all the more delightful. … When the afternoon sunshine is streaming through the throng of comets, ever wasting, ever renewed, the marvelous fineness, firmness and variety of their forms are beautifully revealed. At the top of the fall they seem to burst forth in irregular spurts from some grand, throbbing mountain heart. Now and then one mighty throb sends forth a mass of solid water into the free air far beyond the others, which rushes alone to the bottom of the fall with long streaming tail, like combed silk, while the others, descending in clusters, gradually mingle and lose their identity. … The heads of these comet-like masses are composed of nearly solid water, and are dense white in color like pressed snow, from the friction they suffer in rushing though the air, the portion worn off forming the tail, between the white lustrous threads and films of which faint, grayish pencilings appear, while the outer, finer sprays of water-dust, whirling in sunny eddies, are pearly gray throughout.

FOR FURTHER REFLECTION

Ostensibly a guidebook, *The Yosemite* is filled with the rhapsodic prose of one who regarded the wilderness as sacred. Notice how skillfully Muir captures the sublime power and beauty of a Yosemite waterfall with such precise yet imaginative metaphors as "combed silk" and "comet-like" to describe the plunging water.

......................................TRY THIS....................................

Bodies of water are endlessly fascinating. Write an extended description of a lake, river, tide pool, marine preserve, waterfall, lagoon, or estuary, using vivid sensory details. Strive to be both informative and evocative.

MARCH 20
"Virtual Memory"
by Suzanne K. Langer
from Feeling and Form: A Theory of Art

Everything actual must be transformed by imagination into something purely experiential; that is the principle of poesis. The normal means of making the poetic transformation is language; the way an event is reported gives it the appearance of being something casual or something momentous, trivial or great, good or bad, even familiar or new. A statement is always a formulation of an idea, and every known fact or hypothesis or fancy takes its emotional value largely from the way it is presented and entertained.

The power of words is really astounding. Their very sound can influence one's feeling about what they are known to mean. The relation between the length of rhythmic phrases and the length of chains of thought makes thinking easy or difficult, and may make the ideas involved seem more or less profound. The vocal stresses that rhythmicize some languages, the length of vowels in others, or the tonal pitch at which words are spoken in Chinese and some less known tongues, may make one way of wording a proposition seem gayer or sadder than another. ...

Virtual life, as literature presents it, is always a self-contained form, a unit of experience, in which every element is organically related to every other, no matter how capricious or fragmentary the items are to appear. ... Memory is the great organizer of consciousness.

FOR FURTHER REFLECTION

One of the most lucid writers among twentieth-century philosophers, Suzanne Langer enables us to comprehend the complex relationship between language and experience—how language not only gives shape to our ideas and experiences, but in the guise of literature, greatly enlarges our experience of the world.

....TRY THIS....................................

Write a poem or a prose meditation on the role that language plays in shaping experience—firsthand experience (interaction with people, facing the challenges of daily life), and virtual experience (as shaped by books, television, and cyberspace).

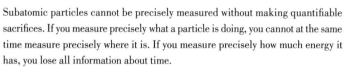

MARCH 21

The Universe and the Teacup:
The Mathematics of Truth and Beauty
by K.C. Cole

Subatomic particles cannot be precisely measured without making quantifiable sacrifices. If you measure precisely what a particle is doing, you cannot at the same time measure precisely where it is. If you measure precisely how much energy it has, you lose all information about time.

Subatomic physics gives some people the willies because of this inherent uncertainty. But knowledge is also lost with the most mundane measurements of everyday life. You cannot chemically analyze your dinner and eat it (or at least the very same bit), too. You cannot dissect the mathematics underlying Mozart and at the same time feel the emotional impact. A Picasso, viewed through a powerful microscope, dissolves into a grainy pattern of dots. ... Something is lost for every measure that's gained.

FOR FURTHER REFLECTION

Our complex brains enable us to be both analytical and artistic, but not at the same time—at least not according to *Los Angeles Times* science writer K.C. Cole, whose engaging commentary on new ideas in physics and mathematics has made her one of the most admired science commentators since Carl Sagan and Stephen Jay Gould. (See the entries for April 3 and March 7, respectively.) But is it true that just because we cannot simultaneously observe a subatomic particle's behavior and compute its location, we likewise cannot both enjoy a Mozart symphony and analyze its harmonic patterns? Or experience the romantic sensations of a star-filled night and still be able to think about the stars as far-distant suns undergoing thermonuclear fusion like our own sun?

.................................TRY THIS...................................

Can one be both romantic and analytic at the same time? Stage a debate with a friend or family member on the issue. Afterwards, write an essay presenting both sides of the debate, and then taking one side or the other.

The World Is Flat:
A Brief History of the Twenty-First Century
by Thomas L. Friedman

If you own a Toshiba laptop computer that is under warranty and it breaks and you call Toshiba to have it repaired, Toshiba will tell you to drop it off at a UPS store and have it shipped to Toshiba, and it will get repaired and shipped back to you. But here's what they don't tell you: UPS doesn't just pick up and deliver your Toshiba laptop. UPS actually repairs the computer in its own UPS-run workshop dedicated to computer and printer repairs at its Louisville hub. ...

But this is just a sliver of what UPS does today. Eaten a Papa John's pizza lately? If you see the branded Papa John's supply truck go by, ask who's dispatching the drivers and scheduling the pickups of supplies, like tomatoes, pizza sauce, and onions. Answer: UPS. UPS comes inside a lot of companies now and takes over their branded vehicles to assure on-time delivery. ...

What is going on here? It's a process that has come to be called "in-sourcing"—a whole new form of collaboration and creating value horizontally, made possible by the flat world and flattening it even more.

FOR FURTHER REFLECTION

Technology and industry in a twenty-first-century global culture is "flattening"—Thomas Friedman's term for the compression (and sometimes erasure) of distance, national boundaries, cultural differences—the world in order to make the work of the world more efficient and more profitable—but not necessarily more protective of quality.

...................................TRY THIS...................................

What is your view of in-sourcing (or outsourcing, for that matter) in our global culture? Have we gone too far? Write an essay about whether flattening the world, in Friedman's sense of the word, is ultimately a good thing or a bad thing for the United States and/or for the world.

MARCH 23

The Undiscovered Self
by C.G. Jung
Translated by R. F. C. Hull

Today, our basic convictions have become increasingly rationalistic. Our philosophy is no longer a way of life, as it was in antiquity; it has turned into an exclusively intellectual and academic affair. Our denominational religions with their archaic rites and conceptions—justified enough in themselves—express a view of the world which caused no great difficulties in the Middle Ages but has become strange and unintelligible to the man of today. Despite this conflict with the modern scientific outlook, a deep instinct bids him hang on to ideas which, if taken literally, leave out of account all the mental developments of the last five hundred years. The obvious purpose of this is to prevent him from falling into the abyss of nihilistic despair.

FOR FURTHER REFLECTION
Science and religion both embrace the wonders of creation; but unlike scientific understanding, religious belief is based upon faith. If religious rituals seem archaic to anyone today it is because that person is regarding those rituals intellectually and is not experiencing the rituals subjectively, intimately, as part of one's faith. Without the faith that religion provides, Jung is suggesting, we risk plunging into despair because the phenomenal world gives us no indication of a supernatural realm or the possibility of salvation.

..................................TRY THIS..................................

Construct a dialogue between a person of faith—one who accepts intrinsically the promise of salvation and the reality of an almighty spirit governing the universe—and an existentialist, who insists that natural phenomena is all there is, that our mortal existence is all there is.

MARCH 24

Word Freak: Heartbreak, Triumph, Genius, and Obsession in the World of Competitive SCRABBLE Players

by Stefan Fatsis

There are 3,199,724 unique combinations of seven tiles that can be plucked from a virgin Scrabble bag of ninety-eight letters and two blanks. That's the good news. The bad news is that you can draw only one of those combinations at a time. It could be AEINST? With its sixty-seven possible bingos. But it also could be IIUUUWW or any other rack of dross.

Mathematicians have determined that the possibility of choosing an acceptable seven-letter word from a fresh bag is 12.63 percent, or just over one in eight, and that's pretty good news, too. Except for one thing: Those seven letters could be EEEGRUX or CMMOPSY and you don't know that EXERGUE and COMSYMP are acceptable words. Even worse, they could be AELLRSY and you see RAL-LYES but chicken out and learn later that it is a word and means exactly what you thought it meant (the plural of a kind of auto race). Or, even worse than that, the tiles could be AAFIWY? And you fail to see the one obvious bingo, FAIrWAY.

FOR FURTHER REFLECTION

Scrabble, like chess, challenges players to use their game pieces to take the best possible advantage of a given configuration of pieces on the board. Unlike chess, of course, there's a good deal of luck involved in Scrabble: Each player acquires letter tiles via the luck of the draw. Even so, the possibilities of word formation are great. Not only that, one must learn to make words out of a jumble of letters as well as be able to integrate them with existing words on the board and do so in a way that garners a maximum number of points.

...................................TRY THIS....................................

Scrabble is certainly a writer's game. The next time you play Scrabble, keep a record of the words you've generated and, afterwards, use them in a poem or short story. As an alternative, write a feature article, serious or humorous, in which you describe the play-by-play moves of a game in progress—your own or a friend's.

The Teachings of the Compassionate Buddha

by Edwin A. Burtt

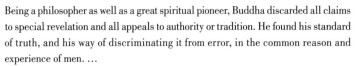

Being a philosopher as well as a great spiritual pioneer, Buddha discarded all claims to special revelation and all appeals to authority or tradition. He found his standard of truth, and his way of discriminating it from error, in the common reason and experience of men. ...

The gist of [Buddha's] basic analysis is given in the famous sermon at Benares. ... It consists of the "Four Noble Truths" ... as follows:

I. Existence is unhappiness.

II. Unhappiness is caused by selfish craving.

III. Selfish craving can be destroyed.

IV. It can be destroyed by following the eightfold path, whose steps are: (1) Right understanding; (2) Right purpose (aspiration); (3) Right speech; (4) Right conduct; (5) Right vocation; (6) Right effort; (7) Right alertness; (8) Right concentration.

FOR FURTHER REFLECTION

Religious experience, we might say, brings the natural world into direct contact with the supernatural world. The legacy of a people, bound by history, is brought into the framework of the divine and the eternal, generating, as a result of this contact, a foundation for ethical and meaningful living. Buddhism offers its followers a succinct framework for living a proper and meaningful life with its Four Noble Truths.

...................................TRY THIS....................................

Drawing from your religious convictions as well as from your life's experiences, write an essay titled "My _____ Noble Truths," listing as many truths as you consider to be valuable, and explaining (with concrete examples) why each truth has proven to be valuable for you.

Naked Beneath My Clothes: Tales of a Revealing Nature

by Rita Rudner

Women look forward to shopping for a bathing suit with much the same anticipation that baby seals look forward to clubbing season. Men don't know what we go through, so if you are a man, … I am going to tell you. (After all, we only wear those skimpy things to look good for you. If it were up to us, we'd wear bathing suits that had feet.) We go into these little cells that have mirrors everywhere, and very cruel lighting, so we can see exactly what's wrong with our bodies from every conceivable angle. I think after you leave those rooms they should offer you some kind of counseling—or at least a sign on the mirror that says, "Caution: objects in mirror may appear larger."

FOR FURTHER REFLECTION

We live in an appearance-obsessed society, and it sometimes takes a fine comedienne like Rita Rudner to remind us with a comic jolt of that fact. When Ms. Rudner writes that there ought to be counseling services outside of fitting rooms, she's probably not too far from the literal truth. The images of attractiveness—male or female—that are promulgated by all the media almost inevitably encourage us to think disparagingly of ourselves if we don't possess the figures of fashion models.

...................................TRY THIS...................................

Write a humorous or satirical essay that pokes fun at mass-media visions of male and/or female attractiveness or stylishness.

MARCH 27

The Martian Chronicles
by Ray Bradbury

[Spender to Captain Wilder]

"No matter how we touch Mars, we'll never touch it. And then we'll get mad at it, and you know what we'll do? We'll rip it up, rip the skin off, and change it to fit ourselves."

"We won't ruin Mars," said the captain. "It's too big and too good."

"You think not? We Earth Men have a talent for ruining big, beautiful things. The only reason we didn't set up hot-dog stands in the midst of the Egyptian temple of Karnak is because it was out of the way and served no large commercial purpose. And Egypt is a small part of Earth. But here, this whole thing is ancient and different, and we have to set down somewhere and start fouling it up." … Spender looked at the iron mountains. "They know we're here tonight, to spit in their wine, and I imagine they hate us."

The captain shook his head. "There's no hatred here." He listened to the wind. "From the look of their cities they were a graceful, beautiful, and philosophical people. They accepted what came to them."

FOR FURTHER REFLECTION

The episodes that comprise Bradbury's novel, one of the best-loved science fiction novels of the twentieth century, are essentially parables of the human condition, and Mars is like a mirror held up to magnify that condition. Ancient and mysterious, the Red Planet becomes a place of hope and comfort for the Earth men—but it also proves to be a place that will not be exploited so easily.

...................................TRY THIS....................................

Try your hand at composing a story set on Mars (or some imaginary, strange world) that emulates the tone and mood of one of the Martian Chronicle episodes. For example, you might build conflict between two characters: one who wants to exploit Mars for its mineral resources, and the other who sees Mars as a spiritual mecca.

"Rappaccini's Daughter"
by Nathaniel Hawthorne
from *Tales and Sketches*

"Beatrice," asked [Giovanni], abruptly, "whence came this shrub?"

"My father created it," answered she, with simplicity.

"Created it! Created it!!" repeated Giovanni. "What mean you, Beatrice?"

"He is a man fearfully acquainted with the secrets of Nature," replied Beatrice, "and, at the hour when I first drew breath, this plant sprang from the soil, the off-spring of his science, of his intellect, while I was but his earthly child. Approach it not!" continued she, observing with terror that Giovanni was drawing nearer to the shrub. "It has qualities that you little dream of. But I, dearest Giovanni, I grew up and blossomed with the plant and was nourished with its breath. It was my sister, and I loved it with a human affection; for, alas!—hast thou not suspected it?—there was an awful doom."

Here Giovanni frowned so darkly upon her that Beatrice paused and trembled. ...

"There was an awful doom," she continued, "the effect of my father's fatal love of science, which estranged me from all society of my kind."

FOR FURTHER REFLECTION

Like Mary Shelley's Victor Frankenstein, Rappaccini stops at nothing, not even the welfare of his daughter Beatrice's soul, to learn the secrets of nature. In this Garden of Eden story with a twist, Hawthorne is considering the possibility that it's not so much knowledge itself that is the root of original sin; it is the insatiable, Faustian quest for it that poses a danger to humanity.

............................TRY THIS....................................

Write a story in which your protagonist is obsessed with her scientific or medical research. To what extremes will this person go in this quest? What sacrifices will she be willing to make? What will be the consequences?

Against Technology: From the Luddites to Neo-Luddism
by Steven E. Jones

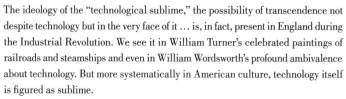

The ideology of the "technological sublime," the possibility of transcendence not despite technology but in the very face of it ... is, in fact, present in England during the Industrial Revolution. We see it in William Turner's celebrated paintings of railroads and steamships and even in William Wordsworth's profound ambivalence about technology. But more systematically in American culture, technology itself is figured as sublime.

During the twentieth century, the sublimity of modern technology shifted away from bridges to computers, what one recent book calls "the digital sublime" [Vincent Mosco, *The Digital Sublime*; MIT Press, 2004]. The conventional mode of the sublime, a sense of transcendence in the face of scenes of natural or manmade grandeur, gigantic bridges and seemingly infinite railways which competed with the divine in provoking terror and awe gave way to a more slippery, "liquid" kind of technological sublimity that is everywhere and nowhere at once and whose material synecdoche—the symbolic part that represents the larger whole—became the Internet.

FOR FURTHER REFLECTION

Technology can lead us down two very different paths. One is the path of industrial blight, of smog-choked cities and polluted rivers; the other is the path of spiritual and aesthetic transcendence that Steven Jones discusses: machines and other engineering marvels as icons of sublime power and beauty.

..................................TRY THIS..................................

Compose a poem or meditative essay about a machine, building, or bridge that possesses symbolic, transcendent value for you. Perhaps it's an engineering marvel like a dam or a suspension bridge; or perhaps it's a complex machine, like the supercollider in Switzerland.

MARCH 30

Notes and Counternotes: Writings on the Theatre

by Eugène Ionesco

Translated by Donald Watson

It was not for me to conceal the devices of the theatre, but rather make them still more evident, deliberately obvious, go all-out for caricature and the grotesque, way beyond the pale irony of witty drawing-room comedies. No drawing-room comedies, but farce, the extreme exaggeration of parody. Humor, yes, but using the methods of burlesque. Comic effects that are firm, broad and outrageous. … Everything raised to paroxysm, where the source of tragedy lies. A theatre of violence: violently comic, violently dramatic. …

We need to be virtually bludgeoned into detachment from our daily lives, our habits and mental laziness, which conceal from us the strangeness of the world. Without a fresh virginity of mind, without a new and healthy awareness of existential reality, there can be no theatre and no art either; the real must be in a way dislocated, before it can be re-integrated.

FOR FURTHER REFLECTION

Eugène Ionesco, along with Samuel Beckett, Harold Pinter, and Edward Albee, revolutionized drama by developing what critic Martin Esslin has termed "theatre of the absurd"—an effort to get closer to the human condition by confronting rather than concealing the artifice not only of society but of art, including theatrical illusions. Many of Ionesco's plays, such as *Rhinoceros*, are in effect metaphysical farces. In this play, while a charging rhinoceros is wreaking havoc in a French village, two logicians are furiously debating whether the species of rhino in question is African or Asian.

.....................................TRY THIS.....................................

Write a skit that pokes fun at a long-standing tradition in order to expose its inherent faults. Example: a confrontation between a teacher and a student over a supposedly indisputable historical fact.

MARCH 31
Eats, Shoots & Leaves: The Zero Tolerance Approach to Punctuation
by Lynne Truss

To those who care about punctuation, a sentence such as "Thank God its Friday" (without the apostrophe) rouses feelings not only of despair but of violence. The confusion of the possessive "its" (no apostrophe) is an unequivocal signal of illiteracy and sets off a simple Pavlovian "kill" response in the average stickler. The rule is: the word "it's" (with apostrophe) stands for "it is" or "it has." If the word does not stand for "it is" or "it has," then what you require is "its." *This is extremely easy to grasp.* Getting your itses mixed up is the greatest solecism in the world of punctuation. No matter that you have a PhD and have read all of Henry James twice. If you still persist in writing, "Good food at it's best," you deserve to be struck by lightning, hacked up on the spot and buried in an unmarked grave.

FOR FURTHER REFLECTION

Why are so many people, even highly literate people, sloppy with punctuation? Perhaps it has something to do with the digital age we're living in, the age of e-mail and texting, of rapid-fire, unedited communication. Perhaps it has something to do with the fact that people are contemptuous (consciously or not) of punctuation, which conjures up bad memories of their wrist-slapping, red-ink-wielding schoolteachers. Whatever the reason, the British journalist Lynne Truss wittily reminds us of the important role punctuation plays in clear communication.

..................................TRY THIS....................................

1. Make a list of your pet punctuation and sentence-construction peeves, and then write a humorous commentary in the manner of Lynne Truss on one or two of them.
2. Write a play or short story in which one of your characters, for comic or satiric purposes, flagrantly abuses the English language.

APRIL 1

The Descent of Man
by Charles Darwin

He who believes in the advancement of man from some low organized form will naturally ask, how does this bear on the belief in the immortality of the soul? ... Few persons feel any anxiety from the impossibility of determining at what precise period in the development of the individual, from the first trace of a minute germinal vesicle, man becomes an immortal being; and there is no greater cause for anxiety because the period cannot possibly be determined in the gradually ascending organic scale.

I am aware that the conclusions arrived at in this work will be denounced by some as highly irreligious; but he who denounces them is bound to shew why it is more irreligious to explain the origin of man as a distinct species by descent from some lower form through the laws of variation and natural selection, than to explain the birth of the individual through the laws of ordinary reproduction. The birth both of the species and of the individual are equally parts of that grand sequence of events, which our minds refuse to accept as the result of blind chance.

FOR FURTHER REFLECTION

If we accept the analogy between the natural birth and development of an individual and the natural birth and development of a species, Darwin reasons, then on what legitimate grounds can we dismiss the latter as irreligious? For some fundamentalists, the answer is simple: Scripture says that God created man in His own image, end of discussion. But if we value rational thought, we cannot foreclose discussion of a debatable premise—and the premise need not be dualistic (i.e., humans either evolved naturally with all other life-forms *or* they were divinely and separately created).

. . . . TRY THIS . . . .

The creation vs. evolution debate shows no sign of diminishing. Create a dialogue between a creationist and an evolutionist on the following topic: "Creationism (or intelligent design) should be taught as an alternative theory to evolution in the public-school science classroom." Represent both views as accurately as you can.

APRIL 2

"Loving and Loathing Science at the Fin de Siècle"

by Lynn Gamwell

from *Exploring the Invisible: Art, Science, and the Spiritual*

Artists in the closing decades of the nineteenth century could not ignore the irresistible rise of science and technology, and responded from the heart and the mind. The most extreme reactions—of great enthusiasm and bitter apprehension—came from two groups, respectively, Neo-Impressionists and Symbolists. Perched at the borderland of art and science, the Neo-Impressionist Georges Seurat employed an experimental painting method that relied on the latest optical theory.* Ever since his brief career in the 1880s, he has been associated with those who deliberately brought science to their art. Artists in Symbolist circles took an opposite approach, finding only bad news in science—decadence, degeneracy, entropy. Symbolist artists and poets rejected the objective mind-set of the realist and scientist, preferring subjectivity and fantasy. Nostalgic about decorative styles from prescientific eras and resigned to their bitter fate of being trapped in a world where they did not feel at home, some Symbolists** expressed dismay, even scorn, at what the scientific age promised.

FOR FURTHER REFLECTION

Art thrives on paradox, which is why an artist can be either pro-science or anti-science in his or her artistic vision, and still produce great art. Seurat's (and other neo-Impressionists') studies of new ways of reproducing the effects of light with pigment, and the Symbolists' revolt against naturalism, have produced equally powerful masterpieces that, collectively, capture the spectrum of human experience, intellectual as well as emotional and spiritual.

...................................TRY THIS...................................

Discuss a famous painting from any period from two different perspectives, a "scientific" one, in which you describe the painting's ability, say, to capture nature accurately; and an aesthetic one, that focuses more on the mood or emotions it generates.

---

* Seurat's paintings may be viewed via the website of the Art Institute of Chicago: www.artic.edu/aic/collections/search/citi/artist%3ASeurat

** For example, the Austrian painter Alfred Kubin, whose painting "The North Pole," depicts a mountain with a peak in the shape of a skull.

Pale Blue Dot: A Vision of the Human Future in Space
by Carl Sagan

The exploration of other worlds has opened our eyes in the study of volcanoes, earthquakes, and weather. It may one day have profound implications for biology, because all life on Earth is built on a common biochemical master plan. The discovery of a single extraterrestrial organism—even something as humble as a bacterium—would revolutionize our understanding of living things. But the connection between exploring other worlds and protecting this one is most evident in the study of Earth's climate and the burgeoning threat to that climate that our technology now poses. Other worlds provide vital insights about what dumb things not to do on earth.

Three potential environmental catastrophes—all operating on a global scale—have recently been uncovered: ozone layer depletion, greenhouse warming, and nuclear winter. All three discoveries, it turns out, have strong ties to the exploration of the planets.

FOR FURTHER REFLECTION

We can learn a great deal about our home world by studying other worlds. The planet Venus, for example, teaches us what a runaway greenhouse effect can do to an environment. Venus's thick atmosphere of mostly carbon dioxide has produced a surface environment of hellish temperatures (hot enough to melt lead) and crushing air pressure. Robotic probes such as those currently exploring the surface of Mars are providing us with new information about whether hostile environments can still be conducive to life.

................................TRY THIS................................

1. Speculate, in an essay, on the practical applications of space exploration, either by humans, robots, or orbiting high-resolution probes.
2. Write a feature article for young people on some of the great discoveries made as a result of exploring space with robotic probes or with the Hubble Space Telescope.

APRIL 4

The Periodic Table
by Primo Levi

Translated by Raymond Rosenthal

Night lay beyond the walls of the Chemical Institute, the night of Europe: ... Hitler had marched into Prague ..., Franco had subdued Barcelona. ... Fascist Italy, the small-time pirate, had occupied Albania, and the premonition of imminent catastrophe condensed like grumous dew. ... Fascist censorship itself, the regime's masterwork, kept us shut off from the world, in a white, anesthetized limbo. About thirty of us had managed to surmount the harsh barrier of the first exams and had been admitted to the second year's Qualitative Analysis laboratory. ...

Professor D ... handed each of us precisely one gram of a certain powder: by the next day we had to complete the qualitative analysis, that is, report what metals and non-metals it contained. Report in writing, like a police report, only yes and no, because doubts and hesitations were not admissible. ... Some elements, such as iron and copper, were easy and direct, incapable of concealment; others, such as bismuth and cadmium, were deceptive and elusive. There was a method, a toilsome, age-old plan for systematic research, a kind of combined steamroller and fine-toothed comb which nothing (in theory) could escape, but I preferred to invent each time a new road, and with swift, extemporaneous forays, as in a war of movement, instead of the deadly grind of a war of position. Sublimate mercury into droplets, transform sodium into chloride, and identify it as trough-shaped chips under my microscope. One way or another, here the relationship with Matter changed, became dialectical.

FOR FURTHER REFLECTION

Working as a chemist for the Italian Fascist government not only helped Primo Levi survive the Holocaust (although he was eventually sent to Auschwitz in 1944), it provided him by way of the Periodic Table of elements with a rich body of metaphors from which to fashion a memoir. Thus argon, one of the inert gases, reminded him of his relatives, kept apart from the rest of the villagers; and iron represented the element of military conquest and oppression.

..................................TRY THIS....................................

Use a chemical element to serve as a metaphor for a memorable incident or person in your life. For example, silver might conjure memories of your grandmother, who entertained with heirloom silverware, candelabras, trays, and pitchers.

Leave Me Alone, I'm Reading: Finding and Losing Myself in Books
by Maureen Corrigan

For all readers, male and female, there is a discrepancy between the possibilities offered by the world of the imagination and the possibilities offered by real life. That's one of the reasons we read fiction: to fantasize about what might be. But, until the social revolution of the Second Women's Movement, that discrepancy, generally speaking, had been more gaping for women readers. Because so many of fiction's heroes are, well, heroes instead of heroines, women readers, out of pleasant necessity, have learned to step into the roomier footwear of the Deerslayer, Beowulf, Ulysses, Ishmael, David Copperfield, and so on. These heroes lead lives of on-the-road adventure, recklessness, and big dreams—all played out in the public sphere. And therein lies the bad-boy allure of these tales. Victorian and turn-of-the-century patriarchs worried that middle-class female readers would get all stirred up by "questionable" literature—like romances and adventure sagas—and, for a time, live through their imaginations like men. They would squeeze back into their own overstuffed parlors with their heads full of mutinous androgynous possibilities.

FOR FURTHER REFLECTION

Society, collectively, seems to be of two minds when it comes to gender differences: On the one hand there's a strong compulsion to maintain and reinforce those differences; on the other hand, both men and women (but especially women) strive to break down those distinctions, which tend to fossilize into stereotypes (e.g., women are weaker than men—an especially damaging stereotype that has resulted in job discrimination). There's nothing like reading, as Maureen Corrigan points out, to awaken the possibilities of living once assumed to be restricted only to men.

...................................TRY THIS....................................

Write a story about a woman whose interests and ambitions do not conform to what is stereotypically female, yet at the same time is one who enjoys her femininity.

APRIL 6

Fast Food Nation: The Dark Side of the All-American Meal
by Eric Schlosser

Congress should ban advertising that preys upon children, it should stop subsidizing dead-end jobs, it should pass tougher food safety laws, it should protect American workers from serious harm, it should fight against dangerous concentrations of economic power. Congress should do all those things, but it isn't likely to do any of them soon. The political influence of the fast food industry and its agribusiness suppliers makes a discussion of what Congress should do largely academic. The fast food industry spends millions of dollars every year on lobbying and billions on mass marketing. The wealth and power of the major chains make them seem impossible to defeat. And yet those companies must obey the demands of one group—consumers—whom they eagerly flatter and pursue. As the market for fast food in the United States becomes increasingly saturated, the chains have to complete fiercely with one another for customers. According to William P. Foley II, the chairman of the company that owns Carl's Jr., the basic imperative of today's fast food industry is "Grow or die."

FOR FURTHER REFLECTION

It might seem as though consumers are at the mercy of mega-corporations like fast-food restaurants and their agribusiness suppliers; yet, consumers are what keep these enterprises thriving, as Eric Schlosser notes. If there is widespread outrage over the way the fast-food industry is ruining the nation's health, then consumers must find ways to channel their outrage and resist with moratoriums and counter-advertising.

.... TRY THIS ....

Prepare a manifesto in which you reflect the collective voice of consumers who wish to put an end to—or at least significantly reform—the fast-food industry as it currently exists. Lay out specific recommendations for improvement.

APRIL 7

"The Metaphors of Geology"

by John McPhee

from *Basin and Range* and *Annals of the Former World*

I used to sit in class and listen to the terms come floating down the room like paper airplanes. Geology was called a descriptive science, and with its pitted outwash plains and drowned rivers, its hanging tributaries and starved coastlines, it was nothing if not descriptive. It was a fountain of metaphor—of isostatic adjustments and degraded channels, of angular unconformities and shifting divides, of rootless mountains and bitter lakes. Streams eroded headward, digging from two sides into mountain or hill, avidly struggling toward each other until the divide between them broke down, and the two rivers that did the breaking now became confluent (one yielding to the other, giving up its direction of flow and going the opposite way) to become a single stream. Stream capture. In the Sierra Nevada, the Yuba captured the Bear. … There was fatigued rock and incompetent rock and inequigranular fabric in rock. If you bent or folded rock, the inside of the curve was in a state of compression, the outside of the curve was under great tension, and somewhere in the middle was the surface of no strain. Thrust fault, reverse fault, normal fault—the two sides were active in every fault. … There seemed, indeed, to be more than a little of the humanities in this subject.

FOR FURTHER REFLECTION

Few literary journalists have captured the metaphoric richness of scientific language—especially the language of geology—more than John McPhee, who takes us on what we might call geological safaris (accompanied by prominent geologists) across the continental United States.

························· TRY THIS ·······················

With a dictionary of geology at your elbow, write an essay about a favorite landform or body of water, making use of as many relevant geological terms as possible. For example, you might describe a prominent rock outcrop. Describe the types of rocks present (perhaps granite, feldspar, limestone, mica, basalt), the different layers of sediment, erosion, and so on. You may first want to read one or more of McPhee's four geology books (collected in *Annals of the Former World*) before proceeding with your own essay.

APRIL 8
"Babylon"
by Robert Ingpen and Philip Wilkinson

from *Encyclopedia of Mysterious Places:*
The Life and Legends of Ancient Sites Around the World

Babylon has lived longer in the human imagination than any other city in the world. Even today the stories of the Tower of Babel and the Babylonian captivity of the Jews under King Nebuchadnezzar have a haunting power. Although the events these stories describe were separated by many centuries they convey a consistent image of the city—a place of great riches and magnificent buildings, but at the same time a city of luxury and decadence, doomed to perish in a terrible apocalypse. ...

It is thanks to the Bible that this image of Babylon has prevailed. The first picture of Babylon that has come down to us in this way is in ... the Book of Genesis. This tells how Noah's descendants, at the time when all the people on earth spoke the same language, started to build a great tower that was designed to reach all the way to heaven. God ... realised that the only way to prevent them would be to stop them understanding each other. So he unleashed the "babble after Babel," the confusion of different languages, and scattered the people over the earth.

The second great story ... is in the later books of the Old Testament that deal with the conquest of Jerusalem and the exile of the Jews. These accounts have given us a host of enduring scenes—form the exiles weeping by the waters of Babylon, to the adventures of the prophet Daniel in the lions' den.

FOR FURTHER REFLECTION

Few tales can set a writer's imagination racing more than those of lost cities. Babylon is among the most famous because of its Biblical representation, and the wonderful legend of the Tower of Babel with its grim lesson about the consequences of mortals attempting to reach heaven.

......................................TRY THIS....................................

Explore the history and archaeology of a lost, mysterious city such as Knossos, Delphi, or Rhodes in Europe; Mohenjo-daro, Ur, or Ellora in Asia; Karnak, Abu Simbel or Alexandria in Africa; or Chichen Itza, Tenochtitlan, or Machu Picchu in the New World (all of which are portrayed in the *Encyclopedia of Mysterious Places*). Next, write a story that dramatizes a struggle between good and evil in this city.

A Short History of India and Pakistan; From Ancient Times to the Present
by T. Walter Wallbank

Up to 1000 A.D. India had been able to assimilate the numerous invaders who had pushed through the narrow passes of her northern mountain wall. But not long after the death of King Harsha in the seventh century and the collapse of a strong government in the north, a new invasion movement began to take form that would seriously challenge the traditional capacity of Hinduism to absorb alien cultures.

As early as the year 711 Muslim Arabs came in conflict with Indians when an expedition of Arab marauders reached the mouth of the Indus and captured the area of Sind. Further expansion in this region, however, was blocked, and Muslim raids into India were started in earnest from the northwest late in the tenth century. Under the redoubtable Amir Mahmud of Ghazni, an Afghan Turk who began raiding in 998, seventeen looting expeditions were carried out. ... To his Muslim horsemen, India was a land handed over by Allah for pillage and plunder. Fiercely monotheistic, detesting idolatry, and believing in the equality of man, the Muslims abhorred the "Hindu infidels and unbelievers" with their idols and their caste system.

FOR FURTHER REFLECTION

So much of history is a history of religiously motivated conquest and subjugation. This is dramatically illustrated by the conflict, spread over centuries, between Muslims, for whom iconography is blasphemous, and Hindus, for whom iconography is foundational to worship.

.....................................TRY THIS....................................

Explore one facet of the Muslim-Hindu conflict in depth and write an essay in which you focus on the particular clashing religious ideologies. As an alternative, write a love story between a Muslim and a Hindu, and dramatize their struggle to resolve their religious differences.

APRIL 10
The Fifties
by David Halberstam

If Stalin had represented the worst of Soviet Communism, then Khrushchev to many Americans was even more threatening, for he seemed to reflect the peasant vigor of this new state. Was America finally attaining a broad affluence only to find that the comforts of middle-class existence had weakened it? …

Many Americans worried that the very material success of America in the postwar years—all those cars, kitchen amenities, and other luxuries—had made us soft and vulnerable to the Soviet Union, where people were tougher and more willing to sacrifice for their nation. Was there strength and truth in poverty? Styles Bridges, a conservative Republican senator, seemed to talk in this vein when he said that Americans had to be less concerned with "the height of the tail fin in the new car and be much more prepared to shed blood, sweat and tears, if this country and the free world are to survive."

FOR FURTHER REFLECTION

In the eyes of the world, American society has always seemed highly materialistic. Aside from the moral concerns of being materialistic, was Senator Bridges correct in suggesting that Americans needed to be more self-sacrificing if they wanted to prevail in a hostile world? Some would argue that materialism and courage are not incompatible; others would agree that materialism blinds one to higher values.

................................TRY THIS................................

1. Write a story that would illustrate your views about materialism and courage. Does one preclude the other?
2. Choose one of your favorite personalities from the 1950s and write a detailed, colorful profile of him or her.

"Immortal Aphrodite of the Broidered Throne"

by Sappho

from *Sappho: Memoir, Text, Selected Renderings,*
and a Literal Translation. Translated by Henry Wharton

Immortal Aphrodite of the broidered throne, daughter of Zeus, weaver of wiles, I pray thee break not my spirit with anguish and distress, O Queen. But come hither, if ever before thou didst hear my voice afar, and listen, and leaving thy father's golden house camest with chariot yoked, and fair fleet sparrows drew thee, flapping fast their wings around the dark earth, from heaven through mid sky. Quickly arrived they; and thou, blessed one, smiling with immortal countenance, didst ask, What now is befallen me, and Why now I call, and What I in my mad heart most desire to see. "What Beauty now wouldst thou draw to love thee? Who wrongs thee, Sappho? For even if she flies she shall soon follow, and if she rejects gifts shall yet give, and if she loves not shall soon love, however loth." Come, I pray thee, now too, and release me from cruel cares; and all that my heart desires to accomplish, accomplish thou, and be thyself my ally.

FOR FURTHER REFLECTION

Among the finest of the ancient Greek lyric poets, Sappho is known to have written the equivalent of seven volumes of poetry, but her poems have survived only in fragments. Most of the poems are expressions of romantic love—homosexual and heterosexual (the word *lesbian* is derived from Sappho's island home of Lesbos). In "Immortal Aphrodite" the speaker prays to the love goddess to release her from the anguish of unrequited love.

............................TRY THIS....................................

Write a poem, perhaps addressed to a god or goddess, or to God, in which the speaker describes the anguish of unrequited love and prays for the loved one's affections.

The Divine Comedy: Hell

by Dante

from *The Comedy of Dante Alighieri, the Florentine.*
Translated by Dorothy L. Sayers

I am now in the Third Circle: that of rain—
One ceaseless, heavy, cold, accursed quench,
Whose law and nature vary never a grain;

Huge hailstones, sleet and snow, and turbid drench
Of water sluice down through the darkened air,
And the soaked earth gives off a putrid stench.

Cerberus, the cruel, misshapen monster, there
Buys in his triple gullet and doglike growls
Over the wallowing shades, his eyeballs glare

A bloodshot crimson, and his bearded jowls
Are greasy and black; pot-bellied, talon-heeled,
He clutches and flays and rips and rends the souls.

They howl in the rain like hounds; they try to shield
One flank with the other; with many a twist and squirm,
The impious wretches writhe in the filthy field.

FOR FURTHER REFLECTION

Few poems kindle the imagination like *Hell* (*Inferno*), the first book in the
Divine Comedy trilogy. Who cannot shudder as we descend, circle by circle,
observing the lost souls being tormented for their transgressions—gluttony,
avarice, treachery, impiety (as witnessed in the Third Circle). With graphic
imagery that is both horrifying and eloquent, we witness the meting out of
grotesque punishments that match the grotesqueness of the sins.

.................................TRY THIS...................................

Write your own version of one of the circles of Hell by describing the punishment
of one of its victims. Use graphic imagery to convey the horror of the punishment
being administered.

"A Poem Sacred to the Memory of Sir Isaac Newton"

by James Thomson

All intellectual eye, our solar round
First gazing thro', he by the blended power
Of gravitation and projection, saw
The whole in silent harmony revolve.
From unassisted vision hid, the moons
To cheer remoter planets numerous form'd,
By him in all their mingled tracts were seen.
He also fix'd the wandering Queen of Night,
Whether she wanes into a scanty orb,
Or, waxing broad, with her pale shadowy light,
In a soft deluge overflows the sky.
Her every motion clear-discerning, he
Adjusted to the mutual main, and taught
Why now the mighty mass of water swells
Restless, heaving on the broken rocks,
And the full river turning, till again
The tide revertive, unattracted, leaves
A yellow waste of idle sands behind.

FOR FURTHER REFLECTION

The Age of Enlightenment is so named because of the way it championed rational thought in all endeavors—not just in the investigation of nature, but in the arts, history, politics, and even religion. Poets like Thomson looked to Isaac Newton, who demystified the forces of the cosmos with his three laws of motion (including the laws that explained why the moon orbited the earth), elucidated the properties of light and optics, and coinvented the calculus as the crown prince of the Enlightenment.

. . . . TRY THIS. . . . .

Write a poem celebrating a scientist and his or her contributions. Great scientists like Copernicus, Galileo, Newton, Darwin, Einstein, Curie, and Freud are good choices, but also consider writing about lesser-known figures such as William Harvey, Anton van Leeuwenhoek, and James Clerk Maxwell.

Hard Times

by Charles Dickens

[Coketown] was a town of red brick, or of brick that would have been red if the smoke and ashes had allowed it; but as matters stood it was a town of unnatural red and black like the painted face of a savage. It was a town of machinery and tall chimneys, out of which interminable serpents of smoke trailed themselves forever and ever, and never got uncoiled. It had a black canal in it, and a river than ran purple with ill-smelling dye, and ... where the piston of the steam-engine worked monotonously up and down like the head of an elephant in a state of melancholy madness. It contained several large streets all very like one another, inhabited by people equally like one another, who all went in and out at the same hours, with the same sound upon the same pavements, to do the same work, and to whom every day was the same as yesterday and tomorrow, and every year the counterpart of the last and the next.

FOR FURTHER REFLECTION

The Industrial Revolution began transforming European culture around the beginning of the nineteenth century. By mid-century it was in full swing; the urban blight due to pollution from manufacturing was ugly and oppressive, as Dickens conveys so vividly in *Hard Times*. Dickens also makes a connection between the inhuman forces of industrial mechanization and those twin destroyers of humanistic culture and imagination, the rise of mass conformity and the relentless monotony of life in an industrial society.

..................................TRY THIS...................................

Write a short story, poem, or essay in which you convey the deleterious effects of a monotonous, uninspiring job (assembly-line work, for example) on the quality of life.

APRIL 15

Things Fall Apart
by Chinua Achebe

The arrival of the missionaries had caused a considerable stir in the village of Mbanta. There were six of them and one was a white man. Every man and woman came out to see the white man. Stories about these strange men had grown since one of them had been killed in Abame and his iron horse tied to the sacred silk-cotton tree. And so everybody came to see the white man. It was the time of the year when everybody was at home. The harvest was over.

When they had all gathered, the white man began to speak to them. He spoke through an interpreter who was an Ibo man, though his dialect was different and harsh to the ears of Mbanta. ... He said he was one of them, as they could see from his color and his language. The other four black men were also their brothers, although one of them did not speak Ibo. The white man was also their brother because they were all sons of God. And he told them about this new God, the Creator of all the world and all the men and women. He told them that they worshipped false gods, gods of wood and stone.

FOR FURTHER REFLECTION

One of the finest novels from twentieth-century Africa, *Things Fall Apart* (the title comes from Yeats's famous 1921 poem, "The Second Coming": "Things fall apart; the centre cannot hold; / Mere anarchy is loosed upon the world") dramatizes the clash of values between Ibo culture (in what is now Biafra) and the Christian missionaries with their conversion and colonial agendas.

..................................TRY THIS..................................

After reading in depth about a clash of cultures through missionary work or military coup (examples: Roman conquests in Africa and Britain; the Crusades; Christian missionary infiltration of Hawaii; America's forced relocation of Native American peoples), write a story that brings the culture clash down to the level of two individuals.

"Why Vegetables Are Good for You"
by Natalie Angier
from *The Beauty of the Beastly: New Views on the Nature of Life*

Cached away in the soul of every red-blooded American who fondly recalls when carnivory was a virtue and supper wasn't supper without a centerpiece of pork chops or prime ribs lies the frail hope that all the recent emphasis on fruits, grains, and vegetables, vegetables, vegetables will somehow turn out to be a terrible mistake.

Abandon that hope, ye who succor it. The truth is that the more we learn about the ingredients found in fruits, vegetables, beans, and herbs, the more impressive appears the power of those compounds to retard the bodily breakdown that results in cancer and other chronic diseases. Nutritionists and epidemiologists have long observed that people who eat a plant-rich diet suffer lower rates of cancer than do meat loyalists, and now scientists are on their way to understanding why. ...

In the course of metabolizing energy and using oxygen, the body's cells constantly generate hazardous molecules called free radicals, which can mutate genes and set the foundation for cancer. Most of the radicals are sopped up by the body's native antioxidant enzymes, but yellow and green vegetables, as well as melons and citrus fruits, also offer a wealth of antioxidant compounds, including vitamins C, E, and beta carotene, the precursor to vitamin A.

FOR FURTHER REFLECTION

Natalie Angier, a Pulitzer Prize–winning science writer for *The New York Times*, has a knack for explaining complex ideas about chemistry, physics, medicine, and health in a manner that is at once precise, clear, and engaging. One of her techniques, apparent in the above passage, is first explaining causes and effects in accessible language and then showing how the causes lead to the effects, as in the case with the way in which yellow and green vegetables help the body to absorb the hazardous molecules it continuously generates.

..................................TRY THIS....................................

People yearn to understand the principles of physics, astronomy, chemistry, biology, and medicine that are often obscured by jargon. Write a feature for young readers that explains a phenomenon in one of the sciences. Use analogies to make the concept(s) understandable to this age group.

The Private Lives of Albert Einstein
by Roger Highfield and Paul Carter

Einstein's purported dimness as a schoolboy is one of the most seductive parts of his legend: it gives hope to the rest of us. Classmates at primary school taunted him with the nickname "Biedermeier," which roughly translates as "Honest John," because of his blunt and unsophisticated manner. His sister remarked that he was considered only moderately talented because he took so long to mull things over. She wrote, "Nothing of his special aptitude for mathematics was noticeable at the time; he wasn't even good at arithmetic in the sense of being quick and accurate, though he was reliable and persevering." Stories of this early backwardness are easily overplayed, however, and as early as seven he had started to show real promise. Pauline [Einstein's mother] wrote to her own mother in August 1886 that he had been placed top of the class "once again" and had received a "splendid" school report. It became part of family folklore that she had declared that her little Albert would become a great professor one day.

FOR FURTHER REFLECTION

Famous people tend to become mythologized and some of their traits distorted. This is certainly true of Einstein—a mathematical genius who is purported to have been poor at math in school. It is always important to place things in context, however. If rapidity of response is a criterion, for example, then Einstein the student was "slow." If originality of insight into the properties of the fundamental forces of nature—of time, space, and motion—is the criterion, then Einstein has no equal.

...................................TRY THIS...................................

Write a biographical sketch of a famous person, aiming especially to overturn inaccurate ideas or outright falsehoods about that person. You might want to speculate on how the mistaken ideas took root. Perhaps they were based on misunderstandings or half-truths.

Perfume: The Story of a Murderer
by Patrick Süskind
Translated by John E. Woods

[Setting: Paris, 1738]

For a moment [Jean-Baptiste Grenouille] was so confused that he actually thought he had never in all his life seen anything so beautiful as this girl—although he only caught her from behind in silhouette against the candlelight. He meant, of course, he had never smelled anything so beautiful. But since he knew the smell of humans, knew it a thousandfold, men, women, children, he could not conceive of how such an exquisite scent could be emitted by a human being. Normally human odor was nothing special, or it was ghastly. Children smelled insipid, men ruinous, all sour sweat and cheese, women smelled of rancid fat and rotting fish. Totally uninteresting, repulsive—that was how humans smelled. And so it happened that for the first time in his life, Grenouille did not trust his nose and had to call on his eyes for assistance if he was to believe what he smelled.

FOR FURTHER REFLECTION

In a milieu with smells that would be intolerable to modern-day humans—the stench of manure in the streets, of blood from the slaughterhouses, of people from whose mouths "came the stench of rotting teeth," we find ourselves in the mind of a monstrous protagonist with a capacity for smell so developed that all his other senses were useless by comparison. He could determine someone's entire nature through his or her odor alone. Süskind imbues the sense of smell to the level of myth and parable; indeed, we experience reality anew through this bizarre sensory perspective.

························· TRY THIS ·····························

Write a story focusing on any one of the senses except sight—a story, for example in which the protagonist is blind but has an exceptionally developed sense of hearing.

"Dandelions"

by Diane Ackerman

from *Cultivating Delight: A Natural History of My Garden*

It's funny what things we identify as enemies. Dandelions, for instance. Mushy daylilies or slightly putrid rose petals are easy to categorize as loathsome, but dandelions? Dandy lions with yellow manes? Puff balls that predict love's truth? Let me praise dandelions. They carpet the fields with a yellow so loud it croons in the sun. They're streetwise and hardy, thriving in sidewalk cracks as easily as they do in a topiary garden. Their greens taste good, and they make a light, summery wine. … They're fun to play with when they go to seed, because the lightest shake or breath launches their parachutes. … And yet, only poison ivy is more despised. Why are dandelions regarded as the pinwheels of Satan? Perhaps because they're too short to qualify as model flowers. The same shape and yellow on a lanky stem—coreopsis, for example—we find classy. They multiply fast because they gush with nectar, and manufacture loads of pollen, so all sorts of insects visit them and spread their pollen. But they're also self-contained, and if no insects were to visit they could still produce seeds without pollen. One way or the other, they quickly dominate a yard. I suppose they're too ordinary to prize. Common as ants, they're easy to overlook. Some people may feel they ruin the solid green method of the lawn. I've watched many homeowners patrol their lawns like serial killers, flashing a pair of scissors with which they methodically decapitate every dandelion.

FOR FURTHER REFLECTION

In the eyes of a poet-naturalist like Diane Ackerman, the commonplace—even the ignored or spurned—becomes an object of beauty and wonder. Rich in nearly forgotten lore, the dandelion suddenly appears as luminous through Ackerman's poetic sensibility.

...............................TRY THIS...................................

Celebrate the commonplace in nature by writing a poem or short essay about a blade of grass, a snail, an earthworm, or a dandelion as *you* see it (which may be very different from the way Diane Ackerman sees it).

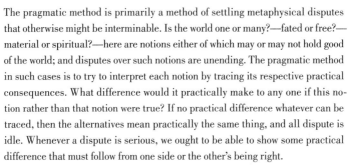

APRIL 20
"What Pragmatism Means"
by William James
from *Pragmatism and Other Essays*

The pragmatic method is primarily a method of settling metaphysical disputes that otherwise might be interminable. Is the world one or many?—fated or free?—material or spiritual?—here are notions either of which may or may not hold good of the world; and disputes over such notions are unending. The pragmatic method in such cases is to try to interpret each notion by tracing its respective practical consequences. What difference would it practically make to any one if this notion rather than that notion were true? If no practical difference whatever can be traced, then the alternatives mean practically the same thing, and all dispute is idle. Whenever a dispute is serious, we ought to be able to show some practical difference that must follow from one side or the other's being right.

… Pragmatism represents a perfectly familiar attitude in philosophy, the empiricist attitude, but it represents it as it seems to me, both in a more radical and in a less objectionable form than it has ever yet assumed. A pragmatist turns his back resolutely … upon a lot of inveterate habits dear to professional philosophers. He turns away from abstraction and insufficiency, from verbal solutions, from bad a priori reasons, from fixed principles, closed systems, and pretended absolutes and origins. He turns towards concreteness and adequacy, towards facts, towards action and towards power.

FOR FURTHER REFLECTION

Pragmatism, or what William James (1842–1910) thought of as radical empiricism, brought philosophy down to earth. Instead of arguing about a particular facet of truth or state of being, for example, the pragmatic philosopher will say: Enough abstract philosophizing! Let's translate our insights into practical situations. Is beauty a form of truth? Then demonstrate it by showing how a beautiful object conveys truth, as Keats tried to do in his famous "Ode on a Grecian Urn."

......................................TRY THIS....................................

Try your hand at a bit of pragmatic philosophy by taking an abstract principle (e.g., love is blind) and putting it to the test in a concrete real-life situation. Pay close attention to the behavior of a couple in love and then reflect on your findings in an essay (or use the couple as a springboard for a short story).

The Emperor's New Mind: Concerning Computers, Minds, and the Laws of Physics

by Roger Penrose

The profound breakthrough that the seventeenth century brought to science was the understanding of *motion*. The ancient Greeks had a marvellous understanding of things static—rigid geometrical shapes, or bodies in *equilibrium* (i.e. with all forces balanced, so there is no motion)—but they had no good conception of the laws governing the way that bodies actually *move*. What they lacked was a good theory of *dynamics*, i.e. a theory of the beautiful way in which Nature actually controls the change in location of bodies from one moment to the next. Part (but by no means all) of the reason for this was an absence of any sufficiently accurate means of keeping time, i.e. of a reasonably good "clock." Such a clock is needed so that changes in position can be accurately timed, and so that the speeds and accelerations of bodies can be well ascertained. Thus, Galileo's observations in 1583 that a pendulum could be used as a reliable means of keeping time had a far-reaching importance for him (and for the development of science as a whole!) since the timing of motion could then be made precise.

FOR FURTHER REFLECTION

We sometimes think of time as fluid, like a steadily flowing river; but time is more precisely a progression of measurable units—with emphasis on the word *measurable*. Without the ability to measure time, it would not be possible to compute the movement of bodies, which is fundamental to modern science.

...................................TRY THIS...................................

Write a meditation on the many ways in which time impacts our lives—our jobs, our daily routines, the stages of our lives, the seasons of the year, and so on.

Screams of Reason:
Mad Science and Modern Culture
by David J. Skal

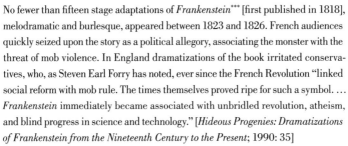

No fewer than fifteen stage adaptations of *Frankenstein**** [first published in 1818], melodramatic and burlesque, appeared between 1823 and 1826. French audiences quickly seized upon the story as a political allegory, associating the monster with the threat of mob violence. In England dramatizations of the book irritated conservatives, who, as Steven Earl Forry has noted, ever since the French Revolution "linked social reform with mob rule. The times themselves proved ripe for such a symbol. ... *Frankenstein* immediately became associated with unbridled revolution, atheism, and blind progress in science and technology." [*Hideous Progenies: Dramatizations of Frankenstein from the Nineteenth Century to the Present*; 1990: 35]

There is no evidence that Mary Shelley followed the progress of the myth she set in motion, though it is difficult to believe she was unaware of the many adaptations and the controversies they raised. But since she tried to dissociate herself from radical themes generally, perhaps it is not surprising that she did not comment on that burgeoning Frankenstein industry and the passions it aroused.

FOR FURTHER REFLECTION

Some stories so captivate the collective imagination that they spawn numerous adaptations in a wide variety of genres and can even influence the language. *Frankenstein*, with its archetypal story of the revolt of the created against the creator, is such a story. It inevitably brings to mind the rebelliousness of colonies against the imperial powers that control them; of children rebelling against their parents; of humans rebelling against God.

..................................TRY THIS..................................

Try writing a Frankenstein-type story of your own, one in which, say, a colony of genetically engineered persons who possess superior intellectual skills but have serious physiological deficiencies revolt against the geneticists who gave them life.

*** See the entry for February 28, which includes a passage from Mary Shelley's novel.

....

"The Art of Seeing Things"
by John Burroughs

from Birch Browsings: A John Burroughs Reader

The eye sees what it has the means of seeing, and its means of seeing are in proportion to the love and desire behind it. The eye is informed and sharpened by the thought. My boy sees ducks on the river where and when I cannot, because at certain seasons he thinks ducks and dreams ducks. ... Some people have an eye for four-leaved clovers; they see them as they walk hastily over the turf, for they already have them in their eyes. I once took a walk with the late Professor Eaton of Yale. He was just then specially interested in the mosses, and he found them, all kinds, everywhere. I can see him yet, every few minutes upon his knees, adjusting his eye-glasses before some rare specimen. The beauty he found in them and pointed out to me, kindled my enthusiasm also. I once spent a summer day at the mountain home of a well-known literary woman and editor. She lamented the absence of birds about her house. I named a half-dozen or more I had heard or seen in her trees within an hour—the indigo-bird, the purple finch, the yellowbird, the veery thrush, the red-eyed vireo, the song sparrow.

"Do you mean to say you have seen or heard all these birds while sitting here on my porch?" she inquired.

"I really have," I said.

"I do not see them or hear them," she replied, "and yet I want to very much."

"No," said I; "you only want to want to see and hear them."

You must have the bird in your heart before you can find it in the bush.

FOR FURTHER REFLECTION

The great naturalist John Burroughs (1837–1921) engagingly illustrates how our capacity for keen observation is governed by our predetermined enthusiasm for the things we set out to observe. To observe well, one must prepare.

................................TRY THIS....................................

Prepare for your next field trip by doing some background reading—and thereby kindling greater knowledge and enthusiasm for whatever it is you hope to observe, be it different species of insects, birds, trees, or rocks and minerals.

APRIL 24

The Stones of Florence
by Mary McCarthy

The palette of the great Florentine innovators is decidedly autumnal or frostbitten. The brown robes of Franciscan friars, the grey beards of patriarch saints, the ashy flesh of the hanging Christ, grey slabs of rock and desert-brown desolation of hermits penetrate the *trecento* with a chill that can still be felt in the rusts, greys, and sepias of Masaccio, the purply browns of Andrea del Castagno, the tawny oranges of Michelangelo, just as, even in mid-summer, the thick stone walls of the fortress-palaces remain, on certain narrow streets where the sun does not strike them, cold and damp to the touch. Iron and iron rust entered the souls of these masters; Masaccio's shivering boy, waiting by the riverbank to be baptized; Adam and Eve, driven naked and howling from the Garden into the cold world. ... Fallen leaves, bare boughs, burnt sedge are evoked by all these masters' tonality. Uccello's favourite medium, *terra verde*, suggests greenish fields coated with rime. Leonardo's brown-skinned witch-women sit in blue-green, northern grottoes, and the strong hues of the Pollaiuoli have a darkish, raisiny cast.

"Pollaiuolo," observed a Florentine, pointing to a dish of the small green shrunken second-crop figs that appear on local tables towards the end of September, and Pollaiuolo, too, are the last velvet pom-pom dahlias, in yellow, wine-red, and purple, that come into the florists' shops, a fall harvest, just before the *vendemmia*, when the turning grapes are picked. ... Late September is the most beautiful time in Florence. San Miniato flashes the green and gold of its mosaic into the setting sun; deep-blue distance is framed sharply in the three honey-coloured arches of Ponte Vecchio.

FOR FURTHER REFLECTION

Travel feeds the soul, especially writers' souls, and few places on the planet are as soul-nourishing as Florence, the cradle of the Renaissance. You'll find yourself at once immersed in the glories of art and architecture, cuisine, music, and fashion. Writers like Mary McCarthy beautifully capture the spirit of the place and inspire us to take up our pens and do likewise.

. . . . TRY THIS . . . .

The next time you take a trip, make it a writer's trip. First read up on the history and lore of the destination. Read essays or books about the place, not just travel guides. When you arrive, select places that intrigue you most and observe them keenly, taking copious notes.

APRIL 25

"Cain and Abel"

by Bill Moyers

from *Genesis: A Living Conversation*

BILL [MOYERS]: Few stories match the longevity and power of the story of Cain and Abel. Augustine, Dante, Shakespeare—this story has fired the imagination of so many. How do you account for it?

OSCAR [HIJUELOS]: The conflict depicted in this story happens in so many families. It's a premise of human experience.

JACK [JOHN BARTH]: And we must remember that Cain and Abel are the first fully human beings not made by God but produced by natural parents. The first fully human being is a murderer—and the second is his victim. …

REBECCA [GOLDSTEIN]: The first murder, yes, but also the first death. Death was hanging around as a concept in the first three chapters with the Tree of Knowledge. … But now death actually enters the world.

FOR FURTHER REFLECTION

The stories in the Bible are archetypal: They capture the deepest truths of human experience; in the case of the Cain and Abel story, the enmity between siblings (and by extension nations), and the grim reality of death. All the while we are reminded of God's presence in human destiny, and how human actions influence that destiny.

························TRY THIS························

1. After rereading the story of Cain and Abel in the Book of Genesis, write a story in which you make Cain and Abel brothers living in the modern world—perhaps they are rival businessmen or leaders of rival nations.
2. Dramatize a conversation about a story in the Book of Genesis (or in any other book in the Bible) between two or more participants, in the manner of Bill Moyers.

Going Around in Academic Circles: A Low View of Higher Education
by Richard Armour

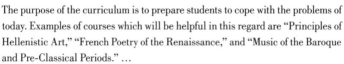

The purpose of the curriculum is to prepare students to cope with the problems of today. Examples of courses which will be helpful in this regard are "Principles of Hellenistic Art," "French Poetry of the Renaissance," and "Music of the Baroque and Pre-Classical Periods." ...

Every student must take a foreign language for two years. This does not mean that the requirement is satisfied after the student has spent two years on First Year French. ... Latin will be accepted as satisfying the language requirement, since otherwise not enough students would enroll to justify keeping the Professor of Classics, who has no other way to make a living.

FOR FURTHER REFLECTION

There is much to satirize in academe, as Richard Armour, once a professor himself, certainly knows. No facet of academic life goes unnoticed, from fraternities and athletic activities to school history and academic administration. Underneath the humor often lurk genuine concerns about academic functions.

...................................TRY THIS....................................

Write a humor piece that focuses on one facet of academic life. Draw from your own experiences in college, or from someone else's.

APRIL 27

Changing Planes
by Ursula K. Le Guin

On the Frinthian plane, dreams are not private property. A troubled Frin has
no need to lie on a couch recounting dreams to a psychoanalyst, for the doctor
already knows what the patient dreamed last night, because the doctor dreamed it
too; and the patient also dreamed when the doctor dreamed; and so did everyone
else in the neighborhood.

To escape from the dreams of others or to have a private, a secret dream, the
Frin must go out alone into the wilderness. And even in the wilderness, their
sleep may be invaded by the strange dream visions of lions, antelope, bears, or
mice. ...

In a village or town, with people asleep in all the houses around, the Frin
spend at least part of every night in a shifting phantasmagoria of their own and
other people's dreams which I find hard to imagine.

FOR FURTHER REFLECTION

The protagonist of this enchanting novel slips out of ordinary reality (she's
literally waiting for a connecting flight in Cincinnati) and discovers that she
can change *reality* planes. Using a narrative style reminiscent of ethnographic
studies—which adds to the verisimilitude of these linked tales, Ursula Le
Guin takes us on a grand tour of parallel universes that are at once similar
to and startlingly unlike our own.

..................................TRY THIS................................

Compose an alternate universe story adapting Le Guin's style of anthropological narrative in your own way.

The Mummy, or Ramses the Damned
by Anne Rice

[The archaeologist Lawrence Stratford] turned and looked at the mummy, at the features clearly molded beneath the tight wrappings. The man who claimed to be Ramses had been tall, and perhaps robust.

Not an old man, like the creatures lying in the Cairo Museum. But then this Ramses claimed that he had never grown old. He was immortal, and merely slept within these bandages. Nothing could kill him, not even the poisons in this room, which he had tried in quantity, when grief for Cleopatra had left him half-mad. On his orders, his servants had wrapped his unconscious body; they had buried him alive, in the coffin he had had prepared for himself, supervising every detail; then they had sealed the tomb with the door and that he himself had inscribed.

But what had rendered him unconscious? That was the mystery. Ah, what a delicious story. And what if—?

He found himself staring at the grim creature in its bindings of yellow linen. Did he really believe that something was alive there?

FOR FURTHER REFLECTION

In this gripping novel, the legendary pharaoh Ramses, having drunk the elixir of life, not only becomes Cleopatra's lover a thousand years after his reign, but is also reawakened to become a modern day Egyptologist, one who cannot bear to be without the Queen of the Nile. Anne Rice's vampire stories are filled with such profound insight into the human heart, we almost (but not quite) forget that we are reading a supernatural horror thriller. Like Poe, Rice skillfully unfolds an extraordinary tale that feels believable.

. . . . TRY THIS . . . .

It is important when writing horror fiction to create a sense of verisimilitude, as if the narrator were providing an eyewitness report. Write a short story in which your protagonist, say a disobedient Roman slave who had been fed to the lions, awakens after two thousand years to find himself in a large American city.

The Pencil: A History of Design and Circumstance
by Henry Petroski

A lead pencil today might seem to be but a piece of graphite cleverly enclosed in a case of wood, but it actually involves an exacting process employing a multiplicity of raw materials. And the materials required for its manufacture make the pencil an object that depends on the most modern and cosmopolitan of political, economic, and technological systems. The lead in a single American-made pencil in the late twentieth century, for example, might be a proprietary mixture of two kinds of graphite, from Sri Lanka and Mexico, clay from Mississippi, gums from the Orient, and water from Pennsylvania. The wooden case would most likely be made of western incense cedar from California, the ferrule possibly of brass or aluminum from the American West, and the eraser perhaps of a mixture of South American rubber and Italian pumice stone.

FOR FURTHER REFLECTION

Who would have thought that one could write a book of more than four hundred pages about the lowly pencil? Yet as Henry Petroski, a historian and engineer, makes dramatically clear, there is nothing lowly about the pencil: It is the product of a long history and a synthesis of manufacturing techniques and materials.

....................................TRY THIS....................................

Fascinating stories are locked away in even the most seemingly mundane, non-descript objects. Choose one such object—an eraser, a pair of scissors, a stapler, a spatula or other kitchen utensil—research it in depth, including its history, and make it the subject of an expressive essay.

APRIL 30
The Story of Jazz
by Marshall Stearns

The basis of jazz is a march rhythm but the jazzman puts more complicated rhythms on top of it. He blows a variety of accents between and around, above and below, the march beat. It's a much more complicated process than syncopation, which is usually defined as stressing the normally weak beat. ...

At the start of a recording session Louis Armstrong, handkerchief in one hand and trumpet in the other, stands in front of the microphone and stamps out a steady rhythm. As the band picks it up, Armstrong's foot doubles the beat and starts tapping twice as fast. And as he sings and plays the trumpet he stresses accents *around* and *between* the taps of his foot. ...

Erroll Garner is justly famous for what jazzmen call "fooling around with the beat," because he doesn't seem to let his left hand know what his right hand is doing. In general, his left hand plays a steady 4/4 march rhythm, quite opposite to the modern trend, but his right hand is playing the melody in a variety of changing tempos: first he drags behind and then he more than catches up in constantly varying fractions of the beat. The effect is schizophrenic. ...

FOR FURTHER REFLECTION

Jazz is deliciously paradoxical: It is American born and bred, yet its roots are African (specifically West African) and Caribbean; its sounds and rhythms are at once traditional and innovative. Jazz embraces the modern spirit while at the same time acknowledging the traditional musical foundations upon which it has built itself. Jazz shares several traits with modern poetry, and many poets have been influenced by the rhythmic complexities of jazz.

..................................TRY THIS....................................

Write a poem that tries to embody the rhythmic textures of a jazz piece. Try to create a theme that meshes jazz's fusion of cultures and of old and new ideas.

MAY 1

Guns, Germs, and Steel: The Fates of Human Societies
by Jared M. Diamond

The striking differences between the long-term histories of peoples of the different continents have been due not to innate differences in the peoples themselves but to differences in their environments. I expect that if the populations of Aboriginal Australia and Eurasia could have been interchanged during the Late Pleistocene, the original Aboriginal Australians would now be occupying most of the Americas and Australia, as well as Eurasia, while the original Aboriginal Eurasians would be the ones now reduced to downtrodden population fragments in Australia. One might at first be inclined to dismiss this assertion as meaningless, because the experiment is imaginary and my claim about its outcome cannot be verified. But historians are nevertheless able to evaluate related hypotheses by retrospective tests. For instance, one can examine what did happen when European farmers stemming ultimately from China emigrated to the Chatham Islands, the rain forests of Borneo, or the volcanic soils of Java or Hawaii. These tests confirm that the same ancestral peoples either ended up extinct, or returned to living as hunter-gatherers, or went on to build complex states, depending on their environments.

FOR FURTHER REFLECTION

Environment is destiny. External forces influence the cultural and migratory habits of an entire people. A desert environment will affect ways of living that an arctic or tropical environment cannot. This is not to say that humans are mere pawns in the face of planetary forces—but it does say that we cannot dissociate environmental factors from our values or the way we interact with the land we inhabit.

......................................TRY THIS....................................

How has your way of life, your upbringing, been influenced by your environment? Write an autobiographical essay, or a chapter for your memoir-in-progress, describing your interaction with the region you call home. Perhaps your story is one of changing environments.

"Sandro Botticelli"

by Walter Pater

from *The Renaissance: Studies in Art and Poetry*

Botticelli lived in a generation of naturalists, and he might have been a mere naturalist among them. There are traces enough in his work of that alert sense of outward things, which, in the pictures of that period, fills the lawns with delicate living creatures, and the hillsides with pools of water, and the pools of water with flowering reeds. But this was not enough for him; he is a visionary painter, and in his visionariness he resembles Dante, Giotto, the tried companion of Dante, Masaccio, Ghirlandaio even, do but transcribe, with more or less refining, the outward image; they are dramatic, not visionary painters; they are almost impassive spectators of the action before them. But the genius of which Botticelli is the type usurps the data before it as the exponent of ideas, moods, visions of its own. ...

The peculiar character of Botticelli is the result of a blending in him of a sympathy for humanity in its uncertain condition, its attractiveness, its investiture at rarer moments in a character of loveliness and energy, with his consciousness of the shadow upon it of the great things from which it shrinks. ... He paints the story of the goddess of pleasure in other episodes besides that of her birth from the sea, but never without some shadow of death in the gray flesh and wan flowers.

FOR FURTHER REFLECTION

A distinguished art historian and aesthetician, Walter Pater (1839–1894), like John Ruskin, raised art criticism itself to the level of art. In an age before full-color mechanical reproduction of artworks was possible, the critic had to rely on his gifts of visual language and expressiveness to convey the genius of the artists whose works he described—as in this case, Botticelli, one of the most gifted of the Florentine Renaissance painters.

.................................TRY THIS....................................

Spend a half hour or so studying the works of one of the Renaissance master painters that Pater discusses in his book—Botticelli, Michelangelo, Leonardo, Pico della Mirandola, Giorgione—and write your own expressive commentary on three or four of his paintings. Refrain from reading Pater's critique until you have finished your own.

The Planets

by Dava Sobel

The vast variegated clouds, which are all anyone ever sees of Jupiter, constitute only a thin veneer surrounding the planet; they comprise less than 1 percent of its forty-five thousand mile radius. Underneath the clouds the atmosphere grows denser and hotter because of mounting pressure. ... Here the carbon content of methane and other trapped gases may be crushed to tiny diamonds in the sky. Gradually the gases cease to behave as gas, as they dissolve into a sea of liquid hydrogen.

Some five thousand miles down into this milieu, where the pressure reaches at least a million times Earth's norm, the liquid hydrogen turns opaque, metallic, molten, and electric. By far the greatest part of Jupiter consists of hydrogen compressed to this exotic phase.

FOR FURTHER REFLECTION

The heavens have always enchanted humankind, even long before the rise of modern astronomy; indeed, the Romans named them after the gods. Modern astronomy has not diminished the enchantment, as science writer Dava Sobel skillfully demonstrates. To read of gases compressed into diamonds, or seas of liquid hydrogen, is to realize that the universe is as filled with wonder as an epic fantasy novel.

...................................TRY THIS...................................

Read up on one of your favorite planets and then write an expressive essay on that planet in the manner of Dava Sobel. Emphasize bizarre or recently discovered phenomena.

MAY 4

"Safflower"

by Victoria Finlay

from *Color: A Natural History of the Palette*

Safflower is unusual: if you add alkalis to the dye broth it is yellow; with acids it goes a beautiful crimson pink which is the color of the original "red" tape once tied around legal documents in England and now gives its name to any bureaucratic knotty procedures. It would have been known to traders in the busy North African bazaars for more generations than anyone could count: Ancient Egyptians used it to dye mummy wrappings and to turn their ceremonial ointments an oily orange. They valued it so much that they put garlands of safflowers entwined with willow leaves in their relatives' tombs, to comfort them after death.

It is also a plant to be wary of. Throughout its five thousand years of cultivation, safflower pickers have been easily spotted going to work in the fields—they have been the ones with leather chaps from thigh to boot to protect them from its spines. Today, if safflower stems get into the throat of a combine harvester, it is almost impossible to get them out.

FOR FURTHER REFLECTION

There is a great deal to learn about the role that colors—and the materials from which they're derived—play in civilization. The safflower plant with its unusual properties is an ideal example, as Victoria Finlay, a British journalist based in Hong Kong, reveals in her fascinating manner of synthesizing facts from disciplines as disparate as etymology, chemistry, Egyptian archaeology, medicine, religion, agriculture, and textiles.

...................................TRY THIS...................................

Write an essay on your favorite color. Pay attention to its source (e.g., rocks and minerals, plants) and its personal, religious, industrial, and artistic applications. You may want to read Alexander Theroux's *The Primary Colors* and *The Secondary Colors*, in addition to Finlay's book, for background information.

MAY 5
How to Read and Why
by Harold Bloom

I turn to reading as a solitary praxis, rather than as an educational enterprise. The way we read now, when we are alone with ourselves, retains considerable continuity with the past, however it is performed by academics. My ideal reader (and lifelong hero) is Dr. Samuel Johnson, who knew and expressed both the power and the limitation of incessant reading. Like every other activity of the mind, it must satisfy Johnson's prime concern, which is "what comes near to ourself, what we can put to use." Sir Francis Bacon, who provided some of the ideas that Johnson put to use, famously gave the advice: "Read not to contradict and confute, nor to believe and take for granted, nor to find talk and discourse, but to weigh and consider." … Ultimately we read … in order to strengthen the self, and to learn its authentic interests.

FOR FURTHER REFLECTION

We read to become better educated; but for Harold Bloom, the prolific literary and Biblical scholar and defender of the traditional canon of great books, the most important reason to read is to learn who we are, to discover our own personal connections with the legacy of humanity.

............................TRY THIS....................................

Most people, and certainly writers, have been profoundly changed by a book. Think about the book that profoundly changed you—perhaps there are several. Choose one and write an essay about how it changed the way you think, or even how you live.

MAY 6

"Easy as Pie"

by Teresa Lust

from *Pass the Polenta, and Other Writings From the Kitchen*

The method for making pie dough is diametrically opposed to that of bread baking. A successful yeast bread depends upon vigorous kneading so the dough can expand and trap the gases given off by the yeast. The result is the chewy, heavenly texture of fresh baked bread. Pie dough, lacking the yeast, turns into a pliable piece of cardboard.

What you strive for in pie dough is a sort of gestalt-mixture. Indeed, the whole is greater than the sum of its parts, yet the crux lies in each part retaining a bit of its own identity. The finished product should possess elements of lumpiness and untidiness—chunks of butter, a dusting of unincorporated flour. When you roll the pastry into two dimensions, the butter blobs should appear as distinguishable streaks throughout the dough. During baking the butter melts back into the dough, but the nooks and crannies the chunks occupied are puffed with steam from the evaporating water. *Et voilà!* A flaky crust.

FOR FURTHER REFLECTION

Essays on food, like food itself, can be an epicurean's delight. Reading Teresa Lust's essay on pie making is as satisfying, on a language level, as eating pie. Like an effective TV commercial, except more artistically satisfying, Lust's sensuous description of pie ingredients heightens our gastronomic memory.

.....................................TRY THIS....................................

1. Study the ingredients of your favorite dessert and write a short piece describing it in as much sensuous detail as you can conjure.
2. Write a short story about a young man or woman who turns to cooking exotic dishes as a way of overcoming depression or hardship.

MAY 7

Krakatoa: The Day the World Exploded, August 27, 1883

by Simon Winchester

"Everyone was frozen with horror," wrote the resident of Lampong, Mr. Altheer, of the moment when he heard the almighty explosion, just after ten on that Monday morning [of August 27, 1883]. He well knew, from what had already happened disastrously three of four times before in the previous twenty hours, just what to expect: Another tidal wave, probably much larger than before since this was so great an explosion, would now come racing out from the island, and it would arrive within minutes. That is, of course, had there been an island: Altheer had no means of knowing that Krakatoa was no more, having just been blown to oblivion.

The wave reached Telok Betong at 11:03. One anonymous European, writing some days later in a Batavia [later renamed Jakarta] newspaper ... saw a tall front of water rearing up and rushing toward him at a barely believable speed. There was a thunderous noise as it hit the beach and began rushing, crashing upward, through the town. ...

Each of those snared by the Telok Betong wave speaks of running, wildly, panicked, trying madly to stay ahead of the wave, following natives running wildly too; and, in the case of the anonymous European writing in the Java *Bode*, of running behind a woman who stumbled and dropped her baby and could not abandon it and so was swept away.

FOR FURTHER REFLECTION

We are astonished by the destructive power of natural forces like earthquakes, hurricanes, tsunamis, and volcanoes, and read eyewitness accounts of these tragic events with fascination—not so much out of morbid curiosity as to remind ourselves of both our helplessness and our ingenuity for survival when faced with disaster.

....TRY THIS....................................

Write a moment-by-moment account of being caught in a severe storm, earthquake, or other natural disaster. What did people do to protect themselves? What did you do? What was the outcome of these survival efforts (or the lack of them)?

A History of Their Own: Women in Europe from Prehistory to the Present

by Bonnie S. Anderson and Judith P. Zinsser

In the ancient world and for many centuries thereafter, the most likely way for a woman to enter the sciences or the arts was to be born into a family which specialized in those fields. There are some epitaphs to women doctors in Greek and Roman cities from the first century A.D. on; a number of them associate the woman with a medical family. "You guided straight the rudder of life in our home and raised high our common fame in healing—though you were a woman you were not behind me in skill," went a tribute to Panthia from her husband Glycon in the second century A.D. Of the eight women artists mentioned by ancient authors, a number are described as the "daughter and student" of a father who painted. The fullest account [by Pliny the Elder] is of Iaia of Cyzicus, who worked in Rome about 100 B.C.:

> She used both the painter's brush and, on ivory, the graving tool. She painted women most frequently, including a panel picture of an old woman in Naples, even a self-portrait for which she used a mirror. No one's hand was quicker to paint a picture than hers; so great was her talent that her prices far exceeded those of the most celebrated painters of her day.

FOR FURTHER REFLECTION

One of the most important contributions to revisionist history is the reassessment of the roles that women have played in all facets of culture through the ages. The oversights are not due, generally, to records that have been lost, but rather to historians' blind spots.

. . . . TRY THIS . . . .

Anderson and Zinsser tell us, provocatively, that there were women doctors in the ancient world (also in the Middle Ages and the Renaissance). Write a profile of one of these female physicians. If you prefer, create a short story, drawing from as much factual information as you can find, in which she is the central character.

MAY 9

"The Two Christendoms"
by Felipe Fernández-Armesto
from *Millennium: A History of the Last Thousand Years*

Nothing divided the two Christendoms of east and west like religion. ... This was in part a matter of language, for Greek tongues could utter theological subtleties inexpressible in Latin. Untranslatability was at the basis of mutual misunderstanding. Dogmas which started the same in east and west turned out differently in Latin and Greek. But religion is more a matter of practice than of dogma, and of behaviour than belief. The differences between the Roman Catholic and Orthodox traditions accumulated over centuries of relative mutual isolation. The process began, or became continuous, as early as the mid-sixth century, when the eastern churches resisted or rejected the universal primacy of the pope. Allegiance to Rome gave the west a basis of common doctrine and common liturgical practice, which gradually took shape until, by the time of the crusades, Rome had established itself as the arbiter of doctrinal questions, the fount of patronage, and the source of liturgical usage. ... In 794 ... for reasons that probably had less to do with Christianity than with the political relationship between the empire of Byzantium and the kingdom of the Franks, a western synod had arbitrarily altered the wording of the creed. To this day the western churches ... profess their belief that "the Holy Spirit proceeds from the Father and the Son" while the easterners omit mention of the Son and limit to the Father the explicit source of this heavenly emanation.

FOR FURTHER REFLECTION

Politics, military conquest, and geographical isolation all affect religious practice. Just as language acquires distinctive characteristics in different nations over time, so too will religious practice, especially if the nations in question were overtaken militarily or experienced an internal ideological revolution.

......................................TRY THIS....................................

1. Write an essay in which you reflect on the role of politics, colonialism, or military conquest on religion in a particular region.
2. Write a short story, set in the Middle Ages or the Renaissance, in which a group of crusaders confronts so-called primitive or pagan peoples with the intention of converting them.

MAY 10
"The Blitz"
by Winston S. Churchill
from *The Second World War*

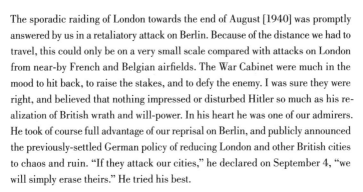

The sporadic raiding of London towards the end of August [1940] was promptly answered by us in a retaliatory attack on Berlin. Because of the distance we had to travel, this could only be on a very small scale compared with attacks on London from near-by French and Belgian airfields. The War Cabinet were much in the mood to hit back, to raise the stakes, and to defy the enemy. I was sure they were right, and believed that nothing impressed or disturbed Hitler so much as his realization of British wrath and will-power. In his heart he was one of our admirers. He took of course full advantage of our reprisal on Berlin, and publicly announced the previously-settled German policy of reducing London and other British cities to chaos and ruin. "If they attack our cities," he declared on September 4, "we will simply erase theirs." He tried his best.

FOR FURTHER REFLECTION
Churchill understood the enemy, understood the complex motives of a tyrant like Hitler; hence, retaliatory strikes against Berlin were crucial (because they unsettled Hitler), even though they could only be conducted on a small scale (because British bombers had to travel much greater distances—between London and Berlin—than the Germans, who could launch their attacks from the northernmost part of France, the country they had already occupied).

...................................TRY THIS...................................

Write an article about one specific World War II battle, focusing on the defensive and offensive strategies between, say, the United States and one of the Axis powers. Depending on the battle's outcome, analyze why the strategies were successes or failures.

Daphnis and Chloe

by Longus

from *Three Greek Romances*. Translated by Moses Hadas

Dorcon, that cowherd ... was a brisk young fellow, newly bearded, who knew not only the name but the facts of love, and ... was smitten with Chloe. ... He [was] determined to work his will either by gifts or by force. ... Having no experience of a lover's wiles, she received the gifts very gladly. ... But now it was time for Daphnis too to know the effects of love, and he and Dorcon fell into a dispute concerning their respective beauty. Chloe was the umpire, and the victor's prize was to kiss Chloe. ...

"I, my girl, am bigger than Daphnis, and I am a cowherd while he is a goatherd; I am, therefore, as much better than he as cows are better than goats. ... I was brought up by a mother, not an animal [a goat]. That fellow is puny, unbearded like a woman ... He is so poor that he cannot keep even a dog."

Such ... were Dorcon's words, and after him Daphnis spoke: "True, I was suckled by a goat; so was Zeus. The goats I keep are bigger than his cows ... . I am beardless, sure, but so is Dionysus ... And remember, girl, that you too were nursed by an animal, but still you are beautiful."

Chloe waited no longer, but partly out of pleasure at his praise and partly because she had long yearned to kiss Daphnis, she leaped up and gave him the prize.

FOR FURTHER REFLECTION

Ah, the trials and tribulations of lovers competing for love! Not much has changed in 1,800 years: Today a lover probably wouldn't brag that being a cowherd is better than being a goatherd, but clever repartee is still highly prized. Daphnis certainly wins the debate when he reverses the negative associations of being suckled by a goat by noting that that was also true of the king of the gods. Wit and wisdom trump accident of birth.

...................................TRY THIS....................................

Imagine a love triangle that is resolved through clever debate. Set your story in the distant past, the present, or the future, but take care to make your characters three-dimensional.

MAY 12

"Of Revenge"

by Francis Bacon

from *The Essays*

Revenge is a kind of wild justice, which the more man's nature runs to, the more ought law to weed it out. For as for the first wrong, it doth but offend the law; but the revenge of that wrong putteth the law out of office. Certainly, in taking revenge a man is but even with his enemy, but in passing it over he is superior, for it is a prince's part to pardon. And Solomon … saith, *It is the glory of a man to pass by an offence.* That which is past is gone and irrevocable, and wise men have enough to do with things present and to come: therefore they do but trifle with themselves that labour in past matters. There is no man doth a wrong for the wrong's sake, but thereby to purchase himself profit or pleasure or honour or the like. Therefore why should I be angry with a man for loving himself better than me? And if any man should do wrong merely out of ill nature, why, yet it is but like the thorn or briar, which prick and scratch, because they can do no other.

FOR FURTHER REFLECTION

In this pithy essay, Francis Bacon (1561–1626), a defender of empiricism over scholasticism (crucial in the development of modern science), demonstrates his worldly insights into human nature in his essays. Revenge is *wild* justice: That is, Bacon reminds us that the impulse to punish wrongdoing stems from motives not unlike the impulse for wrongdoing itself (e.g., "to purchase himself profit or pleasure or honour or the like"), and so must be tempered by rule of law if society is to function properly. Without laws and their enforcement, vengeance would lead to anarchy.

. . . . TRY THIS . . . .

Develop a short story in which one of your characters is overtaken by the need for revenge, and another character struggles to keep her from taking the law into her own hands.

"Ode on the Death of a Favourite Cat, Drowned in a Tub of Gold Fishes"

by Thomas Gray

The hapless nymph with wonder saw:
A whisker first and then a claw,
　With many an ardent wish,
She stretch'd in vain to reach the prize.
What female heart can gold despise?
　What cat's averse to fish?

Presumptuous maid! with looks intent
Again she stretch'd, again she bent,
　Nor knew the gulf between.
(Malignant Fate sat by, and smil'd)
The slipp'ry verge her feet beguil'd,
　She tumbled headlong in.

Eight times emerging from the flood,
She mew'd to ev'ry wat'ry god,
　Some speedy aid to send.
No Dolphin came, no Nereid stirr'd:
Nor cruel Tom, nor Susan heard.
　A fav'rite has no friend!

From hence, ye beauties, undeceiv'd,
Know, one false step is ne'er retriev'd,
　And be with caution bold.
Not all that tempts your
　wand'ring eyes
And heedless hearts, is lawful prize;
　Nor all that glisters, gold.

FOR FURTHER REFLECTION

At once a fable and an elegy, this clever poem, like the mock epics of Gray's contemporaries John Dryden and Alexander Pope, evokes the heroes of classical mythology to convey the morality tale of a cat who could not resist the fatal lure of gold.

. . . . TRY THIS . . . .

Compose a verse fable of your own, rhymed or unrhymed. Perhaps you might tell your own story of a pet cat whose encounter with a ball of yarn or the neighbor's dog resulted in calamity.

MAY 14
"Self-Reliance"
by Ralph Waldo Emerson
from *Essays*

Society everywhere is in conspiracy against the manhood of every one of its members. Society is a joint-stock company, in which the members agree, for the better securing of his bread to each shareholder, to surrender the liberty and culture of the eater. The virtue in most requests is conformity. Self-reliance is its aversion. It loves not realities and creators, but names and customs.

Whoso would be a man, must be a nonconformist. ... Nothing is at last sacred but the integrity of our own mind. Absolve you to yourself, and you shall have the suffrage of the world. I remember an answer which when quite young I was prompted to make to a valued adviser who was wont to importune me with the dear old doctrines of the church. On my saying, What have I to do with the sacredness of traditions, if I live wholly from within? my friend suggested,—"But these impulses may be from below, not from above." I replied, "They do not seem to me to be such; but if I am the devil's child, I will live then from the devil." No law can be sacred to me but that of my nature. Good and bad are but names very readily transferable to that or this; the only right is what is after my constitution; the only wrong is what is against it.

FOR FURTHER REFLECTION

Emerson's metaphor of society as a joint stock company skillfully embodies a disturbing truth: We, the individual members, agree to surrender a certain amount of our liberty in order to preserve stability. But Emerson does not ever advocate selling out. Is it possible to be both member and self-sufficient nonconformist? It has got to be so; for if we do indeed sell out, we become a mindless cog in the system; but if we proclaim absolute sovereignty over society, we become anarchists and lose the privileges that come with membership. The cost of being civilized, to move from Emerson to Freud, is to effect a compromise between our individual impulses and our social obligations.

.... TRY THIS.....................................

What price are you willing to pay to achieve autonomy, self-reliance? Where do you draw the line between conforming to the status quo and venturing out on your own, societal expectations be damned? Write an essay that explores the extent of your personal declaration of independence.

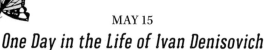

One Day in the Life of Ivan Denisovich

by Alexander Solzhenitsyn

Translated by Ronald Hingley and Max Hayward

The prisoners undid their coats and held them open. They marched up by fives, and five warders were waiting for them. They put their hands inside the prisoners' coats and felt their jackets. They patted the pocket (the only one allowed) on the right knee. They had gloves on, and if they felt something odd they didn't yank it out right away but asked, taking their time: "What do you have there?"

What did they hope to find on a prisoner in the morning? Knives? But knives don't get taken out of camp, they get brought in. What they had to watch out for in the mornings was people carrying a lot of food to escape with. There was a time when they were so worried about bread—a six-ounce ration for the noon meal—that an order was issued for each gang to make itself a wooden box and put everybody's bread together in it. ... Most likely the idea was to make things even tougher for people and add to their troubles—you took a bite out of it to put your mark on it, and threw it in the box. But all these hunks looked alike anyway. It was all the same bread. Then all the way you worried yourself sick about not getting your own piece back.

FOR FURTHER REFLECTION

In this short, harrowing novel, Solzhenitsyn (1918–2008) powerfully captures, through minute and graphic detail, what life was like in a Soviet prison camp during a single day. By the time we reach the ending, we feel as if we ourselves have been incarcerated with the prisoners. "There were three thousand six hundred and fifty-three days like this in his sentence, from reveille to lights out. ..."

...................................TRY THIS...................................

Write a short story in which your protagonist endures the rigors of incarceration—either in an actual prison (or labor camp), or in a future society ruled by a dictator—a police state like that of Orwell's *Nineteen Eighty-Four*.

"The Reconstitution of the Hospital"
by Paul Starr

from *The Social Transformation of American Medicine*

We now think of hospitals as the most visible embodiment of medical care in its technically most sophisticated form, but before the last hundred years, hospitals and medical practice had relatively little to do with each other. From their earliest origins in preindustrial societies, hospitals had been primarily religious and charitable institutions for tending the sick, rather than medical institutions for their cure. While in Europe from the eighteenth century they played an important part in medical education and research, systematic clinical instruction and investigation were neglected in America until the founding of Johns Hopkins. Before the Civil War, an American doctor might contentedly spend an entire career in practice without setting foot on a hospital ward. ...

But in a matter of decades, roughly between 1870 and 1910, hospitals moved from the periphery to the center of medical education and medical practice. From refuges mainly for the homeless poor and insane, they evolved into doctors' workshops for all types and classes of patients. From charities, dependent upon voluntary gifts, they developed into market institutions, financed increasingly out of payments from patients. What drove this transformation was not simply the advance of science, important though that was, but the demands and examples of an industrializing capitalist society, which brought larger numbers of people into urban centers, detached them from traditions of self-sufficiency.

FOR FURTHER REFLECTION

Progress in medicine and health care has been rapid and dramatic, and nowhere is this more apparent than in the evolution of hospitals. The centrality of the hospital as a result of the free-market system has led to greater interconnectedness among the medical profession's numerous specialties, which in turn has led to greater progress in both medical research and patient care.

......................................TRY THIS....................................

Plan a novel set inside a hospital. Develop five viewpoint characters. Create a central story situation, and tell the story through the lives of each of your viewpoint characters.

Angela's Ashes
by Frank McCourt

There are three cows in a field with their heads over a stone wall and they say moo to us. Paddy says, Bejasus, 'tis milkin' time, and he's over the wall, stretched on his back under a cow with her big udder hanging into his face. He pulls on a teat and squirts milk into his mouth. He stops squirting and says, Come on, Frankie, fresh milk. 'Tis lovely. Get that other cow, they're all ready for the milkin'.

I get under the cow and pull on a teat but she kicks and moves and I'm sure she's going to kill me. Paddy comes over and shows me how to do it, pull hard and straight and the milk comes out in a powerful stream. The two of us lie under the one cow and we're having a great time filling ourselves with milk when there's a roar and there's a man with a stick charging across the field.

FOR FURTHER REFLECTION

We call a book great when it stirs not just one emotion, but many. Readers want a novel, biography, or memoir to enlighten them, astonish them with unusual and unexpected incidents, and maybe even bring them to tears. Frank McCourt's Pulitzer Prize—winning memoir, many would agree, accomplishes this, mainly because of his ability to portray the people in his life (including himself!) both wittily and realistically.

......................................TRY THIS....................................

So you are itching to write your memoir? Start by writing out a dramatic incident from your life—a moment of mischief, like trying to milk a cow, or a moment of danger or foolishness. Focus sharply on *details*—dialogue, setting, character description—to bring the moment to life.

MAY 18
The Alienist
by Caleb Carr

Rarely have I felt so strongly the truth of [Dr.] Kreizler's belief that the answers one gives to life's crucial questions are never truly spontaneous; they are the embodiment of years of contextual experience, of the building of patterns in each of our lives that eventually grow to dominate our behavior. Was [Police Commissioner] Theodore—whose credo of active response to all challenges had guided him through physical sickness in youth and political and personal trials in adulthood—truly free to refuse [alienist Laszlo] Kreizler's offer [of assistance in solving a murder]? And if he accepted it, was I then free to say no to these two friends, with whom I had lived through many escapades and who were now telling me that my extracurricular activities and knowledge—so often dismissed as useless by almost everyone I knew—would prove vital in catching a brutal killer? Professor [William] James would have said that, yes, any human being is free, at any time, to pursue or decline anything; and perhaps, objectively, that is true. But as Kreizler loved to say (and Professor James ultimately had a hard time refuting), you cannot objectify the subjective, you cannot generalize the specific.

FOR FURTHER REFLECTION

In many works of fiction the "made-up" story is embedded in historical fact. Theodore Roosevelt was indeed a New York City police commissioner before entering national politics; William James was one of the nineteenth century's most esteemed psychologists (then known as "alienists" because those who suffered from mental illness were considered alienated from real life). Thus, we learn quite a bit about criminal investigation and the burgeoning discipline of psychology in America during the 1890s while being engrossed in the fictional mystery.

......................................TRY THIS....................................

Outline a murder mystery that involves individuals who actually lived. Of course, you will need to read their biographies to get a feel for the kinds of persons they were and to create convincing imaginary scenes in which they interact with your fictional characters.

A Green History of the World: The Environment and the Collapse of Great Civilizations

by Clive Ponting

Probably the most terrible example of mass slaughter in the history of wildlife was not the bison but the passenger pigeon—a story that almost defies belief. The early Europeans in North America frequently commented on the huge numbers of blue, long-tailed, fast and graceful pigeons in the country. One of the first settlers in Virginia wrote that "There are wild pigeons in winter beyond number or imagination, myself have seen three or four hours together flocks in the air, so thick that even have they shadowed the sky from us." ...

One reason why the passenger pigeon existed in such prodigious numbers was the lack of natural predators apart from hawks and eagles. It was, however, surprisingly vulnerable to human intervention. Each female laid only one egg a year, which made it difficult to replace any losses quickly. The birds fed mainly on acorns, chestnuts, and beechnuts in the extensive woodlands of North America and so when these were steadily cut down their habitat and food supplies were reduced. ... The real onslaught began [however] with the onset of large-scale commercial hunting carried out by well-organised trappers and shippers in order to supply the developing cities on the east coast of the United States with a cheap source of meat. ... By 1855 300,000 pigeons a year were being sent to New York alone. ...

FOR FURTHER REFLECTION

It is difficult to envision the extinction of a species, even when their numbers have dwindled. But as in the sad case with the passenger pigeon, even when a species numbers in the hundreds of millions, wanton slaughter will put an end to them in a very short time. Unless we collectively recognize the fact that nature comprises a complex weave of interspecies symbiosis, and that species extinction can wreak havoc on the whole balance of nature, our planet, including ourselves, will suffer.

..................................TRY THIS....................................

Write a poem or essay praising the balance of nature, and the harmonious interrelationships among species. Or explain to young readers how the balance is maintained, using relationships between a few species as examples.

The Birth of Tragedy

by Friedrich Nietzsche

Everything that rises to the surface in the Apollonian portion of Greek tragedy (in the dialogue) looks simple, transparent, beautiful. In this sense the dialogue is a mirror of the Greek mind. … The language of the Sophoclean heroes surprises us by its Apollonian determinacy and lucidity. It seems to us that we can fathom their innermost being, and we are somewhat surprised that we had such a short way to go. However, once we abstract from the character of the hero as it rises to the surface and becomes visible (a character at bottom no more than a luminous shape projected onto a dark wall …) and instead penetrate into the myth which is projected in these luminous reflections, we suddenly come up against a phenomenon which is the exact opposite of a familiar optical one. After an energetic attempt to focus on the sun, we have, by way of remedy almost, dark spots before our eyes when we turn away. Conversely, the luminous images of the Sophoclean heroes—those Apollonian masks—are the necessary productions of a deep look into the horror of nature; luminous spots, as it were, designed to cure an eye hurt by the ghastly night. …

Sophocles conceived doomed Oedipus, the greatest sufferer of the Greek stage, as a pattern of nobility, destined to error and misery despite his wisdom, yet exercising a beneficent influence upon his environment in virtue of his boundless grief.

FOR FURTHER REFLECTION

Apollo and Dionysus, the gods of rational light and irrational darkness respectively, represented to Nietzsche the basic oppositional forces of human nature. A generation later, Sigmund Freud would characterize these forces as strictly psychological phenomena: the public-oriented superego; the primal, self-gratifying id. What is intriguing about Nietzsche's representation is that he embodies these all-too-human impulses with their ancient mythological representations. Indeed, the psychological forces that beviled the likes of Oedipus or Electra 2,500 years ago continue to bedevil us today.

. . . . TRY THIS . . . .

Outline a dramatic scenario in which the two principal characters—hero and villain, say—are patterned after Apollo and Dionysus respectively. Or, if you wish make these gods themselves the characters in your play.

"The Myth of Passage"
by Donald C. Williams
from *The Philosophy of Time*

True motion … is motion at once in time and space. Nothing can "move" in time alone any more than in space alone, and time itself cannot "move" any more than space itself. "Does this road go anywhere?" asks the city tourist. "No, it stays right along here," replies the countryman. Time "flows" only in the sense in which a line flows or a landscape "recedes into the west." That is, it is an ordered extension. And each of us proceeds through time only as a fence proceeds across a farm: that is, parts of our being, and the fence's, occupy successive instants and points, respectively. There is passage, but it is nothing extra. It is the mere happening of things, their existence strung along in the manifold. The term "the present" is the conventional way of designating the cross section of events which are simultaneous with the uttering of the phrase "the present moves" only in that when similar words occur at successively different moments, they denote, by a twist of language essentially the same as that of all "egocentric particulars," like "here" and "this," different cross sections of the manifold.

FOR FURTHER REFLECTION

When it comes to understanding time, we must recruit the finest minds from physics, philosophy, psychology, and theology to help us get a handle on this mystery of mysteries—or perhaps we should say paradox of paradoxes. Time moves yet it is motionless, like that fence across a farm Donald Williams describes. From the perspective of eternity—or God, a theologian might argue—past, present, and future are coexistent.

. . . . TRY THIS . . . .

Do your own meditating on the nature of time. Describe moments in your life when time seems to behave in different ways, depending on whether your experience with time is "subjective," as in dreams or when you're engrossed in an exciting game, book, or movie; or "objective," when you're determining the length of time necessary to complete a task or drive a certain distance.

MAY 22
Reinventing Womanhood
by Carolyn Heilbrun

Womanhood must be reinvented. Woman has too long been content to accept as fundamental the dependent condition of her sex. We avoid aggressive behavior, fear autonomy, feel incomplete without the social status only a man can bestow. In the past those women who have made their way successfully into the male-dominated worlds of business, the arts, or the professions have done so as honorary men, neither admiring nor bonding with other women, offering no encouragement to those who might come after them, preserving the socially required "femininity," but sacrificing their womanhood. …

What becomes evident in studying women like myself, women who moved against the current of their times, is that some condition in their lives insulated them from society's expectations and gave them a source of energy, even a sense of destiny, which would not permit them to accept the conventional female role. Some condition of being an outsider gave them the courage to be themselves.

FOR FURTHER REFLECTION

Heilbrun's call for women to reinvent themselves is really a call to *un*invent themselves, to stop shaping their identities in the context of male values. Thus, instead of being reluctant to pursue a career because it has been traditionally defined as "male" (a firefighter or commercial airline pilot, say), or repressing an urge to be competitive in the marketplace because such competitiveness is considered aggressive (hence, "masculine," as in "tomboy"), stop inventing a stereotypically "feminine" nature and simply follow their own individualistic nature. Or, to put it another way, why not make "feminine" (or, for that matter, "masculine") relative to being true to one's own female or male nature?

. . . . TRY THIS . . . .

To what extent do women consciously or subconsciously reject their authentic natures in order to follow male-based expectations for how women should appear and behave? Write a profile of four women: two who have adapted their personalities and pursuits to male-derived criteria, and two who have resisted the pressure to adapt and, like Heilbrun, faithfully adhered to their own criteria.

MAY 23

The Myth of Mental Illness: Foundations of a Theory of Personal Conduct

by Thomas S. Szasz, M.D.

It is important to understand clearly that modern psychiatry—and the identification of new psychiatric diseases—began not by identifying such diseases by means of the established methods of pathology, but by creating a new criterion of what constitutes disease: to the established criterion of detectable alteration of *bodily structure* was now added the fresh criterion of *bodily function*; and, as the former was detected by observing the patient's body, so the latter was detected by observing his behavior. This is how and why conversion hysteria became the prototype of this new class of diseases—appropriately named "mental" to distinguish them from those that are "organic," and appropriately called also "functional" in contrast to those that are "structural." Thus, whereas in modern medicine new diseases were *discovered*, in modern psychiatry they were *invented*. Paresis [paralysis] was *proved* to be a disease; hysteria was *declared* to be one.

It would be difficult to overemphasize the importance of this shift in the criteria of what constitutes illness. Under its impact, persons who complained of pains and paralyses but were apparently physically intact in their bodies—that is, were healthy, by the old standards—were now declared to be suffering from a "functional illness." Thus was hysteria invented.

FOR FURTHER REFLECTION

A veteran psychiatrist who was cofounder of the American Association for the Abolition of Involuntary Mental Hospitalization, Dr. Szasz alerts us to the dangers of diagnosing behavior. Too many persons have been incarcerated in mental institutions for exhibiting "abnormal" behavior, as if any deviance from normalcy (however it is perceived) constitutes illness.

...................................TRY THIS....................................

Explain in an essay how you draw the line between genuine mental illness and deviant behavior. Refer to individuals (actual or imaginary) to illustrate. Consider including cases that are difficult to diagnose. What should be done with such cases?

Birth of the Chess Queen: A History
by Marilyn Yalom

In India, where chess had originated in the fifth century, it would have made no sense to have a queen on the board. Chess was resolutely and exclusively a war game enacted between male fighters mounted on animals or marching on foot. The same pattern made its way into Persia and the Arabic lands, with only slight modifications. To this day, the Arabic game is played with a vizier and an elephant, having resisted the changes that took place in Europe a thousand years ago.

When the Arabs carried the game across the Mediterranean into Spain and Sicily, chess began to reflect Western feudal structures and took on a social dimension. The queen replaced the vizier, the horse was transformed into a knight, the chariot into a tower (today's castle or rook), the elephant into a bishop (though in France, it became a jester, and in Italy, a standard bearer). Only the king and the foot soldier (pawn) at the two ends of the hierarchy remained exactly the same.

FOR FURTHER REFLECTION

We can learn about history through games; and chess, having been around since medieval times, reflects not only the history of warfare, but as Stanford University scholar Marilyn Yalom points out, of social relationships—particularly the role of women in feudal society. Where the vizier (the royal adviser) once stood beside the king on the chessboard, the queen now stands—and over the last thousand years she has evolved into the most powerful piece on the chessboard.

....................................TRY THIS....................................

Explore the history of your favorite game, be it Monopoly, Scrabble (see the entry for March 24), roulette, or a card game like poker. Write an essay that not only traces its origin and evolution, but profiles the people who helped bring it into being.

Contemplative Prayer
by Thomas Merton

The dimensions of prayer in solitude are those of man's ordinary anguish, his self-searching, his moments of nausea at his own vanity, falsity and capacity for betrayal. Far from establishing one in unassailable narcissistic security, the way of prayer brings us face to face with the sham and indignity of the false self that seeks to live for itself alone and to enjoy the "consolation of prayer" for its own sake. This "self" is pure illusion, and ultimately he who lives for and by such an illusion must end either in disgust or in madness.

On the other hand, we must admit that social life, so-called "worldly life," in its own way promotes this illusory and narcissistic existence to the very limit. The curious state of alienation and confusion of man in modern society is perhaps more "bearable" because it is lived in common, with a multitude of distractions and escapes—and also with opportunities for fruitful action and genuine Christian self-forgetfulness.

FOR FURTHER REFLECTION

Our daily lives inevitably immerse us in materialistic concerns, which is why we need to remove ourselves from worldly matters now and then in order to renew our perspective and to attend to our neglected spiritual lives, through contemplative prayer—that is, through the kind of prayer that addresses the needs of the soul rather than the desires of the self.

..................................TRY THIS....................................

Compose a meditation or contemplative prayer that penetrates beyond the long-ings of the materialistic or worldly self in order to reflect on the value of selfless-ness, of compassion for and service to others, of living in the world without succumbing to its materialistic temptations.

"You Bet Your Life: A Selection of One-Liners"

by Groucho Marx

from *The Essential Groucho*

To a cartoonist: If you want to see a comic strip, you should see me in a shower.

To a tree surgeon: Have you ever fallen out of a patient?

To a skywriter: When you're up there skywriting do you ever feel that someone is looking over your shoulder?

To elderly newlyweds: I'll never forget my wedding day … they threw vitamin pills.

To an author: It won't do you any good to plug your book on my show, because none of our listeners can read.

To a choreographer: Oh, you make maps?

To an economist: I made a killing on Wall Street a few years ago. I shot my broker.

FOR FURTHER REFLECTION

From 1947–1960, Groucho Marx hosted a half-hour quiz show called *You Bet Your Life*—first on radio, then on television. The show brought him an even larger audience than his movies. It wasn't the quiz portion of the show so much as Groucho's witty repartee with his guests (as the above one-liners indicate) that made the show so popular.

......................................TRY THIS....................................

Write a string of Groucho-esque one-liners to imaginary guests on your show, using their careers as the basis for the joke—try a computer programmer, a Washington lobbyist, a rock singer, a hot-air balloonist, a masseur or masseuse.

MAY 27
Flowers for Algernon
by Daniel Keyes

3d progris riport

martch 5—Dr Strauss asked me how come you went to the Beekman School all by yourself Charlie. How did you find out about it. I said I don't remember.

Prof Nemur said but why did you want to lern to reed and spell in the frist place. I tolld him because all my life I wanted to be smart and not dumb. ...

Progris riport 5 mar 6

They found my sister Normal who lives with my mother in Brooklin and she have permissen for the operashun. So their going to use me. Im so exited I can hardly write it down ... . Dr Strauss said I had something that was very good. He said I had a good motor-vation. I never even knowed I had that. I felt good when he said not everbody with an eye-Q of 68 had that thing like I had it. I don't know what it is or where I got it but he said Algernon had it too. Algernons motor-vation is the chees they put in his box. ...

Progress Report 9

I'm getting a little smarter every day. I know punctuation, and I can spell good. I like to look up all the hard words in the dictionary and I remember them. And I try to write these progress reports very careful but that's hard to do. I'm reading a lot now, and Miss Kinnian says I read very fast.

FOR FURTHER REFLECTION

Charlie's odyssey from retardation to genius as the result of a daring medical experiment is both frightening and heartwarming. Through his protagonist, Keyes reminds us that while "smartness" may increase, the human heart remains steadfast. A selfish person remains selfish and will use his intelligence for personal gain; a compassionate person continues to be compassionate and will use his intelligence to help others and the world. The novel also calls attention to the widespread mistreatment of persons whose intelligence has been considered substandard.

......................................TRY THIS....................................

Write a story about two individuals—a hero and a villain—both of whom receive brain boosts. The hero is moral and kindhearted; the villain is power hungry and ruthless. Bring the two of them together in a climactic showdown.

MAY 28
The Shining
by Stephen King

Jack stared at the curtain. His face felt as if it had been heavily waxed, all dead skin on the outside, live, hot rivulets of fear on the inside. ...

There was something behind the pink plastic shower curtain. There was something in the tub.

He could see it, ill defined and obscure through the plastic, a nearly amorphous shape. It could have been anything. A trick of the light. The shadow of the shower attachment. A woman long dead and reclining in her bath, a bar of Lowila in one stiffening hand as she waited patiently for whatever lover might come.

Jack told himself to step forward boldly and rake the shower curtain back. To expose whatever might be there. Instead he turned with jerky, marionette strides, his heart whamming frightfully in his chest, and went back into the bed/sitting room.

The door to the hall was shut.

He stared at it for a long, immobile second. He could taste his terror now. ...

He turned off the light with a fumbling gesture, stepped out into the hall, and pulled the door shut without looking back. From inside, he seemed to hear an odd wet thumping sound, far off, dim, as if something had just scrambled belatedly out of the tub.

FOR FURTHER REFLECTION

One of the obstacles to successfully capturing a powerful horror novel like *The Shining* on film, is that in order to experience the horror fully, we must get inside the head of the viewpoint character, not just see him reacting outwardly. Stanley Kubrick did a memorable job of capturing on film the eeriness of the haunted Overlook Hotel and the behavior exhibited by the demonically possessed Jack Torrance (superbly performed by Jack Nicholson)—but only through Stephen King's masterful storytelling can we *feel* what it is like to be possessed.

......................................TRY THIS......................................

Write a scene, later to be incorporated into a horror novel, in which your viewpoint character begins to experience his surroundings differently, and change his feelings towards his family or friends, as a result of an evil spirit gradually taking over his mind and body.

Technopoly: The Surrender of Culture to Technology
by Neil Postman

Technological change is neither additive nor subtractive. It is ecological. I mean "ecological" in the same sense as the word is used by environmental scientists. One significant change generates total change. If you remove caterpillars from a given habitat, you are not left with the same environment minus caterpillars: you have a new environment, and you have reconstituted the conditions of survival; the same is true if you add caterpillars to an environment that has had none. This is how the ecology of media works as well. A new technology does not add or subtract something. It changes everything. In the year 1500, fifty years after the printing press was invented, we did not have old Europe plus the printing press. We had a different Europe. After television, the United States was not America plus television; television gave a new coloration to every political campaign, to every home, to every school, to every church, to every industry. And that is why the competition among media is so fierce. Surrounding every technology are institutions whose organization—not to mention their reason for being—reflects the world-view promoted by the technology. Therefore, when an old technology is assaulted by a new one, institutions are threatened. When institutions are threatened, a culture finds itself in crisis.

FOR FURTHER REFLECTION

A new kind of machine—the printing press, the automobile, the airplane, radio and television, computers and the Internet—not only augments society, but profoundly changes it. For that reason, as Neil Postman, a communications theorist, suggests, we must be attentive to the way in which technology changes us: Will the change be good for us in the long run, or will it undermine our humanity?

. . . . TRY THIS . . . .

If you are old enough to remember what society was like before computers or cell phones or iPods, write an essay about the changes in human nature that have occurred as a result of one or more of these inventions. If you are not old enough, then do the opposite: Write an essay in which you imagine what society would be like without one or more of these inventions.

"The Birth of Harmony"
by Robert Jourdain

from *Music, the Brain, and Ecstasy:*
How Music Captures Our Imagination

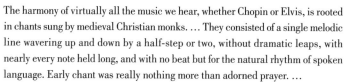

The harmony of virtually all the music we hear, whether Chopin or Elvis, is rooted in chants sung by medieval Christian monks. ... They consisted of a single melodic line wavering up and down by a half-step or two, without dramatic leaps, with nearly every note held long, and with no beat but for the natural rhythm of spoken language. Early chant was really nothing more than adorned prayer. ...

In time, vocal range expanded toward high notes and low notes that not all singers could manage. And so chants were separated into two or more vocal lines—parts—that were identical in every way but for being separated by several steps. ...

This way of singing prayers, called *organum*, continued for hundreds of years. But starting in the eleventh century, the individual parts of organum began to go separate ways. The upper part was often made more complex than the others, taking on more embellishments. And lower parts began to follow their own melodic line, sometimes moving in contrary directions to the treble. Still, all voices remained synchronized upon the same words. It was not until the thirteenth century that the most crucial development took place. Particularly at Notre Dame Cathedral in Paris, a group of church composers wrote music in which voices shifted out of sync and moved independently across time for long stretches, though alternately falling back into unison in the older style.

To medieval ears this new music sounded revolutionary, and rightly so. Chant had become multimelodic—*polyphonic*—with several independent lines sung simultaneously.

FOR FURTHER REFLECTION

We say of beautiful music that it is *ecstatic*—a word that literally means being taken out of ourselves, of being transported, *moved*. That is why music is so closely associated with spirituality and romance, and why music inspires us.

·································TRY THIS···································

Play a selection of music from your CD collection that makes you ecstatic. What thoughts are stirred by the music? Write them down without editing. Later, fashion your notes into a poem, short story, or essay.

Writing the Breakout Novel
by Donald Maass

If there is one single principle that is central to making any story more powerful, it is simply this: Raise the stakes. ... Everyone knows that stakes are important. It is as fundamental as putting a period at the end of a sentence. Why, then, do so few fiction writers put this principle into effective practice? ...

Think hard. Be honest with yourself. Are the stakes in your current manuscript as high as they possibly can be? Can you define the stakes right now? Can you point to the exact pages in which the stakes escalate, locking your protagonist into his course of action with less hope of success than before?

Low stakes are easy to diagnose in the work of beginning novelists. In one-on-one meetings at writers conferences, I can usually stop a story pitch dead in its tracks by interjecting the following: "Hold on, your protagonist wants to (insert *goal* here), but let me ask you this, if he is not successful, so what?" What follows that question is generally a stare of disbelief or, if I am lucky, choked stammering. "So what? Well, if he didn't then ... then. ..."

Then what? That is the essence of defining what is at stake. What would be lost? A day? A job? A love? A life?

FOR FURTHER REFLECTION

Stories are all about people who go to great lengths, take great risks, to achieve a goal they long for or urgently need. The risk factor—or as literary agent Donald Maass would say, the high-stakes factor—exists because of opposing forces: Someone or something (which can sometimes be the protagonist's own alter ego) does not want the protagonist to succeed and will stop at nothing to sabotage the protagonist's efforts. Without such high-stakes conflict, there is no dimension of excitement, no wondering what will happen next ... and therefore no story.

............................TRY THIS....................................

Begin writing a story you've always wanted to write but were afraid to take the plunge, for whatever reason. You can always revise or discard what you've written if you're not satisfied with the results. Taking risks is important in creative writing.

JUNE 1
"Hierarchy Has Taken a Bad Rap"
by Deborah Tannen, Ph.D.

from *Talking From 9 to 5: How Women's and
Men's Conversational Styles Affect Who Gets Heard,
Who Gets Credit, and What Gets Done at Work*

Part of the reason Americans feel hierarchy is negative is that we tend to think of its benefits as flowing one way only: The person in the superior position has the right to tell a subordinate what to do, and the person in the subordinate position has to obey. In this spirit, if someone says he is being treated like a child, he is sure to be heard registering a complaint, synonymous with saying he is being humiliated. ...

In our assumption that equality is good and hierarchy is bad, Americans tend to regard the sibling relationship as the ultimate in reciprocity. Such statements as "We're like sisters" or "He's like a brother to me" are usually understood as references to closeness, not hierarchy. It is as if to say, "We're so close, there are no power games between us." And yet anyone who has had a flesh-and-blood sibling knows that age differences resulting from birth order are the ultimate in hierarchy: Older siblings can both protect and torment younger ones, who, in return, idolize or resent them or both. And none of this means that they cannot be close.

FOR FURTHER REFLECTION
Hierarchic relationships are useful and healthy; but like anything else, they can be abused. Those in positions of leadership are as obligated to adhere to ethical principles of supervision as their charges are obligated to follow the supervisor's directions. A hierarchic relationship must function properly both ways or not at all.

.................................TRY THIS.................................

Scrutinize one of the hierarchic relationships in your life: your relationship with your children or your parents; your relationship with your boss or employees; your relationship with your teachers or your students. Record both the positive and the negative aspects of the relationship. Finally, discuss your findings in an essay in which you offer suggestions for improving such relationships.

JUNE 2
"Theater Architecture of the Seventeenth Century"
by Spiro Kostof
from A History of Architecture: Settings and Rituals

In the course of the seventeenth century the theater, both popular and courtly, moved toward one, more or less canonical layout. The catalyst was the opera, a new form of musical drama of Italian origin which caught on fast and became the favorite entertainment of cultured Europe. For it the theater reorganized its component parts, so that the auditorium and the stage behind a curtain were now two clearly separate worlds. ... The auditorium which could be U-shaped, horseshoed, or bell-shaped was subdivided into two main sections to segregate the lower classes from the wealthy—one taking up the cheaper seats in the orchestra, the other reserving boxes that had replaced the old galleries. On the stage, a principal innovation was the replacement of *periaktoi** by flat scenic wings that moved on grooves on the stage floor, a flexible system that allowed for a multiplicity of quick changes.

FOR FURTHER REFLECTION
The physical design of a stage has played an important role in the way a dramatic work is presented. The world of the play or opera was an artistically distinct world, set distinctly apart from the real world (the world inhabited by the audience), and so was expected to be larger than life. Theater architecture helped to reinforce that illusion.

...................................TRY THIS...................................

Write a scene for a children's play in which the setting and characters are strikingly different from those of the everyday world. Suggest props such as furnishings or set architecture that would enhance the illusion of otherworldliness.

---

* Triangular prisms on either side of the stage that revolve for scene changes.

JUNE 3

The Alchemy of the Heavens: Searching for Meaning in the Milky Way
by Ken Croswell

The Milky Way Galaxy is mighty and immense, and both its center and edge lie far, far from Earth. From end to end the Milky Way's disk, which radiates most of the Galaxy's light, stretches 130,000 light-years. A photon that set out during the peak of the last ice age and raced at light speed across the disk would by now have covered only a seventh of its extent. The Sun and Earth lie within this disk, 27,000 light-years from the Galaxy's center, or about 40 percent of the way from the center to the edge. If the Milky Way were a huge metropolis, the Sun and Earth would reside in an inner suburb.

Yet from what we see in the night sky, we glimpse only a fraction of the Milky Way's magnificence. The most distant first-magnitude star in the sky is the white supergiant Deneb, 1500 light-years away. Carve a large sphere in the Galaxy by scooping out all the stars closer than Deneb and gather them like colorful jewels extracted from a celestial mine. In your arms would be 50 million stars, some shining red, others yellow, and still others white, orange, or blue. Nearly every star you can see in the night sky lies within this huge sphere: Antares, Betelgeuse, Sirius, Alpha Centauri, Polaris, Vega, Rigel, Arcturus, and all the other stars that set the sky afire. Sprinkled among these gems are millions of red, orange, and white dwarfs that glow so feebly they do not appear in even the largest star catalogue.

FOR FURTHER REFLECTION

It is easy to understand why a galaxy is sometimes called an "island universe": It is so vast—hundreds of thousands of light-years across (i.e., hundreds of thousands of trillions of miles across) that it is difficult to imagine anything beyond them. When we gaze up at the night sky we are gazing at the tiniest fraction—a few thousand at most—of the total number of stars in the galaxy, which is estimated to be around two hundred billion. It is easy to become overwhelmed by the immensity of the heavens.

. . . . TRY THIS . . . .

Children are naturally fascinated by astronomy. Write an article aimed at, say, fifth or six graders, that describes the properties of our Milky Way Galaxy.

JUNE 4

Sex on the Brain: The Biological Differences Between Men and Women

by Deborah Blum

There seems to be a complex and life-reinforcing chemistry to parenting and partnership. Research suggests that once that route is chosen, and the single life abandoned, the brain itself changes. And this makes sense, of course, because if parents are going to be any good at all at what they do, they have to change in some fundamental ways. To a great extent, you have to kiss self-absorption goodbye, accommodate a partner, and care for a small child whose survival may depend on that commitment. …

There's also some very distinct hormonal chemistry associated with being a good partner. Many scientists place two particular hormones—oxytocin and vasopressin—right at the heart of monogamous behavior, although other hormones, including testosterone and the estrogens, may play a supporting role. Researchers suspect that oxytocin and vasopressin play an influential role in romantic love and parental love. The fact that there are two of them also suggests a significant gender difference. Both sexes make both hormones. But oxytocin is the hormone linked to emotional connection in females. In males, it's vasopressin. And one of the mysteries of monogamy is why the sexes might need two different hormones to achieve the same things—a sense of partnership, the urge to care for a child.

FOR FURTHER REFLECTION

We may be creatures of free will, but brain chemistry can determine our behavior to some extent—as in the case of the hormones oxytocin and vasopressin, which help to prepare couples for parenting as well as to maintain marital stability. Perhaps through deeper understanding of neurochemistry and brain function, medical researchers can help couples better prepare for parental responsibilities.

....TRY THIS....................................

Learn more about the body's production of hormones and the role they play in behavior. Write an essay in which you reflect on the role that hormones play in romantic and/or marital relationships.

JUNE 5
The Pleasures of Reading in an Ideological Age
by Robert Alter

A discriminating awareness of the distinctive resources of literary expression—style, allusion, structure, perspective and much else—can amplify the pleasure and the precision of the reading experience. But let me hasten to add that, having earlier objected to the mechanical nature of the conception of literature assumed by Structuralism and some of its heirs, I do not propose still another mechanical model. The formal aspects of the literary text may deserve the nicest attention, but reading is not a matter of nuts and bolts, and an account of formal categories cannot serve as a simple checklist, like the directions for assembling a bicycle. A work of literature ... consists of too many disparate elements engaged in constant, shifting interplay for reading ever to be a linear assemblage of parts by even the most patient analyst. Most literary works, moreover, turn on an experiential dimension that is not finally reducible to the formal vehicles through which it is conveyed.

FOR FURTHER REFLECTION

The reading experience, like any other intellectual or physical activity, matures with practice. As Robert Alter, a professor of comparative literature at the University of California, Berkeley, points out, there are numerous facets to the reading experience; the more one reads, the greater one's capacity for recognizing and appreciating the aesthetic effects produced by style, point of view, symbolism, allusion, and the like.

...................................TRY THIS...................................

Spend several days monitoring your reading experience. Read or reread a novel by an author you admire, and after each stint of reading, jot down as many of the novel's aesthetic qualities as you can. After you finish the novel, write an essay in which you reflect on the processes involved in reading a novel. Later on, you might try a similar experiment with a long poem or a play.

"The Garden"

by Andrew Marvell

from *Miscellaneous Poems*

When we have run our
  passion's heat,
Love hither makes his best retreat.
The gods, that mortal beauty chase,
Still in a tree did end their race:
Apollo hunted Daphne so,
Only that she might laurel grow;
And Pan did after Syrinx speed,
Not as a nymph, but for a reed.

What wondrous life in this I lead!
Ripe apples drop about my head;
The luscious clusters of the vine
Upon my mouth do crush their wine;
The nectarine and curious** peach

Into my hands themselves do reach;
Stumbling on melons, as I pass,
Ensnared with flowers, I fall on grass.

Meanwhile the mind
  from pleasure less
Withdraws into its happiness;
The mind, that ocean where each kind
Does straight its own re-
  semblance find;
Yet it creates, transcending these,
Far other worlds and other seas,
Annihilating all that's made
To a green thought in a green shade.

FOR FURTHER REFLECTION

It sometimes takes a poet—in the case of Andrew Marvell, a great poet—to capture the sensory pleasures of succumbing to the temptation of various foods in a post-Eden garden. But even more important than those momentary pleasures of savoring "the luscious clusters of the vine" and such are the transcendent ecstasies, the pleasures of the mind that those sensory pleasures ignite. Marvell's wonderful poem is its own demonstration of that body-to-mind sublimation of palatal to intellectual delight.

.....................................TRY THIS.....................................

Compose an ode to your favorite food—filet mignon or king salmon, heirloom tomatoes or asparagus, raspberries or chocolate—conjuring up as many sensory impressions and associations as you can.

** exotic

JUNE 7
"Fossils"
by Richard Dawkins
from *The Ancestor's Tale: A Pilgrimage to the Dawn of Evolution*

In spite of the fascination of fossils, it is surprising how much we would still know about our evolutionary past without them. If every fossil were magicked away, the comparative study of modern organisms, of how their patterns of resemblances, especially of their genetic sequences, are distributed among species, and of how species are distributed among continents and islands, would still demonstrate, beyond all sane doubt, that our history is evolutionary, and that all living creatures are cousins. Fossils are a bonus. A welcome bonus, to be sure, but not an essential one. It is worth remembering this when creationists go on (as they tediously do) about "gaps" in the fossil record. The fossil record could be one big gap, and the evidence for evolution would still be overwhelmingly strong. At the same time, if we had only fossils and no other evidence, the fact of evolution would again be overwhelmingly supported. As things stand, we are blessed with both. ...

When we speak of a fossil, we normally mean that the original material has been substituted or infiltrated by a mineral of a different chemical composition. ... An imprint of the original form may be preserved in stone for a very long time indeed, perhaps mixed with some of the original material. ...

By hopping around the world, from site to site where different strata happen to be accessibly near the surface, the palaeontologist can aspire to piece together something approaching a continuous record. Of course individual palaeontologists don't hop from site to site. They hop from museum to museum looking at specimens in drawers.

FOR FURTHER REFLECTION

Fossils represent a record of life from the geologic past. Fossils tell a story not only of how life forms evolved, but how the earth itself evolved. In deserts, for example, one finds dinosaur fossils, telling us that a hundred million years ago, the area was heavily vegetated. Fossils also represent a second body of evidence for species evolution—the other being the genetic record.

·······························TRY THIS····································

Many misconceptions about evolution exist because it is not the easiest concept to understand. Write an essay in which you explain, in the simplest yet most accurate language possible, the basic principles of biological evolution.

JUNE 8
"Ancient Black Africa"
by Fernand Braudel
from *A History of Civilizations*. Translated by Richard Mayne

Black Africa has had few outlets to the rest of the world—a serious handicap, because all progress in civilization is made easier by mutual contact and influence. This relative isolation explains the important gaps which were scarcely filled, if at all, before the arrival of the Europeans and the establishment of their colonies. The wheel, for example, was unknown: so were the plough and the use of pack-animals: so was writing except in Ethiopia (which is not really part of Black Africa) and the countries of the Sudan and the East coast (where writing came from Islam, which they soon adopted). ...

Even so, the disadvantages should not be overstressed. First, Black Africa made progress in ancient times that was no less rapid than in prehistoric Europe. There were also artistic triumphs, and not only in the fine Benin bronzes of the eleventh to fifteenth centuries, or the equally fine textiles made from various vegetable fibres. Last but not least, Africa was an early pioneer in metallurgy—as early as 3000 BC in the case of iron. It is absurd—and untrue—to claim that Black Africans were introduced to iron only after the Portuguese reached Cape Bojador on the coast of the Western Sahara in AD 1354. Iron weapons were known very early on. ... Tin-working was probably practiced in Upper Nigeria 2,000 years ago.

FOR FURTHER REFLECTION

History is always being revised, not just as a result of new archaeological discoveries, but also because of new criteria applied to what is already known or what has been inadequately understood. Until relatively recently, historians tended to overlook Black Africa (i.e., sub-Saharan Africa—the Africa of Egypt and Ethiopia being more associated with Biblical lands of the Middle East) as a major player on the world stage; but a closer look reveals artistic and technological activity in this region that goes back to the Stone Age. As Braudel notes, historians have sometimes read too much into the influences of explorers from Europe during the Middle Ages and Renaissance.

.... TRY THIS ....

Conduct in-depth research on the ancient history of one sub-Saharan African nation, such as Mali, Ghana, Senegal, Nigeria, Cameroon, or Angola, and write an essay highlighting your most intriguing findings.

JUNE 9
"The Origin of Modern Banking"
by James Burke
from *Connections*

The Tuscans had been pre-eminent in finance since the thirteenth century, when a Pisan called Leonardo Fibonacchi brought the Arabic numerical system back from North Africa, and double-entry bookkeeping appeared. This made it easier to run complex accounts in an orderly manner, instead of in the jumbled, narrative way it had been done up to then with each transaction written as a separate credit-and-debit account. In the fourteenth century the Italians had also developed the bill of exchange, as a means of handling the increasing international trade of the time without requiring merchants to carry large amounts of cash on unsafe roads. The bill took the form of a credit note for a certain amount, payable at a rate agreed before the merchant left his home, in a specified foreign location for a certain sum of foreign currency. This system needed banks to run it, and these evolved gradually from the counters at international fairs such as those of the Champagne area, where the exchange of money or of credit note for money took place. Monopoly of these techniques had by the fifteenth century given the Italians control of the European money market.

FOR FURTHER REFLECTION

Systems of credit and monetary exchange evolve as society evolves and spreads across the globe. One of the great contributions of the European Renaissance, which first took place in Italy, was a system of accounting and banking that laid the foundation for our modern international economy.

.... TRY THIS ....

Reflect on the intricacies of our modern system of economics—of credit, investments, international trade—and write an introductory essay (say, aimed at high school seniors) on the way these systems function, as well as how they can be abused.

"The New Woman"
by Lynn Dumenil

from *The Modern Temper: American Culture and Society in the 1920s*

Many observers in the twenties, noting the emphasis on the new woman's sexuality, argued that the dislocations of war had turned traditional morals upside town. The causes, however, are far more complex and, moreover, predate the war. An emerging new morality was already evident in the 1910s. As one journal put it in 1913, the nation "has struck sex o'clock." The emphasis on women's sexuality coincided with the trend of women seeking more freedom in their social life. At the forefront of this change were the working-class young women who by the turn of the century were seeking, in historian Kathy Peiss's words, "cheap amusements." Looking for an escape in part from parental authority and in part from the harsh conditions of work, many young women took advantage of the new urban amusements—dance halls, amusement parks, theaters. This unchaperoned, relatively anonymous environment inevitably led to more sexual experimentation. Relaxing sexual standards may also have stemmed from the widespread practice of "treating." Poorly paid and often contributors to family incomes, these women had little left to pay for their entertainments. Men could and did "treat" them, but frequently with the implicit assumption of sexual favors as part of the exchange.

FOR FURTHER REFLECTION

Society changed dramatically in the 1920s for many reasons, but four of them are fundamental: feminism (kindled by women having won the right to vote), a rapidly expanding industrial workforce, the mass-production of automobiles, and motion pictures, which influenced the way young men and women viewed themselves. Add to these the revolutions in music and the secretive nightlife inspired by speakeasies as a result of Prohibition, and it is no surprise that a sexual revolution accompanied the social one. (See also the entry for June 15.)

.................................TRY THIS...................................

Write a story about a young woman who wants to become sexually liberated yet cannot quite break away from the Victorian values of her family.

JUNE 11
Oedipus the King
by Sophocles

Translated by Paul Roche

TIRESIAS [to Oedipus]: You'll not be rid of me until I've spoken
what I came to say. You do not frighten me.
There's not a thing that you can do to hurt.
I tell you this: the man you've searched for
all along with threats and fanfares for the murder
Of King Laius—that man, I say, is here.
He was a stranger in our midst, they thought;
but in a moment you shall see
him openly displayed a Theban born,
and shattered by the honor. Blind
instead of seeing; beggar instead of rich;
he'll grope through foreign places tapping out
his way with stick in hand. Oh yes, detected
in his very heart of home: his children's father
and their brother; son and husband of his mother;
bed-rival to his father and assassin.
Ponder this and go inside,
and when you think you've caught me at a lie,
then come and tell me I'm not fit to prophecy.

FOR FURTHER REFLECTION

One cannot escape one's destiny, not even when it is foretold to us by the Delphic Oracle or by the seer Tiresias. Oedipus finds it preposterous to take Tiresias seriously, having left his home in Corinth to avoid the Oracle's horrific prophecy. Unable to consider the possibility that he himself was the murderer that Tiresias mentions, Oedipus accepts the reward offered him by Thebes in gratitude for slaying the Sphinx: to replace Laius (his real father, the old man he had murdered) and marry the Queen.

...................................TRY THIS....................................

Plan a story that centers around a prophecy and the effort of your protagonist to avoid that prophecy at all costs.

"O Shepherd of Souls" and "O Glittering Starlight"

by Hildegard of Bingen

from *Lieder*. Translated by Lawrence Rosenwald

O Pastor Animarum

O pastor animarum
et o prima vox
nunc tibi, tibi placeat
per quam omnes create sumus,
ut digneris
nos liberare de miseriis
et languoribus nostris

O Shepherd of Souls

O shepherd of souls
O first voice
by which we have all been created,
may you, may you now be willing
to release us
from our miseries
and our frailties

O Choruscans Lux Stellarum

O choruscans lux stellarum,
o splendidissima specialis forma
regalium nuptiarum,
o fulgens gemma:
tu es ornate in alta persona
que non habet maculatam rugam.
Tu es etiam social angelorum
et civis sanctorum.
Fuge, fuge speluncam
antique perditoris,
et veniens veni in palatium regis.

O Glittering Starlight

O glittering starlight,
O most splendid and special form
of regal marriage,
O shining gem:
you are adorned like a noble lady
who has no blemish.
And you are a companion of angels
and a citizen among the saints.
Flee, O flee the cave
of the old betrayer,
and come, O come into
 the Lord's palace.

FOR FURTHER REFLECTION

Hildegard of Bingen was a German Benedictine abbess, visionary mystic, poet, and one of the most important and beloved composers of the Middle Ages. Her verses, which often employ sensuous images to evoke spiritual visions and states of mind, are both prayers and songs.

....TRY THIS....................................

Try to capture a spiritual vision in a poem that could serve as both a prayer and a chant.

"Of Poetry"
by Sir William Temple
from *Miscellanea*

Besides the heat of invention and liveliness of wit, there must be [in poetry] the coldness of good sense and soundness of judgment, to distinguish between things and conceptions which at first sight or upon short glances seem alike; to choose among infinite productions of wit and fancy which are worth preserving and cultivating, and which are better stifled in the birth, or thrown away when they are born, as not worth bringing up. Without the forces of wit, all poetry is flat and languishing without the succors of judgment. ... there must be a great agitation of mind to invent, a great calm to judge and correct; there must be upon the same tree, and at the same time, both flower and fruit. To work up this metal into exquisite figure there must be employed the fire, the hammer, and chisel, and the file. There must be a general knowledge both of nature and of arts. ...

When I speak of poetry I mean not an ode or an elegy, a song or a satire, nor by a poet the composer of any of these, but of a just poem [i.e., a poem of high ambition, such as an epic]; and after all I have said, 'tis no wonder there should be so few that appeared in any parts or any ages of the world.

FOR FURTHER REFLECTION

For the neo-Platonic philosopher-statesman-essayist William Temple (1628–1699), great poetry was, like prophecy, a manifestation of the divine spirit in the world. But such poetry is uncommon because too few poets understood what poetry must achieve to become great. It must first be the product of exceptional judgment, of deep knowledge combined with impassioned execution of form.

...................................TRY THIS...................................

After reading Temple's essay on poetry (or, perhaps, other great essays on poetry through the ages by Percy B. Shelley, Matthew Arnold, and T.S. Eliot), write your own essay on what you consider to exemplify greatness in the works of three or four contemporary poets.

JUNE 14

Vanity Fair

by William Makepeace Thackeray

[Miss Rebecca Sharp to Miss Sedley]

"… For two years I have only had insults and outrages from her [Miss Pinkerton, headmistress of an academy for young ladies]. I have been treated worse than any servant in the kitchen. I have never had a friend or a kind word, except from you. I have been made to tend the little girls in the lower schoolroom, and to talk French to the Misses until I grew sick of my mother-tongue. But that talking French to Miss Pinkerton was capital fun, wasn't it? She doesn't know a word of French and was too proud to confess it. I believe it was that which made her part with me; and so thank Heaven for French. *Vive la France! Vive l'Empereur! Vive Bonaparte!*"

"O Rebecca, Rebecca, for shame!" cried Miss Sedley; for this was the greatest blasphemy Rebecca had as yet uttered; and in those days, in England, to say "Long live Bonaparte!" was as much as to say "Long live Lucifer!" "How can you—how dare you have such wicked, revengeful thoughts?"

"Revenge may be wicked, but it's natural," answered Miss Rebecca. "I'm no angel." And, to say the truth, she certainly was not.

FOR FURTHER REFLECTION

Thackeray subtitled this delightful human comedy "a novel without a hero"— and Becky Sharp is its prized non-heroine: a young woman memorable for all her flaws, most especially her impulsive and outspoken manner.

..................................TRY THIS....................................

Keeping in mind that readers love colorful, even outrageous characters, write a profile of one such person you would like to inhabit your novel. Focus on behavioral more than on physical characteristics: Is he or she obsessed with certain ideas or goals and willing to take great risks—or perhaps he or she is neurotic, abnormally shy and subject to dark depression one moment and sudden elation the next.

This Side of Paradise
by F. Scott Fitzgerald

[Code of the Young Egoist]

He had realized that his best interests were bound up with those of a certain variant, changing person, whose label, in order that his past might always be identified with him, was Amory Blaine. Amory marked himself a fortunate youth, capable of infinite expansion for good or evil. He did not consider himself a "strong char'c'ter," but relied on his facility (learn things sorta quick) and his superior mentality (read a lotta deep books). He was proud of the fact that he could never become a mechanical or scientific genius. From no other heights was he debarred.

Physically.—Amory thought that he was exceedingly handsome. He was. He fancied himself an athlete of possibilities and a supple dancer.

Socially.—Here his condition was, perhaps, most dangerous. He granted himself personality, charm, magnetism, poise, the power of dominating all contemporary males, the gift of fascinating all women.

Mentally.—Complete, unquestioned superiority.

Now a confession will have to be made. Amory had rather a Puritan conscience. Not that he yielded to it—later in life he almost certainly slew it—but at fifteen it made him consider himself a great deal worse than other boys ... unscrupulousness ... the desire to influence people in almost every way, even for evil ... a certain coldness and lack of affection, amounting sometimes to cruelty ... a shifting sense of honor ... an unholy selfishness ... a puzzled, furtive interest in everything concerning sex.

FOR FURTHER REFLECTION

Egoism was a prominent character trait during the Roaring Twenties, a time of great technological progress and artistic experimentation, especially in fashion and in music. It was a time when secularism and romantic idealism overshadowed Puritan conformity. (See also the entry for June 10.)

..................................TRY THIS....................................

Read some of F. Scott Fitzgerald's Jazz Age stories ("Bernice Bobs Her Hair" and "The Camel's Back," for example); then write a jazz-age story of your own in which a young man dares to express himself in ways that would most likely shock his employer as well as his parents. How does he resolve the conflict, if at all?

JUNE 16
Tending Lives:
Nurses on the Medical Front
by Echo Heron

9:47 A.M.

Georgia is directing the traffic inside the ER, when she sees a woman go by on a carrier with what looks like half her face torn off. She notices an ear is missing and the muscles to her neck and shoulder are exposed.

Georgia's most vivid memory, besides [the patient's] face, will be the amount of blood draining off of carriers, carts, and people. It is more blood than she has ever seen in her life. ...

9:50 A.M.

Dana is treating a primary blast injury patient who has a variety of fractures, lacerations, and a large chunk of flesh and tissue missing from her neck. The patient is awake and alert, although she is intubated and cannot speak. Dana starts an IV and splints her fractures. Almost immediately the injured woman is sent upstairs to surgery. ...

Dana's next patient is a man with a bad laceration whom she will not forget because he is so happy to be alive. In shock he repeats the same question that is on most of the victims' lips—"What happened?"

FOR FURTHER REFLECTION

The answer to the man's question is that Timothy McVeigh, in the worst act of domestic terrorism before 9/11, had blown up the Murrah Federal Building in Oklahoma City. Bestselling author and former emergency room nurse, and activist for nurses' and patients' rights, Echo Heron vividly dramatizes throughout this book (as well as in her previous books, *Intensive Care* and *Condition Critical*) the extraordinary dedication, talent, and heroism of nurses, who have been all too often maligned and treated as second-class citizens in the medical community.

..................................TRY THIS....................................

Write a story about a nurse who has helped you or a loved one during a moment of medical urgency. To make your characters three-dimensional, consider flashing back to earlier events in their respective lives—events that helped shape their personalities and lead up to the present circumstance.

JUNE 17
Elvis Presley
by Bobbie Ann Mason

Elvis turned out to be a great natural showman—spontaneous onstage, with an easy rapport with the audience and a sense of what they wanted and needed. With that assurance, he could move extravagantly, his raunchiness arousing raw reactions. In the early days, he was often crude onstage, telling off-color jokes and gesturing lewdly. He spit. Oblivious to the rules of professional showmanship, he hammed it up with a teenage rebellious energy and a country innocence, throwing decorum to the wind.

There are hardly any fragments of film portraying the early Elvis. People described him as behaving wildly, agog at the commotion he was creating. He was a sight to see. His hair was unconventionally long, wafted up into a pompadour, and he sported sideburns. He wore a colorful shirt, baggy pants, a narrow belt, a loose jacket, and buckskin shoes. Or he wore pink pants with a black shirt, or perhaps purple pants with a green shirt. By mid-1955 he was playing a D-28 Martin guitar with a tooled-leather cover bearing his name. He banged his guitar so fervently he often broke the strings.

FOR FURTHER REFLECTION

Elvis has got to be a biographer's dream come true: the bizarre dress, the outrageous behavior, the wild appearance—Elvis practically writes himself. However, it takes a gifted writer like Bobbie Ann Mason to *orchestrate* those details into a three-dimensional portrait.

.................................TRY THIS...................................

1. Describe "The King" in the context of one of his live concerts or television. Include a description of the crowd's reactions.
2. Profile Elvis Presley the movie actor. Refer in detail to at least two of his movies.

JUNE 18
Treasure
by Clive Cussler

[Oceanographer and historian Mel Redfern to archaeologist
Lily Redfern and hero Dirk Pitt]

"In [A.D. 391] Emperor Theodosius and the patriarch of Alexandria, Theophilos, who was a religious nut case, decided all reference to anything except newly formed Christian principles was paganism. They masterminded the destruction of the library's contents. Statues, fabulous works of art in marble, bronze, gold and ivory, incredible paintings and tapestries, countless numbers of books inscribed on lambskin or papyrus scrolls, even Alexander's corpse: all were to be smashed into dust or burned to ashes."

"What kind of numbers are we talking about?" Pitt asked.

"The books alone numbered in the hundreds of thousands."

Lily shook her head sadly. "What a terrible waste." ...

"The earlier masterworks that took centuries to collect were lost, gone forever," Pitt summed up.

"Lost," Redfern agreed. "So historians have thought until now. But if what I just read rings true, the cream of the collection is not gone forever. It lies hidden somewhere."

FOR FURTHER REFLECTION

For anyone who has bemoaned what is arguably one of the most tragic cultural losses of all time, the destruction of the great Library of Alexandria, Cussler's novel offers a satisfying if fictive momentary reprieve: the discovery of tantalizing clues leading scientists to suspect that the treasure of ancient books, once considered gone forever, could actually still exist. Cussler skillfully infuses an exciting adventure story with fascinating background details about the Alexandrian library, ancient maritime history, and archaeology.

..................................TRY THIS....................................

The ancient Alexandrian library was pillaged not once but several times between the first century B.C.E. and the seventh century C.E. Write a story that takes place during one of these periods in which the guardians of the library confront its enemies, who regard books as a threat to their totalitarian ideologies.

JUNE 19

Lame Deer, Seeker of Visions

by John (Fire) Lame Deer and Richard Erdoes

For the white man each blade of grass or spring of water has a price tag on it. And that is the trouble, because look at what happens. The bobcats and coyotes which used to feed on prairie dogs now have to go after a stray lamb or a crippled calf. The rancher calls the pest-control officer to kill these animals. This man shoots some rabbits and puts them out as bait with a piece of wood stuck in them. That stick has an explosive charge which shoots some cyanide into the mouth of the coyote who tugs at it. The officer has been trained to be careful. He puts a printed warning on each stick reading, "Danger, Explosive Poison!" The trouble is that our dogs can't read, and some of our children can't either.

And the prairie becomes a thing without life—no more prairie dogs, no more badgers, foxes, coyotes. The big birds of prey used to feed on prairie dogs, too. So you hardly see an eagle these days. The bald eagle is your symbol. You see him on your money, but your money is killing him. When a people start killing off their own symbols they are in a bad way.

FOR FURTHER REFLECTION

In plain yet poetic and forceful language, Lame Deer highlights the essential difference in worldview between the white man, for whom land is a commodity, and the Native Americans, for whom land cannot be owned because it, and all that is a part of it (including the animals) are sacred.

. . . . TRY THIS . . . .

Do some research on the way one or two Native American nations—Navajo, Sioux, Cherokee, Kiowa, Hopi, for example—interact with the land they respectively inhabit. How does each nation's perception of land reflect their worldview? Their day-to-day way of life?

The Life of the Mind
by Hannah Arendt

Thinking … plays an enormous role in every scientific enterprise, but it is the role of a means to an end; the end is determined by a decision about what is worthwhile knowing, and this decision cannot be scientific. Moreover, the end is cognition or knowledge, which, having been obtained, clearly belongs to the world of appearances; once established as truth, it becomes part and parcel of the world. Cognition and the thirst for knowledge never leave the world of appearances altogether; if the scientists withdraw from it in order to "think," it is only in order to find better, more promising approaches, called methods, toward it. Science in this respect is but an enormously refined prolongation of common-sense reasoning in which sense illusions are constantly dissipated just as errors in science are corrected. The criterion in both cases is evidence, which as such is inherent in a world of appearances. And since it is the nature of appearances to reveal and to conceal, every correction and every dis-illusion "is the loss of one evidence only because it is the acquisition of another evidence," in the words of [Maurice] Merleau-Ponty.

FOR FURTHER REFLECTION

Most of us take our ability to think—that is, to think things out—for granted, but thinking is extraordinarily complex. Scientific thinking in particular is one of the mind's greatest achievements in that it is, in a sense, thinking carefully about thinking—weeding out flawed assumptions or lines of reasoning, for example.

......................................TRY THIS....................................

Spend some time thinking about the way you think. Do you often rush to judgment or do you take the time to examine an assumption from all sides in order to be assured of its validity? Write an essay—which you may later wish to incorporate into your memoir—about your habits of thought, how they have changed over the years, and what may have influenced those changes.

JUNE 21
Mathematics for the Nonmathematician
by Morris Kline

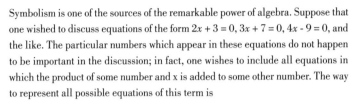

Symbolism is one of the sources of the remarkable power of algebra. Suppose that one wished to discuss equations of the form $2x + 3 = 0$, $3x + 7 = 0$, $4x - 9 = 0$, and the like. The particular numbers which appear in these equations do not happen to be important in the discussion; in fact, one wishes to include all equations in which the product of some number and x is added to some other number. The way to represent all possible equations of this term is

$$ax + b = 0 \qquad (1)$$

Here a stands for any number, and so does b. These numbers are known, but their precise value is not stated. The letter x stands for some unknown number. By reasoning about the general form (1) the mathematician covers the millions of separate cases which arise when a and b have specific values. Thus, by means of symbolism, algebra can handle a whole class of problems in one bit of reasoning.

FOR FURTHER REFLECTION
It is perhaps a bit startling to realize that symbolism plays just as important a role in science and mathematics as it does in literature and art. The only difference is that whereas mathematical symbols represent very specific quantities, ratios, or forces, literary or artistic symbols generally do not represent any universally agreed-upon ideas or meanings.

.....................................TRY THIS.....................................

To the uninitiated, an equation or set of algebraic computations looks like some kind of arcane gibberish, quite off-putting. In an article aimed at young readers, write about a mathematical or geometric principle (e.g., the ratio of the diameter of a circle to its circumference) in nonmathematical language.

"Myth America"
by Camryn Manheim
from *Wake Up, I'm Fat!*

Every year the Praying Mantis Brigade had a little pageant of its own in protest of the Miss California Pageant called the "Myth California Pageant." Women could come wearing gowns made entirely of meat, wearing sashes that said "Miss Used," "Miss Treated," "Miss Understood." At the end of the parade was a Cadillac convertible with a 500-pound woman sitting on the back, wearing a bikini and a tiara with her fat flowing over the sides of the car. She looked absolutely regal, doing the obligatory elbow, elbow, wrist, wrist; elbow, elbow, wrist, wrist wave.

One year the Praying Mantis Brigade asked women who had at one time been raped to donate blood to be used in a protest against the pageant. And on the night of the Miss California Pageant, the Praying Mantis took raped women's blood, went up to the Civic Auditorium where the pageant was being held, and threw the blood on the stairs so all the gowns and tuxedo pants would have to drag through it.

It was just like *Carrie*, only, y'know, more political.

FOR FURTHER REFLECTION

Camryn Manheim is a representative voice among women who are fed up with America's preoccupation with women's bodies as evidenced by so-called beauty pageants that do more to reinforce stereotypes of women and even increase violence against them than to celebrate them. Even after decades of heightened awareness regarding the harmful effects of treating women as sex objects, pageants, fashion shows, movies, and commercials still foster stereotypes of beauty and feminine behavior as ideal. The Praying Mantis Brigade aims to put a stop to it once and for all.

...................................TRY THIS....................................

In an essay, trace the probable origins of current stereotypes of female (or for that matter, male) attractiveness and how these stereotypes are perpetuated. Explain why these stereotypes are harmful and suggest ways in which they might be eliminated.

JUNE 23

Mindset: The New Psychology of Success
by Carol S. Dweck, Ph.D.

People in a growth mindset don't just *seek* challenge, they thrive on it. The bigger the challenge, the more they stretch. And nowhere can it be seen more clearly than in the world of sports. You can just watch people stretch and grow.

Mia Hamm, the greatest female soccer star of her time, says it straight out. "All my life I've been playing up, meaning I've challenged myself with players older, bigger, more skillful, more experienced—in short, better than me." First she played with her older brother. Then at ten, she joined the eleven-year-old boys' team. Then she threw herself into the number one college team in the United States. "Each day I attempted to play up to their level … and I was improving faster than I ever dreamed possible."

Patricia Miranda was a chubby, unathletic high school kid who wanted to wrestle. After a bad beating on the mat, she was told, "You're a joke." First she cried, then she felt: "That really set my resolve. I had to keep going and had to know if effort and focus and belief and training could somehow legitimize me as a wrestler."

FOR FURTHER REFLECTION

The road to success is filled with obstacles. Like Miranda, we must set our resolve not merely to meet those challenges but to look forward to conquering them. Overcoming challenges makes us strong; looking forward to challenges and preparing for them makes us stronger still.

...................................TRY THIS....................................

For your memoir in progress, write a chapter about an episode in which you failed at something you wanted to do badly, but then capitalized on that failure by strengthening your skills and meeting the challenge later on.

JUNE 24

The Romance of the Postage Stamp
by Gustav Schenk
Translated by Mervyn Savill

In [1863, in] the harbour town of Plymouth [England] it was not unusual to meet sailors, but they seldom appeared in [Stanley] Gibbons's shop as buyers of stamps. However, one morning which was to be a decisive one in Gibbons's life, two sailors stopped outside his window. From their appearance they had just come ashore after a very long trip. They whispered together for some time before they shyly and hesitantly entered the shop. The embarrassed seamen explained that they had not come to buy stamps, but wanted to sell some. At a charity bazaar in the Cape they had been unlucky enough to win in a lottery a pile of stamps which the women of Cape Province had collected for many years for charity. In the eyes of their husbands, mostly businessmen who threw such rubbish into the waste-paper basket, it was an odd and whimsical occupation, for what could they hope to do with this booty? ...

Stanley Gibbons listened to the sailors' story without betraying his excitement. He merely said that he would like to see the stamps. On the following day the seamen shook out a whole ditty-bag full of stamps on to his counter—thousands of triangular Cape of Good Hopes which had been designed by the Cape Province postmaster, Charles Bell, with the allegorical figure of Hope and an anchor as watermark. ... In addition to single copies, there were pairs, strips, and blocks of four, six, or eight. Even in those days it was a fabulous treasure trove. Gibbons gave the sailors £5 and they considered themselves well paid.

FOR FURTHER REFLECTION

Stamp collecting became a popular hobby very shortly after the first stamps were issued in England in 1840. Because there were so many stamps, collectors began to specialize in single countries or topics and themes; wealthier collectors specialized in rarities, like the Cape of Good Hope triangles.

...................................TRY THIS....................................

Today collectors' specialties include topics like presidents on stamps, chess on stamps, and so on. Write a feature article on some of the more unusual specialized areas stamp collectors might pursue.

JUNE 25

Religio Medici

by Sir Thomas Browne

How shall the dead arise is no question of my Faith; to believe only possibilities is not Faith, but mere Philosophy. Many things are true in Divinity, which are neither inducible by reason, nor confirmable by sense; and many things in Philosophy confirmable by sense, yet not inducible by reason. Thus it is impossible by any solid or demonstrative reasons to persuade a man to believe the conversion of the Needle to the North; though this be possible and true, and easily credible, upon a single experiment unto the sense. I believe that our estranged and divided ashes shall unite again; that our separated dust after so many Pilgrimages and transformations into the parts of Minerals, Plants, Animals, Elements, shall at the Voice of God return into their primitive shapes, and join again to make up their primary and predestinate forms. As at the Creation there was a separation of that confused mass into its pieces; so at the destruction thereof there shall be a separation into its distinct individuals. As at the Creation of the World, all the distinct species that we behold lay involved in one mass, till the fruitful Voice of God separated this united multitude into its several species: so at the last day, when those corrupted reliques shall be scattered in the Wilderness of forms, and seem to have forgot their proper habits, God by a powerful Voice shall command them back into their proper shapes.

FOR FURTHER REFLECTION

At the dawn of modern science, the philosopher-physician Sir Thomas Browne (1605–1682), thought deeply about reconciling reason with faith. There are simply facets of existence that are not relevant to scientific inquiry, and vice versa.

......................................TRY THIS....................................

Reflect on the interplay of faith and reason in your daily life. How do you reconcile any perceived contradictions, such as the apparent contradiction between the creation story in Genesis and the creation story suggested by the findings of modern geology, astronomy, and anthropology?

"Reading While Traveling"
by Tom Raabe

from *Biblioholism: The Literary Addiction*

Books and traveling. There's something about the clickety-clack of the rails un-
derfoot, something about the jet engines idling and the evacuation procedures
being recited, that simply begs us to unsheath a volume and dive into it, bar cars
and in-flight movies notwithstanding. ... I know of one biblioholic who walks onto
airplanes dragging a briefcase the size of a Toyota Camry. None of those sleek
attaché cases for him. It usually takes two flight attendants to help him heft the
thing up to the bin. After all, there is a larger question at play here: How many is
enough? Are two dozen paperbacks going to stay one's mind for two solid weeks at
the in-laws, when even a day at the beach requires at least three? Can one book
delight and satisfy for two or three long hours in the sky? What if we experience a
mood swing as the plane encounters engine trouble in mid-flight and want to switch
to something more practical—like the Twenty-third Psalm? ...

One book is never enough. Biblioholics always carry with them a portable
library for traveling.

FOR FURTHER REFLECTION

It isn't easy to satirize biblioholics, as biblioholism sort of satirizes itself. As
Tom Raabe makes clear, the addicted book lover can never have enough books
in his duffle bag or on his shelves. Reading is an all-consuming passion, the
raison d'etre for traveling, vacationing, or simply living.

. . . . TRY THIS . . . .

On a scale of one to ten, how do you rank yourself or a member of your family as
a book lover? Do you take books with you everywhere you go (even if it's to buy
groceries and you're afraid you might have to wait in line for five minutes without
a book to read)? Or do you fall at the other end of the spectrum, reading only
when it its absolutely necessary to do so? Write a humorous essay about the
bibliophile or bibliophobe in your family.

JUNE 27

A Voyage to Arcturus
by David Lindsay

Another remarkable plant [that Maskull encountered] was a large, feathery ball, resembling a dandelion fruit ... sailing through the air. Joiwind caught it with an exceedingly graceful movement of her arm. ... It had roots and presumably lived in the air and fed on the chemical constituents of the atmosphere. But what was peculiar about it was its color. It was an entirely new color—not a new shade or combination, but a new primary color, as vivid as blue, red, or yellow, but quite different. When he inquired, she told him that it was known as "*ulfire.*" Presently he met with a second new color. This she designated "*jale.*" The sense impressions caused in Maskull by these two additional primary colors can only be vaguely hinted at by analogy. Just as blue is delicate and mysterious, yellow clear and unsubtle, and red sanguine and passionate, so he felt ulfire to be wild and painful, and jale dreamlike, feverish, and voluptuous.

FOR FURTHER REFLECTION

Maskull's journey across the dreamscape of the planet Tormance is like a journey through the psyche. The novel reads like an allegory of the soul's transmigration into a plane beyond mortal life—hence the bizarre new appendages that give Maskull new sensory experiences, including the ability to perceive new primary colors.

..................................TRY THIS...................................

Compose a fantasy story that reads like an unfolding dream. Give yourself the freedom to suspend natural laws or create new ones. You might give your characters the ability to fly, to change shape, to read each other's minds, or to participate in each other's dreams.

Song of Kali

by Dan Simmons

The room was very small and dark. A tiny oil lamp, open flame sputtering above a pool of rancid *ghee*, sat in the center of a square wooden table but the little light it produced was swallowed by the tattered black curtains which hung on every side. The chamber was less a room than a black-shrouded crypt. Two chairs waited at the table. On the splintered table's surface lay a book, its title not quite legible in the sick light. I did not have to read the cover to know what book it was. It was *Winter Spirits*, the collection of my poetry. …

The door had opened on a [narrow] corridor. … The black gauze curtain hanging just inside the room struck my face as I entered. It swept aside easily enough, crumbling at my touch like a spider's abandoned web. …

I remained standing four feet from the table. … "All right, let's get this show on the road," I said and stepped forward, pulled the chair out, and sat at the table. … I waited.

Then the flame bent to an unfelt movement of air.

Someone was coming through the black curtains.

A tall form brushed back the netting, paused while still in shadow, and then shuffled hesitantly into the light.

I saw the eyes first—the moist, intelligent eyes tempered by time and too great a knowledge of human suffering. … They were the eyes of a poet. I was looking at M. Das. He stopped closer, and I gripped the edge of the table in a convulsive movement.

FOR FURTHER REFLECTION

What causes the narrator, the poet Robert Luczak, to convulse is the sight of the poet M. Das entering the room—a person who was supposed to be dead, a victim of a bizarre occult ritual in Calcutta. Even before the moment of confrontation, Simmons skillfully creates an atmosphere of foreboding that makes the reader's skin crawl.

······························TRY THIS····························

Write a chapter that slowly creates a feeling of dread for what is about to happen—a zombie breaking into someone's bedroom, for example. Take care to ensure that every description contributes to the atmosphere of dread.

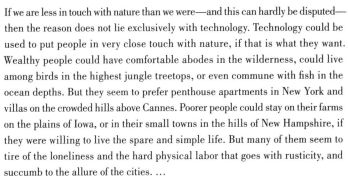

JUNE 29

The Existential Pleasures of Engineering

by Samuel C. Florman

If we are less in touch with nature than we were—and this can hardly be disputed—then the reason does not lie exclusively with technology. Technology could be used to put people in very close touch with nature, if that is what they want. Wealthy people could have comfortable abodes in the wilderness, could live among birds in the highest jungle treetops, or even commune with fish in the ocean depths. But they seem to prefer penthouse apartments in New York and villas on the crowded hills above Cannes. Poorer people could stay on their farms on the plains of Iowa, or in their small towns in the hills of New Hampshire, if they were willing to live the spare and simple life. But many of them seem to tire of the loneliness and the hard physical labor that goes with rusticity, and succumb to the allure of the cities. ...

The antitechnologists talk a lot about nature without clearly defining what they mean by the word. Does nature consist of farms, seashores, lakes, and meadows ...? Does not nature consist also of scorched deserts, fetid tropical forests, barren ice fields, ocean depths, and outer space—environments relentlessly hostile to human life? If farms and meadows are considered "natural" even though they have been made by men out of the stuff of the universe, what is "unnatural"? A stone wall and a farm cottage are still "good," I suppose, but a bridge and a dam become "bad." ... Must one be in the wilds to be in touch with nature? Will not a garden in the back yard suffice?

FOR FURTHER REFLECTION

What does it mean to be drawn to nature? Perhaps it has something to do with being overwhelmed by the harshness of urban life. Perhaps we resist technology despite the conveniences it provides because technology also has an unpleasant side: machines break down; machines remove much of the human element from labor. On the other hand, as Samuel Florman notes, nature is not all sweetness and light. Maybe what we crave is *peace*: the peace that comes from relaxing beside a pond and listening to birds chirping; the peace that comes from not having to spend eight hours a day doing unsatisfying work.

...................................TRY THIS....................................

Create a character who is suffering from job burnout. What does he or she do to make life more fulfilling? What obstacles does this person face?

"Mozart and Beauty"
by Maynard Solomon
from *Mozart: A Life*

As we probe the nature of beauty in Mozart, many apparently disparate themes converge and blend. Classical and neoclassical formulas dissolve—notions of proportion, symmetry, order, and decorum are suffused with their opposites. We gaze at consolation and find terror; we examine grief and find love; we cannot think of bliss without awakening fears of abandonment; a commonplace musical figure with martial connotations reveals, through the flattening of the third degree of the scale, a rare and strange kind of beauty; a perfectly regular periodic phrase turns out to be a potent symbol of a pull to inertia that will require heroic efforts to overcome. The chaste, sublimated surface of Mozart's music conceals turbulent, potentially eruptive currents of feeling. The strange, the terrible, the uncanny, and the deadly aspects of beauty … are interwoven with its erotic implications. It may be worth observing that, owing to the circumstances of his upbringing, where sexual expression was surrounded by prohibitions, Mozart had good reason to associate punishment, destructiveness, disease, and death with the pursuit of beauty and pleasure.

FOR FURTHER REFLECTION

Music is a wonderful fusion of art, philosophy, and spirituality distilled as pure sound; and few composers could make the fusion so pleasurable and profound as Mozart. In his symphonies and piano sonatas, mighty opposites dance around each other, sometimes collide head-on, sometimes merge together. The net result is always a stirring musical experience.

..................................TRY THIS....................................

Write a poem in which you "translate" your emotional response to a Mozart symphony, such as the *Jupiter*; or opera overture, such as the one he wrote for *Don Giovanni*. Try to capture the opposing life forces, such as love and hate, birth-death-rebirth.

The Interpretation of Cultures
by Clifford Geertz

We need to look for systematic relationships among diverse phenomena, not for substantive identities among similar ones. And to do that with any effectiveness, we need to replace the "stratigraphic" conception of the relations between the various aspects of human existence with a synthetic one; that is, one in which biological, psychological, sociological, and cultural factors can be treated as variables within unitary systems of analysis [instead of one aspect underlying another like geological layers]. ...

In attempting to launch such an integration from the anthropological side and to reach, thereby, a more exact image of man, I want to propose two ideas. The first of these is that culture is best seen not as complexes of concrete behavior patterns—customs, usages, traditions, habit clusters—as has, by and large, been the case up to now, but as a set of control mechanisms—plans, recipes, rules, instructions ... —for the governing of behavior. The second idea is that man is precisely the animal most desperately dependent upon such extragenetic, outside-the-skin control mechanisms, such cultural programs [in other words], for order his behavior.

FOR FURTHER REFLECTION

Unlike cultural anthropologists before him, Clifford Geertz presents a new paradigm for understanding the nature of humankind: Instead of a static approach based on timeless universals, Geertz introduces a more dynamic model that recognizes human complexity and diversity, especially the complexity of symbolic systems. To put it another way, human beings are best defined through their dynamic (i.e., ever-changing) cultural complexity rather than through any predetermined, static biological, psychological, and sociological external givens.

..................................TRY THIS..................................

Develop an idea for a novel that rests on the premise that people interact dynamically and complexly with their environment instead of being mere passive products of their environment. For example, you might create a protagonist whose personality gradually changes from being passive and cowardly to one who learns to take active control of his life and to engage in courageous actions out of a rich combination of social interaction, intellectual development, chance encounters, and so on.

JULY 2

On Photography
by Susan Sontag

A new sense of the notion of information has been constructed around the photographic image. The photograph is a thin slice of space as well as time. In a world ruled by photographic images, all borders ("framing") seem arbitrary. Anything can be separated, can be made discontinuous, from anything else: all that is necessary is to frame the subject differently. (Conversely, anything can be made adjacent to anything else.) Photography reinforces a nominalist view of social reality as consisting of small units of an apparently infinite number—as the number of photographs that could be taken of anything is unlimited. Through photographs, the world becomes a series of unrelated, freestanding particles; and history, past and present, a set of anecdotes and *faits divers*. The camera makes reality atomic, manageable, and opaque. It is a view of the world which denies interconnectedness, continuity, but which confers on each moment the character of a mystery. Any photograph has multiple meanings; indeed, to see something in the form of a photograph is to encounter a potential object of fascination.

FOR FURTHER REFLECTION

Ever since the invention of the camera and photographic reproduction in the early nineteenth century, people have been fascinated by what we might call the metaphysics of photography. Compared to a painting, which involves manipulation of reality, a photograph represents the thing itself—an image of reality without human intervention other than the selecting of the image, the manipulation of "technicalities" such as focus, depth of field, and exposure time. This tension between the thing in itself and the fact of its having been selected and transformed into an art object has generated a rich metaphysics of the photograph, which Sontag brilliantly conveys.

. . . . TRY THIS . . . .

Write a profile of a close friend or family member based on a series of photographs of this person, taken at different times in his or her life. Don't just summarize; rather, bring the moment in time each photograph represents to life through action and dialogue.

JULY 3

Are We Alone? Philosophical Implications of the Discovery of Extraterrestrial Life

by Paul Davies

At the present state of our knowledge, the origin of life remains a deep mystery. That is not to say, of course, that it will always be so. Undoubtedly the physical and chemical processes that led to the emergence of life from non-life were immensely complicated, and it is no surprise that we find such processes hard to model mathematically or to duplicate in the laboratory. In the face of this basic obstacle, one can distinguish between three philosophical positions concerning the origin of life: (i) it was a miracle; (ii) it was a stupendously improbable accident; and (iii) it was an inevitable consequence of the outworking of the laws of physics and chemistry, given the right conditions.

I wish to state at the outset that I shall argue strongly for (iii), which seems to be the position adopted by most of the SETI [Search for Extraterrestrial Intelligence] scientists. It is based on the adoption of three philosophical principles [uniformity of nature—nature is the same everywhere in the universe; plentitude—whatever is possible becomes realized; and the Copernican principle that earth is not a special case].

FOR FURTHER REFLECTION

Part of our fascination with the heavens is that life—especially intelligent life—might exist on other worlds. However, the findings of the robotic probes that have been exploring Mars and the outer planets since the 1970s suggest that the likelihood of discovering anything other than microbial life in our solar system is unlikely. Mars is a frozen, arid desert; Venus is a toxic hothouse; the moons of the outer planets are far too cold to support life. Of course, Earth-like worlds may exist in orbit around other stars, but the distances are so vast it doesn't seem possible that physical contact could ever take place—although radio contact may be a possibility.

...................................TRY THIS ....

1. Contact with extraterrestrials has been a popular theme in science fiction since H.G. Wells. Write your own alien-contact story but avoid the movie clichés of reptilian monsters, malicious invaders, and cuddlesome ETs.
2. Write an essay on the importance of pursuing radio searches for alien civilizations.

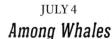

JULY 4

Among Whales

by Roger Payne

One reason whales maintain such a hold on our imaginations seems to be their omnipossibility—their unexpected and unpredictable appearances off all coasts, invariably arriving on their own schedules, showing up for reasons we do not understand. Sometimes whales even make their way up rivers. Humphrey the wrong-way humpback whale was the most famous of these river vagrants. Humphrey somehow got headed up the Sacramento River toward the city of Sacramento, the great seat of the California government, and it took a small navy of boats to turn him around. (One wonders what it was that Humphrey so urgently wished to convey to the California Congress, and why he wasn't aware of how powerless they would almost certainly be to do anything whatever for him.) …

Whales can pass along your coast, or come into any harbor or bay that is deep enough to float them, no matter where you live, and sometimes they do. When it happens it always sends a message that speaks to you directly—one capable of setting up waves that propagate right into the core of your being.

FOR FURTHER REFLECTION

It's no wonder that whales feed our imaginations and have inspired legends and works of art and literature through the ages. In size, behavior, and mysteriousness, there are no other creatures quite like them. Yet despite their endless fascination, some whale species, like the blue whale, are endangered. It would be a great loss to humanity if whales went extinct—a scenario that served as the basis of the 1986 movie, *Star Trek IV: The Voyage Home*.

...................................TRY THIS...................................

1. Write a story for young readers in which the protagonist befriends a lost whale and helps him finds his way home. The whale, in turn, to show his gratitude, bestows a special gift on the protagonist.

2. Research one facet of whale studies (cetology)—whale migration, whale song, misinformation about whales, efforts to protect whales from hunting—and write an article for general readers on the topic.

Dreaming by the Book
by Elaine Scarry

The quality of instruction in a poem or prose narrative brings about a radical change from daydreaming to vivid image-making. The vibrancy of perception—the rush of color, the spill of light, the thrilling density or discontinuity of sound—is less likely to be duplicated during undirected daydreaming than when dreaming-by-the-book. Our freely practiced imaginative acts bear less resemblance to our freely practiced perceptual acts than do our constrained imaginative acts occurring under authorial direction.

It would be an easy, but also a serious, intellectual error to think that this element of direction comes about as a result of authoritarian motives, either a poet's wish to dominate, or a reader's wish to be dominated, though each may along the way become a secondary or tertiary entailment and may heighten the need for contractual entry into this process of directed image-making. Rather, direction comes about to suppress our own awareness of the voluntary, which interferes with the mimesis of perception. Artists themselves provide strong evidence that successful image-making entails suppressing awareness of volition, since they have, over many centuries, reported the ease of writing under the dictation, the direction, or the instruction of a muse: "Having formed these beings," says Charlotte Brontë of Emily Brontë's Catherine and Heathcliff, "she did not know what she had done."

FOR FURTHER REFLECTION

How poets and fiction writers instruct us to imagine—i.e., form images from their literary creations—is the subject of Elaine Scarry's book. Along the way, she gives important psychological insight into the way writers enable their readers to process imaginative literature—an insight that can prove valuable to any aspiring writer.

..................................TRY THIS..................................

Examine one of your poems or short stories in terms of what, exactly, you want your readers to imagine. What do you need to revise in order to enrich your readers' imaginative experience?

JULY 6

The Omnivore's Dilemma: A Natural History of Four Meals
by Michael Pollan

I enjoy shopping at Whole Foods nearly as much as I enjoy browsing a good bookstore, which, come to think of it, is probably no accident: Shopping at Whole Foods is a literary experience, too. That's not to take anything away from the food, which is generally of high quality, much of it "certified organic" or "humanely raised" or "free range." But right there, that's the point: It's the evocative prose as much as anything else that makes this food really special, elevating an egg or chicken breast or bag of arugula from the realm of ordinary protein and carbohydrates into a much headier experience, one with complex aesthetic, emotional, and even political dimensions. Take the "range-fed" sirloin steak I recently eyed in the meat case. According to the brochure on the counter, it was formerly part of a steer that spent its days "living in beautiful places" ranging from "plant-diverse, high-mountain meadows to thick aspen groves and miles of sagebrush-filled flats." Now a steak like that has got to taste better than one from Safeway, where the only accompanying information comes in the form of a number: the price, I mean, which you can bet will be considerably less. But I'm evidently not the only shopper willing to pay more for a good story.

FOR FURTHER REFLECTION
Evocative sensory description contributes as much to our enjoyment of food as does visualizing it. Think about, for example, the descriptions of menu selections in a quality restaurant. Describing an entrée in terms of its preparation ("sesame-crusted"; "honey-glazed") or manner of production ("free-range") or source ("Maine coastal") enhances our appetites.

······························TRY THIS································

1. Write a scene for your novel in progress in which one of your characters is preparing a fancy meal. Go into detail about how he or she prepares the meal and the nature of the ingredients used.
2. Write a poem filled with the sensory descriptions (taste, smell sight, perhaps even sound) of a fancy seafood or meat entrée in the process of being prepared.

JULY 7
Wind in the Rock
by Ann Zwinger

[Johns Canyon, Utah]

I stand on a knife edge of rock, testing the morning wind, feeling as a falcon must just before it's ready to cast off and soar. At my feet, goldenweed wreathes the rock crevices, and five hundred feet below, two small side canyons, grinding their way southward, meet at the foot of this promontory. The wavering sandy lines of their dry streambeds are interrupted but once by the green of cottonwood and willow. In contrast to the somber green piñon-juniper blanket that covers the Cedar Mesa Plateau, from which these lateral canyons descend down into Johns Canyon proper, the white Cedar Mesa Sandstone canyon walls shine clean, looking as if they had been bitten out—I remember how Cedar Mesa looks from the air: a dark green jigsaw puzzle with the canyon heads like missing pieces, rock layers looking like the layers of plywood. ...

From the end of this wind-fretted promontory I can see two miles down the throat of Johns Canyon, where the walls are wider and the floor is leveled off, filled in with alluvium. Down there on that flat, cattle can be run if there is enough water for them and to promote a good growth of grass; still, around here it takes a minimum of fifty acres per head.

FOR FURTHER REFLECTION

Understanding the earth's physical features—its rock formations, its dynamics (like erosion, seismic and volcanic activity) can contribute much to one's aesthetic perception of a particular geographic region, as Ann Zwinger demonstrates with her vivid and detailed description of Utah's Green River canyon-land region. Learning to evoke the feel of a region is important for storytellers; and part of the knack for creating vivid landscape descriptions comes from familiarity with geological features.

...................................TRY THIS...................................

Prepare a detailed description of the setting for a story, emphasizing geological features like bedrock, mountain terrain, canyons, rivers, and so on. (See also the entries for April 7 and September 7.)

A History of Egypt, From the Earliest Times to the Persian Conquest

by James Henry Breasted

The Egyptian [of the Old Kingdom, approx. 3000 B.C.E.] was passionately fond of nature and of outdoor life. The house of the noble was always surrounded by a garden, in which he loved to plant figs and palms and sycamores, laying out vineyards and arbours, and excavating before the house a pool, lined with masonry coping, and filled with fish. A large body of servants and slaves were in attendance, both in house and garden; a chief steward had charge of the entire house and estate, while an upper gardener directed the slaves in the care and culture of the garden. This was the noble's paradise; here he spent his leisure hours with his family and friends, playing at draughts, listening to the music of the harp, pipe and lute, watching his women in the slow and stately dance of the time, while his children sported about the trees, splashed in the pool, or played with ball, doll or jumping-jack. Again in a light boat of papyrus reeds, accompanied by his wife and sometimes by one of his children, the noble delighted to float about in the shade of the tall rushes, in the inundated marshes and swamps.

FOR FURTHER REFLECTION

Learning about the everyday lives of people who lived centuries, even millennia ago, helps make the concept of ancient history seem less abstract, more connected to our own lives. The ancient Egyptians, like ourselves, raised children, tended gardens, played games. The larger social structure might have been radically different—living under a pharaoh or keeping slaves is alien to us; but basic human needs and pleasures were not so different from our own.

.................................TRY THIS...................................

Write a short story, either for young readers or adults, about an ancient Egyptian family and an incident that threatens to disrupt their peaceful lives, such as a slave revolt or a flood. You will want to thoroughly familiarize yourself with a specific period in Egyptian history by reading James Breasted's and more recent histories of Egyptian civilization.

JULY 9

The Elizabethan World Picture
by E.M.W. Tillyard

The Middle Ages derived their world picture from an amalgam of Plato and the Old Testament, invented by the Jews of Alexandria and vivified by the new religion of Christ. It was unlike paganism (apart from Platonism and some mystery cults) in being theocentric, and it resembled Platonism and other theocentric cults in being perpetually subjected to the conflicting claims of this and another world. ... Those who know most about the Middle Ages ... assure us that humanism and a belief in the present life were powerful by the twelfth century, and that exhortations to condemn the world were themselves powerful at that time for that very reason. The two contradictory principles co-existed in a state of high tension. Further, it is an error to think that with the Renaissance the belief in the present life won a definitive victory. Till recently Petrarch's imaginary dialogue between himself and St. Augustine, known as his *Secret*, was thought to typify the transition from Middle Ages to Renaissance because it deals with this same conflict as if there might be a doubt about the result. Actually it does not differ greatly in spirit from the most popular of all moral treatises during the Middle Ages, the dialogue Boethius held between himself and Divine Philosophy[*]; it shows no slackening of ardour in presenting the old arguments for despising the world.

FOR FURTHER REFLECTION

One must be careful not to overstate the distinction between the Middle Ages and the Renaissance. There was considerable fascination with "the present life" during the former, as well as widespread adherence to a theocentric worldview during the latter. Eventually, the steady rise of modern science, the roots of which extend as far back as ancient Greece, brought greater attention to the here and now, to the phenomenal world, than to the divine milieu. But as Tillyard points out, the two contradictory views continued to coexist in a state of high tension.

...................................TRY THIS..................................

One could argue that even in the twenty-first century, tension exists between the scientific and the theological worldviews. Comment on the nature of this tension in a personal essay. Include firsthand experiences you've had with this tension.

---

[*] *The Consolation of Philosophy* (ca. 524 C.E.) was written while Boethius was imprisoned by Theodoric the Great for treason.

JULY 10
"The Irish Home Rule Debate"
by W.E. Lunt
from *History of England*, 4th Edition

The chief arguments advanced in favor of [Irish] home rule were three. (1) The Irish, on account of common traditions, race, and religion, constituted for purposes of government a nation. Since they were in a minority in the imperial parliament, without power to influence its decisions on Irish policies, they would always be discontented with the legislation enacted by that body. The separation by water would prevent the destruction of that nationality, and home rule would maintain a sufficient connection to avoid the danger of a separate Ireland on Britain's flank. (2) The British government of Ireland had been a constant and a complete failure. (3) Home rule would relieve the British parliament of the obstruction of the Irish members and of the burden of Irish business. ... The chief objections brought against the [1886] bill were also three. (1) Home rule would endanger the union. An Ireland so far independent would be dangerous to Great Britain in time of war. (2) Ireland was not fitted for self-government. Its people were not sufficiently advanced to govern themselves, as was witnessed by their recent turbulence. (3) It would subject the Protestant minority to the tyranny of the Catholic majority. Protestant Ulster would not be safe from a vengeful Catholic Ireland.

FOR FURTHER REFLECTION

Independence versus imperial rule has been, and continues to be, a major source of conflict in the world. As colonies grow, they mature and, like individuals, wish to govern their own lives; but there are always compromises and sacrifices for both the parent nation and the independence-seeking colony.

.....................................TRY THIS....................................

Write a short story set in Ireland in 1886, when the Home Rule bill was introduced. Dramatize, via an Irish rebel and a British ambassador, the clash of reasoning between Ireland and England, drawing from the three reasons in favor, and the three reasons against, mentioned by Lunt.

The Epic of Gilgamesh

Translated by N.K. Sandars

With the first light of dawn a black cloud came from the horizon; it thundered within where Adad, lord of the storm, was riding. In front over hill and plain Shullat and Hanish, heralds of the storm, led on. Then the gods of the abyss rose up; Nergal pulled out the dams of the nether waters, Ninurta the war-lord threw down the dykes, and the seven judges of hell, the Annunaki, raised their torches, lighting the land with their livid flame. A stupor of despair went up to heaven when the god of the storm turned daylight to darkness, when he smashed the land like a cup. One whole day the tempest raged gathering fury as it went, it poured over the people like the tides of battle; a man could not see his brother nor the people be seen from heaven. Even the gods were terrified of the flood, they fled to the highest heaven, the firmament of Anu. ...

For six days and six nights the winds blew, torrent and tempest and flood overwhelmed the world, tempest and flood raged together like warring hosts. When the seventh day dawned the storm from the south subsided, the sea grew calm, the flood was stilled. I looked at the face of the world and there was silence, all mankind was turned to clay.

FOR FURTHER REFLECTION

In *Gilgamesh*, the oldest extant epic in world literature, we also have the oldest description of a great flood, antedating the account in Genesis by a thousand years. Such stories are archetypal, appearing in the stories (sacred and secular) of many cultures, and may well have been triggered by actual events.

...................................TRY THIS...................................

Stories of a great flood have been told and retold through the ages. As recently as 2007, the motion picture *Evan Almighty* comically retells the story of the Biblical flood when a businessman is transformed into Noah and commanded to build an ark in preparation for a second Great Flood. Retell the flood story in your own way.

JULY 12
Beowulf
Transltated by David Wright

[Beowulf to King Hrothgar]

"Venerable king, do not grieve. It is better for a man to avenge his friend than to mourn him long. We must all expect an end to life in this world; let him who can win fame before death, because that is a dead man's best memorial. Rise, King Hrothgar, and let us go at once to pick up the spoor of Grendel's mother. She can go where she likes, but I promise you that she shall find no cover from me, whether in the bowels of the earth, in mountain thickets, or in the depths of the ocean. Have patience in your grief today, as I know you will."

The old king sprang up and thanked the Almighty for the hero's words. A horse with plaited mane was bridled for Hrothgar, and the prince set out in state, accompanied by a troop of foot. The spoor was clearly visible on the ground and in the forest paths. She had gone straight over the somber moors carrying the lifeless body of the best chieftain that had held watch in Hrothgar's hall. Over rocky, broken ground the princely company made their way, along meager tracks, narrow, forbidding bridle-paths, uncertain ways, and beetling crags, past holes of the waterdemons. Hrothgar pushed ahead with a few experienced men to find the place.

FOR FURTHER REFLECTION

The earliest English epic, *Beowulf* fascinates us with its fusion of pagan with early Christian motifs. Grendel and Grendel's mother are demons, but at the same time they are said to have descended from Cain; Beowulf's sword, Hrunting, having been forged by wizards, possesses magical properties; and so on.

......................................TRY THIS................................

Write a fantasy story in which a benevolent wizard and a treacherous evil wizard clash. In plotting the story, include both "pagan" (such as magic and sorcery) and Christian motifs (such as baptism and being in a state of grace through Confession of sins and Eucharistic Communion).

JULY 13

"Two Meditations on Meditation"
by Thomas Traherne

from *Centuries of Meditations*

What is more easy and sweet than meditation? Yet in this hath God commended his Love, that by meditation it is enjoyed. As nothing is more easy than to think, so nothing is more difficult than to think well. The easiness of thinking we received from God, the difficulty of thinking well proceeded from ourselves. Yet in truth, it is far more easy to think well than ill, because good thoughts be sweet and delightful. Evil thoughts are full of discontent and trouble.

To think well is to serve God in the interior court: to have a mind composed of divine thoughts, and set in frame, to be like Him within. To conceive aright and to enjoy the world is to conceive the Holy Ghost and to see His Love, which is the mind of the Father. And this more pleaseth Him than many worlds, could we create as fair and great as this. For when you are once acquainted with the world, you will find the goodness and wisdom of God so manifest therein that it was impossible another or better could be made. Which being made to be enjoyed, nothing can please or serve Him more than the soul that enjoys it. For that soul doth accomplish the end of His desire in creating it.

FOR FURTHER REFLECTION

To the poet and Christian mystic Thomas Traherne (1637–1674), thinking is a divine gift, but it is up to us to think well—and to learn to do so brings us ever closer to the divine. Of course, it is necessary to ensure that we know what thinking well entails, how it differs from thinking ill or badly. Traherne seems to imply that the simple God-given ability to think includes the ability to make that distinction.

. . . . TRY THIS . . . .

Compose a meditation or a poem in which you reflect on thinking well as a means of enhancing one's spiritual awareness. Focus on specific kinds of thinking—concepts that are philosophically complex and that might also inspire spiritual contemplation, such as predestination vs. free will.

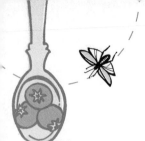

JULY 14
Wuthering Heights
by Emily Brontë

[Catherine to Nelly Dean]

My great miseries in this world have been Heathcliff's miseries, and I watched and felt each from the beginning; my great thought in living is himself. If all else perished, and *he* remained, I should still continue to be; and, if all else remained, and he were annihilated, the Universe would turn to a mighty stranger. I should not seem a part of it. My love for [Edgar] Linton is like the foliage in the woods. Time will change it, I'm well aware, as winter changes the trees—my love for Heathcliff resembles the eternal rocks beneath—a source of little visible delight, but necessary. Nelly I *am* Heathcliff—he's always, always in my mind—not as a pleasure, any more than I am always a pleasure to myself—but, as my own being—so, don't talk of our separation again—it is impracticable; and—"

She paused, and hid her face in the folds of my gown; but I jerked it forcibly away. I was out of patience with her folly!

"If I can make any sense of your nonsense, Miss," I said, "it only goes to convince me that you are ignorant of the duties you undertake in marrying; or else, that you are a wicked, unprincipled girl. But trouble me with no more secrets. I'll not promise to keep them."

FOR FURTHER REFLECTION

Few love stories in literature can equal that of Catherine's love for the foundling Heathcliff. For Catherine, he was a force of nature, one that she could not separate from her very being—and the sad irony is that she is only able to acknowledge this powerful love after Heathcliff has gone away.

......................................TRY THIS....................................

Write a story about two people who love each other very much, yet for one reason or another, cannot bring themselves to express it, except to a friend or relative. Will this third party find a way to help the lovers finally convey their feelings for each other, perhaps just before it's too late?

JULY 15

Roger's Version
by John Updike

Really, what a preposterous glib hope, his [Dale Kohler's] of extracting God from the statistics of high-energy physics and Big Bang cosmology. Whenever theology touches science, it gets burned. In the sixteenth century astronomy, in the seventeenth microbiology, in the eighteenth geology and paleontology, in the nineteenth Darwin's biology all grotesquely extended the world-frame and sent churchmen scurrying for cover in ever smaller, more shadowy nooks, little gloomy ambiguous caves in the psyche where even now neurology is cruelly harrying them, gouging them out from the multifolded brain like wood lice from under the lumber pile. [Karl] Barth had been right: *totaliter aliter*. Only by placing God totally on the other side of the humanly understandable can any final safety for Him be secured. The positivism of revelation, as [Friedrich] Bonhoeffer described it. All else is mere philosophy, churning the void in the hope of making butter, as it was put by the junior Oliver Wendell Holmes, the Supreme Court justice.

FOR FURTHER REFLECTION

In this novel of ideas in which a professor of theology and a brilliant student in computer science come head-to-head, the late Pulitzer Prize–winning author John Updike (1932–2009) takes us into the heart of one of civilization's greatest debates, science vs. religion. Which comes closest to the essential reality—the physical universe as it is revealed through scientific analysis, or the divine cosmos as it is revealed through Scripture and religious dogma? The central drama—and irony—of the novel is that the student is convinced he has found a way to prove God's existence via a computer program.

................................TRY THIS................................

Dramatize a confrontation scene between a deeply religious person and a scientific rationalist over the existence of God. Before you do, you ought to read *Roger's Version* in its entirety, as well as examine the philosophical arguments for and against the existence of God.

"The Arrival of Cholera in London"
by Stephen Inwood
from *A History of London*

Although public attitudes towards government intervention were slowly becoming more favourable [in the early nineteenth century], it usually took a well-publicized crisis or disaster to awaken aristocratic politicians to an awareness of their new social responsibilities. The arrival of cholera, a dramatic bacterial infection of the gut previously unknown in Europe, whose westward progress had been watched with dread since it appeared in India in 1818, was such a crisis. Cholera reached ... London in February 1832, and killed over 31,000 in Great Britain (5,000 in London) by a process of rapid and painful dehydration. Cholera fell far short of tuberculosis, typhus or influenza in the numbers it killed ... but its newness, its dramatic impact on its victims, and fears that it might become a new plague forced politicians to act.

Sadly, ignorance of the causes of cholera meant that the response to it was often ineffective and sometimes harmful. Cholera was transmitted by the ingestion of the faeces of infected people, sometimes from contaminated food or clothing, but most often from sewage-polluted water. It thus entered London households in buckets and pipes.

FOR FURTHER REFLECTION

Disease has had a significant influence on human history—particularly when epidemics of bubonic plague, cholera, and tuberculosis spurred politicians into becoming more aware of the needs of the common people. Even though such actions had little effect before physicians understood the bacterial basis for disease, such political reform was an important step toward the establishment of government agencies to protect the public welfare.

.... TRY THIS ....

Write a story about the way a family coped with a dangerous epidemic, such as a cholera epidemic, in the days before vaccinations or antibiotics. As an alternative, write a story set during the very first attempts to inoculate against disease.

The Better Angel:
Walt Whitman in the Civil War
by Roy Morris, Jr.

Determined to find his brother [George]—dead or alive—Whitman plunged head-long into the maelstrom of war. In the confused aftermath of Fredericksburg, thousands of similarly frantic relatives had embarked for the front, thronging railroad stations and riverboat docks from Maine to Wisconsin. His own three-day journey, Whitman told his mother, entailed "the greatest suffering I ever experienced in my life." He crowded aboard a ferry to Manhattan, took a second across the Hudson River to New Jersey, and caught the night train to Philadelphia. Pressing his way through a mob of fellow travelers, he had his pocket picked while changing trains, and he arrived in Washington without a penny to his name. ...

It was anything but an auspicious beginning to Whitman's new life, and his first view of the nation's capital did little to elevate his sagging spirits. Senator George Randolph's fabled "city of magnificent distances" had become a teeming jumble of close-pressed squalor. ... A fetid canal bordered the northern edge of the mall, floating with dead cats, broken whiskey bottles, and rotting garbage. ...

Hungry, exhausted, and increasingly footsore, he trudged dispiritedly from hospital to hospital, hoping to find his wounded brother. There were dozens of facilities to choose from. The largest, Armory Square, through some inexplicable lapse of medical logic, backed up against the stagnant canal.

FOR FURTHER REFLECTION

Walt Whitman's compassion for humanity is not only vividly apparent through-out his poetry but in his visitations to battlefields and hospitals in order to comfort the wounded, and occasionally to assist nurses. In a poem titled "The Wound-Dresser," he graphically captures this experience: "From the stump of the arm, the amputated hand, / I undo the clotted lint, remove the slough, wash off the matter and blood, / Back on his pillow the soldier bends with curv'd neck and side-falling head, / His eyes are closed, his face is pale, he dares not look on the bloody stump ..."

......................................TRY THIS....................................

Write a war story from the point of view of a doctor, nurse, or wounded soldier. You will need to familiarize yourself with the nature of medical care during the time of this war.

Déjà Dead
by Kathy Reichs

Denis placed two cardboard boxes on the end of the table, one large and one small, each sealed and carefully labeled. I eased the lid from the larger box, selected portions of Isabelle Gagnon's skeleton, and laid them out on the right half of the table.

Next I opened the smaller box. Though Chantale Trottier's body had been returned to her family for burial, segments of bone had been retained as evidence, a standard procedure in homicide cases involving skeletal injury or mutilation.

I removed sixteen Ziploc bags and put them on the left side of the table. Each was marked as to body part and side. Right wrist. Left wrist. Right knee. Left knee. Cervical vertebrae. Thoracic and lumbar vertebrae. I emptied each bag and arranged the contents in anatomical order. The two segments of femur went next to their corresponding portions of tibia and fibula to form the knee joints. Each wrist was represented by six inches of radius and ulna. The ends of the bones sawed at autopsy were clearly notched. I would not confuse these cuts with those made by the killer.

FOR FURTHER REFLECTION

As you can tell from the above selection, Kathy Reichs, like her protagonist, is a forensic anthropologist. An anthropologist's deep understanding of human physiology, including the effects of trauma on organs and bone, can prove to be invaluable in helping to solve a crime.

.................................TRY THIS...................................

Try your hand at writing a mystery story in which evidence derived from anthropological evidence, such as the details of a bone or skull fracture, is necessary for solving the crime.

Ecospeak: Rhetoric and Environmental Politics in America

by M. Jimmie Killingsworth and Jacqueline S. Palmer

Instead of placing developmentalism (nature as resource) as the absolute opposite of environmentalism or deep ecology (nature as spirit, or presence), the [following] map extends in two directions … placing at one extreme the perspective of traditional science, which, due to its concern with objectivism and its rejection of anthropocentric thinking, would depart from the view of nature as a resource.

nature as object		nature as resource			nature as spirit
traditional or mainstream science	government	business and industry	agriculture	social ecology (humanistic enviromentalism)	deep ecology (wilderness ethic, nature mysticism)

We are thinking here of experimental science as it has developed since the seventeenth century, with its fabled detachment from all natural objects (including human beings). This view of science has been encapsulated and rigidified in government and industry in the form of "scientific management." At the opposite pole is "deep ecology," which departs from both objectivity and anthropocentricity, asserting instead a mythic involvement with nature, an identity in which the spirit of creation wraps the human and the nonhuman in an indissolvable unity with definite ethical consequences. From the anthropocentric perspective … which holds that nature is a bounty of resources for human use and enjoyment, both the scientific and the deep ecological outlooks could prove threatening.

FOR FURTHER REFLECTION

Modern environmental thinking has shifted away from extremist ideas of nature. From the perspective of environmental stewardship, it makes sense to find a middle ground: nature as a vital resource that must be safeguarded for future generations as well as for ourselves.

.....................................TRY THIS.....................................

Think of ways in which we humans are interconnected with the natural world. For example, the near match between the salinity of the ocean and the salinity of our blood. Write a meditative essay or a poem about this interconnectedness.

The Rise of Scientific Philosophy
by Hans Reichenbach

[Socrates] wishes to illustrate [in Plato's *Meno*] his contention that in order to know what is virtue, and what is the good, one has to perform an act of insight of the same kind as is required for the understanding of geometrical proofs. Ethical judgments are thus presented as being found through a peculiar form of vision, comparable to the visualization of geometrical relations. By the use of this argument, ethical insight is presented as a parallel to geometrical insight. ...

With this thesis, Plato and Socrates established ... the theory that ethical insight is a form of cognition, that is, of knowing. If a man commits immoral actions, he is ignorant in the same sense that a man who makes mistakes in geometry is ignorant; he is unable to perform the act of vision which shows him the good, a vision of the same kind as the one that shows him geometrical truth. ...

The laws of nature and of mathematics had first to be recognized as laws, as relations that impose recognition upon us and do not tolerate any exceptions, before they could be conceived as parallels of ethical laws. The double meaning of the world "law," as moral command and as the rule of nature or of reason, bears witness to the construction of this parallelism.

FOR FURTHER REFLECTION

The ancient Greek ideal of paralleling ethical behavior with mathematical principles has had a far-reaching influence on modern thought. Underlying both mathematical (and geometric) principles and sound ethical judgment is knowledge and deep understanding (or wisdom). Without knowledge or wisdom, human judgment is impaired. The rise of scientific understanding (at least in Reichenbach's view) has led to the rise of modern ethics.

.....................................TRY THIS....................................

In an essay, present a view of the impact of science on ethics. Some might argue that science can negatively influence ethics. For example, biological Darwinism has given rise to social Darwinism, in which the principal of "survival of the fittest" has been applied to competition in society, such as the workplace, with consequences that many find distinctly unethical.

A Beautiful Mind: A Biography of John Forbes Nash, Jr., Winner of the Nobel Prize in Economics 1994

by Sylvia Nasar

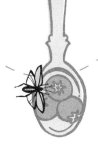

Nash wrote his first paper, one of the great classics of modern economics, during his second term at Princeton [in 1949]. "The Bargaining Problem" is a remarkably down-to-earth work for a mathematician, especially a young mathematician. Yet no one but a brilliant mathematician could have conceived the idea. In the paper, Nash, whose economics training consisted of a single undergraduate course taken at Carnegie, adopted "an altogether different angle" on one of the oldest problems in economics and proposed a completely surprising solution. By so doing, he showed that behavior that economists had long considered part of human psychology, and therefore beyond the reach of economic reasoning, was, in fact, amenable to systematic analysis.

The idea of exchange, the basis of economics, is nearly as old as man, and deal-making has been the stuff of legend since the Levantine kings and the pharaohs traded gold and chariots for weapons and slaves. Despite the rise of the great impersonal capitalist marketplace, with its millions of buyers and sellers who never meet face-to-face, the one-on-one bargain—involving wealthy individuals, powerful governments, labor unions, or giant corporations—dominates the headlines. But two centuries after the publication of Adam Smith's *The Wealth of Nations*, there were still no principles of economics that could tell one how the parties to a *potential* bargain would interact, or how they would split up the pie.

FOR FURTHER REFLECTION

We are endlessly fascinated by innovative thinkers who change the way we think about the world and ourselves. Nobel Laureate John Nash is such a person. His insights into game theory—by developing a systematic way of computing highly complex, highly variable interactions—revolutionized economics.

...................................TRY THIS...................................

Reflect on the nature of probability or potentiality in a game such as chess, Monopoly, or a card game like poker or twenty-one. For example, you might consider how knowing the odds might give you a competitive edge. At one point does chance phase into likelihood, and likelihood into inevitability?

JULY 22

The Second Sex

by Simone de Beauvoir

Translated by H.M. Parshley

A man's clothes, like his body, should indicate his transcendence and not attract attention[**]; for him, neither elegance nor good looks call for his setting himself up as object; moreover, he does not normally consider his appearance as a reflection of his ego.

Woman, on the contrary, is even required by society to make herself an erotic object. The purpose of the fashions to which she is enslaved is not to reveal her as an independent individual, but rather to cut her off from her transcendence in order to offer her as prey to male desires; thus society is not seeking to further her projects but to thwart them. The skirt is less convenient than trousers, high-heeled shoes impede walking; the least practical of gowns and dress shoes, the most fragile of hats and stockings, are most elegant; the costume may disguise the body, deform it, or follow its curves; in any case it puts it on display. That is why dressing up is an enchanting game for the little girl, who loves to contemplate herself; later her childish independence rises in rebellion against the constraint imposed by light-colored muslins and patent-leather shoes; at the awkward age the girl is torn between the wish and the refusal to display herself; but when she has once more accepted her vocation as sexual object, she enjoys adorning herself.

FOR FURTHER REFLECTION

One of the greatest voices in twentieth century feminist thought, Simone de Beauvoir (1908–1986) here argues how clothes have been made to entrap women as sex objects, unable to transcend their physicality in order to function fully as human beings, to reinforce their role as dependent upon males for their support and even for their sense of identity.

.................................TRY THIS ....

1. Many would argue that considerable progress has been made in the past fifty-eight years since *The Second Sex* first appeared with regard to women's rights as well as to the way women are perceived and treated. Write an essay in which you discuss this progress (or lack of it).
2. Compose a humorous or satiric piece on how men prefer women to dress, or on the nature of some types of women's clothing.

[**] Exception must be made for homosexuals. (Simone de Beauvoir's note)

"Praise and Blame Are All the Same"
by Richard Carlson
from Don't Sweat the Small Stuff ... And It's All Small Stuff

One of the most unavoidable life lessons is having to deal with the disapproval of others. Praise and blame are all the same is a fancy way of reminding yourself of the old cliché that you'll never be able to please all of the people all the time. Even in a landslide election victory in which a candidate secures 55 percent of the vote, he or she is left with 45 percent of the population that wishes someone else the winner. Pretty humbling, isn't it?

Our approval rating from family, friends, and the people we work with isn't likely to be much higher. The truth is, everyone has their own set of ideas with which to evaluate life, and our ideas don't always match those of other people. For some reason, however, most of us struggle against this inevitable fact. We get angry, hurt, or otherwise frustrated when people reject our ideas, tell us no, or give us some other form of disapproval.

The sooner we accept the inevitable dilemma of not being able to win the approval of everyone we meet, the easier our lives will become.

FOR FURTHER REFLECTION

We work hard to ensure that others agree with our way of seeing things, share our values, approve of us. The most independent and self-sufficient among us understand that we are part of the human community and must interact to some degree with that community. On the other hand, it is foolish to try and win approval at all costs. In psychologist Richard Carlson's view, it is healthy to accept the reality that many will disagree with us, and to retain our integrity, feeling confident in the rightness of our thoughts and deeds.

...................................TRY THIS....................................

Write an Aesop-like fable about a young man or woman who tried too hard to be likeable, who could not bear disapproval or criticism. Conceive of some incident that would enable this person to learn to accept disapproval.

JULY 24

"Bloomsbury Walk"

by Barbara Sloan Hendershott and Alzina Stone Dale

from *Mystery Reader's Walking Guide: London*

Begin this walk at the Euston Square Underground Station. Leave the station and take Melton Street to Euston Road. Cross Euston Road and go right to Gower Street. Parallel with Gower Street, a couple of streets off to the right, is Tottenham Court.

In Patricia Wentworth's *The Case Is Closed*, a model called Celia refused to show a "ghastly pink rag" because it was not her style, and "she wouldn't be seen dead in it in Tottenham Court Road."

In the stage directions of *Busman's Honeymoon*, Dorothy L. Sayers referred to the bargains in cheap furniture for which Tottenham Court Road is known.

Sherlock Holmes bought his Stradivarius violin from a pawnbroker in Tottenham Court Road.

The Knightsbridge School of English had been in business for 12 years. Before setting it up, Ned Nurse had been employed by a series of schools around Tottenham Court Road (*English School Murder* by Ruth Dudley Edwards).

FOR FURTHER REFLECTION

Like many European cities, London is rich in literary lore. If you're a mystery fan, for example, Hendershott and Dale's walking guide will help you to enjoy London in a delightfully new way, by visiting real sites where well-known fictional characters have experienced adventures of one sort or another.

............................TRY THIS............................

Write a travel feature in which you describe a city or region in the context of its literary legacy. For example, if you visit Oxford, Mississippi, the town where William Faulkner used to live, you will want to compare the similarities between that region and his imaginary Yoknapatawpha County, which is based on that region.

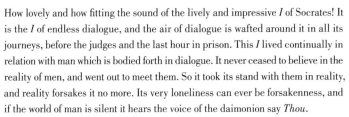

JULY 25
I and Thou
by Martin Buber
Translated by Ronald Gregor Smith

How lovely and how fitting the sound of the lively and impressive *I* of Socrates! It is the *I* of endless dialogue, and the air of dialogue is wafted around it in all its journeys, before the judges and the last hour in prison. This *I* lived continually in relation with man which is bodied forth in dialogue. It never ceased to believe in the reality of men, and went out to meet them. So it took its stand with them in reality, and reality forsakes it no more. Its very loneliness can ever be forsakenness, and if the world of man is silent it hears the voice of the daimonion say *Thou*.

How lovely and how legitimate the sound of the full *I* of Goethe! It is the *I* of pure intercourse with nature; nature gives herself to it and speaks unceasingly with it, revealing her mysteries to it but not betraying her mystery. ...

And ... how powerful, even to being overpowering, and how legitimate, even to being self-evident, is the saying of *I* by Jesus! For it is the *I* of unconditional relation in which the man calls his Thou Father in such a way that he himself is simply Son, and nothing else but Son. Whenever he says *I* he can only mean the *I* of the holy primary world that has been raised for him into unconditional being. If separation ever touches him, his solidarity of relation is the greater; he speaks to others but only out of this solidarity.

FOR FURTHER REFLECTION

We sometimes think that the self, the "I" must exist apart from others in order to shape its own identity, its selfhood; but in the mystical vision of the Jewish philosopher and theologian Martin Buber (1878–1965), the "I" acquires its greatest significance through intimate relationship—with nature, with the spiritual other (father, spouse, etc.), which becomes intertwined with the self as "I-Thou."

..................................TRY THIS....................................

Compose a poem or short story in which a son or daughter becomes emotionally separated from his or her father or mother, and then for some compelling reason strives to reestablish an intimate, loving relationship. What obstacles must the child overcome to achieve this? What obstacles must the parent overcome?

JULY 26
Candide
by Voltaire
Translated by John Butt

Those who have never seen two well-trained armies drawn up for battle can have
no idea of the beauty and brilliance of the display. Bugles, fifes, oboes, drums,
and salvoes of artillery produced such a harmony as Hell itself could not rival.
The opening barrage destroyed about six thousand men on each side. Rifle-fire
which followed rid this best of worlds of about nine or ten thousand villains who
infested its surface. Finally, the bayonet provided "sufficient reason" for the death
of several thousand more. The total casualties amounted to about thirty thousand.
Candide trembled like a philosopher, and hid himself as best he could during this
heroic butchery.

When all was over and the rival kings were celebrating their victory with Te
Deums in their respective camps, Candide decided to find somewhere else to
pursue his reasoning into cause and effect. He picked his way over piles of dead
and dying, and reached a neighbouring village on the Abar side of the border. It
was now no more than a smoking ruin, for the Bulgars had burned it to the ground
in accordance with the terms of international law.

FOR FURTHER REFLECTION
Just as the devil can quote scripture for his purpose, Shakespeare reminds us
in *The Merchant of Venice*, philosophers who place too much trust in rationality
can rationalize anything away. Voltaire (1694–1778) relentlessly attacked this
worldview in his satiric masterpiece, *Candide*.

. . . . TRY THIS . . . .

In a poem or story, poke fun at a famous adage that you consider to be ultimately
false, misleading, or simplistic. Many clichés fit this category; e.g., "You can't
teach an old dog new tricks" or "Whatever is, is right" (one of the prevalent views
of the Enlightenment, which Voltaire ruthlessly attacked).

Wicked: The Life and Times of the Wicked Witch of the West

by Gregory Maguire

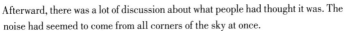

Afterward, there was a lot of discussion about what people had thought it was. The noise had seemed to come from all corners of the sky at once.

Journalists, armed with the thesaurus and apocalyptic scriptures, fumbled and were defeated by it. "A gulfy deliquescence of deranged and harnessed air"; "A volcano of the invisible, darkly construed" …

To the essentialists, it seemed as if the world had suddenly found itself too crammed with life, with cells splitting by the billions, molecules uncoupling to annihilation, atoms shuddering and juggernauting in their casings.

To the superstitious it was the collapsing of time. It was the oozing of the ills of the world into one crepuscular muscle, intent on stabbing the world to its core. …

To the more traditionally religious it was the blitzkrieg of vengeful angel armies, the awful name of the Unnamed God sounding itself at last—*surprise*—and the evaporation of all hopes for mercy.

One or two pretended to think it was squadrons of flying dragons overhead, trained for attack, breaking the sky from its moorings by the thrash of tripartite wings.

In the wake of the destruction it caused, no one had the hubris or courage (or the prior experience) to lie and claim to have known the act of terror for what it was: a wind twisted up in a vertical braid.

In short, a tornado.

FOR FURTHER REFLECTION

One of the most successful retellings of a modern fairy tale, *Wicked* gives us the richly imagined backstory of L. Frank Baum's beloved *Wizard of Oz*, only this time from the point of view of the Wicked Witch of the West. Gregory Maguire reminds us that fairy tales, like the tales from ancient mythology, can always be revisited and mined for new possibilities.

......................................TRY THIS......................................

Retell one of your favorite fairy tales from the point of view of the story's villain or secondary character—*Cinderella* from the viewpoint of one of the stepsisters or the Prince; *Jack and the Beanstalk* from the viewpoint of the giant; and so on.

Dracula

by Bram Stoker

The great box was in the same place, close against the wall, but the lid was laid on it, not fastened down, but with the nails ready in their places to be hammered home. I knew I must reach the body for the key, so I raised the lid, and laid it back against the wall, and then I saw something which filled my very soul with horror. There lay the Count, but looking as if his youth had been half renewed, for the white hair and moustache were changed to dark iron-grey; the cheeks were fuller, and the white skin seemed ruby-red underneath; the mouth was redder than ever, for on the lips were gouts of fresh blood, which trickled from the corners of the mouth and ran over the chin and neck. Even the deep, burning eyes seemed set amongst swollen flesh, for the lids and pouches underneath were bloated. It seemed as if the whole awful creature were simply gorged with blood. He lay like a filthy leech, exhausted with his repletion. I shuddered as I bent over to touch him, and every sense in me revolted at the contact; but I had to search, or I was lost.

FOR FURTHER REFLECTION

Although not the first vampire story (most likely based on folk legends that go back centuries), *Dracula*, by Bram Stoker (1847–1912), has been the most influential, largely because of its vivid imagery and its degree of verisimilitude. Stoker gives us a veritable photographic depiction of the Count lying in his coffin, "gouts of fresh blood" trickling from his mouth, the flesh bloated around his eyes.

......................................TRY THIS....................................

A successful horror story gives the impression that this is really happening in the familiar, everyday world. Begin a horror story in which you emphasize the ordinary over the extraordinary. Treat the supernatural and horrific elements with journalistic objectivity.

JULY 29
"The First Women Pioneers of Flight"
by John H. Lienhard

from *Inventing Modern: Growing Up With X-Rays,*
Skyscrapers, and Tailfins

The Montgolfier brothers created the first manned hot air balloon, which made its first ascent on November 21, 1783. Eleven days later, Alexandre Charles tested a manned hydrogen-filled balloon. When one early hydrogen balloonist, Jean Pierre Blanchard, finally suffered a fall and died, his wife Sophie continued in his barnstorming business. She had taken up flying in 1805. Sophie Blanchard was the first woman we know to have flown on her own, and she made 59 ascents before she too died. She accidentally set her hydrogen on fire, and, as it burned off, the balloon fell to the Paris rooftops below.

Even before Sophie Blanchard, women had been taking part in another kind of aerial display, which is powerfully evocative of the Daedalus story. In 1797, André Garnerin became the first person to parachute from a balloon. Like Daedalus's wings, the inherent purpose of a parachute is to provide a safe avenue of escape. Garnerin talked his wife into making one jump, but it was his niece who saw the parachute as a path to a new and richer life. She took up exhibition parachuting for a living, and women continued to make exhibition jumps throughout the following century.

FOR FURTHER REFLECTION

More than a century before the Wright Brothers, men and women were not only flying in hot air balloons but performing daredevilish stunts in them. Of course, human daring through artificial flight can be seen in ancient myths, like that of Daedalus and Icarus. By the time heavier-than-air flight became a reality in 1903, the human impulse to extend the technology of flight to its limits had already been well-rehearsed.

...................................TRY THIS....................................

Write a short story based on one of the eighteenth- or nineteenth-century hot air balloonists, such as the Montgolfier brothers, Sophie Blanchard, or André-Jaques Garnerin. Go into detail regarding the technical aspects of flight, such as how the balloon's flight path is controlled, and how it returns to the surface.

"Playmaking"

by William Archer

from *European Theories of the Drama*

The essence of drama is crisis. A play is a more or less rapidly-developing crisis in destiny or circumstances, and a dramatic scene is a crisis within a crisis, clearly furthering the ultimate event. The drama may be called the art of crises, as fiction is the art of gradual developments. It is the slowness of its process which differentiates the typical novel from the typical play. If the novelist does not take advantage of the facilities offered by his form for portraying gradual change, whether in the way of growth or of decay, he renounces his own birthright in order to trespass on the domain of the dramatist. Most great novels embrace considerable segments of many lives; whereas the drama gives us only the culminating points—or shall we say, the intersecting culminations?—of two or three destinies. Some novelists have excelled precisely in the art with which they have made the gradations of change in character or circumstance so delicate as to be imperceptible from page to page, and measurable, as in real life, only when we look back over a considerable period. The dramatist, on the other hand, deals in rapid and startling changes, the *peripeties*, as the Greeks called them, which may be the outcome of long, slow processes, but which actually occur in very brief space of time. Nor is this merely a mechanical consequence of the narrow limits of stage presentation. The crisis is as real, though not as inevitable, a part of human experience as the gradual development.

FOR FURTHER REFLECTION

It is useful for aspiring playwrights to contemplate the differences between stage plays and novels. The early twentieth–century playwright and drama theorist William Archer highlighted the essential ones: a rapid, crisis-generated unfolding of plot involving few people instead of a gradual unfolding involving many people; rapid and startling changes in predicament instead of slow and nearly imperceptible changes.

......................................TRY THIS...................................

Prepare a synopsis of a three-act play in which each act is generated by a crisis, which in turn affects the play's central crisis, which will be resolved by the end of the third act.

Reading Like a Writer: A Guide for People Who Love Books and for Those Who Want to Write Them

by Francine Prose

Mediocre writing abounds with physical clichés and stock gestures. Opening a mass-market thriller at random, I read: "Clenching her fists so hard she can feel her nails digging into the palms of her hand she forces herself to walk over to him. ... She snuggled closer to Larry as she felt his arms tighten around her and his sweet breath warm the back of her neck. ... She adjusted her cap as she crunched down the gravel driveway. ... Tom bit his lip." All of these are perfectly acceptable English sentences describing common gestures, but they feel generic. They are not descriptions of an individual's very particular response to a particular event, but rather a shorthand for common psychic states. He bit his lip, she clenched her fists—our characters are nervous. The cap-adjuster is wary and determined, the couple intimate, and so forth.

Writers cover pages with familiar reactions (her heart pounded, he wrung his hands) to familiar situations. But unless what the character does is unexpected or unusual, or truly important to the narrative, the reader will assume that response without having to be told.

FOR FURTHER REFLECTION

One distinction we might draw between "literary" and "nonliterary" fiction is that the former is more devoted to developing characters as individuals rather than as types. This is not to disparage conventional genre fiction, which often relies on personality stereotypes; but it is good to be aware, as writers, that although formula plotting and formula character traits may be comforting to many readers, to others such devices do not usually become recognized as literature—as having the distinction of shedding new light on human nature.

································ TRY THIS ································

Compose a profile sheet of your three or four principal characters in your novel in progress. Now examine these profiles in terms of stereotypes. Do your characters adhere to or violate conventional expectations? Make the necessary adjustments if your goal is to create distinctive individuals.

"Stock-Breeding and Pastoralism"
by Ashley Montagu

from *Man: His First Million Years:*
A Brief Introduction to Anthropology

It is interesting to note that the earliest domestication of animals should have taken place at approximately the same time as the cultivation of cereals. The principles underlying the two forms of food production are the same: the control of reproduction.

... The earliest animals to be domesticated for the purposes of food are those we still use, cattle, sheep, goats, and pigs. Their bones are found in the earliest agricultural settlements of Jarmo in Kurdistan and in the settlements of the Faiyumis, Merimdeans, and Badarians in Neolithic Egypt. That the horse was used as a domestic animal in Elam, at the head of the Persian Gulf, earlier than 3500 B.C., is known from a representation of a man riding one. From Sumerian art of about 3000 B.C. we know that the wheeled cart was invented with horses and cattle as draft animals.

Pastoral communities, living largely off their herds, were well established by 4000 B.C., and there are many peoples today in Mongolia and Arabia who still follow this mode of subsistence, as do the Navahos of our own Southwest.

FOR FURTHER REFLECTION

Some of the very earliest food-production practices at the dawn of civilization six thousand years ago are still in use today, namely self-sufficient livestock domestication and breeding communities among some Native Americans and in eastern Asia. Civilization is often characterized by deeply rooted customs and amazing innovations.

.................................TRY THIS....................................

In an essay, reflect on the progress of civilization over the millennia. What do you identify as the most important humanizing forces? What forces would you identify as the most damaging to humanity?

AUGUST 2
Arts and the Man:
An Introduction to Aesthetics
by Irwin Edman

It is one of the chief functions of the artist to render experience arresting by rendering it alive. The artist, be he poet, painter, sculptor, or architect, does something to objects, the poet and novelist do something to events, that compel the eye to stop and find pleasure in the beholding, the ear to hear for the sheer sake of listening, the mind to attend for the keen, impractical pleasure of discovery or suspense or surprise. The chair ceases to be a signal to a sitter; it becomes a part and a point in a composition, a focus of color and form. It becomes in a painting pictorially significant; it becomes alive. That passing face is not something to be persuaded or conquered or forgotten. It is to be looked at; it is an object of pictorial interest, at once satisfying and exciting. It ceases to be an incident or an instrument; it is not a precipitate to action, a signal to anger or to lust. It is a moment crowded with vitality and filled with order; it is knowledge for its own sweet sake of something living and composed; it is beautiful, as we say, to look at, and its beholding is a pleasure.

FOR FURTHER REFLECTION

As writers, we should occasionally reflect on the power of art to heighten everyday reality and imbue it with meaning. Whether the tools are paints, sounds, clay, or words, art is the means by which painters, musicians, sculptors, and writers direct attention to what is significant and beautiful, dangerous and ugly, in the world and in ourselves.

.....................................TRY THIS....................................

List as many contributions of art to humanity as you can think of. Afterward, write an essay that reflects on why these contributions are so beneficial. You might single out one or two as the most beneficial and explain why.

AUGUST 3

Our Cosmic Habitat

by Martin Rees

Just as geologists infer climatic history by drilling through successive layers of Antarctic ice, astronomers infer the history of our galaxy by studying, and trying to date, the various populations of stars within it. But astronomers have an advantage over geologists: they can actually see the remote past by looking at galaxies so far away that their light was emitted billions of years ago. ... In a completely random universe ... distant regions might not resemble anything in our vicinity and might have quite different histories. The large-scale uniformity of our universe is crucial here. It is only because of the overall smoothness of the universe that we have grounds for believing that all of its parts have evolved similarly. ...

The most detailed pictures of the sky that we have so far obtained came from week-long exposures with the Hubble Space Telescope. Each of these images shows a patch of sky so small that it would cover less than a hundredth the area of the full moon. Such a patch looks blank when viewed with an ordinary telescope. But it reveals many hundreds of faint smudges, each of them actually an entire galaxy, thousands of light-years across. They appear small and faint because they are so far away: their light began its travels 10 billion years ago. We see them as they were in the remote past, when all their stars were still young.

FOR FURTHER REFLECTION

Everything in the universe is separated not only by distance, but by time; thus, the farther away something is from us the farther back in time it is from us as well. The moon, a quarter of a million miles away, is also 1.5 seconds farther back in time from us, because that's how long it takes light to travel to us from the moon, and nothing can exceed the speed of light. When it comes to inter-galactic distances, the time factor becomes much stranger: Our "neighboring" galaxy, Andromeda, is two *million* light-years away: We see it as it existed two million years ago.

......................................TRY THIS....................................

Children are fascinated by astronomy, but some of the concepts like the relativity of time and space can be quite challenging. Write an article in which you explain this relationship to preteen readers.

A Feeling for the Organism:
The Life and Work of Barbara McClintock
by Evelyn Fox Keller

What enabled McClintock to see further and deeper into the mysteries of genetics than her colleagues? Her answer is simple. Over and over again, she tells us one must have the time to look, the patience to "hear what the material has to say to you," the openness to "let it come to you." Above all, one must have "a feeling for the organism."

One must understand "how it grows, understand its parts, understand when something is going wrong with it. [An organism] isn't just a piece of plastic, it's something that is constantly being affected by the environment, constantly showing attributes of disabilities in its growth. ... No two plants are exactly alike. They're all different, and as a consequence, you have to know that difference," she explains. "I start with the seedling, and I don't want to leave it. I don't feel I really know the story if I don't watch the plant all the way along. So I know every plant in the field. I know them intimately. ..."

This intimate knowledge, made possible by years of close association with the organism she studies, is a prerequisite for her extraordinary perspicacity. "I have learned so much about the corn plant that when I see things I can interpret [them] right away." ...

Good science cannot proceed without a deep emotional investment on the part of the scientist. It is that emotional investment that provides the motivating force for the endless hours of intense, often grueling, labor.

FOR FURTHER REFLECTION

Barbara McClintock was a creative thinker among scientists, one for whom intuition played as important a role as formal experimentation and analysis. A molecular geneticist who studied higher organisms, like maize, she applied techniques that seemed more appropriate for the naturalist than the microbiologist. Whereas biologists like Jacques Monod and François Jacob "sought a molecular mechanism," Keller writes, "she sought a conceptual structure."

................................TRY THIS..................................

Write a biographical sketch of a scientist like Barbara McClintock, who makes use of nontraditional or creative methods of problem solving. Take pains to undo some of the clichés that distort or caricature science or scientists.

AUGUST 5

The Yellow-Lighted Bookshop
by Lewis Buzbee

Part of the allowable leisure in a bookstore comes from the product it sells. Books are slow. They require time; they are written slowly, published slowly, and read slowly. A four-hundred page novel might take years to write, longer to publish, and even after the novel is purchased, the reader can expect to spend hours with it at one sitting over a number of days, weeks, sometimes months.

But it's not the just the nature of the book that determines the bookstore's permissiveness. The modern bookstore has long been associated with the coffeehouse and the café. In eighteenth-century Europe, when coffee and tobacco conquered the continent, the coffeehouse provided a public gathering place for writers, editors, and publishers. The stimulant coffee and the sedative tobacco, in combination, made sitting at a table all day a pleasant equilibrium, perfect for writing, reading, long conversations, or staring out the window. This was the Age of Enlightenment: literacy was on the rise, books were cheaper and more abundant.

FOR FURTHER REFLECTION

"Books are slow": These words do not sit comfortably with many people in the digital age. But it is the "slowness" of reading books, or of browsing in bookstores, that is conducive to patient reflection—a habit of mind, and of life, that we must take care not to forsake in favor of speed and efficiency.

..................................TRY THIS..................................

1. Describe, in a poem or essay, the pleasures you experience (a) while reading a book (in contrast to accessing a document on the Internet) or (b) browsing in a bookstore (in contrast to shopping for books online).
2. Argue for or against the preservation of "brick and mortar" bookstores, independent or otherwise. Are they still important even though (some would argue) Internet shopping is more convenient?

AUGUST 6

"The Empress's Omelet"
by Isabel Allende

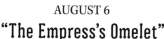

from *Aphrodite: A Memoir of the Senses*

For two people in love, you need 5 eggs, fresh from the nest of a virgin hen, salt and pepper, fresh country butter, chopped chives, 4 fine but succulent slices of Norwegian smoked salmon, ½ cup of beluga caviar, if possible from the Baltic Sea, 2 teaspoons sour cream, and, of course, toast. Ever so delicately break the eggs into a fine porcelain bowl—porcelain for reasons of elegance, nothing more—and heat lightly, adding salt and pepper. Warm the butter in the omelet pan sacred to every good cook, and as soon as the butter begins to turn the tint of warm Caribbean skin, pour in the eggs. When the omelet is half cooked on the bottom, loosen it with infinite gentleness, whispering encouragingly, because if you are rough, it will lose its enchanting disposition; add the chives and salmon and fold it over, exactly as you would close a book. To free it entirely, experts move the skillet back and forth with the pulsing syncopation of a good dancer and then, with a sudden flip of the wrist, toss it up in the air and catch it, now reversed, so it will cook to a golden brown on both sides—although I admit that every time I've tried that move, the omelet has landed on my head. These gyrations are pure exhibitionism, because when you make an omelet, as when you make love, affection counts for more than technique. Serve your omelet on your most beautiful plates, already warmed in the oven.

FOR FURTHER REFLECTION

Food and lovemaking, as the Chilean novelist Isabel Allende poetically demonstrates in this eloquent, often erotic, and sometimes funny memoir, enhance each other in all sorts of ways. Being artful, inventive, and sensitive to cultural tradition when preparing meals is a fine way to enhance the pleasures of life, especially romantic relationships.

· TRY THIS ·

1. With Allende's "Empress's Omelet" as your inspiration, turn one of your favorite recipes into an evocative, sensual piece of creative nonfiction.
2. Write a short story in which the protagonist uses food or cooking in an effort to win the other's affections.

The World of Gold Today
by Timothy Green

Going down a gold mine is rather like a trial run for Hades. You even leave all your clothes, including underwear, behind on the surface and, shrouded in white overalls, enter a steel cage which plummets through a mile of rock in two minutes. There below is a noisy, hot, wet world lit by the dancing fireflies of the lamps on miners' helmets. A ten-minute walk along a gallery cut through rock whose natural temperature is over 100° Fahrenheit, and any visitor is soaked by a combination of sweat and humidity. Then, above the constant hum of the air conditioning and the rumble of trucks along steel rails, comes the sound of compressed air drills biting into solid rock. On one side of the tunnel a narrow opening begins plunging down at an angle of nearly 25 degrees toward the bowels of the earth. ... Almost hidden in a fine spray of water to subdue dust, the long needle nose of a drill chatters into a hole in the rock marked with a blob of red paint. ... This mine, Free State Geduld in the Orange Free State, is one of the very few in which the gold between the pebbles can actually be seen by the naked eye, for it is blessed with one of the riches reefs ever discovered in South Africa.

FOR FURTHER REFLECTION

There is something almost mythological about burrowing deep into the earth in search of gold. Indeed, descending into a South African gold mine reminds Timothy Green, a London freelance journalist, of descending into the underworld. Add to that the physical hardships and extreme dangers of mining, and we can indeed begin to see the elements of a modern dark myth.

..................................TRY THIS...................................

Plan a short story about gold miners, drawing from Greek mythology for metaphors. Of course, you will want to become familiar with the technology of mining for gold as well as the hazards involved.

AUGUST 8

"Agricola"

by Tacitus

from *On Britain and Germany*. Translated by H. Mattingly

Agricola [governor of Roman Britain; Tacitus's father-in-law] understood the feelings of a province and had learned from the experience of others that arms can effect little if injustice follows in their train. He resolved to root out the causes of war. Beginning with himself and his staff, he enforced discipline in his own household first—a task often found as difficult as the government of a province. He made no use of freedmen or slaves for official business. He would not be influenced by personal feelings, recommendations or petitions in choosing his centurions and men. The best, he was sure, would best justify his trust. He knew everything, but did not always act as if he knew. He could condone minor offences, but had no kind of mercy for major ones. Sometimes he would omit to punish and be satisfied by a change of heart. He preferred to appoint to official positions and duties men whom he could trust not to transgress, rather than punish the transgressor. He eased the levy of corn and tribute by distributing the burden fairly, and cancelled those charges, contrived by profiteers, which were more bitterly resented than the tax itself. The provincials had actually been compelled to wait at the doors of closed granaries, buy back their own corn and pay farcical prices.

FOR FURTHER REFLECTION

In great military leaders like Agricola, one often finds paradoxical views and behaviors—a warrior who longs for peace, a disciplinarian who had trouble punishing his troops for transgressions. Such, perhaps is the paradoxical nature of war itself.

..................................TRY THIS..................................

Write a short story about Agricola, or any other military leader, past or present. Focus more on the leader's personality and psyche than on external events. It would help to read deeply into the life of the leader.

"The Great European Explorations and Their World-Wide Consequences"

by W.H. McNeill

from *The Rise of the West: A History of the Human Community*

Europeans of the Atlantic seaboard possessed three talismans of power by 1500 which conferred upon them the command of all the oceans of the world within half a century and permitted the subjugation of the most highly developed regions of the Americas within a single generation. These were: (1) a deep-rooted pugnacity and recklessness operating by means of (2) a complex military technology, most notably in naval matters; and (3) a population inured to a variety of diseases which had long been endemic throughout the Old World ecumene. ... Only when one remembers the all but incredible courage, daring, and brutality of Cortez and Pizarro in the Americas, reflects upon the ruthless aggression of Almeida and Albuquerque in the Indian Ocean, and discovers the disdain of even so cultivated a European as Father Matteo Ricci for the civility of the Chinese, does the full force of European warlikeness, when compared with the attitudes and aptitudes of other major civilizations of the earth, become apparent. ... Moslem merchants usually cringed before the violence held in high repute by their rulers and seldom dared or perhaps cared to emulate it. Hence Moslem commercial enterprise lacked the cutting edge of naked, well-organized, large-scale force which constituted the chief stock-in-trade of European overseas merchants in the sixteenth century.

FOR FURTHER REFLECTION

It's a sad irony that westward expansion often carried the price of ruthlessness, subjugation of cultures, and destruction. Any positive connotations associated with Manifest Destiny are undermined if not altogether negated by the brutal relocation and decimation of Native Americans. The harsh details of history often negate the romantic legends that arise after enough time has passed.

....TRY THIS....................................

1. Tell the story of the conquest of Mexico and South America by the Spanish Conquistadors from the point of view of the Mayans or the Aztecs.
2. Write an essay on the idea of Manifest Destiny, which served as a powerful rationale for moving the United States westward. Reflect on both the positive and the negative aspects of this concept.

Mao: The Unknown Story
by Jung Chang and Jon Halliday

Mao arrived in Changsha in spring 1911, on the eve of the Republican Revolution that was to end over two thousand years of imperial rule. Though Changsha seemed "just like a medieval town" to the British philosopher Bertrand Russell a decade later ... it was not merely in touch with new ideas and trends, it seethed with Republican activity.

The Manchu court had promised a constitutional monarchy, but the Republicans were dedicated to getting rid of the Manchus entirely. To them Manchu rule was "foreign" domination, as the Manchus were not Han Chinese, the ethnic group that formed the bulk—about 94 per cent—of the population. The Republicans lit sparks through newspapers and magazines that had sprung up all over China in the previous decade and through the entirely new practice of public debates, in what had hitherto been an almost totally private society. They formed organizations and launched several—unsuccessful—armed uprisings.

Mao quickly caught up on the issues through newspapers, which he read for the first time now, at the age of seventeen—the start of a lifelong addiction. He wrote his first, rather confused, political essay expressing Republican views and pasted it up on a wall at his school, in line with the latest trend. Like many other students in the school, he cut off his pigtail, which, as a Manchu custom, was the most obvious symbol of imperial rule. With a friend, he then ambushed a dozen others and forcibly removed their queues with scissors.

FOR FURTHER REFLECTION
Revolutionary figures in history often reveal a volatile spirit early on. The teenage Mao Zedong's impulsive act of cutting off his and his fellow students' emblem of imperial subjugation strikingly encapsulates his future as the Communist ruler of over a billion and a half people.

.................................TRY THIS....................................

In a biographical sketch, compare the childhoods of two or three famous (or notorious) military and/or political leaders in modern history. Possible subjects: Theodore Roosevelt, Eva Perón, Charles de Gaulle, Mahatma Ghandi, Lech Walesa, Golda Meir, George Patton.

"Dinner With Trimalchio"

by Petronius Arbiter

from *The Satyricon, and the Fragments.* Translated by John Sullivan

[Trimalchio to his dinner guests]

"We've got to display some culture at our dinner. My patron—God rest his bones!—wanted me to hold up my head in any company. ... Look now, these here heavens, as there are twelve gods living in 'em, changes into that many shapes. First it becomes the Ram. So whoever is born under that sign has a lot of herds, a lot of wool, a hard head as well, a brassy front, and a sharp horn. Most scholars are born under this sign, and most muttonheads as well."

We applauded the wit of our astrologer and he went on:

"Then the whole heavens turns into the little old Bull. So bull-headed folk are born then, and cow-herds and those who find their own feed. Under the Heavenly Twins on the other hand—pairs-in-hand, yokes of oxen, ... and people who have it both ways. I was born under the Crab, so I have a lot of legs to stand on and a lot of property on land and sea, because the Crab takes both in his stride. ... Under Leo are born greedy and domineering people. Under the Virgin, effeminates, runaways, and candidates for the chain-gang. Under the Scales butchers, perfume-sellers, and anyone who weighs things up. Under Scorpio poisoners and murderers. ... Under Capricorn, people in trouble who sprout horns through their worries. Under the Water-Carrier bartenders and jugheads. Under the Fishes, fish-fryers and people who spout in public. So the starry sky turns round like a mill-stone, always bringing some trouble, and men being born or dying."

FOR FURTHER REFLECTION

Being at one time Nero's courtier and arbiter of elegance, Petronius had the license, in effect, to poke fun at social conventions—always a risky thing to do, license or not, in Imperial Rome, especially under this emperor. Eventually, Petronius was accused of plotting against Nero, who ordered him to commit suicide.

.................................TRY THIS....................................

Compose a farcical scene—either for a screenplay or stage play—between an astrologer and a gullible person who dreads doing anything without first consulting his or her horoscope.

AUGUST 12

Utopia

by Sir Thomas More

from *The Renaissance in England: Non-dramatic Prose and Verse of the Sixteenth Century.* Translated by Raphe Robynson

[The Utopians] embrace chiefly the pleasures of the mind. ... The chief part of them, they think, doth come of the exercise of virtue, and conscience of good life. Of those pleasures that the body minist'reth they give the preeminence to health. For the delight of eating and drinking, and whatsoever hath any like pleasantness, they determine to be pleasures much to be desired, but no other ways than for health's sake. ...

Beauty, strength, nimbleness, these, as peculiar and pleasant gifts of nature, they make much of. But those pleasures which be received by the ears, the eyes, and the nose, which nature willeth to be proper and peculiar to man—for no other kind of living beasts doth behold the fairness and the beauty of the world, or is moved with any respect of savors, but only for the diversity of meats, neither perceiveth the concordant and discordant distances of sounds and tunes—these pleasures, I say, they accept and allow as certain pleasant rejoicings of life. But in all things this cautel [trick, deceit] they use, that a less pleasure hinder not a bigger, and that the pleasure be no cause of displeasure, which they think to follow of necessity if the pleasure be unhonest. But yet to dispise the comeliness of beauty, to waste the bodily strength, to turn nimbleness into sloughishness, to consume and make feeble the body with fasting, to do injury to health, and to reject the other pleasant motions of nature ... this to do they think it a point of extreme madness and a token of a man cruelly minded towards himself and unkind toward nature.

FOR FURTHER REFLECTION

We are likely to respond to utopian visions—and More's is one of the most famous—with skepticism and sometimes laughter (as if to say, "Yeah, right, that'll never happen"). At the same time, we find ourselves prodded a little: Maybe we can improve our lot if we limited our pleasures only to those activities that resulted in better health and well-being.

..................................TRY THIS....................................

Describe your ideal society. Begin writing your own "Utopia"–but as you work on it, ask yourself whenever you introduce a directive: What would the consequences be?

"How Love Tyrannizeth Over Men"
by Robert Burton
from *The Anatomy of Melancholy*

You have heard how this tyrant Love rageth with brute beasts and spirits; now let us consider what passions it causeth amongst men. ... I am almost afraid to relate, amazed and ashamed, it hath wrought such ... prodigious effects, such foul offenses. Love indeed (I may not deny) first united provinces, built cities, and by a perpetual generation makes and preserves mankind, propagates the Church; but if it rage, it is no more love, but burning lust, a disease, frenzy, madness, hell ...; 'tis no virtuous habit this, but a vehement perturbation of the mind, a monster of nature, wit, and art. ... It subverts kingdoms, overthrows cities, towns, families, mars, corrupts, and makes a massacre of men; thunder and lightning, wars, fires, plagues, have not done that mischief to mankind, as this burning lust, this brutish passion. Let Sodom and Gomorrah, Troy ... and I know not how many cities bear record. ...

There is an honest love, I confess, which is natural ... a secret snare to captivate the hearts of men ... a strong allurement, of a most attractive, occult, adamantine property and powerful virtue, and no man living can avoid it. ... He is not a man but a block, a very stone ... he hath a gourd for his head, a *pepon* [pumpkin] for his heart, who hath not felt the power of it, and a rare creature to be found.

FOR FURTHER REFLECTION

Robert Burton has captured the almost demonic power that love has on us, especially in the countless ways it manifests itself—as spiritual frenzy, as romantic abandon, as self-sacrificing devotion to another. Perhaps it is love—more than any other emotion—that shapes our humanity.

.....................................TRY THIS....................................

Over the next several days or weeks, keep a running list of the different ways in which you experience love, in all of its manifestations. Eventually, you'll have enough raw material to compose your own treatise on love.

AUGUST 14

The Brothers Karamazov

by Fyodor Dostoevsky

Translated by Constance Garnett

[Fyodor Pavlovich Karamazov to his son Alyosha]

"You don't suppose he [Ivan, one of Alyosha's three brothers] … came to murder me, do you? He must have had some object in coming."

"What do you mean? Why do you say such things?" said Alyosha, troubled.

"He doesn't ask for money, it's true, but yet he won't get a farthing from me. I intend living as long as possible, you may well know … and so I need every farthing, and the longer I live, the more I shall need it," he continued, pacing from one corner of the room to the other, keeping his hands in the pockets of his loose greasy overcoat made of yellow cotton material. "I can still pass for a man at five and fifty, but I want to pass for one for another twenty years. As I get older, you know, I shan't be a pretty object. The wenches won't come to me of their own accord, so I shall want my money. So I am saving more and more, simply for myself, my dear son Alexey Fyodorovitch. You may as well know. For I mean to go on in my sins to the end, let me tell you. For sin is sweet; all abuse it, but all men live in it, only others do it on the sly, and I openly. And so all the other sinners fall upon me for being so simple. And your paradise … is not to my taste, let me tell you that; and it's not the proper place for a gentleman, your paradise, even if it exists. I believe that I fall asleep and don't wake up again, and that's all. You can pray for my soul if you like. And if you don't want to, don't, damn you! That's my philosophy.

FOR FURTHER REFLECTION

Few novelists have been able to probe the minds of the tyrant, the spiritualist, the criminal, as deeply as Dostoevsky. In the above passage we get a keen sense of the tyrannical Fyodor Karamazov sharing his own self-serving attitude toward growing old—and, in the process, as is characteristic of so many domineering and insensitive fathers, sneering at his son Alexey's [Alyosha's] spiritual ideals.

....TRY THIS....................................

Write a story about a father-son relationship in which the son—no matter how valiantly he tries—can never please his father or meet his expectations. What does the son finally do (or not do)?

AUGUST 15

The Fountainhead
by Ayn Rand

[Gail Wynand to Howard Roark]

"I want you to design all my future commercial structures—as the public wishes commercial structures to be designed. You'll build Colonial houses, Rococo hotels and semi-Grecian office buildings. You'll exercise your matchless ingenuity within forms chosen by the taste of the people—and you'll make money for me. You'll take your spectacular talent and make it obedient. Originality and subservience together. They call it harmony. ... But the house you've designed for me shall be erected as you designed it. It will be the last Roark building to rise on earth. Nobody will have one after mine. ... For the rest of your life you'll obey the will of the majority. ... You have a simple choice: if you refuse, you'll never build anything again; if you accept, you'll build this house which you want so much to see erected, and a great many other houses you won't like, but which will make money for both of us. ... That is what I want." ...

"Why, of course," said Roark gaily. "I'll be glad to do it. That's easy." He reached over, took a pencil and the first piece of paper he saw on Wynand's desk. ... He drew rapidly on the back of the letter. ... "Is this what you want?"

Wynand's house stood drawn on the paper—with Colonial porches, a gambrel roof, two massive chimneys ... It was not a parody, it was a serious job of adaptation in what any professor would have called excellent taste.

"Good God, no!" The gasp was instinctive and immediate.

FOR FURTHER REFLECTION

The Fountainhead powerfully dramatizes the clash between individual artistic integrity and commercialism. There is always some give and take, but for Howard Roark, to compromise one's architectural vision for the sake of the marketplace is akin to selling one's soul to the devil. Writers, like architects, also must find the best way to combine individual vision and manner of presentation with the reality of the marketplace. Is it possible to preserve one's artistic integrity and still reach a wide audience?

....TRY THIS....................................

Without thinking about audience, write a short story that embodies a theme close to your heart. Follow your deepest creative impulses as you structure the story, develop the characters, setting, tone. Set the story aside for awhile; then critique it from the perspective of a typical reader, and revise accordingly.

AUGUST 16

The Mindbody Prescription:
Healing the Body, Healing the Pain

by John E. Sarno, M.D.

We know that the purpose of physical symptoms like TMS [Tension Myositis Syndrome] and its equivalents is to keep attention focused on the body. If the pain disappears but you are still fearful of physical activity, recurrent pain, injury and progressive degeneration of spinal elements, the battle has not yet been won. The pain will return unless you overcome those fears. So patients are advised to resume normal, unrestricted physical activity once the pain is gone. ... Patients have reported that becoming active may take months, which is not difficult to understand considering their years of exposure to misconceptions about the presumed fragility of the back.

Never do this or that, do it this way, we're told; be careful, you'll hurt yourself your spine is out of line ... one of your legs is shorter than the other; you've got flat feet ...

All of these admonitions and prohibitions, enhanced by poor medical advice, keep your attention riveted on your body, which is your brain's intention.

The path to resumption of full physical activity, without fear, may be slow and uneven. Don't worry if you begin to exercise too soon and experience some pain. You cannot hurt yourself; TMS is a benign process. Continuing pain with activity means the brain is still in the process of changing its programming. ...

FOR FURTHER REFLECTION

Mind and body are inextricably intertwined. Back pain is not just a matter of neuromuscular or spinal problems, it is also governed by emotional responses to the work that gives rise to the physical problems. Dr. Sarno, a professor of clinical rehabilitation medicine, lays out a means of "deprogramming" the brain's efforts to keep attention restricted only to the physical side of things in order to overcome these afflictions.

.... TRY THIS ....

After reading *Mind Body Prescription* in its entirety, and consulting with your personal physician, begin working toward alleviating one of your physical distresses. Keep a detailed log of your progress, and afterward use your log to write a feature article about the experience.

AUGUST 17

After the Stroke: A Journal
by May Sarton

(Sunday, April 13.) Having a disability has one good effect. I am far more aware of and sympathetic about the illnesses some of my friends are struggling to surmount than I was when I was well. It is companionable to share some of the day-to-day triumphs and despairs. I'm afraid terribly cheerful, well people are no help at all!

I am aware for the first time perhaps what courage it takes to grow old, how exasperating it is no longer to be able to do what seemed nothing at all even a year ago.

And I am learning some of the things *not* to say to a person who has had a stroke. It's a good idea not to seem to expect great improvement. "Are you feeling better?" when there is no chance that the person addressed *can* feel better quickly. For instance, work. Several people suggested I keep a journal—in the first weeks after February twentieth. This caused me to shout and weep. "I can't write a *line*! I'm not myself and shan't be for a long time." It felt like cruelty—like saying to a cripple in a wheelchair, "it will do you good to take a walk."

FOR FURTHER REFLECTION

May Sarton demonstrates through her journal—through the very fact that she has written this post-stroke journal—the mind's, as well as the body's, great potential for rehabilitation. At first it seems impossible, and the stroke victim (and by extension anyone else who has suffered a severe affliction) teeters on the edge of despair. Once again, we see how powerfully therapeutic writing can be.

.................................TRY THIS....................................

Begin a journal (or series of entries in your existing journal) following an illness or accident–your own or someone else's. Chronicle the progress of improvement but also keep tabs of the changes in temperament as a result of the illness or accident.

AUGUST 18
Crimson Joy
by Robert B. Parker

[Spenser to his psychiatrist sweetheart
Susan Silverman while they're having dinner]

"What we know basically is that it's a white guy killing black women. Certainly sounds like a racial crime," I said.

"And the semen traces?" Susan said.

"Certainly sounds like a sexual crime," I said.

"A dysfunctional one," Susan said.

"Because there's no penetration," I said.

"Except with a gun," Susan said. "Think how frightened of women he must be, to tie them up and gag them and render them helpless, and still he cannot actually connect. He can only find sexual expression the way he does." ...

"Why black women?" I said.

Susan shook her head. "No way to know," she said. "Psychopaths, and we must assume that we've got one here, have their own logic, a logic rooted in their own symbolism."

"In other words, just because he's white and they're black is not enough reason to assume he's killing them for racial reasons," I said.

"That's right. What the women represent to him, why he needs to treat them as he does, may be a function of their blackness, or their status on the social scale. Or it may be that there is some idiosyncratic association for him that no one can imagine."

FOR FURTHER REFLECTION

In his Hemingway-esque minimalist prose style that enables us to see as clearly as possible through the language to the people and the drama at hand, Robert Parker keeps the reader fully engrossed in Spenser's efforts to make sense of a psychopathic serial killer's M.O. His conversation with Susan subtly directs the reader to think like a psychologist—to see the details of the murders as symbolic acts.

..................................TRY THIS....................................

Outline a mystery story in which the killer's M.O. is laden with symbolism. For example, you might have him shove a bar of soap in the victim's mouth to symbolize how his father used to punish him by washing out his own mouth with soap.

"Eagle Transforming Into Itself"
by Alison Hawthorne Deming
from *Temporary Homelands*

[The bald eagles'] decline has been attributed to loss of habitat, pesticide and toxic waste exposure, and human predation. Protection began in the lower forty-eight under the National Emblem Law of 1940, which forbade killing eagles. Killing bald eagles was encouraged in Alaska with a bounty of two dollars for each pair of eagle feet until 1953. Bounty was paid on more than one hundred thousand bald eagles shot in Alaska between 1915 and 1951. People feared the birds would deplete the salmon fishery, though the birds are more often timid carrion feeders than voracious hunters. Bald eagles are now protected under federal legislation making it illegal to kill or possess any part of an eagle. Penalties range up to ten thousand dollars and two years in jail. It is also illegal to disturb an eagle nesting site. But laws are unlikely to curb the predatory curiosity of a ten-year-old boy out stalking with his brand-new BB gun or the business-as-usual of a logging corporation with its head office in the profit making clouds.

FOR FURTHER REFLECTION

Environmental protection comes fraught with conflicts: On one side we have industry and agriculture and hundreds of thousands of workers whose goals of earning a living are always short-range; on the other side, we have environmental protection issues, the goals of which are long-range. Both are equally important to the welfare of the nation and the planet, which means that solutions must be carefully considered, with both sides involved. Eagles are being restored, thanks in part to more accurate knowledge of eagle behavior.

.....................................TRY THIS.....................................

Select a current environmental problem such as reduction in salmon or trout populations as a result of dams, water pollution, or other factors. Write an article evaluating the severity of both sides of the problem and propose a solution.

An Essay on Man: An Introduction to a Philosophy of Human Culture
by Ernst Cassirer

No longer in a merely physical universe, man lives in a symbolic universe. Language, myth, art, and religion are parts of this universe. They are the varied threads which weave the symbolic net, the tangled web of human experience. All human progress in thought and experience refines upon and strengthens this net. No longer can man confront reality immediately; he cannot see it, as it were, face to face. Physical reality seems to recede in proportion as man's symbolic activity advances. Instead of dealing with the things themselves man is in a sense constantly conversing with himself. He has so enveloped himself in linguistic forms, in artistic images, in mythical symbols or religious rites that he cannot see or know anything except by interposition of this artificial medium. His situation is the same in the theoretical as in the practical sphere. Even here man does not live in a world of hard facts, or according to his immediate needs and desires. He lives rather in the midst of imaginary emotions, in hopes and fears, in illusions and disillusions, in his fantasies and dreams. "What disturbs and alarms man," said Epictetus, "are not the things, but his opinions and fancies about the things."

FOR FURTHER REFLECTION

Cassirer posits a provocative way that modern humans perceive the real world: We can do so only by representing (that is re-presenting, reconstructing) the world symbolically, through language, storytelling (which consists of language), and image-making. Reality, then, is what we make of it through words and images; we cannot separate the real world from the way we represent with our symbolic tools.

.....................................TRY THIS....................................

Develop a short story consisting of three characters who all witness the same event (baseball game, family reunion, wedding, etc.), but who all perceive it very differently, depending on their feelings about the team, the relatives, the bride and groom, etc. You might make your viewpoint character omniscient—able to comment on the impossibility of gaining a completely objective account of the event.

AUGUST 21
"Thermal Disorder"
by George Gamow
from *One, Two, Three ... Infinity*

Although molecular motion as well as molecules themselves are not directly discernible to the human eye, it is molecular motion that produces a certain irritation in the nervous fibres of the human organism and produces the sensation that we call heat. For those organisms that are much smaller than human beings, such as, for example, small bacteria suspended in a water drop, the effect of thermal motion is much more pronounced, and these poor creatures are incessantly kicked, pushed, and tossed around by the restless molecules that attack them from all sides and give them no rest. This amusing phenomenon, known as Brownian motion, named after the English botanist Robert Brown, who first noticed it more than a century ago in a study of tiny plant spores, is of quite general nature and can be observed in the study of any kind of sufficiently small particles suspended in any kind of liquid, or of microscopic particles of smoke and dust floating in the air.

If we heat the liquid the wild dance of tiny particles suspended in it becomes more violent; with cooling the intensity of the motion noticeably subsides. This leaves no doubt that we are actually watching here the effect of the hidden thermal motion of matter, and what we usually call temperature is nothing else but a measurement of the degree of molecular agitation. By studying the dependence of Brownian motion on temperature, it was found that at the temperature of -273°C or -459°F, thermal agitation of matter completely ceases, and all its molecules come to rest. This apparently is the lowest temperature and it has received the name of *absolute zero.*

FOR FURTHER REFLECTION
Heat is just another way of talking about movement—molecular movement that can result in physical and chemical changes and that causes the nervous system to register a distinct sensation such as comfort or pain (without which illness or injury could result). This is yet another way in which scientific understanding helps to demystify the way things work.

..................................TRY THIS...................................

Write an article in which you describe the changes that take place in a substance (hydrogen, oxygen, carbon dioxide, methane) when it is heated to certain temperatures.

Blood Struggle: The Rise of Modern Indian Nations
by Charles Wilkinson

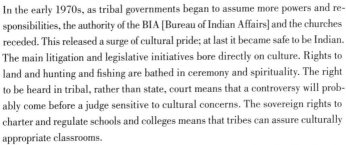

In the early 1970s, as tribal governments began to assume more powers and responsibilities, the authority of the BIA [Bureau of Indian Affairs] and the churches receded. This released a surge of cultural pride; at last it became safe to be Indian. The main litigation and legislative initiatives bore directly on culture. Rights to land and hunting and fishing are bathed in ceremony and spirituality. The right to be heard in tribal, rather than state, court means that a controversy will probably come before a judge sensitive to cultural concerns. The sovereign rights to charter and regulate schools and colleges means that tribes can assure culturally appropriate classrooms.

It is the great irony of nineteenth-century Indian policy that the sharply reduced tribal landholdings, which Native people bitterly protested, later became cherished homelands and the foundation for the modern sovereignty movement. The great irony of the twentieth century is that contemporaneously with the rise of Indian entrepreneurship in general and gaming in particular, Indian people experienced a resurgence in traditionalism. Everywhere there are more dances, songs, and ceremonies, more pottery, jewelry, and rugs, more longhouses and tribal museums, more native language classes.

FOR FURTHER REFLECTION

For more than two centuries, Native American culture has endured profound hardships and threats to its existence. Who would have guessed that as Native peoples became involved in so ultra-Western an activity as gaming entrepreneurship, they would be creating a resurgence of traditional cultural values? Perhaps it has something to do with a minority culture finding itself at the brink of erasure by the predominant culture and channeling capitalist-generated revenues into the old traditions.

. . . . TRY THIS . . . .

Focus on a current facet of Native American life, such as education, the arts, tribal politics, land stewardship, spirituality—and write a short story that captures dramatically the problems this part of Native American culture is facing.

"Neurobiology and Ethical Behaviors"
by Antonio R. Damasio

from *Looking for Spinoza: Joy, Sorrow, and the Feeling Brain*

The construction we call ethics in humans may have begun as part of an overall program of bioregulation. The embryo of ethical behaviors would have been another step in a progression that includes all the nonconscious, automated mechanisms that provide metabolic regulation; drives and motivations; emotions of diverse kinds; and feelings. Most importantly, the situations that evoke these emotions and feelings call for solutions that include cooperation. It is not difficult to imagine the emergence of justice and honor out of the practices of cooperation. ...

It is reasonable to believe that humans equipped with this repertoire of emotions and whose personality traits include cooperative strategies would be more likely to survive longer and leave more descendants. That would have been the way to establish a genomic basis for brains capable of producing cooperative behavior. This is not to suggest that there is a gene for cooperative behavior, let alone ethical behavior in general. All that would be necessary would be a consistent presence of the many genes likely to endow brains with certain regions of circuitry and with the attendant wiring.

FOR FURTHER REFLECTION

Ethics may well have a physiological, medical basis. Just as the human organism, like other organisms, possesses internal regulatory systems, so must they also possess external regulatory systems—systems of cooperation among different individuals, groups, nations—paralleling cooperation between, say, the sensation of thirst and the body's need for fluid replenishment. The more successful the systems of cooperation, internal or external, the greater the likelihood of survival.

...................................TRY THIS...................................

Compose a parable for children in which different organs in the body go to war because of unresolved differences (for example, the tongue disputing with the stomach over the eating of chocolate or jalapeño peppers).

AUGUST 24

"Bear Creek"

by Kathleen Dean Moore

from *Riverwalking: Reflections on Moving Water*

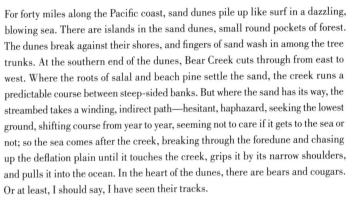

For forty miles along the Pacific coast, sand dunes pile up like surf in a dazzling, blowing sea. There are islands in the sand dunes, small round pockets of forest. The dunes break against their shores, and fingers of sand wash in among the tree trunks. At the southern end of the dunes, Bear Creek cuts through from east to west. Where the roots of salal and beach pine settle the sand, the creek runs a predictable course between steep-sided banks. But where the sand has its way, the streambed takes a winding, indirect path—hesitant, haphazard, seeking the lowest ground, shifting course from year to year, seeming not to care if it gets to the sea or not; so the sea comes after the creek, breaking through the foredune and chasing up the deflation plain until it touches the creek, grips it by its narrow shoulders, and pulls it into the ocean. In the heart of the dunes, there are bears and cougars. Or at least, I should say, I have seen their tracks.

It's hard to get into the dunes, since they are protected by a tangle of swamps, sunken forests, and high hills so thickly forested with salal, salmonberry, sword ferns, and vine maples that nothing but small animals travel there—white-footed deer mice, maybe, or vagrant shrews, to judge from their tracks.

FOR FURTHER REFLECTION

We are drawn to the wild, especially when water runs through it. Here, our senses are heightened, our primal connections to the natural world restored. Thoreau famously wrote, "In wilderness is the preservation of the world"; he could well have added, "and ourselves."

.................................TRY THIS....................................

Plan a trek along a river, creek, pond, or other body of water, and take ample notes of all that you observe and feel. Capture the moment. Take time to rest and meditate. When you return home, begin writing a poem or essay about this excursion.

Myth and Ritual in Christianity
by Alan W. Watts

The Old Testament—the Law of Moses, the Prophets, and the history of Israel—is significant to the Catholic mind only because it is a symbolical foreshadowing of Christ. Thus the Old Testament stories enter into the Christian story in so far as they seem appropriate "types" of the various "mysteries" of the life of Christ which are celebrated through the course of the Christian year. …

It must be understood that with the Fall of the Angels and of Man the whole created universe of time and space, material and immaterial, became corrupt—so much so that at one period the deeds of men became so evil that the Lord God sent a flood upon the waters in an Ark built at the commandment of God. For Christianity, the Ark of Noah is naturally a type of the Church—the Nave or Ship of Salvation, wherein men are saved from the Flood of everlasting damnation. However, when God the Son came into the world as Jesus of Nazareth, the universe was redeemed from this curse, and time itself became holy so that the very years are reckoned from his birth—Anno Domini, in the Year of the Lord. Furthermore, the seasons of the year are themselves transformed from the pagan Spring, Summer, Autumn, and Winter to the Christian Advent, Christmas, Epiphany, Lent, Passiontide, Easter, and Pentecost.

FOR FURTHER REFLECTION

In Christianity, as Alan Watts deftly makes apparent, the scriptural past—the Old Testament—is prologue, signs of what is going to be the central event in human history, the coming of the Savior of mankind. Thus, the history of humankind from the perspective of the Bible truly is a story, with a beginning, middle, and end.

. . . . TRY THIS . . . .

Describe any event that appears in the Old Testament—for instance, Moses on Mount Sinai, receiving the Ten Commandments from God or Job's trials and tribulations—as a prefiguring of Christ.

Lake Wobegon Days
by Garrison Keillor

In Lake Wobegon, car ownership is a matter of faith. Lutherans drive Fords, bought from Bunsen Motors, the Lutheran car dealer, and Catholics drive Chevies from Main Garage, owned by the Kruegers, except for Hjalmar Ingqvist, who has a Lincoln. Years ago, John Tollerud was tempted by Chevyship until … Pastor Tommerdahl took John aside after church and told him it was his (Pastor Tommerdahl's) responsibility to point out that Fords get better mileage and have a better trade-in value. And he knew for a fact that the Kruegers spent a share of the Chevy profits to purchase Asian babies and make them Catholics. So John got a new Ford Falcon. It turned out to be a dud. The transmission went out after ten thousand miles. … In a town where car ownership is by faith, however, a person doesn't complain about these things, and John figured there must be a good reason for his car trouble. …

The Brethren, being Protestant, also drove Fords, of course, but we distinguished ourselves from Lutherans by carrying small steel Scripture plates bolted to the top of our license plates. The verses were written in tiny glass beads so they showed up well at night. We ordered these from the Grace & Truth Scripture Depot in Erie, Pennsylvania, and the favorites were "The wages of sin is death. Rom.6:23" and "I am the way, the truth and the life. Jn.10:6."

FOR FURTHER REFLECTION

Satire comes in different flavors, from harsh and bitter, to gently—sometimes even lovingly—tart. Keillor's brand of satire is always in the latter category. Those folks up there in the North Star State, with their distinctive fusion of religion and automobile maintenance, Scandinavian cuisine and winter sports, generate a lot of affectionate chuckles while at the same time illuminating an infrequently explored facet of American life.

..................................TRY THIS....................................

What facets of American life do you find most amusing or troubling, or a combination of both? List several possibilities—small town customs, behavior at sports or musical events, driving habits, holiday celebrations, etc.—and then choose one to satirize.

Oryx and Crake
by Margaret Atwood

Jimmy's father spent more and more time at his work, but talked about it less and less. There were pigoons at NooSkins, just as at OrganInc Farms, but these were smaller and were being used to develop skin-related biotechnologies. The main idea was to find a method of replacing the older epidermis with a fresh one … a genuine start-over skin that would be wrinkle- and blemish-free. For that, it would be useful to grow a young, plump skin cell that would eat up the worn cells in the skins of those on whom it was planted and replace them with replicas of itself, like algae growing on a pond.

The rewards in the case of success would be enormous, Jimmy's father explained, doing the straight-talking man-to-man act he had recently adopted with Jimmy. What well-to-do and once-young, once-beautiful woman or man, cranked up on hormonal supplements and shot full of vitamins but hampered by the unforgiving mirror, wouldn't sell their house, their gated retirement villa, their kids, and their soul to get a second kick at the sexual can? NooSkins for Olds, said the snappy logo. Not that a totally effective method had been found yet: the dozen or so ravaged hopefuls who had volunteered themselves as subjects, paying no fees but signing away their rights to sue, had come out looking like the Mould Creature from Outer Space—uneven in tone, greenish brown, and peeling in ragged strips.

FOR FURTHER REFLECTION

Will biotechnology create more problems than it tries to solve? One of Atwood's satiric targets in this dystopian parable of a world ravaged by a biogenetic catastrophe can be discerned from the product trademarks—NooSkins, OrganInc Farms, etc. We are in a world in which biotech companies were given carte blanche in manipulating genetic material to meet public demand, without regard to environmental consequences.

······························TRY THIS······························

1. What are your feelings toward genetically engineered foods, cosmetics, medicines? After doing some research into one aspect of biotechnology, weigh both the advantages and the disadvantages, and argue your position in a persuasive essay.

2. Write a short story in which a genetic engineering project has gotten out of hand—such as the inadvertent creation of a superintelligent rat by infusing its brain with human brain cells.

The Night Boat

by Robert R. McCammon

Steven Kip [Constable of Police] grunted, "I can understand a dead boat going down. I *can't* understand a dead one coming back up. This beats all I've ever seen. … World War II crate, I'd say. No markings. Could be British, American, Italian, German … who knows? They all prowled these waters during the war. Now that it's up we're going to have to do something with it. I can't leave it out here, but for the life of me I'm stumped as to …"

There was another sharp noise of something striking iron. Kip peered over the bulwark, expecting to see one of the islanders again trying to gather up that heavy-duty cable.

But the men were all standing together at the bow. They had been talking quietly, and now they stared up at the constable, their faces frozen, their lips drawn into tight lines. The others on the trawler stood where they were, watching and listening.

And all around a deep, hollow booming—something striking iron with a rising, feverish intensity.

One of the islanders cried out in fear; they all backed away from the tower, moving towards the gangplank and the safety of the trawler.

FOR FURTHER REFLECTION

"Evil has infinite forms," reads one of the epigraphs (by Pascal) that horror master Robert McCammon has selected for this novel. Evil here manifests itself in the form of a Nazi U-Boat that has just returned to the surface of a Caribbean lagoon after nearly half a century.

······································TRY THIS····································

Prepare a list of five or more plot synopses for a horror novel of your own. Let each one demonstrate the truth of Pascal's claim regarding the infinite forms that evil can assume.

Dark Sun: The Making of the Hydrogen Bomb
by Richard Rhodes

The team that Marshall Holloway [director of weapons development at Los Alamos] assembled to design and build the first megaton-scale thermonuclear—the Panda Committee, also known as the Theoretical Megaton Group—met for the first time on October 5, 1951, two days after the White House announced the detection of a second Soviet atomic-bomb explosion. ...

It was clear from the beginning that the test device would be large, since it would have to accommodate a fission primary at one end: the smallest fission bomb available of sufficient yield was forty-five inches in diameter, almost four feet. The complicated device needed thick walls of dense metal to hold it together long enough for a good burn to proceed. Steel was the metal of choice. Who could fabricate thick pieces of steel more than four feet in diameter? Whoever it was would have to be security-checked and cleared. The biggest heavy-equipment manufacturer in the United States was American Car and Foundry of Buffalo, New York, which had built blockbuster bomb casings for the US Air Force for use in Korea. Los Alamos began negotiations with ACF in October aimed at initiating engineering design; ACF started fabrication before the end of the month.

FOR FURTHER REFLECTION

Weapons manufacture requires a complex network of subsidiary projects, like bomb casings thick enough to withstand the ignition of a hydrogen bomb. Along with the networking, there must be high-level security clearances for every subcontractor.

..............................TRY THIS...................................

Writers of thriller novels often need to become familiar not only with weapons of mass destruction but with the infrastructure required to produce them and the security systems required to protect them. Outline a synopsis for a novel in which an enemy manages to plant a bomb in a government building. Include details about the bomb, how it will detonate, and where and how it was hidden.

AUGUST 30
Mad as Hell: The Life and Work of Paddy Chayefsky
by Shaun Considine

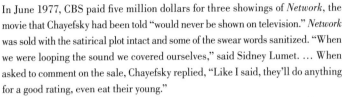

In June 1977, CBS paid five million dollars for three showings of *Network*, the movie that Chayefsky had been told "would never be shown on television." *Network* was sold with the satirical plot intact and some of the swear words sanitized. "When we were looping the sound we covered ourselves," said Sidney Lumet. ... When asked to comment on the sale, Chayefsky replied, "Like I said, they'll do anything for a good rating, even eat their young."

As the only writer to win three Academy Awards, [Chayefsky] found he was frequently lionized by new young writers wanting to know his "formula" for success. When he had the time, he answered each call and letter soliciting advice. "My father had such a caring for people starting out, for writers who were not sure about themselves at the beginning," said Dan Chayefsky. "He knew how difficult it was. Sometimes he would take me to the clubs to see the new comics. At the end of their act they would wind up talking to my dad about their work. And he was always generous with his advice and suggestions."

FOR FURTHER REFLECTION
One could say of CBS's decision to air the most caustic satire ever written about television on television that truth will win out in the end. We could also say that *Network* is not just a criticism of the television industry, it is a criticism of how corporate greed can corrupt our most precious human values.

....TRY THIS....................................

Many people harbor a love-hate attitude toward television. How would you describe yours? Make two lists: one for positive attributes, one for negative attributes. Then write your own Chayefsky-esque satire on some facet of television, or write an essay on how television programming could be improved.

AUGUST 31

If You Want to Write: A Book About Art, Independence and Spirit

by Brenda Ueland

I learned that you should feel when writing, not like Lord Byron on a mountain top, but like a child stringing beads in kindergarten—happy, absorbed and quietly putting one bead on in front of another.

Once I posed for a lot of twelve-year-old girls who wanted to try some oil painting. I said that I would sit for them for three days and all day long, until their portraits of me were all entirely finished and the very best that they could do. None of these children had painted with oil paints before. ... Everyone knows what a mysteriously difficult thing it is to draw something if you are not used to it: the weird difficulty of expressing the third dimension on flat paper! ... Moreover, to paint with oil paints for the first time—I can only describe it by saying it is like trying to make something exquisitely accurate and microscopically clear out of mud pies with boxing gloves on.

Well, that's what these children were trying to do. Yet while they were painting me there was utter dead silence in the room. You could hear their breathing. Only those burning eyes were looking up at me and down again. ...

Now these children worked for five or six hours at a stretch (and this will be the way you are going to work at your writing) for two and a half days—working with the blissful, radiant power of a Michelangelo or Blake. Their paintings were all remarkable—all different, astonishing in their own way, because the creative impulse was working innocently, not egotistically or to please someone.

FOR FURTHER REFLECTION

Writing should emulate the joyous, absorbed attentiveness of children at play, allowing the creative imagination to predominate, momentarily suspending the "rules" and expectations. Everyone sees the world differently, and these individual differences speak to what is essential in artistic expression.

..................................TRY THIS....................................

Begin writing a poem, essay, stage play, short story, or chapter of a novel, and allow yourself the complete freedom to let the piece unfold any way you wish. Keep thinking of yourself as a child at play, throwing all caution to the wind.

Anatomy of Love: The Natural History of Monogamy, Adultery, and Divorce
by Helen E. Fisher

We seem emotionally unfinished. Attached lovers, for example, tend to suffer during a period of separation such as a business trip or school vacation. [Psychiatrist Michael] Liebowitz thinks that, while apart, neither partner is getting his or her daily dose of natural narcotic drugs. Levels of the endorphins plunge. Then, as withdrawal sets in, lovers deeply miss, even crave, each other.

This romantic wiring is probably also partly responsible for the psychological and physical abuse that some men and women are willing to endure. Some rebuffed lovers make ridiculous compromises or accept hideous battering for fear of losing "him" or "her." Liebowitz proposes that these "attachment junkies" are suffering from low levels of these natural narcotic drugs, so they cling to a partner rather than risking a drop in these opiates. Like heroin addicts, they are chemically wedded to their partners. What is equally compelling, some battered partners have learned to associate the pain inflicted on them with pleasure. So as they receive abuse, levels of endorphins may actually rise—driving them to return for more pain and its corresponding high.

FOR FURTHER REFLECTION

When we say that being in love is like being drugged, we may think we're speaking metaphorically, but psychological findings suggest something much closer to literal truth.

......................................TRY THIS....................................

1. Speculate in an essay on how becoming more aware of the biochemistry of love can prove helpful (or maybe even harmful) in love relationships.
2. Write a humorous story in which the protagonist, a chemistry researcher, is experiencing (enduring?) a romantic relationship.

Icon & Idea: The Function of Art in the Development of Human Consciousness
by Herbert Read

Aldous Huxley has … shown that under the influence of the drug called mescalin a heightened sense of reality, of the "isness" of things, is induced: forms are more clearly defined, colors are more intense, etc., and this heightened sense of reality is due, according to his theory, not to an extension of normal faculties but rather to a relaxing of the inhibitions that normally reduce consciousness to manageable proportions. An artist like Cezanne, it would seem, may be attempting by intense concentration to reach a clarity of perception that can be more quickly reached by drugs, the difference being that the drugged person shows no desire or ability to record his vision in plastic images. But to record this mere sense of "isness" … is not in itself a sufficient aim of art: art is its own reality: it is the revelation or creation of an objective world, not the representation of one. This was Cezanne's great, though perhaps incidental, discovery. He found himself giving to reality—to real things like mountains, trees, and people—a structural configuration which was not the surface appearance of these things but rather their supporting geometry, their spatial depth, their immaculate colors devoid of highlights or shadows. His pictures became what he called "constructions after nature, based on the methods, the sensations and developments suggested by the model."

FOR FURTHER REFLECTION

The very *raison d'etre* of art lies in its power to convey its own reality—call it "artreality"—each individual artist's ability to bring forth a new reality fashioned out of creative imagination and skill. Unlike drug-induced "heightened" perception, artistic perception is active, intentional, and not passive.

......................................TRY THIS....................................

The next time you begin an artistic project, keep a detailed record of your activities. After the project is completed, write an essay in which you reflect on artistic production, on using the materials of reality to fashion a new reality out of your imagination.

SEPTEMBER 3

A Traveler's Guide to Mars: The Mysterious Landscapes of the Red Planet
by William K. Hartmann

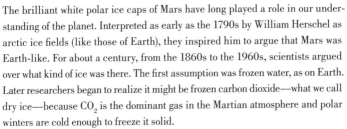

The brilliant white polar ice caps of Mars have long played a role in our understanding of the planet. Interpreted as early as the 1790s by William Herschel as arctic ice fields (like those of Earth), they inspired him to argue that Mars was Earth-like. For about a century, from the 1860s to the 1960s, scientists argued over what kind of ice was there. The first assumption was frozen water, as on Earth. Later researchers began to realize it might be frozen carbon dioxide—what we call dry ice—because CO_2 is the dominant gas in the Martian atmosphere and polar winters are cold enough to freeze it solid.

It turns out both arguments were correct! Each cap apparently has a relatively permanent central core of H_2O ice and a much larger seasonal deposit of CO_2 frost. There are two key facts to realize about the frosts and ices of the Martian polar regions: first, Mars is so cold that water is almost permanently frozen; second, CO_2 is to Mars as H_2O is to Earth. On Earth, during winter, it is water vapor in the atmosphere that condenses into frost or snowflakes, creating ice, ground-frost, or snow deposits. On Mars, during winter, it is carbon dioxide in the atmosphere that condenses into frost and frost deposits on the ground.

FOR FURTHER REFLECTION

No planet in our solar system has captivated the imagination like Mars, and it continues to do so as robotic exploration of the red planet continues, from Martian orbit and on its surface. Yes, Mars is largely a frigid, arid world; but water ice has been detected, and there's some possibility that primitive vegetation and microbial life might exist below the surface.

.................................TRY THIS....................................

1. Argue for or against the importance of Martian exploration—or of planetary exploration in general.
2. Write a story in which a human expedition to Mars discovers some form of life there. Where on Mars will they find it? What measures does the crew take to protect it (and perhaps themselves)? What impact does the discovery have on the crew? On Earth after the news is received?

The Norton History of Chemistry
by William H. Brock

In September 1931 during the celebrations of the 150th anniversary of the birth of Michael Faraday, a combined electrical and chemical exhibition was held at the Albert Hall in London. The chemical section, arranged by Henry Armstrong, aimed to illustrate how Faraday's discovery of benzene in 1825 had, through the development of chemical industry, brightened people's lives with colourful fabrics and perfumes, produced new synthetic materials such as Bakelite, casein plastics and viscose artificial silks, promoted the introduction of colour photography, aided an understanding of the chemistry of the human body, especially that of internal secretions (hormones), and revolutionized health through the drugs industry. Dominating the exhibits close by the great organ was a fourteen-foot high banner bearing benzene's signature, the sign of the hexagon, surrounding which was a frieze carrying a rainbow spectrum built up from the extensive range of subtle dyestuffs available three-quarters of a century after Perkin's discovery of mauve.

Fifty years later, although no comparable exhibition was mounted in honour of Faraday's bicentennial, the magnitude of chemists' contributions to the benefit of society goes beyond anything that Armstrong could have imagined—despite his lyrical enthusiasm for the exploits of industry. Underlying what the American chemical firm of Du Pont called "better living through chemistry" has been the chemists' ability to synthesize new products and the chemical engineers' ingenuity in industrializing invention.

FOR FURTHER REFLECTION

Chemistry, like science in general, has proven to benefit humankind in countless ways. At the same time, it has led to harmful and shameful events: the poisoning of the biosphere by dangerous pesticides; the use of napalm to defoliate the jungles of Vietnam and Cambodia, and in the process kill villagers in a hideous manner.

...................................TRY THIS...................................

Research Faraday's contributions to chemistry and write an essay about one of them, taking time to consider the long-range benefits to society—as well as any negative consequences.

The Reading of Books
by Holbrook Jackson

Unlike music, the theatre, or pictures, books can be wherever we are. They are the readiest as well as the most influential passports to territories of the mind and the imagination. It would be absurd to argue that they take the place of experience. They do nothing of the sort. What they do is to give, in the first place, experiences to the emotions and the mind which are not otherwise obtainable, and in the second, they augment the quality of living by predisposing the mind and the emotions to the adventure of contemplation, by sharpening the perceptions so that experience may be more vivid and more memorable. ...

Books may serve many purposes. If we are to take sedatives books are better than drugs. If we need respite from ourselves, what better than to take a holiday by becoming someone else? And there is no more economical or convenient refreshment than a book. Indeed it is because all these purposes are beneficial as well as desirable that readers are instinctively disposed to combine them. That need not cause surprise, for the act of reading is co-ordinative, a merging of several faculties and instincts. When we read we endeavour to satisfy desire or whim by perception and comment, and we bring to our aid all the endowments of the mind from the comparatively simple act of observation to the complex activities of creative imagination.

FOR FURTHER REFLECTION

Books enrich and augment experience; they do not replace it. It is the most effective means of understanding the lives of others, to see the world from perspectives other than our own. Reading books makes us participants in the rich, multidisciplined and multifaceted conversation of humankind. We preserve our humanity through books and the culture of books.

............................TRY THIS..............................

Why is reading important to you? Create a list of books you've read—poetry, fiction, drama, memoir, reportage, humor, and so on. Write an essay in which you reflect on the different ways you've benefited from such reading.

"Debunking Fruitcake"
by James Villas

from *Stalking the Green Fairy and*
Other Fantastic Adventures in Food and Drink

Although fruitcake can be traced back at least to an ancient Roman-baked mixture of dried fruits, seeds, nuts, and the honey wine called *satura*—and while it has modern derivatives throughout the world (German *stollen*, Portugese *morgado*, Italian *panforte*, Caribbean black cake, English Christmas pudding and simnel cake)—nowhere over the centuries has the cake evolved as an intrinsic part of the culture as it has in the American South. Needless to say, everyone in this country is as familiar with fruitcake as with meatloaf. If in recent times this confection has become the object of every bad gastronomic joke imaginable, it is only because most Americans, exposed increasingly to little more than those wretched store-bought or mail-order products, do not know, or have forgotten, what great fruitcake tastes like. This sad predicament applies as much to our professional chefs as to most home cooks, which I suppose is why, disgracefully, the last item you can ever expect to find on restaurant dessert menus is some form of fruitcake.

Southerners like my mother, on the other hand, not only still prepare the same luscious cakes made by their mothers and grandmothers and great-grandmothers but also spend days in the fall planning their baking schedules, searching for just the right ingredients, and indulging in a culinary and social tradition that is as sacred as the preparation of authentic pork barbecue. Southerners are fiercely proud of their fruitcakes. They eat them all year round.

FOR FURTHER REFLECTION

Foods often fall out of favor because culinary tastes change, just like fashion tastes. But sometimes foods will fall out of favor for the wrong reasons, like acquiring an undeserved reputation based on the worst examples rather than the best.

·······························TRY THIS·····························

1. Obtain an authentic Southern fruitcake and in a short feature, compare it with fruitcake of lesser quality.
2. Write an "Ode to Fruitcake" in which you express your sentiments toward the confection.

SEPTEMBER 7

Reading the Rocks:
The Autobiography of the Earth
by Marcia Bjornerud

James Hutton, the enlightened Scotsman who defined uniformitarianism [current geological forces as a basis for understanding geologic forces of the distant past], recognized the profundity of the silences in the rock record. In 1787 at Siccar Point, Berwickshire, near Scotland's border with England, Hutton made an observation that ranks as one of the great epiphanies of intellectual history. At this windy, wave-sculpted promontory, Hutton noted two distinct sequences of layered rock: an upper sequence in which the strata were nearly horizontal (close to the orientation in which they were presumably deposited), and a lower sequence in which the layers were nearly vertical, standing on end like books on a library shelf. Between these two sequences was a non-planar surface along which pebbles derived from the lower rocks were strewn in an irregular layer. Hutton later wrote that on seeing this surface, he "grew giddy from peering into the abyss of time," because he understood that it represented the countless centuries necessary to erode a mountain belt—whose roots were represented by the vertical layers—down to sea level (where the sediments of the overlying rocks were laid down).

FOR FURTHER REFLECTION

Geological time—time expressed in millions and even billions of years—is difficult to imagine because such a scale vastly transcends human experience. But when Hutton came upon vertically laid-out rock strata, the only explanation was that they had been laid down horizontally and then uplifted as mountains formed—a process that had to have taken countless centuries.

..................................TRY THIS..................................

Compose a meditation (in poetry or prose) on deep time. For example, you might compare natural events that can occur within a human lifetime—flooding, erosion, volcanic eruptions—with events that can only occur over countless millennia, like continental drift and the wearing down of mountain ranges. How does insight into deep time contribute to our sense of reality?

"Nero"

by Julius Cicatrix and Martin Rowson

from *Imperial Exits*

Compared to killing his mother, killing a wife or two came relatively easy [for Nero]. The first one, Claudius's daughter Octavia, was banished to a small island and murdered shortly afterwards. He then married Poppaea Sabina, one of the beauties of the age, but she came a cropper when she criticized Nero for coming home late from the races. He kicked her to death in a rage, even though she was pregnant.

His overthrow came in AD 68, and was a curious mix of domestic conspiracy and provincial revolt. The revolt was led by one Julius Vindex, governor of Gaul. Vindex's local levies were easily squashed by the mighty Rhine army, however, and for a moment it looked as if Nero had won. But if the Rhine legions didn't like Vindex (a Gallic upstart) they weren't too keen on Nero either. And in fact Galba, governor of Spain, had already been proclaimed emperor instead.

Nero hung on at Rome, hoping the trouble would pass, but Galba's agents got to work on his officials, and Nero's cruelty and extortion came home to roost.

FOR FURTHER REFLECTION

If power corrupts, then nowhere was corruption through power more blatant than in Imperial Rome, where the emperors (like the Egyptian pharaohs before them) were considered divine. Some divinity! No one in the annals of history exhibited such a lethal combination of insanity and cruelty than Nero, who literally brought the city to ruin by the time his reign (and his decadent life) came to an end.

. . . . TRY THIS . . . .

Create a one-act play starring Nero and one of his wives or one of his generals. Dramatize scenes that call attention to Nero's madness as well as his cruelty in the way he interacts with others close to him.

SEPTEMBER 9

The Waning of the Middle Ages
by J. Huizinga

In the blind passion with which people followed their lord or their party, the unshakable sentiment of right, characteristic of the Middle Ages, is trying to find expression. Man at that time is convinced that right is absolutely fixed and certain. Justice should prosecute the unjust everywhere and to the end. Reparation and retribution have to be extreme, and assume the character of revenge. In this exaggerated need of justice, primitive barbarism, pagan at bottom, blends with the Christian conception of society. The Church, on the other hand, had inculcated gentleness and clemency, and tried, in that way, to soften judicial morals. On the other hand, in adding to the primitive need of retribution the horror of sin, it had, to a certain extent, stimulated the sentiment of justice. And sin, to violent and impulsive spirits, was only too frequently another name for what their enemies did. The barbarous idea of retaliation was reinforced by fanaticism. The chronic insecurity made the greatest possible severity on the part of the public authorities desirable; crime came to be regarded as a menace to order and society, as well as an insult to divine majesty. Thus it was natural that the late Middle Ages should become the special period of judicial cruelty. That the criminal deserved his punishment was not doubted for a moment. The popular sense of justice always sanctioned the most rigorous penalties.

FOR FURTHER REFLECTION

Justice in the Middle Ages was tempered with revenge: not surprising in an age when good and evil were unambiguous and absolute, and enemies of the state or the church were placed in the same category as demons and devils. It took a long time before rule of law could finally detach itself from supernatural or divine directives.

................................TRY THIS................................

Write a medieval or Renaissance courtroom drama in which modern secular notions of justice collide with divine or supernatural ones. Think, for example, of Arthur Miller's *The Crucible*, a play based on the Salem witch hunts and trials.

SEPTEMBER 10
Man of the People:
A Life of Harry S. Truman
by Alonzo L. Hamby

The refusal to face reality in Tokyo imparted nearly unstoppable momentum to the planning for military use of the bomb. Of those with whom Truman talked in the final stages, no one was more important than [Secretary of War Henry] Stimson, who had his total respect and was directly responsible for the Manhattan Project. When Stimson insisted on dropping Kyoto from the target list for the atomic bomb, Truman concurred, in Stimson's words, "with the utmost emphasis." The military saw Kyoto as a prime industrial target; Stimson saw it as a city of shrines and cultural centers that could not be destroyed without alienating the Japanese population.

Stimson was probably also the key figure, if only through his refusal to wield a veto, in persuading Truman to adopt a strategy of dropping the first two bombs in rapid succession; the idea was to convince the Japanese that the United States had a large stockpile. As to the decision to use the bomb, there was no dissent among the primary advisers. ...

Issued from Potsdam on July 26 [1945] in the names of Truman, Attlee, and Chiang Kai-shek of China, the proclamation demanding the unconditional surrender of Japan was a stern document that presented as the alternative "the inevitable and complete destruction of the Japanese armed forces and the utter devastation of the Japanese homeland." ... Two days later, Japanese prime minister Kantaro Suzuki issued a statement at a press conference rejecting the Potsdam ultimatum.

FOR FURTHER REFLECTION

History, as Ralph Waldo Emerson reminds us, is essentially biography: Before we can begin to understand the reasons underlying a historical event, such as the decision to bomb or not bomb a given city, or the reason for rejecting a surrender ultimatum, we need to understand the thoughts and motives, as well as actions, of the men and women involved.

......................................TRY THIS....................................

Revisit a pivotal moment in recent history—such as the decision behind going to war, passing or rescinding a law, or launching a new scientific or economic program—and, in a short story or essay, present it from the perspective of the individuals most responsible for its enactment.

SEPTEMBER 11

The Voyage of Argo
by Apollonius of Rhodes
Translated by E.V. Rieu

Jason wept as he turned his eyes away from the land of his birth. But the rest struck
the rough sea with their oars in time with Orpheus's lyre, like young men bringing
down their quick feet on the earth in unison with one another and the lyre, as they
dance for Apollo round his altar at Pytho, or in Ortygia, or by the waters of Ismenus.
Their blades were swallowed by the waves, and on either side the dark salt water
broke into foam, seething angrily in answer to the strong men's strokes. The armour
on the moving ship glittered in the sunshine like fire; and all the time she was followed by a long white wake which stood out like a path across a green plain.

All the gods looked down from heaven that day, observing Argo and the spirit
shown by her heroic crew, the noblest seamen of their time; and from the mountain
heights the Nymphs of Pelion admired Athene's work and the gallant Argonauts
themselves, tugging at the oars. ... Till they had left the harbour and its curv-
ing shores behind them, the ship was in the expert hands of Tiphys, wise son of
Hagnias, who used the polished steering-oar to keep her on her course. But now
they ... hauled the sail up to the masthead and unfurled it. The shrill wind filled
it out; and after making the halyards fast on deck, each round its wooden pin, they
sailed on at their ease past the long Tisaean headland, while Orpheus played his
lyre and sang them a sweet song of highborn Artemis, Saver of ships.

FOR FURTHER REFLECTION
In the ancient myths, mortals and gods interacted, the latter bestowing favors,
taking sides, meting out severe punishments against transgressors. In the
Voyage of Argo, Jason and his fellow Argonauts emerge as individuals rather
than types, so that we gain a keener sense of the struggle one must go through
to overcome terrible obstacles.

................................TRY THIS................................

The ancient myths have been retold many times. Select a favorite story, such as
Jason's quest for the Golden Fleece or Perseus slaying the Medusa, and retell
it in a modern context.

"My Mistress' Eyes Are Nothing Like the Sun"

by William Shakespeare

My mistress' eyes are nothing like the sun;
Coral is far more red than her lips' red;
If snow be white, why then her breasts are dun;
If hairs be wires, black wires grow on her head.
I have seen roses damasked red and white,
But no such roses see I in her cheeks;
And in some perfumes is there more delight
Than in the breath that from my mistress reeks.
I love to hear her speak, yet well I know
That music hath a far more pleasing sound;
I grant I never saw a goddess go:
My mistress, when she walks, treads on the ground.
    And yet, by heaven, I think my love as rare
    As any she, belied with false compare.

FOR FURTHER REFLECTION

Many a sonneteer during the Renaissance used this versatile poetic form to adulate the beloved. Not surprisingly, such love poetry became a convention, and Shakespeare himself made good use of it—but not with this sonnet, where he defies the conventional expectation of comparing the beloved's eyes to the sun, her cheeks to roses, and so on. The result is a delightful, startlingly modern effort to celebrate female beauty for its naturalistic attributes.

......................................TRY THIS....................................

Compose a love poem in which you describe the loved one in naturalistic language, without resorting to clichés or exaggerated description.

SEPTEMBER 13

"The Effect of Newness on the Imagination," *Spectator* No. 412
by Joseph Addison

Everything that is new or uncommon raises a pleasure in the imagination because it fills the soul with an agreeable surprise, gratifies its curiosity, and gives it an idea of which it was not before possessed. We are indeed so often conversant with one set of objects, and tired out with so many repeated shows of the same things, that whatever is new or uncommon contributes a little to vary human life, and to divert our minds, for a while, with the strangeness of its appearance. It serves us for a kind of refreshment, and takes off from that satiety we are apt to complain of in our usual and ordinary entertainments. It is this that bestows charms on a monster, and makes even the imperfections of nature please us. It is this that recommends variety, where the mind is every instant called off to something new, and the attention not suffered to dwell too long, and waste itself on any particular object. It is this, likewise, that improves what is great or beautiful, and makes it afford the mind a double entertainment. Groves, fields, and meadows are at any season of the year pleasant to look upon, but never so much as in the opening of the spring, when they are all new and fresh, with their first gloss upon them, and not yet too much accustomed and familiar to the eye. For this reason there is nothing that more enlivens a prospect than rivers, *jets d'eau*, or falls of water, where the scene is perpetually shifting, and entertaining the sight every moment with something that is new.

FOR FURTHER REFLECTION

The eighteenth century is often called the Age of Reason or the Enlightenment. It was a time when modern empirical science—thanks largely to the momentous discoveries of Isaac Newton—blossomed. But it was also the age of aesthetic taste, the cultivation of beauty in the arts. This led essayists and journalists like Joseph Addison and Richard Steele to extol the virtues of the imagination, of the artistic temperament—the wellspring of the arts.

......................................TRY THIS....................................

How do imagination and reason contradict or complement each other? You might consider certain examples of scientific discovery (Newton's work on optics and the properties of light, for example) that may have had a profound influence on philosophy, art, or literature. Convey your thoughts in an essay.

Moby-Dick
by Herman Melville

There seemed no sign of common bodily illness about [Ahab], nor of the recovery from any. He looked like a man cut away from the stake, when the fire has overrunningly wasted all the limbs without consuming them, or taking away one particle from their compacted aged robustness. His whole high, broad form seemed made of solid bronze, and shaped in an unalterable mould, like Cellini's cast Perseus. Threading its way out from among his grey hairs, and continuing right down one side of his tawny scorched face and neck, till it disappeared in his clothing, you saw a slender rod-like mark, lividly whitish. It resembled that perpendicular seam sometimes made in the straight, lofty trunk of a great tree, when the upper lightning tearingly darts down it, and without wrenching a single twig, peels and grooves out the bark from top to bottom, ere running off into the soil, leaving the tree still greenly alive, but branded. Whether that mark was born with him, or whether it was the scar left by some desperate wound, no one could certainly say. By some tacit consent, throughout the voyage little or no allusion was made to it, especially by the mates. But once Tashtego's senior, an old Gay-Head Indian among the crew, superstitiously asserted that not till he was full forty years old did Ahab become that way branded, and then it came upon him, not in the fury of any mortal fray, but in an elemental strife at sea.

FOR FURTHER REFLECTION

Few works of literature embody so many truths and pose so many quandaries, on so many levels, as *Moby-Dick*; the whale-quest of the *Pequod* crew embodies humanity's quest to probe the deepest mysteries of reality. But this is also a story of the rich diversity of the human community, from Queequeg's pagan spirituality to Ahab's Faustian desire to overpower the forces of nature.

.................................TRY THIS..............................

Ships—self-contained societies embarked upon some voyage—can be a powerful symbol for society. Write a story that takes place on a ship (such as a riverboat, that has set out to study an obscure tribe of rain forest dwellers). Create a conflict situation among the crew members—say, for example, between the captain's insistence on noninterference and some crew members' insistence that they interact with the natives.

SEPTEMBER 15

The Story of Edgar Sawtelle
by David Wroblewski

In all his life, Edgar had seen only one real dog fight. That had been broken up
when his parents sprayed water on the antagonists, hauling them away by their
tails. Later, his father said a person never, *ever* reached between fighting dogs.
To make his point, he'd pulled up his sleeve and shown Edgar the puckered scar
running along the axis of his forearm, jagged and shiny. A dog in a fight will bite
before it realizes what it's doing, he'd said. It won't mean to hurt you, but it will
see motion and react.

Some of the dogs were backing away from Finch and Epi, hackles raised.
Edgar clapped his hands, grabbed two dogs, and hauled them into the nearest
pen. Then another two. … He kenneled Tinder, Essay, and Pout. Baboo had
already retreated to his run; Edgar shoved Opal and Umbra in after him and
ran down the aisle wrestling dogs into their pens one after another and slinging
shut the doors.

When he turned, only three dogs remained in the kennel aisle: Finch, Epi, and
Almondine. Finch lay on his back. Epi stood over him, jaws buried in the fur at
the base of his throat. On her muzzle there was a smear of red. Finch alternately
lay limp and struggled to escape. A pace away, Almondine stood with her lips
raised, growling, but the moment she stepped forward, Epi released Finch and
lashed her muzzle toward Almondine, ears flattened. Almondine jerked her head
away but stood her ground.

FOR FURTHER REFLECTION

We are endlessly fascinated by canine behavior partly because dogs can teach
us a lot about ourselves. Edgar Sawtelle, a deaf-mute, has acquired an intimate knowledge of dogs not only from training them, but from tapping deeply
into their psyches and learning to see the world through their eyes.

·· TRY THIS ································

Write a boy-and-his-dog or girl-and-her-dog adventure story for young readers.
One possibility: The boy or girl gets lost in the woods, but the dog leads him
or her to safety. Another possibility: The dog teaches the boy or girl a valuable
lesson about survival in the wilderness.

Prozac Diary
by Lauren Slater

I wanted to tell the Prozac Doctor about my hands. I wanted to splay them across his desk and say, "Look at them. What are they seeking?" I wanted him to touch my hands, not really an odd desire, the laying on of hands a practice as ancient as the Bible itself. The Prozac Doctor was biblical to me. I invited him to take on that role, the role every sick person needs her healer to play—not only technician, but poet, priest, theologian, and friend. I know this was asking a lot, poor man, but few people are as full of need and desire as the patient.

Instead, he reached down, opened a desk drawer, and pulled out a sample pill packet. He did not need to ask me many questions, as he had my entire chart before him, thick as an urban phone book. The packet was rather unimpressive, plain white, with a perforated top. To my surprise, he lifted it to his lips and tore at it with his teeth, then gently tapped at it until a smooth pill slid from its foiled pouch into the clean cup of his palm.

There it lay, cream and green. Tiny black letters were stamped down its side—DISTA—which sounded to me like an astronomy term, the name of a planet in another galaxy. On and on my mind went, making from this small capsule many private metaphors—it was candy, no poison; protein, no plastic.

FOR FURTHER REFLECTION

Where do we draw the line between spiritual healing and medicinal healing? In her absorbing and beautifully written memoir about living with OCD (obsessive compulsive disorder), Lauren Slater, who holds a master's degree in psychology from Harvard and a doctorate from Boston University, gives us the impression that the distinction is ambiguous. Psychological disorders like OCD, Slater suggests, demand that the doctor become a Healer with a capital H.

. . . . TRY THIS . . . .

Think back to when you or someone you know suffered from an emotional disturbance of some kind. How did you recover from it? Who helped you through the ordeal, and how? Write a narrative in which you capture this harrowing experience vividly, dramatically.

The Liars' Club: A Memoir
by Mary Karr

Of all the men in the Liars' Club, Daddy told the best stories. When he started one, the guys invariably fell quiet, studying their laps or their cards or the inner rims of their beer mugs like men in prayer. No matter how many tangents he took or how far the tale flew from its starting point before he reeled it back, he had this gift: he knew how to be believed. He mastered it the way he mastered bluffing in poker, which probably happened long before my appearance. His tough half-breed face would move between solemn blankness and sudden caricature. He kept stock expressions for stock characters. When his jaw jutted and stiffened and his eyes squinted, I expected to hear the faint brogue of his uncle Husky. ...

Cooter has just asked Daddy if he had planned to run away from home. "They wasn't no planning to it," Daddy says, then lights a cigarette to stall, picking a few strands of tobacco off his tongue as if that gesture may take all the time in the world. "Poppa give me a silver dollar and told me to get into town and buy some coffee. Had to cross the train tracks to get there. When that old train come around the turn, it had to slow up. Well, when it slowed up, I jumped, and that dollar come with me. ..."

FOR FURTHER REFLECTION

The art of storytelling lies largely in the manner of telling—the pacing, the buildup of anticipation, the careful selection of minute details to add an aura of authenticity. Karr's memoir, like her father's tall tales, also draws us irresistibly into the situations she recreates—except that these situations are factual, not invented.

............................TRY THIS................................

Narrate an event in your life using the techniques of a fiction writer—suspense buildup, sensory impressions, use of dialogue, mood-setting descriptions. Make sure, however, that the events you describe actually happened.

SEPTEMBER 18

The Carbon Murder:
A Periodic Table Mystery
by Camille Minichino

"According to your statement, Dr. Frederick, you added illegal compounds to microchips intended for use as identification codes for horses, is that correct?"

"I manipulated the ketone using a Grignard reagent. It involves adding a carbon anion. It's not illegal, just not approved for wide distribution."

"Not approved, thank you. And to your knowledge is it legal to use chemicals *not approved* by the Food and Drug Administration?"

Lorna sighed and leaned into her lawyer. Mr. Di Marco said something inaudible, covering the side of his face with long, slender fingers, one of which sported a large school ring.

"No, it is not," Lorna said.

"Not legal to use chemicals unapproved by the Food and Drug Administration?"

"No, it is not legal," Lorna said, with an exasperated sigh.

FOR FURTHER REFLECTION

Imagine learning a lot about chemistry by reading suspenseful murder mysteries. Such is the case with Camille Minichino's Periodic Table mysteries—each novel unfolding around a chemical element. Minichino reminds us of the important role that scientific knowledge, along with Sherlock Holmes–like logical deduction, can play in solving mysteries.

...................................TRY THIS....................................

Put your knowledge of science to use in a mystery story. For example, you might write a story about an amateur astronomer who commits certain crimes during certain phases of the moon, or a story about an ex-medical student who uses certain drugs to mimic a heart attack or seizure.

SEPTEMBER 19

The Parrot's Lament, and Other True Tales of Animal Intrigue, Intelligence, and Ingenuity

by Eugene Linden

In nature, deception runs the gamut from trickery that is genetically encoded to sophisticated ruses knowingly perpetrated. In the former category, for instance, the Rafflesia of Borneo, which at three feet across is the world's largest flower, evolved to look and smell like rotting meat to trick carrion-eating flies into serving as its pollinators. Another born liar is one particular moth caterpillar of Meso-america, which has a colored pattern on its underbody that makes the bug look for all the world like a viper. Over time, some animals have learned that it is in their interest to give false signals. For instance, the white-winged shrike tanager serves as a sentinel for other birds in the western Amazon. It provides an early-warning system through its vigilance, but according to ornithologist Charles Munn, the bird also takes advantage of its position by occasionally making the alarm call when no hawk is around. As its feathered colleagues head for cover, it wolfs down all the food in sight.

Another bird that resorts to deception is the zone-tailed hawk, which will initiate the flight pattern of a vulture, complete with rocking wings, in order to lull macaws or parakeets into a false sense of security. (Birds have nothing to fear from a scavenger.) Once the camouflaged predator has gotten overhead, it swoops down to attack the smaller birds.

FOR FURTHER REFLECTION

We sometimes use the word *clever* to describe the ruses that birds and other animals in the wild resort to in order to improve their security, improve their food supplies, and more effectively attract mates; but it isn't so much cleverness or cunning as it is the creature's struggle for survival competing with other creatures also struggling for survival. If they are clever enough, they will survive long enough to breed and pass along those superior survival genes to offspring. This is how species not only survive but evolve.

. . . . TRY THIS . . . .

Children are fascinated by animal behavior. Select a species and describe its survival tactics—camouflage, mimicry—in an article slanted for young readers.

SEPTEMBER 20
"Empiricism"
by T.Z. Lavine

from *From Socrates to Sartre: The Philosophic Quest*

From the very early days of empiricism in the work of John Locke, empiricism shows itself to be a deliberate and defiant rejection of philosophic rationalism, and especially of Descartes. All the empiricists rejected what they came to call Cartesianism—the rationalistic building of great deductive systems of philosophy purporting to have grasped by the powers of reason alone the nature of total reality—man, nature, and God—and to have achieved complete mathematical certainty in this knowledge by the use of logical deduction from self-evident axioms. In sharpest rejection of this, the empiricists are suspicious of metaphysical systems constructed by reason.

Empiricism ... offers no speculations or world views for humans to live by. It remains only a theory of knowledge, a theory of what we can know. Empiricists claim that we can know reliably only what comes to us by sensory experience, by observation and experiment, and by testing through experience. Empiricism is thus basing knowledge upon the senses, upon the flux of the sensible world, which the two great rationalists, Plato and Descartes, rejected as an inferior way of knowing.

FOR FURTHER REFLECTION

It is probably no coincidence that as empiricism began to overshadow rationalism in the seventeenth century, science as we know it—examination and analysis through strict application of experimental method—also began to flourish. The cost of course is the abolition of metaphysical systems like idealism or notions of absolute reality.

.................................TRY THIS....................................

Do you agree or disagree with the empiricists that human knowledge is limited by the senses? Before drawing your conclusions, review the arguments set forth by rationalists, like Descartes, and empiricists, like John Locke.

Hyperspace: A Scientific Odyssey Through Parallel Universes, Time Warps, and the Tenth Dimension

by Michio Kaku

On June 10, 1854, a new geometry was born.

The theory of higher dimensions was introduced when Georg Bernhard Riemann gave his celebrated lecture before the faculty of the University of Göttingen in Germany. In one masterful stroke, like opening up a musty, darkened room to the brilliance of a warm summer's sun, Riemann's lecture exposed the world to the dazzling properties of higher-dimensional space.

His profoundly important and exceptionally elegant essay, "On the Hypotheses Which Lie at the Foundation of Geometry," toppled the pillars of classical Greek geometry, which had successfully weathered all assaults by skeptics for 2 millennia. The old geometry of Euclid, in which all geometric figures are two or three dimensional, came tumbling down as a new Riemannian geometry emerged from its ruins. The Riemannian revolution would have vast implications for the future of the arts and sciences. Within 3 decades of his talk, the "mysterious fourth dimension" would influence the evolution of art, philosophy, and literature in Europe. Within 6 decades of Riemann's lecture, Einstein would use four-dimensional Riemannian geometry to explain the creation of the universe and its evolution. And 130 years after his lecture, physicists would use ten-dimensional geometry to attempt to unite all the laws of the physical universe. The core of Riemann's work was the realization that physical laws simplify in higher-dimensional space.

FOR FURTHER REFLECTION

Once the fourth dimension (time) was perceived as part of physical reality (an object's passage through time becomes a part of its reality), a new geometry needed to be created to describe its properties. Without it, post-Newtonian physics could not have developed.

....................................TRY THIS....................................

Create a diagram that traces your timeline from the time you got out of bed this morning until this moment. The lines that connect your movements from location A to location B to location C and so forth will form a diagram that is not only spatial but temporal. Write a short explanation of this concept for young readers.

"The Origin of Batman"

by Ron Goulart

from *Great American Comic Books*

In its earliest incarnation, *The Bat* was a highly popular Broadway play by Avery Hopwood and Mary Roberts Rinehart. It was filmed for the first time in 1926 and again in 1931 under the title *The Bat Whisper*. ... Basically an "old dark house" story, it had to do with stolen money, secret rooms and hidden passages, and a crazed killer who dresses up like a bat. The night-stalking Bat of the 1931 version certainly seems to be an ancestor of Batman, particularly when prowling the rooftops and casting his weird shadow across walls. [Bob] Kane [creator of Batman] is on record as having been influenced by this movie.

In civilian life Batman was Bruce Wayne, "a bored young socialite." When night fell, however, playboy Wayne became "powerful and awesome," a "weird menace to all crime." Unlike his more sedate contemporaries in the private investigator line, Batman didn't wait for cases to come to him. He prowled the city—New York in the earliest adventures and later Gotham City—looking for trouble. He always found it, dropping down to shock the bejeesus out of burglars, kidnappers, and murderers. ...

Batman's origin, the inside story of "who he is and how he came to be," didn't appear until *Detective* #33 (November 1939). In a terse two-page account readers were told that fifteen years earlier Bruce Wayne's parents were gunned down on the street by a stickup man. The boy, a witness to the crime, vowed to dedicate his life to "warring on criminals." Having no supernatural powers, Wayne had to work at becoming a hero.

FOR FURTHER REFLECTION

Comic book heroes are no less heroic than those from the ancient myths. Much of Batman's heroic appeal, unlike Superman's, lies in the fact that he stretches the limits of what is humanly possible rather than making use of supernatural or extraterrestrial powers.

......................................TRY THIS...................................

Create a comic book hero or heroine, one who achieves astonishing feats through ingenious applications of ordinary human attributes. After compiling a detailed list of this person's heroic attributes and an explanation of his or her origins, write out a scenario that will show your hero or heroine in action.

The Cradle of Thought: Exploring the Origins of Thinking
by Peter Hobson

When a child does not experience the forms of social engagement that are typically human, then both self-awareness and thinking are seriously affected. Even more illuminating is what we learn about the *qualities* of self-awareness and thinking that are defective. It is not that everything goes, but only some aspects of self-consciousness and only some kinds of thinking.

We can see this in the following description of a man who seems unable to follow the normal pathways of thought, but only in specific respects. The selectiveness of his deficits tells us that we are not encountering someone with mental retardation. This is not a person who, for some genetic or environmental reason, lacks adequate hardware in the brain to support thinking processes. On the contrary, he seems to have the potential for quite extraordinary feats of memory and deduction. Yet he is so obviously handicapped when it comes to common-sense thinking. ... His limitations in thinking about things go along with lack of thought about himself.

This person was one of the first people with autism to be described in detail ... in 1945. Despite serious and disabling intellectual difficulties, he was capable of telling the day of the week for any given date between about 1880 and 1950. ... He could spell forwards and backwards. He could play melodies by ear. At the same time, L was unable to understand or create an imaginary situation. He did not play with toys, nor did he show any sign that he understood make-believe. ... In fact L had never shown interest in his social surroundings.

FOR FURTHER REFLECTION

By studying and treating people with neurological disorders like autism, doctors can gain insight into the processes of thinking, of language formation and the ability to communicate with others. One also hopes that such insight will lead toward more successful treatment of these debilitating disorders.

...................................TRY THIS...................................

After reading case histories of children or adults with autism, write a short story in which a person with autism, with the help of doctors, nurses, and parents, gradually learns to overcome much of his disability.

Paris to the Moon
by Adam Gopnik

A French school term that I have learned to love is *leçons des choses*, lessons from things. It refers to a whole field of study, which you learn in class, or used to, that traces civilization's progress from stuff to things. The wonderful posters in Deyrolle, which [my wife] Martha and I love and have collected, were made for *leçons des choses*. They show the passage of coffee from the bean to the porcelain coffeepot, of wine from the vine and soil to the bottle, of sugar from the cane to the *clafoutis*. They always show the precise costume that the beans and grapes and stuff end up in: the chateau bottling, the painted coffeepot, the label on the jam jar. The Deyrolle posters simultaneously remind you that even the best things always have some stuff leaking out their edges—a bit of the barnyard, a stain of soil—and that even the worst stuff is really OK, because it can all be civilized into things. The *choses*, the things, are what matters.

Of all the *leçons des choses* I have absorbed in Paris, the most important has come from learning to cook. I cooked a bit in New York, Thanksgiving dinner and a filet mignon or two, and summers by the grill, like every American guy. But here I cook compulsively, obsessively, waking up with a plate in mind, balancing it with wine and side dishes throughout the working day.

FOR FURTHER REFLECTION

We already know that Paris is famous for fine cuisine, but it is also the city that inspires one's own desire to cook, as Adam Gopnik, author of the Paris Journals for *The New Yorker*, has discovered. Part of the pleasure would certainly be shopping for the meats and produce and spices that would enable one to conjure up memorable dishes.

......................................TRY THIS................................

Write an essay on a gourmet meal you will have prepared for a special occasion, such as an anniversary, birthday, welcome-home celebration, or holiday. To prepare for the essay, take detailed notes of the ingredients you purchased, each step of preparation, the table layout, and the dining experience itself.

"Apollo and Dionysus"

by Camille Paglia

from *Sexual Personae: Art and Decadence From*
Nefertiti to Emily Dickinson

In Egypt, sky-cult and earth-cult were harmonized, but in Greece there is a split. Greek greatness is Apollonian. The gods live on a peak touching the sky. Olympus and Parnassus are mountain shrines of creative power spurning the earth. In that swerve upward is the sublime conceptualism of western intellect and art. Egypt gave Greece the pillar and monumental sculpture, which Greece turns from Pharaoh to *kouros*, from divine king to divine boy. Hidden in these gifts lay Egypt's Apollonianism, which Greek artists so splendidly develop. The orderly mathematic of the Doric temple is an orchestration of Egyptian ideas. Pheidias brings person and building together on the Acropolis or High City, Athens' magic mountain. Egypt invented clarity of image, the essence of Apollonianism. From Old Kingdom Pharaohs to Pheidias is two thousand years but one step in the history of art. ...

In Judeo-Christianity man is made in God's image, but in Greek religion God is made in man's image. The Greek gods have a higher human beauty, their flesh incorruptible yet sensual. Greece, unlike Egypt, never worshipped beast gods. Greek sky-cult kept nature in her place. The visibility of the Greek gods is intellectual, symbolizing mind's victory over matter. Art, a glorification of matter, wins its independence to the gods' perfection.

FOR FURTHER REFLECTION

The gods Apollo and Dionysus represent the two principal aspects of human nature, logic and passion; orderliness and sensuous expression. In ancient Greece both aspects were exploited with great results. The Apollonian was predominant in philosophy, politics, science, and sculpture; the Dionysian in religious cults. In Greek drama and sculpture, however the Apollonian and Dionysian seemed to be in balance.

. . . . .TRY THIS. . . . .

Write two poems on a single subject. Compose the first poem in an Apollonian manner, adhering to a traditional poetic form such as a sonnet or rhymed couplets, and using vivid but not-too-unusual imagery. Next, rewrite the poem in a Dionysian manner, adhering to no preestablished poetic form and using highly unconventional imagery.

SEPTEMBER 26
"Whitman"
by D.H. Lawrence

from *Studies in Classic American Literature*

"And of these one and all I weave the song of myself."

Do you? Well, then, it just shows you haven't *got* any self. It's a mush, not a woven thing. A hotch-potch, not a tissue. Your self.

Oh, Walter, Walter, what have you done with it? What have you done with yourself? With your own individual self? For it sounds as if it had all leaked out of you, leaked into the universe.

Post mortem effects. The individuality had leaked out of him.

No, no, don't lay this down to poetry. These are post mortem effects. And Walt's great poems are really huge fat tomb-plants, great rank graveyard growths.

All that false exuberance. All those lists of things boiled in one pudding-cloth! No, no!

I don't want all those things inside me, thank you.

"I reject nothing," says Walt.

If that is so, one must be a pipe open at both ends, so everything runs through.

Post mortem effects.

"I embrace ALL," says Whitman. "I weave all things into myself."

Do you really! There can't be much left of *you* when you've done. When you've cooked the awful pudding of One Identity.

FOR FURTHER REFLECTION

Literary criticism as *humor*? Who would have believed it possible—yet here, in this acerbic little volume by the great early twentieth-century English novelist and poet D.H. Lawrence, we have a rare masterful example of this unusual subgenre. Other examples include Oscar Wilde's "The Critic as Artist" and Mark Twain's "Fenimore Cooper's Literary Offenses." Lest we fall too quickly under the rhetorical spell of a great poet like Whitman, Lawrence reacts with unaffected, colloquial bluntness to Whitman's grandiose proclamations. Do they make good sense, or are they just examples of bloated rhetoric?

. . . . TRY THIS. . . . .

Read or reread some of Whitman's poetry, then respond to Lawrence's commentary, either in a straightforward or a witty manner.

There Are Doors
by Gene Wolfe

[Mr. Green to Fanny]: "When you've been around someone from the other world, you see doors. Anything that's closed on all four sides can be one. It looks *significant*; that was [Lara's] word. If you go through, you cross over. But then if you turn around to go back, you don't go back. It isn't a door anymore, for you. You have to back out."

He snapped his fingers, and Fanny said, "What is it now?"

"Why is it a door looks the same on both sides?"

"Do they? Beats me."

"Because it is. That's what makes it a door. Shut your eyes. Go on ..."

She did.

"Now, you've eaten here before, and you brought me here. What's the full, official name of this restaurant?"

She considered for a moment. "There's a sign outside with brass letters. *Trattoria Capini.*"

He sighed and said, "All right, now open them again." He handed her a book of matches that had been lying on the table.

Fanny glanced at the cover. "'Capini's Italian Cuisine.' Okay, it's not quite the same."

He put down his fork. "This restaurant—I call it Mama's—in my world. It's the place where I've eaten for years. The other one—the *Trattoria*—is in yours ... Anyway, the door of the *Trattoria* is a Door. People from your world who've been with people from mine can get into mine by walking through it, like you did when you came in with me."

FOR FURTHER REFLECTION

Imagine being able to move back and forth from one reality to another—to enter a world in which, say, men die after having sex, which happens to be one of the bizarre characteristics of the universe where Lara, the goddess-like woman Mr. Green loves, lives.

...................................TRY THIS..................................

Create a love story that takes place in more than one reality—one in which the lover must seek out the beloved in a different (alternate) universe. How does he cross over? What other obstacles must he face in his beloved's reality—geographical boundaries, time reckoning, social customs?

"The Turn of the Screw"
by Henry James

How can I retrace today the strange steps of my obsession? There were times of our being together when I would have been ready to swear that ... they had visitors who were known and were welcome. Then it was that, had I not been deterred by the very chance that such an injury might prove greater than the injury to be averted, my exaltation would have broken out. "They're here, they're here, you little wretches," I would have cried, "and you can't deny it now!" The little wretches [Miles and Flora] denied it with all the added volume of their sociability and their tenderness, just in the crystal depths of which—like the flash of a fish in a stream—the mockery of their advantage peeped up. The shock in truth had sunk into me still deeper than I knew on the night when, looking out either for Quint or Miss Jessel under the stars, I had seen there the boy over whose rest I watched and who had immediately brought in with him—had straightway there turned on me—the lovely upward look with which, from the battlements above us, the hideous apparition of Quint and played. If it was a question of a scare my discovery on this occasion had scared me more than any other, and it was essentially in the scared state that I drew my actual conclusions.

FOR FURTHER REFLECTION

Can children—who, practically by definition, are supposed to be innocent—become corrupted by evil spirits? Like Nathaniel Hawthorne before him, Henry James explores the gray zone between good and evil, reality and illusion, the natural and the supernatural.

......................................TRY THIS..................................

Compose a short story or novella set in a house or forest, in which strange occurrences may or may not be caused by the supernatural. Either sustain the ambiguity throughout or disclose in a climactic scene whether the demons are real or are the result of living (but no less evil) persons masquerading as ghouls.

SEPTEMBER 29
The Myth of the Machine: Technics and Human Development
by Lewis Mumford

Modern man has formed a curiously distorted picture of himself, by interpreting his early history in terms of his present interests in making machines and conquering nature. And then in turn he has justified his present concerns by calling his prehistoric self a tool-making animal, and assuming that the material instruments of production dominated all his other activities. ...

I shall find it necessary as a generalist to challenge this narrow view. There is sound reason to believe that man's brain was from the beginning far more important than his hands, and its size could not be derived solely from his shaping or using of tools; that ritual and language and social organization which left no material traces whatever, although constantly present in every culture, were probably man's most important artifacts from the earliest stages on; and that so far from conquering nature or reshaping his environment primitive man's first concern was to utilize his overdeveloped, intensely active nervous system, and to give form to a human self, set apart from his original animal self by the fabrication of symbols—the only tools that could be constructed out of the resources provided by his own body: dreams, images and sounds.

FOR FURTHER REFLECTION

Has our human destiny been shaped primarily by our toolmaking, nature-conquering capacity or by our large and complex brains and nervous systems? For Mumford the former view is narrow because it does not do justice to the formative powers of symbol-making (including language)—powers of mind that enable human beings to transform dream into reality. One might conclude that our capacity for technology *arose* out of our capacity for symbolic thought.

...................................TRY THIS....................................

Do you agree or disagree with Mumford's thesis that our symbol-making ability is more important than our toolmaking ability? Which is more fundamental to civilization? Express your thoughts in an essay.

Timebends: A Life
by Arthur Miller

In time, *The Crucible* became by far my most frequently produced play, both abroad and at home. Its meaning is somewhat different in different places and moments. I can almost tell what the political situation in a country is when the play is suddenly a hit there—it is either a warning of tyranny on the way or a reminder of tyranny just past. As recently as the winter of 1986 the Royal Shakespeare Company, after touring *The Crucible* through British cathedrals and open town squares, played it in English for a week in two Polish cities. Some important government figures were in the audience, by their presence urging on its message of resistance to a tyranny they were forced to serve. In Shanghai in 1980, it served as a metaphor for life under Mao and the Cultural Revolution, decades when accusation and enforced guilt ruled China and all but destroyed the last signs of intelligent life. The writer Nien Cheng, who spent six and a half years in solitary confinement and whose daughter was murdered by the Red Guards, told me that after her release she saw the Shanghai production and could not believe that a non-Chinese had written the play. "Some of the interrogations," she said, "were precisely the same ones used on us in the Cultural Revolution." It was chilling to realize what had never occurred to me until she mentioned it—that the tyranny of teenagers was almost identical in both instances.

FOR FURTHER REFLECTION

Great literature has the power, in Hamlet's words, to hold a mirror to nature—to capture, in the case of *The Crucible*, the evils of tyranny and religious persecution based on irrational fears and superstitions. A stage play is especially powerful in its ability to capture the reality of such shameful events in human history as the Salem witch trials.

..................................TRY THIS..................................

Write a short play in which a tyrannical body like the Inquisition interrogates a person accused of heresy–of teaching an idea about God that contradicts official church teaching.

OCTOBER 1

"India and Pakistan: Anglo-Asian Synthesis"

by Vera Micheles Dean

from *The Nature of the Non-Western World*

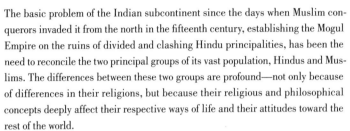

The basic problem of the Indian subcontinent since the days when Muslim conquerors invaded it from the north in the fifteenth century, establishing the Mogul Empire on the ruins of divided and clashing Hindu principalities, has been the need to reconcile the two principal groups of its vast population, Hindus and Muslims. The differences between these two groups are profound—not only because of differences in their religions, but because their religious and philosophical concepts deeply affect their respective ways of life and their attitudes toward the rest of the world.

When a Westerner first looks at Hinduism and at Islam, the differences seem far more striking and far-reaching than the similarities. The Hindus believe in a secular state, and oppose the concept of a state founded on religion. This was the basis for the objections of Nehru and Gandhi to the demand of Mohammed Ali Jinnah, the lawyer who played a key role in the creation of Pakistan, for the establishment of a Muslim state when India achieved independence from Britain in 1947. On the other hand, the Muslims of the Indian subcontinent, like their coreligionists elsewhere, think in terms of a religious state. Not only did they insist on the separation of a Muslim state from India, but once free, they decided that the constitution of Pakistan, with its population of 70 million Muslims and 10 million Hindus, should be squarely based on the Koran, the sacred book of Islam.

FOR FURTHER REFLECTION

Secular states tend to be incompatible with religious ones, India and Pakistan being a case in point. But one wonders if the formation of separate nations based on religious beliefs (or the lack of them) fosters peace and political stability, or instead eventually leads to international tensions.

. . . . TRY THIS . . . .

Can theocracies flourish in the modern world? Write an essay in which you reflect on the possibility, as well as on the reasons why they should or should not flourish. Refer specifically to recent conflicts between secular and religious states.

.

OCTOBER 2

Mont-Saint-Michel & Chartres
by Henry Adams

Like all great churches that are not mere storehouses of theology, Chartres expressed ... an emotion, the deepest man ever felt—the struggle of his own littleness to grasp the infinite. You may, if you like, figure in it a mathematic formula of infinity—the broken arch, our finite area of space; the spire, pointing, with its converging lines, to unity beyond space; the sleepless, restless thrust of the vaults, telling the unsatisfied, incomplete, overstrained effort of man to rival the energy, intelligence, and purpose of God. ...

The world is not a schoolroom or a pulpit, but a stage, and the stage [that is Chartres] is the highest yet seen on earth. In this church the old Romanesque leaps into the Gothic under our eyes; of a sudden, between the portal and the shrine, the infinite rises into a new expression, always a rare and excellent miracle in thought. The two expressions are nowhere far apart; not further than the Mother from the Son. The new artist drops unwillingly the hand of his father or his grandfather; he looks back, from every corner of his own work, to see whether it goes with the old. He will not part with the western portal or the lancet windows; he holds close to the round columns of the choir; he would have kept the round arch if he could, but the round arch was unable to do the work; it could not rise; so he broke it, lifted the vaulting, threw out flying buttresses, and satisfied the Virgin's wish.

FOR FURTHER REFLECTION

Church architecture, with its spires, vast interiors, vaulted ceilings, arches, and so on, has the power to ignite spiritual ecstasy. As the great American historian Henry Adams (1838–1918) explains, cathedrals like Chartres serve as a powerful stage on which the drama of God's presence is conveyed through the interaction of its many graceful and lofty architectural shapes.

..................................TRY THIS....................................

Visit a cathedral in your area and take detailed notes of its architectural features, exterior as well as interior. Also learn about its history. Transform your notes into a poem or essay on how this particular cathedral's architecture heightens religious feelings.

OCTOBER 3

The First Three Minutes: A Modern View of the Origin of the Universe
by Steven Weinberg

If the universe in the first few minutes was really composed of precisely equal numbers of particles and antiparticles, they would all have annihilated as the temperature dropped below 1,000 million degrees, and nothing would be left but radiation. There is very good evidence against this possibility—we are here! There must have been some excess of electrons over positrons, of protons over antiprotons, and of neutrons over antineutrons, in order that there would be something left over after the annihilation of particles and antiparticles to furnish the matter of the present universe. ... The energy density of the nuclear particles did not become comparable to the energy density of radiation until the universe had cooled to about 4,000 degrees K. However, the small seasoning of leftover electrons and nuclear particles has a special claim to our attention, because they dominate the contents of the present universe, and in particular, because they are the main constituents of the author and the reader.

FOR FURTHER REFLECTION

It is always a challenge to try and imagine what at first seems utterly unimaginable, like the very first moments of creation, when matter as we know it had not yet taken its present form, when temperatures were a billion degrees. But as Nobel laureate Steven Weinberg explains, the leftover "seasoning" of electrons and nuclear particles that survived the cooling should be of special interest to us, because they are what we are made of. Whatever exists in the universe today has its origins in those first few minutes of creation.

...................................TRY THIS....................................

Imagine a time during the early days of creation, before stars or planets were born, and the cosmos consisted of nothing but subatomic particles. Write a parable in which your "characters" are, let us say, two electrons wondering about their fate, and speculating between themselves of what they might become. For examples of this type of parable, see *Cosmicomics* by Italo Calvino.

"Order Odonata: Dragonflies"

by Sue Hubbell

from *Broadsides From the Other Orders: A Book of Bugs*

The name "dragonfly" makes them sound fierce, but in European languages they are named more gently. The French *demoiselle* and the Dutch *Juffer* (little miss) echo the name "damselfly," which we use for one kind of dragonfly. The Italian name is *saetta*, an arrow, and Germans, acknowledging that the animal spends most of its life under water, say *Wassernymphe*. But the Russian name is best of all, for careful observation of the insect is built into it. That language calls both a dragonfly and a flighty, lively young girl *strekosa*, which comes from a root word for a rattling, nervous noise: the chatter of a machine gun, the noise of a turning wheel on a gravel road, the *chirrr* of a bug. Dragonflies do not sing, chirp, or call, but when the air is cold their wings do make a whirring noise as they beat them rapidly to elevate their body temperature, giving their flight muscles the strength to carry them into the air. On a cool Russian morning near a lake surrounded by birches, where a group of *strekosa* have spent the night, the most noticeable sound would be the *chirrrrrr* of their warming wings.

The English "dragonfly" is justified by most authorities, who point out that in both the immature, nymphal stages, when the animal lives underwater, and the adult one, when it lives in the air, the dragonfly is a voracious feeder, snatching up gnats, mosquitoes, and even larger prey in a dragonlike way.

FOR FURTHER REFLECTION

The common names we give to creatures tend to be colorful and metaphoric—but that doesn't mean they aren't rooted in empirical truth. Dragonflies are a good example: They may conjure up a creature from fantasy and mythology, but the name is also suited to their feeding behavior, as Sue Hubbell points out. Such nomenclature adds a dimension of enchantment to biology; it never poses a problem because the formal scientific genus-species taxonomy is never compromised.

......................................TRY THIS...................................

Write a fable for adults or children in which the characters are insects. Give them fanciful names, but at the same time let their names reflect their natures, benevolent or sinister.

OCTOBER 5

The Idea of a University
by John Henry Cardinal Newman

Are we to limit our idea of university knowledge by the evidence of our senses? Then we exclude ethics; by intuition? We exclude history; by testimony? We exclude metaphysics; by abstract reasoning? We exclude physics. Is not the being of a God reported to us by testimony, handed down by history, inferred by an inductive process, brought home to us by metaphysical necessity, urged on us by the suggestions of our conscience? It is a truth in the natural order, as well as in the supernatural. So much for its origin; and when obtained, what is it worth? Is it a great truth or a small one? Is it a comprehensive truth? ... The word "God" is a theology in itself, indivisibly one, inexhaustibly various, from the vastness and the simplicity of its meaning. Admit a God and you introduce among the subjects of your knowledge a fact encompassing, closing in upon, absorbing, every other fact conceivable. How can we investigate any part of any order of knowledge, and stop short of that which enters into every order? All true principles run over with it, all phenomena converge to it; it is truly the first and the last. In word indeed, and in idea, it is easy enough to divide knowledge into human and divine, secular and religious, and to lay down that we will address ourselves to the one without interfering with the other; but it is impossible in fact. ... If knowledge of the Creator is in a different order from knowledge of the creature, so, in like manner, metaphysical science is in a different order from physical, physics from history, history from ethics. You will soon break up into fragments the whole circle of secular knowledge if you begin the mutilation of the divine.

FOR FURTHER REFLECTION

Education is paradoxical in that as knowledge in a given discipline advances it tends to become ever more specialized and disconnected from its parent disciplines. But unless there is interconnectedness among the specialized areas, education becomes fragmentary. For Newman, the way to ensure coherence and integrity in higher learning is to acknowledge divinity as central.

...................................TRY THIS...................................

What knowledge and skills should all college students have in common, regardless of concentration? Express your ideas in an essay; use your own educational experience and/or the experiences of others as examples.

Apples

by Frank Browning

Twice each year, down in a valley along Virginia Route 20, halfway between the two great monuments created by Thomas Jefferson, Monticello and the University of Virginia, Tom Burford holds an apple tasting. Dozens of varieties of apples fill wicker baskets that have been lined up on long banquet tables. Some of the varieties grew in Mr. Jefferson's original orchard, which has been restored with Tom Burford's help. Most come from Burford's own nursery, an hour away in Monroe.

"There are collectors who want to have as many different kinds of apples as they can get," Burford begins. "I want as many different flavors as you can get." … He lends his pocketknife to an assistant, who begins to slice the first apples to be tasted.

Before passing the slices around, Burford instructs his audience of about fifty Monticello visitors—who have made their reservations weeks in advance—"how to taste an apple." The apples will be placed on paper plates along with small chunks of bread to clear the palate. Each person has been given a sheet of paper with each apple's name on it and space to write in a numerical ranking. … "Taste," Burford continues," is subjective." He advises them to close their eyes and allow the apple juices to wash the mouth. …

FOR FURTHER REFLECTION

Apples, like wines, come in many varieties and flavors—sufficient for there to be apple-tasting events and apple connoisseurs like Tom Burford. Additionally, the apple is rooted in mythology and ancient history as well as being associated with traditional Americana. Frank Browning notes, for example, that the ancient Romans grew a variety of apple now known as the White Winter Pearmain, which in modern times was brought to America from England.

......................................TRY THIS................................

In a poem or essay, try to capture the personal associations that apples have had for you over the years, from early childhood onward. Use vivid sensory language to capture the experience of eating a favorite apple.

OCTOBER 7

Earth: An Intimate History
by Richard Fortey

The Bay of Naples is where the science of geology started. The description of
the eruption of Vesuvius and the destruction of Pompeii in A.D. 79 by Pliny the
Younger is probably the first clear and objective description of a geological phenomenon. No dragons were invoked, no clashes between the Titans and the gods.
Pliny provided observation, not speculation. Not quite two millennia later, in
1830, Charles Lyell was to use an illustration of columns from the so-called
Temple of Serapis at Pozzuoli, north of Naples, as the frontispiece in volume 1 of
the most seminal work in geology—his *Principles of Geology*. This book influenced the young Charles Darwin more than any other source in his formulation
of evolutionary theory. ...

The country backing the Bay of Naples is known as Campania, and the same
name, Campanian, is applied to a subdivision of geological time belonging to
the Cretaceous period. If you look carefully on some of the weathered surfaces
of the limestones, you will see the remains of seashells that were alive in the age
of the dinosaurs. I saw some obvious clams and sea urchins, belonging to extinct
species, emerging from the cliffs as if they were on a bas-relief. A palaeontologist
can identify the individual fossil species, and use them to calibrate the age of
the rocks, since the succession of species is a measure of geological time. The
implication is clear enough: in Cretaceous times all these hilly regions were
beneath a shallow, warm sea.

FOR FURTHER REFLECTION

Science begins with observation that is free from preconceptions, from systems of thought that lay down certain givens about the nature of reality. This
has taken millennia to evolve even though in the ancient world a few great
minds laid the groundwork for such objective examination of phenomena.
Ancient geological observations must have originated out of necessity—the
annual flooding of the Nile and its impact on agriculture; the search for underground water sources, and so on. Richard Fortey, senior paleontologist at
the Natural History Museum of London, calls attention to the indebtedness of
modern geologists to the groundwork laid by their ancient predecessors.

..............................TRY THIS..............................

Take notes on scientific thinkers of the ancient world, such as Anaximander, Par-
menides, or Empedocles. Then use your notes to fashion biographical profiles.

The Story of Civilization
by Will Durant

China has been called "the paradise of historians." For centuries and millenniums it has had official historiographers who recorded everything that happened, and much besides. We cannot trust them further back than 776 B.C.; but if we lend them a ready ear they will explain in detail the history of China from 3000 B.C., and the more pious among them ... will describe the creation of the world. ...

The earliest kings, says Chinese legend, reigned eighteen thousand years each. ... Then came the emperor Fu Hsi, in precisely 2852 B.C.; with the help of his enlightened Queen he taught his people marriage, music, writing, painting, fishing with nets, the domestication of animals, and the feeding of silkworms for the secretion of silk. Dying, he appointed as his successor Shen Nung, who introduced agriculture, invented the wooden plough, established markets and trade, and developed the science of medicine from the curative values of plants. So legend, which loves personalities more than ideas, attributes to a few individuals the laborious advances of many generations. Then a vigorous soldier-emperor, Huang-ti, in a reign of a mere century, gave China the magnet and the wheel, appointed official historians, built the first brick structures in China, erected an observatory for the study of the stars, corrected the calendar, and redistributed the land.

FOR FURTHER REFLECTION

Ancient historians of any culture tended to mythologize leaders and war heroes, transforming them into larger-than-life icons. Ancient Chinese history is especially fascinating because of the way its ancient historians were both exhaustive chroniclers as well as imaginative storytellers. Although the earliest historians were more concerned with valorizing the great leaders, they still managed to include some historically accurate information, such as the time when observatories were first established and when technological innovations like the plough and fishing nets were developed.

.................................TRY THIS.................................

1. Write a biographical essay on an ancient Chinese emperor, writer, philosopher, or military hero. See if you can distinguish between fact and legend in your account.
2. Write a biographical essay on one or more ancient Chinese historians. If you wish, compare them to ancient historians from other cultures, such as the Athenian historian Herodotus.

OCTOBER 9

The Year of Three Kings: 1483
by Giles St. Aubyn

Sixteenth century writers regarded history as a living source of instruction for the present. They saw the historians' task as essentially didactic: to proclaim the lessons of the past, and to demonstrate their relevance. "He who would foresee what is to happen," says Machiavelli, "should look to what has happened: for all that is has its counterpart in time past."

The Tudors lived through a period of rebellions which threatened the very survival of government. At times in Elizabeth I's reign it seemed as if her life alone preserved the realm from anarchy. Consequently most of her subjects lived in mortal terror of Civil War, and regarded the deposition of an anointed King—to say nothing of regicide—as an atrocious crime. The Tudors were obsessed by the warning signals they deciphered in fifteenth century precedents. As they saw it, what was sown in 1399, when Henry IV usurped the throne, was reaped in the Wars of the Roses: the bloody harvest of that first disobedience. Because "the powers that be are ordained of God," to depose a sovereign was to incur divine displeasure. Nowhere was the work of an almighty hand more evidently proclaimed than in "the disorder, horror, fear and mutiny" [Shakespeare, *Richard II*, IV.i] which plagued the late Middle Ages.

FOR FURTHER REFLECTION

In Medieval and Renaissance England, a monarch's reign was thought to be divinely ordained. To usurp the throne for whatever reason—abuse of power, restoration of the rightful heir—was like usurping nature: There would be consequences from the Almighty to face. Shakespeare, as British historian Giles St. Aubyn points out in his book, was especially sensitive to the political instability that usurpation or regicide could bring; eight of his plays in effect serve as warnings "of the evils of Civil War ... [and] the bitter fruits of rebellion."

..................................TRY THIS..................................

Explore in depth the reign of Richard II, Richard III, or Edward VII and write a short story or play in which the King faces rebellion and accusation (e.g., Richard III's being accused of murdering King Henry VI).

OCTOBER 10

"1906: The Town That Refused to Die"
by Walter Lord

from *The Good Years: From 1900 to the First World War*

It was simply incredible. Cracks yawned in the streets. Water geysered into the air from a hundred ruptured mains. Trolley tracks writhed and buckled. The whole earth ripped and heaved—"Like a man shakes a rug," "like a dog shakes a rat." Everyone had his favorite description. It was worse in the soft, filled land south of Market Street, but it was bad everywhere.

The big and the small crashed together. The Valencia Street Hotel collapsed in a splintered heap—its four wooden floors telescoping into one. A falling telegraph pole sliced a milk wagon in two on Mission Street. An avalanche of bricks buried Patrolman Max Fenner, affectionately known as "the Terrible Swede," at Mason and Ellis. Some 520 cemetery monuments toppled, all falling east or slightly north of east.

Uptown, a marble statue of "The Diving Girl" (the quintessence of Victorian modesty) crumbled on the lawn of 1801 Van Ness Avenue. Downtown, the whole City Hall tumbled in ruins. Tall "stone" columns crashed to the ground—and turned out to be hollow iron, loosely filled with bricks and clay. Huge slabs of masonry clattered off the walls, leaving the dome a gaunt bird cage silhouetted against the morning sky. More than the girders were exposed—the whole corrupt mess of Mayor Eugene Schmitz's administration lay bare for all to see.

FOR FURTHER REFLECTION

History is filled with tragic earthquakes, many of them even more destructive, with greater loss of life, than the San Francisco earthquake of 1906—but because of the quantity and quality of coverage it has received, the San Francisco quake has acquired legendary status. Lord's description of the disaster is memorable for his unusually keen observations.

......................................TRY THIS......................................

Describe the aftermath of a recent storm, earthquake, flood or fire in your area. Ideally you will want to observe the destruction (or the aftermath) firsthand rather than rely on news reports. Use eyewitness descriptions from persons who endured the disaster.

"The Education of Children"

by Plutarch

from *On Love, the Family, and the Good Life*. Translated by Moses Hadas

What can be said regarding the education of freeborn children? What procedures are likely to produce soundness of character? Let us address ourselves to this problem.

Perhaps it is better to begin with parentage as a starting point. Those who desire to become fathers of reputable children I should for my part advise not to consort with any women that happen along, I mean such as courtesans or concubines. Persons not well born, either on their mother's side or their father's are pursued by the indelible disgrace of bad birth throughout their lives. ... Wise indeed was the poet [Euripides] who said ... "And if their birth's foundation be not well and truly laid, of necessity children are unfortunate."

Respectable birth therefore affords a man the treasured freedom to speak his mind openly, and the highest value should be set upon it by anyone whose object is lawful procreation. It is perfectly natural for those whose birth is flawed or tainted to be lamed and humbled in their self-esteem, and the poet [Euripides] is quite right in remarking ... "It makes a slave of a man, however stouthearted he be, when he learns his mother's or father's baseness." By obvious corollary children of distinguished parents are full of proud and lofty temper.

... Nature without learning is blind, learning apart from nature is fractional, and practice in the absence of both is aimless. Agriculture offers an analogy: in the first place there must be good soil, then the cultivator must be expert, and then the seed must be sound; after the same fashion nature corresponds to the soil, the educator to the cultivator, and the substance of his doctrine and his admonitions to the seed.

FOR FURTHER REFLECTION

According to Moses Hadas, this essay is "the only complete treatise on education which has come down from antiquity." Plutarch's wise and elegant insights, conveyed in lucid, aphoristic prose, were a major influence on the great essayists from Montaigne in the Renaissance to our own day.

.................................TRY THIS.................................

Use one of Plutarch's nuggets of wisdom and compose an essay of your own in which you reflect on the implications of that bit of wisdom.

The Romance of Tristan and Iseult
by Joseph Bédier

Translated by Hilaire Belloc and Paul Rosenfeld

One day when the wind had fallen and the sails hung slack Tristan dropped anchor by an island and the hundred knights of Cornwall and the sailors, weary of the sea, landed all. Iseult alone remained aboard and a little serving maid, when Tristan came near the Queen to calm her sorrow. The sun was hot above them and they were athirst and, as they called, the little maid looked about for drink for them and found that pitcher which the mother of Iseult had given into Brangien's keeping. And when she came on it, the child cried, "I have found you wine!" Now she had found not wine—but Passion and Joy most sharp, and Anguish without end, and Death.

The child filled a goblet and presented it to her mistress. The Queen drank deep of that draught and gave it to Tristan and he drank also long and emptied it all.

Brangien came in upon them; she saw them gazing at each other in silence as though ravished and apart. ... She snatched up the pitcher and cast it into the shuddering sea and cried aloud: "Cursed be the day I was born ... Iseult, my friend, and Tristan, you, you have drunk death together."

FOR FURTHER REFLECTION

In this retelling of one of literature's most poignant love stories, the French medievalist Joseph Bédier (1864–1938) eloquently captures the power of love in the face of overwhelming adversity, and how uncannily similar to the sensation of dying, as symbolized by the wine-drinking, love can be.

.....................................TRY THIS.....................................

Begin work on your own version of this love story, placing the two lovers in the modern world, faced with modern-day obstacles—for example, being from clashing religious backgrounds or forced to choose between commitment to their respective vocations and devoting themselves exclusively to each other.

Life of Johnson
by James Boswell

[Johnson's] *Dictionary*, with a *Grammar and History of the English Language*, being now at length published [1755], in two volumes folio, the world contemplated with wonder so stupendous a work achieved by one man, while other countries had thought such undertakings fit only for whole academies. Vast as his powers were, I cannot but think that his imagination deceived him, when he supposed that by constant application he might have performed the task in three years. Let the Preface [to the *Dictionary*] be attentively perused, in which is given, in a clear, strong, and glowing style, a comprehensive, yet particular view of what he had done; and it will be evident, that the time he employed upon it was comparatively short. ... I believe there are few compositions in the English language that are read with more delight, or are more impressed upon the memory, than that preliminary discourse. ...

The extensive reading which was absolutely necessary for the accumulation of authorities, and which alone may account for Johnson's retentive mind being enriched with a very large and various store of knowledge and imagery, must have occupied several years. ... Sir Joshua Reynolds heard him say, "There are two things which I am confident I can do very well: one is an introduction to any literary work, stating what it is to contain, and how it should be executed in the most perfect manner; the other is a conclusion, shewing from various causes why the execution has not been equal to what the author promised to himself and to the publick."

FOR FURTHER REFLECTION

Boswell's massive biography of his close friend Samuel Johnson gains the status of literature through its relentless devotion to those social and intellectual involvements that fed into Johnson's great achievements as a lexicographer and critic. Not only does Boswell portray in meticulous detail the great man in the act of conceiving and assembling his projects, but he also places them in the context of Johnson's correspondence (dozens of letters are reproduced) and the public and academic reception of Johnson's publications.

..................................TRY THIS..................................

Interview a friend, teacher, or employer, learning all you can about his or her accomplishments. Drawing from your notes and (if possible) correspondence or other documents, write a profile of this person. Give special attention to what you consider to be the most noteworthy accomplishment.

OCTOBER 14

"The World Is Too Much With Us"

by William Wordsworth

The world is too much with us; late and soon,
Getting and spending, we lay waste our powers;
Little we see in Nature that is ours;
We have given our hearts away, a sordid boon!
This Sea that bares her bosom to the moon;
The winds that will be howling at all hours,
And are up-gathered now like sleeping flowers;
For this, for everything, we are out of tune;
It moves us not.—Great God! I'd rather be
A Pagan suckled in a creed outworn;
So might I, standing on this pleasant lea,
Have glimpses that would make me less forlorn;
Have sight of Proteus rising from the sea;
Or hear old Triton blow his wreathèd horn.

FOR FURTHER REFLECTION

In this powerful sonnet Wordsworth expresses his anguish over his and his
fellow citizens' inability to experience the spirituality, the enchantment of the
natural world that had enthralled the ancients. Our powers, he laments, have
been thwarted by materialism—which is to say, by the material productivity
of the Industrial Revolution which in 1807 seemed to be usurping nature
with its pollution and noise and worst of all destroying the beauty of nature,
turning it into mere commodity. Far more soul-satisfying to experience nature
like a Pagan—except that once those ancient beliefs have been perceived as
"outworn," one can never go back to them.

......................................TRY THIS................................

1. In a poem, describe your own spiritual relationship (or the lack of it) to
   nature in the context of modern science and technology.
2. Reflect, in an essay, on how one might reconcile one's view of nature
   as resource with nature as an abode of spirit and enchantment.

OCTOBER 15

Native Son
by Richard Wright

[Mary] came out [of the building where there had been a Communist meeting], followed by a young white man. They walked to the car; but, instead of getting into the back seat, they came to side of the car and stood, facing [Bigger]. At once Bigger recognized the man as the one he had seen in the newsreel in the movie.

"Oh, Bigger, this is Jan. And Jan, this is Bigger Thomas."

Jan smiled broadly, then extended an open palm toward him. Bigger's entire body tightened with suspense and dread.

"How are you, Bigger?"

Bigger's right hand gripped the steering wheel and he wondered if he ought to shake hands with this white man. "I'm fine," he mumbled.

Jan's hand was still extended. Bigger's right hand raised itself about three inches, then stopped in mid-air. "Come on and shake," Jan said.

Bigger extended a limp palm, his mouth open in astonishment. He felt Jan's fingers about his own. He tried to pull his hand away, ever so gently, but Jan held on, firmly, smiling.

"We may as well get to know each other," Jan said. "I'm a friend of Mary's."

"Yessuh," he mumbled.

"First of all," Jan continued, putting his foot upon the running-board, "don't say sir to me. I'll call you Bigger and you'll call me Jan. That's the way it'll be between us. How's that?"

FOR FURTHER REFLECTION

In this disturbing classic of African-American literature, Wright conveys the psychological impact of racism on a black man, Bigger Thomas, who is torn between playing the stereotyped role of someone who is persona non grata in white society in order to survive, and taking advantage of the efforts of progressive whites to revolt against racist practices.

.................................TRY THIS................................

1. America has made significant progress in race relations since Richard Wright's day, but few would disagree that further progress is needed. Write an essay in which you target two or three areas in which racial prejudice continues to exist, and how it might be overcome.

2. Write a short story in which an African-American man or woman falls victim to racial prejudice and how he or she manages to triumph over it.

"Saddlebag Drugs"

by Ritchie Calder

from *Medicine and Man: The Story of the Art and Science of Healing*

The backwoods doctors, who followed the covered wagons and the iron tracks of the railroads which opened up the frontiers of America, carried their surgery and their dispensary in their saddlebags. They could ply the knife and the saw, amputate and probe. They might have ether or chloroform, if they had heard of Crawford Long, Morton or Simpson. They might use carbolic if the news of Lister and his antisepsis had reached them. But they knew little of the nature of infections or contagions because the disputations over Pasteur and Koch were far away. They relied on bleeding, cupping and leeching, and their invariable stand-bys were Dover's powder, dragon's blood, Peruvian bark, and calomel, the mercurial drug. Those were the four suits in their medical pack of cards, which they shuffled and dealt for any situation. …

Without questioning the courage, the self-sacrifice and devotion of the pioneer doctors nor underestimating that physicians' other attribute—the giving of confidence and comfort, which is often half the battle—it is more than likely that in frontier days any medicine man or wise squaw of the Five Nations knew more medicine than the medical camp-followers of the victorious white man.

That was the great contradiction of the nineteenth century—that while the science of medicine advanced the art of medicine dragged. This was an age of great discoveries about the body and mind of man. It saw the development of organic chemistry; of physiological chemistry (biochemistry); of anesthetics; bacteriology, and with it antisepsis and asepsis; and the diagnostic identification of manifold diseases.

FOR FURTHER REFLECTION

Modern medicine took a painfully long time to evolve; there was much trial and error; years elapsed between new insights into the nature of disease, into hygiene and anesthetics, and integrating those new insights into actual practice. Also, in nineteenth-century America it took a long time for news of new procedures to reach the frontier.

······································TRY THIS····································

Write a story in which your hero is a physician or nurse devoted to finding new ways of caring for the sick and injured.

OCTOBER 17

Conversations with Kafka
by Gustav Janouch

Translated by Goronwy Rees

Franz Kafka asked me several times to show him some of my "unrhymed scribbles"—
as I myself described them. I therefore looked through my notebook for suitable
extracts, which I put together as a collection of short prose pieces, gave it the title
The Moment of the Abyss, and presented it to Kafka.

He only gave me back the manuscript after several months, when he was preparing to travel to the sanatorium at Tatranské Matlyary. As he did so, he said:

"All your stories are so touchingly young. You say far more about the impressions
which things inspire in you than about the things and objects themselves. That is
lyrical poetry. You caress the world, instead of grasping it."

"So my writing is worthless?"

Kafka grasped my hand. "I did not say that. Certainly these little stories have
a value for you. Every written word is a personal document. But art ..."

"Art is different," I continued bitterly.

"Your writing is not yet art," said Kafka firmly. "This description of feelings and
impressions is most of all a hesitant groping for the world. ... But in time that will
cease and then perhaps the outstretched groping hand will withdraw as if caught by
the fire. Perhaps you will cry out, stammer incoherently, or grind your teeth together
and open your eyes wide, very wide. But—these are only words. Art is always a
matter of the entire personality. For that reason it is fundamentally tragic."

FOR FURTHER REFLECTION

The Franz Kafka we encounter in these conversations with Gustav Janouch
is a compassionate thinker for whom the art of writing cannot be separated
from the existential reality of the human condition. Although a writer can
gain personal value from fashioning stories out of words, it becomes a work
of art only when it can break through the frozen surface and grapple with the
vulnerable human soul underneath the ice.

..................................TRY THIS....................................

Review one of your stories or poems from the perspective of the light it sheds
on human nature. What insights into human nature are generated by your main
character's personality and activities? What can you add to this character's
thoughts and deeds that will make him or her more memorable?

OCTOBER 18

Cat & Mouse

by James Patterson

The victim of the moment was Drew Cabot. He was a chief inspector—of all the hopelessly inane things to do with your life. He was "hot" in London, having recently apprehended an IRA killer. His murder would electrify the town, drive everyone mad. ... Civilized and sophisticated London loved a gory murder as well as the next burg. ...

Mr. Smith had to bend low to talk into Drew Cabot's ear, to be more intimate with his prey. He played music while he worked—all kinds of music. Today's selection was the overture to *Don Giovanni*. Opera buffa felt right to him.

Opera felt right for this *live* autopsy.

"Ten minutes or so after your death," Mr. Smith said, "flies will already have picked up the scent of gas accompanying the decomposition of your tissue. Green flies will lay the tiniest eggs within the orifices of your body. Ironically, the language reminds me of Dr. Seuss—'green flies and ham.' What could that mean? I don't know. It's a curious association, though."

Drew Cabot had lost a lot of blood, but he wasn't giving up. He was a tall, rugged man with silver-blond hair. A never-say-never sort of chap. The inspector shook his head back and forth until Smith finally removed the gag.

"What is it, Drew?" he asked. "Speak."

"I have a wife and two children. Why are you doing this to me? Why me?" he whispered.

"Oh, let's say because you're Drew. Keep it simple and unsentimental. You, Drew, are a piece of the puzzle."

He tugged the inspector's gag back into place. No more chitchat from Drew.

FOR FURTHER REFLECTION

In *Cat & Mouse*, James Patterson takes us into the mind of a truly perverted evil intelligence: someone who is obsessed with wanting his victims to monitor the very progression of dying to the instant of death. To *feel*, as well as understand, how a criminal mind operates, can be both an illuminating and an unsettling aesthetic experience.

.... TRY THIS ....

Begin work on a murder mystery in which you devote alternate chapters between good guy and bad guy. You will want your readers to become startlingly aware of the contrast between the psyches of these two men and/or women.

OCTOBER 19
Ecotopia: The Notebooks and Reports of William Weston: A Novel
by Ernest Callenbach

One surprising similarity between Ecotopia and contemporary America is that they both use huge amounts of plastics. At first I took this as a sign that our ways of life have not diverged so drastically after all. However, closer investigation has revealed that, despite surface resemblances, the two countries use plastics in totally different ways.

Ecotopian plastics are entirely derived from living biological sources (plants) rather than from fossilized ones (petroleum and coal) as most of ours are. Intense research effort went into this area directly after Independence, and it continues. According to my informants, there were two major objectives. One was to produce the plastics, at low cost and in a wide range of types: light, heavy, rigid, flexible, clear, opaque, and so on—and to produce them with a technology that was not itself a pollutant. The other objective was to make them all *biodegradable,* that is, susceptible to decay. This meant that they could be returned to the fields as fertilizer, which would nourish new crops, which in turn could be made into new plastics—and so on indefinitely, in what the Ecotopians call, with almost religious fervor, a "stable-state system."

One interesting strategy for biodegradability involved producing plastics which had a short planned lifetime and would automatically self-destruct after a certain period or under certain conditions. ... Plastics of this type are used to make containers for beer, food of many types, to produce packaging materials that resemble cellophane, and so on. These materials "die" after a month or so, especially when exposed to sunlight's ultraviolet rays.

FOR FURTHER REFLECTION

What is so striking about Callenbach's ecological utopia in which California, Oregon, and Washington have become an independent ecological superstate, is that it is so fully delineated—with detailed ways in which difficult problems like population control, racial relations, education, and use of natural resources might be managed so much more effectively than they are today.

................................TRY THIS................................

Develop your own ecological utopian vision in a sequence of poems or essays. Devote each work to one specific issue.

"The Metaphysics of Aristotle"
by Frederick Copleston, S.J.
from *A History of Philosophy*

"All men by nature desire to know." So does Aristotle optimistically begin the *Metaphysics*, a book, or rather collection of lectures, which is difficult to read … but which is of the greatest importance for an understanding of the philosophy of Aristotle, and which has had a tremendous influence on the subsequent thought of Europe. But though all men desire to know, there are different degrees of knowledge. For example, the man of *mere experience*, as Aristotle calls him, may know that a certain medicine had done good to X when he was ill, but without knowing the reason for this, whereas the man of *art* knows the reason, e.g. he knows that X was suffering from fever, and that the medicine in question has a certain property which abates fever. He knows a universal, for he knows that the medicine will tend to cure all who suffer from that complaint. Art, then, aims at production of some kind, but this is not Wisdom in Aristotle's view, for the highest Wisdom does not aim at producing anything or securing some effect—it is not utilitarian—but at apprehending the first principles of Reality, i.e. at knowledge for its own sake. Aristotle places the man who seeks for knowledge for its own sake above him who seeks for knowledge of some particular kind with a view to the attainment of some practical effect. In other words, that science stands higher which is desirable for its own sake and not merely with a view to its results.

FOR FURTHER REFLECTION

Aristotle is concerned with the relationship between practical knowledge derived from experience, and intrinsic, universal wisdom, derived from underlying or universal reality. Both are necessary, but the latter deserves to be ranked higher, as they constitute the wellspring from which all practical knowledge originates.

..................................TRY THIS....................................

Compose a skit that dramatizes a confrontation between an artistic individual and a practical one, who considers art to be a useless frivolity. Let each character communicate his or her values fully.

OCTOBER 21

Catching the Light:
The Entwined History of Light and Mind
by Arthur Zajonc

Light a candle and notice first the perfect cup formed below the flame to carry the melted wax. The flame, reaching down the wick, melts the wax at the candle's center, while a current of air rising around the candle keeps the rim cool and high, and so creates a vessel perfectly suited to hold its molten contents. The liquid within is drawn up the wick by the same forces that draw sap up a tree or plant: capillary action. Instead of feeding leaves and flowers, however, the liquid wax vaporizes in the dark inner region of the flame closest to the wick, mingles there with the air, and feeds the flame. If this were all, as it is for some flames, a candle would shed little light. The bright yellow cone that spreads its gentle radiance, however, is due to tiny glowing embers of unburned carbon, the same that turn up as soot when the wick is too long. Cold, it is the blackest of substances, but when hot, soot becomes beautifully luminous.

To the poetic eye of Gaston Bachelard, the candle flame is a model phenomenon. In it "The most vulgar material of all produces light. It purifies itself in the very act of giving off light. Evil is the nourisher of good. In the flame, the philosopher encounters a model-phenomenon, a cosmic phenomenon, a model of humanization." [Bachelard, *The Flame of a Candle*, 20]

FOR FURTHER REFLECTION

Hard science can reveal not only the underlying properties and functions of the material world, they can also convey a transcendent truth, like the darkest of substances proving to be a marvelous source of illumination. Study the mechanisms that generate light deeply enough and one moves almost inevitably from physics to metaphysics. This is a lovely example of how science, far from being insensate, can illuminate a universe filled with enchantment.

.... TRY THIS ....

Write a poem in which you explore a phenomenon of nature in such a way as to bring out its mystical aspects. Possible topics: the influence of the moon on the tides; lightning and thunder; caterpillar-butterfly metamorphosis.

On Liberty
by John Stuart Mill

The general tendency of things throughout the world is to render mediocrity the ascendant power among mankind. In ancient history, in the middle ages, and in a diminishing degree through the long transition from feudality to the present time, the individual was a power in himself; and if he had either great talents or a high social position, he was a considerable power. At present individuals are lost in the crowd. In politics it is almost a triviality to say that public opinion now rules the world. The only power deserving the name is that of masses, and of governments while they make themselves the organ of the tendencies and instincts of masses. This is as true in the moral and social relations of private life as in public transactions. Those whose opinions go by the name of public opinion, are not always the same sort of public: in America they are the whole white population; in England, chiefly the middle class. But they are always a mass, that is to say, collective mediocrity. And what is still a greater novelty, the mass do not now take their opinions from dignitaries in Church or State, from ostensible leaders, or from books. Their thinking is done for them by men much like themselves. … I am not complaining of all this. I do not assert that anything better is compatible, as a general rule, with the present low state of the human mind. But that does not hinder the government of mediocrity from being mediocre government. No government by a democracy or a numerous aristocracy … ever did or could rise above mediocrity, except in so far as the sovereign. Many have let themselves be guided (which in their best times they always have done) by the counsels and influence of a more highly gifted and instructed One or Few. The initiation of all wise or noble things comes and must come from individuals; generally at first from one individual. The honour and glory of the average man is that he is capable of following that initiative; that he can respond internally to wise and noble things.

FOR FURTHER REFLECTION

For excellence to triumph over mediocrity, leaders must break free of mass consciousness, assert their individual vision, and, most importantly, they must find a way to persuade the common people to ascend to their vision.

................................TRY THIS................................

Compose a political satire in which a mediocre candidate is elected to a leadership role on the basis of his or her mediocrity. "We voted for this person because he (or she) is just like us!"

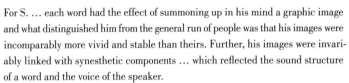

OCTOBER 23
The Mind of a Mnemonist:
A Little Book About a Vast Memory
by A.R. Luria

Translated by Lynn Solotaroff

For S. ... each word had the effect of summoning up in his mind a graphic image and what distinguished him from the general run of people was that his images were incomparably more vivid and stable than theirs. Further, his images were invariably linked with synesthetic components ... which reflected the sound structure of a word and the voice of the speaker.

It was only natural, then, that the *visual quality of his recall* was fundamental to his capacity for remembering words. For when he heard or read a word it was at once converted into a visual image corresponding with the object the word signified for him. Once he formed an image ... it stabilized itself in his memory, and though it might vanish for a time when his attention was taken up with something else, it would manifest itself once again whenever he returned to the situation in which that word has first come up. As he described it:

> When I hear the word *green*, a green flowerpot appears; with
> the word *red* I see a man in a red shirt coming toward me ...
> Even numbers remind me of images. Take the number 1.
> This is a proud, will-built man; 2 is a high-spirited woman;
> 3 a gloomy person (why, I don't know) ...

FOR FURTHER REFLECTION

The five senses can sometimes interact in ways that capture our experience of the world in fascinating new ways. For example, we might associate a given color with a certain taste (that vegetable tastes *green*); or we might describe violin music as *silky*. This is known as synesthesia. Some synesthetic descriptions are rather conventional, but as psychologist A.R. Luria points out, the brain can combine sensations in strange and fascinating ways.

...................................TRY THIS...................................

List some of your own synesthetic associations—what colors do you associate with what numbers? What smells with what physical sensations? Write a poem in which synesthesia is your predominant technique.

OCTOBER 24

Turkish Reflections: A Biography of a Place

by Mary Lee Settle

Even though it may be a romantic illusion, I want to live where I am. So for weeks in Turkey I had been walking, driving, floating, dawdling, talking on the easy street of being part of the places I went to, the way of living by the day, however short the time. But because there seemed no other way to see it, I joined a tour to go to see the Gordium of King Midas [where the young king Alexander is said to have cut the Gordian knot]. ... We floated like skaters across the great plain west of Ankara, and people on the bus bet who could see a camel first in a land that has in the last twenty years been converted to the tractor.

The road we took had been the Silk Road, the great trade route, the road of Alexander, the Crusaders, the Seljuks, the Ottoman and the Türkmen, the Phrygians, Tamerlane, Genghis Khan. It is the artery of Turkish history from east to west and, for the Eurocentric historian, from west to east, across Anatolia. It should clang with the shields of the hoplites. Armor should shine in the sun. ...

We came to that huge desert the color of fawns, with thin lines of black cypresses drawn in the distance across it, dotted with natural and man-made hills. Under the man-made tumuli [mounds] of Gordium there are tombs, and they are so like the natural hills that they made those of us who were amateurs at archaeology wonder which were tumuli. Lulled by the bus, we could dream of treasure, still unfound, in lost tombs.

After an hour or so, we turned off the main road and began to roll across the flat land toward a river, the ancient Sangarius where the reeds of the river whispered in the wind, "King Midas has ass's ears. King Midas has ass's ears."

FOR FURTHER REFLECTION

In Turkey, ancient and modern intertwine, as well as myths and legends with evidence of terrible battles through the ages. In a land where camels share the fields with tractors, it is only natural to want to remain there long enough to let the customs and the land, the complex intertwining of past and present, penetrate the psyche.

......................................TRY THIS......................................

Choose a city with a long history. Write an essay that captures the feel of the place, making sure to bring special moments into dramatic focus.

"Faith and Reason"

by William Barrett

from *Irrational Man: A Study in Existential Philosophy*

What is faith? Philosophers through the centuries have attempted to analyze or describe it, but all their talk cannot reproduce mentally the fact itself. Faith is faith, vital and indescribable. He who has it knows what it is; and perhaps also he who sincerely and painfully knows he is without it has some inkling of what it is, in its absence from a heart that feels itself dry and shriveled. Faith can no more be described to a thoroughly rational mind than the idea of colors can be conveyed to a blind man. Fortunately, we are able to recognize it when we see it in others, as in St. Paul, a case where faith had taken over the whole personality. Thus vital and indescribable, faith partakes of the mystery of life itself. The opposition between faith and reason is that between the vital and the rational—and stated in these terms, the opposition is a crucial problem today. The question is one of where the center of the human personality is to be located: St Paul locates this center in faith, Aristotle in reason; and these two conceptions, worlds apart, show how at its very fountainhead the Christian understanding of man diverges utterly from that of Greek philosophy, however much later thinkers may have tried to straddle this gulf.

FOR FURTHER REFLECTION

Is it possible to reconcile faith and reason or must they forever be mutually contradictory? Some argue that faith doesn't so much contradict reason as transcend it because faith is an emotion like love. We experience how real and powerful it is, yet that experience cannot be embodied by rational explanation.

....TRY THIS..

1. Where do you locate "the center of personality"—in faith or in reason? Argue your convictions in an essay, but be sure to represent the opposing view as objectively as you can.

2. Write a one-act play or short story in which you pit a person of faith against a person of reason.

OCTOBER 26
Small World: An Academic Romance
by David Lodge

In his office at the University of North Queensland, Rodney Wainwright is working at his paper on the Future of Criticism. To try and recover the impetus of his argument, he is copying out what he has already written, from the beginning, as a pole vaulter lengthens his run-up to achieve a particularly daunting jump. His hope is that the sheer momentum of discourse will carry him over that stubborn obstacle which has delayed him for so long. So far it is going well. His hand is moving fluently across the foolscap. He is introducing many new gracenotes and making various subtle revisions of the original text as he proceeds. He tries to suppress his own knowledge of what comes next, tries not to see the crucial passage looming ahead. He is trying to trick his own brain. Don't look! Keep going, keep going! Gather all your strength up into one ball, ready to spring, NOW!

> The question is, therefore, how can literary criticism maintain its Arnoldian function of identifying the best which has been thought and said, when literary discourse itself has been decentered by deconstructing the traditional concept of the author, of "authority." Clearly

Yes, clearly …? … Clearly what?

The vaulter hangs suspended in the air for a moment, his face red with effort, eyes bulging, tendons knotted, the pole bent almost to breaking point under his weight, the crossbar only inches from his nose. Then it all collapses. … Rodney Wainwright slumps forward onto his desk and buries his face in his hands.

FOR FURTHER REFLECTION

Pity the poor literary scholar, caught between the love of great literature and the need to survive in academia by publishing sufficiently complex literary criticism. How easy it is to become swallowed up by one's own jargon!

...................................TRY THIS...............................

Write a satirical story involving members of a college community: a professor seeking revenge after being denied tenure; mayhem at a fraternity or sorority house; a male student who seduces his female professor (or vice versa).

OCTOBER 27

Rollback

by Robert J. Sawyer

[McGavin to Dr. Sarah Halifax]: "Communication between two planets isn't something one generation starts, another continues, and still another picks up after that. Even with the long time frames imposed by the speed of light, interstellar communication is still almost certainly communication between individuals. And you, Dr. Halifax, are our individual. You already proved, all those years ago, that you know how they think. Nobody else managed that."

Her voice was soft. "I—am happy to be the, um, the public face for our reply to the current message, if you think that's necessary, but after that …" She lifted her narrow shoulders slightly as if to say the rest was obvious.

"No," said McGavin. "We need to keep you around for a good long time."

Sarah was nervous; Don [her husband] could tell, even if McGavin couldn't. She lifted her glass and swirled the contents so that the ice cubes clinked together. "What are you going to do? Have me stuffed and put on display?"

"Goodness, no."

"Then what?" Don demanded.

"Rejuvenation," said McGavin.

"Pardon me?"

"Rejuvenation; a rollback. We'll make you young again."

FOR FURTHER REFLECTION

If we were to intercept radio signals sent by aliens from the stars, how could we possibly maintain communication across distances so vast that it would take decades for the messages, traveling at light-speed—the cosmic speed limit—to be received? One way is to ensure that the messenger—astrophysicist Sarah Halifax in this case, the only person on earth who can communicate with the aliens—lives long enough by undergoing an expensive and less-than-fully reliable rejuvenation process called a rollback.

......................................TRY THIS......................................

Work up an outline for a story set in a future in which it is possible for old people to become young again in both mind and body. What possible negative consequences might arise? For example, what would happen to family life if, say, your grandmother rejuvenated herself to become, literally, a woman in her twenties, but your grandfather refused to be rejuvenated?

OCTOBER 28
Lightning
by Dean Koontz

[Kokoschka] looked beyond his reflection again. He had no trouble finding Laura Shane among the swaddled infants, for the surname of each child was printed on a card and affixed to the back of his or her cradle.

Why is there such interest in you, Laura? he wondered. Why is your life so important? Why all this energy expended to see that you are brought safely into the world? Should I kill you now and put an end to the traitor's scheme?

He'd be able to murder her without compunction. He had killed children before, though none quite so young as this. No crime was too terrible if it furthered the cause to which he had devoted his life.

The babe was sleeping. Now and then her mouth worked, and her tiny face briefly wrinkled, as perhaps she dreamed of the womb with regret and longing.

At last he decided not to kill her. Not yet.

"I can always eliminate you later, little one," he murmured. "When I understand what part you play in the traitor's plans, then I can kill you."

Kokoschka walked away from the window. He knew he would not see the girl again for more than eight years.

FOR FURTHER REFLECTION

You would think we could distinguish between guardian angel or malicious evil spirit, but in this supernatural thriller, we're not quite sure what to think. Imagine being able to control one's destiny by intervening at crucial moments and changing the way things were supposed to unfold. This is one "escapist" page-turner that makes us think deeply about the relationship between destiny and free will.

································TRY THIS································

Tell the story of a demon or angel (you might want to keep your readers guessing about this character's true nature and intentions) who goes back in time in an effort to change the course of history for better or worse—but whose plans are disrupted by an opponent.

OCTOBER 29

Eating in the Dark: America's Experiment with Genetically Engineered Food

by Kathleen Hart

On May 27, 1998, a coalition of rabbis, Christian clergy, biologists, and consumers sued the U.S. Food and Drug Administration for failing to require safety testing and labeling of genetically engineered foods. The lawsuit charged that the FDA's policy endangers public health and violates the religious freedom of individuals who wish to avoid foods that have been engineered with genes from animals and microorganisms.

"Genetic engineering is the most radical technology ever devised by the human brain, yet it has been subjected to far less testing than other new products," Steven Druker, president of the Alliance for Bio-Integrity, the lead plaintiff, said at a press conference in Washington, D.C., to announce the lawsuit. "This lax regulatory process is scientifically unsound and morally wrong."

Druker said that Genetic ID, the DNA testing company in Fairfield, Iowa, had tested several soy-based infant formulas in 1997, looking for genetically engineered ingredients. Four baby formulas containing soy ingredients had tested positive.

FDA officials had always maintained that genetically engineered foods were substantially the same as their conventional counterparts. Yet, the plaintiffs argued, if the foods contained new constituents that could be detected and measured, how could government regulators assert they were virtually identical to traditional ones?

FOR FURTHER REFLECTION

It's understandable to be wary about genetically manipulating food, and to insist upon rigorous and repeated testing to ensure that ingesting genes from foreign organisms do not carry subtle or long-term dangers. On the other hand, there's the equal danger of becoming paranoid about potential problems and losing sight of genuine benefits to genetically enhanced foods—e.g., improved flavor, added nutrition, retarded spoilage.

..................................TRY THIS....................................

Locate the most current information about genetically engineered food and weigh this information against the guidelines set by the Alliance for Bio-Integrity and other watchdog organizations. Write an article that details your findings.

The Theater and Its Double

by Antonin Artaud

Translated by Mary Caroline Richards

One of the reasons for the asphyxiating atmosphere in which we live without possible escape or remedy ... is our respect for what has been written, formulated, or painted, what has been given form, as if all expression were not at last exhausted, were not at a point where things must break apart if they are to start anew and begin fresh.

... Masterpieces of the past are good for the past: they are not good for us. We have the right to say what has been said and even what has not been said in a way that belongs to us, a way that is immediate and direct, corresponding to present modes of feeling, and understandable to everyone.

It is idiotic to reproach the masses for having no sense of the sublime, when the sublime is confused with one or another of its formal manifestations, which are moreover always defunct manifestations. And if for example a contemporary public does not understand *Oedipus Rex*, I shall make bold to say that it is the fault of *Oedipus Rex* and not of the public.

In *Oedipus Rex* there is the theme of incest and the idea that nature mocks at morality and that there are certain unspecified powers at large which we would do well to beware of, call them destiny or anything you choose. There is in addition the presence of a plague epidemic which is a physical incarnation of these powers. But the whole in a manner and language that have lost all touch with the rude and epileptic rhythm of our time. Sophocles speaks grandly, perhaps, but in a style that is no longer timely.

FOR FURTHER REFLECTION

How deeply are we moved by a performance of a play by Sophocles or Shakespeare? For Artaud it wasn't enough merely to be "entertained" by the great dramatic works of the past that were occluded by the language and mannerisms of the past; they did not get through to the audiences. These works have become elitist objects of veneration without truly connecting with the contemporary human soul.

.... TRY THIS, ...

Describe an innovative way of staging a pre-twentieth-century drama—Ibsen's *A Doll's House* or Shakespeare's *A Midsummer Night's Dream*.

OCTOBER 31
The Writing Life
by Annie Dillard

The printed word cannot compete with the movies on their ground and should not. You can describe beautiful faces, car chases, or valleys full of Indians on horseback until you run out of words, and you will not approach the movies' spectacle. Novels written with film contracts in mind have a faint but unmistakable, and ruinous, odor. I cannot name what, in the text, alerts the reader to suspect the writer of mixed motives; I cannot specify which sentences, in several books, have caused me to read on with increasing dismay, and finally close the books because I smelled a rat. Such books seem uneasy being books; they seem eager to fling off their disguises and jump onto screens.

Why would anyone read a book instead of watching big people move on a screen? Because a book can be literature. It is a subtle thing. ... In my view, the more literary the book—the more purely verbal, crafted sentence by sentence, the more imaginative, reasoned, and deep—the more likely people are to read it. The people who read are the people who like literature. ... They like, or require, what books alone have.

FOR FURTHER REFLECTION

In an age dominated by visual media, literature must retain its integrity as *literature*—of using language to convey its imaginative richness and powers of insight—instead of selling out to the merely cinematic and sensationalistic. Writing for the screen is an honorable profession, but that is a very different vocation from that of novelist or memoirist.

......................................TRY THIS................................

In your journal describe your true objectives as a writer. Are you writing one kind of fiction or nonfiction but secretly wishing you were writing another kind? Are you trying to write novels when you'd really rather be writing screenplays, or vice versa? Focus sharply on the kind of writing you most sincerely wish to produce, and then spend the next three months pursuing that goal alone.

NOVEMBER 1

The Whisperings Within: Evolution and the Origin of Human Nature

by David Barash

Thomas Hobbes wrote in the seventeenth century that human beings are "by their nature" unrelentingly selfish, and warned of the continuing and unavoidable "warre of each against each" unless society would mediate. In Hobbes's view, the role of society is to restrain those biological tendencies that may be beneficial to individuals but potentially ruinous for the whole. As social creatures, we each have a very low fitness unless we associate with our fellows; we therefore live in social groups, for our personal gain. At the same time, these social groups must, for the survival of the society, restrain our more flagrantly self-centered acts. We are placed in a frustrating bind: we need the society of others for our benefit, but successful functioning within that society requires us to renounce conspicuous pursuit of that benefit.

If human society requires that each of us sublimate our selfish fitness-maximizing strategies, then much of our social behavior is greatly constrained and actually a complex web of lies and deceptions. "The self," wrote Reinhold Niebuhr, "is tempted to hide its desire to dominate behind its pretended devotion to the world. All mature conduct is therefore infected with an element of dishonesty and insincerity. The lie is always intimately related to the sin of egoism."

… The product of this repression is the unconscious, an internal core of biologically evolved, ravenous selfishness (similar to Freud's concept of the id), which has combined with our personalized coping devices.

FOR FURTHER REFLECTION

Is altruism a myth? Is selfishness our most natural state, as Hobbes argued, and do our moral actions arise out of social conditioning? From a Freudian perspective, we need not see ourselves as phonies if Hobbes's conclusions are true. We can counterargue that our ability to suppress our selfishness is also natural; that we also desire to be compassionate toward others.

...................................TRY THIS....................................

How do you react to Reinhold Niebuhr's claim that "all mature conduct is infected with an element of dishonesty and insincerity"? Express your thoughts in an essay on the psychology of honesty.

NOVEMBER 2
My Life
by Marc Chagall

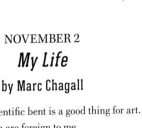

Personally I do not think a scientific bent is a good thing for art.

Impressionism and Cubism are foreign to me.

Art seems to me to be above all a state of soul.

All souls are sacred, the soul of all the bipeds in every quarter of the globe.

Only the upright heart that has its own logic and its own reason is free.

The soul that has reached by itself that level which men call literature, the illogic, is the purest.

I am not speaking of the old realism, not of the symbolism-romanticism that has contributed very little; nor of mythology either, not of any sort of fantasy, but of what, my God?

You will say, those schools are merely formal trappings.

Primitive art already possessed the technical perfection towards which present generations strive, juggling and even falling into stylization.

FOR FURTHER REFLECTION

In Chagall's painting we see a fusion of spirituality with whimsy. Old Testament figures are brought vibrantly to life. It is not surprising, therefore, that he asserts in his cryptic autobiography that the realm of illogic comes closest to the essence of art, and to the essence of the soul.

......................................TRY THIS....................................

1. Study several of Chagall's paintings, along with his famous stained glass windows, and compose a poem or two that captures the emotions that one or more of these works trigger.
2. Write an essay analyzing the biblical motifs in Chagall's paintings.

Lonely Hearts of the Cosmos: The Story of the Scientific Quest for the Secret of the Universe

by Dennis Overbye

What does it mean to say the universe is expanding? Few statements sound so glib and cause so much trouble when people try to visualize what is really going on. Most laymen think of the galaxies as exploding from some point and flying outward through space. According to Einstein's general relativity, however, it is really space that is exploding, carrying the galaxies along like twigs on a current. A popular analogy is a raisin cake baking in the oven. As the yeast expands the dough, the cake gets larger, carrying the raisins farther apart from each other.

Although we see individual galaxies receding at different speeds, space expands at the same speed everywhere in all directions at once. In fact it is this uniform expansion that gives the illusion that everything is racing away from *us*. Suppose the universe doubles in size in an hour. In that time span a galaxy originally 1 mile distant will become 2 miles distant and thus seem to be moving away at 1 mile per hour. But a galaxy 10 miles away at the start of the hour will be 20 miles away at the end—it will seem to be going ten times faster than the other one.

These cosmic speeds are all relative. At the other end of the universe or of the raisin cake, a galaxy or a raisin would see itself at rest and its own neighbors moving modestly while *we* would appear to be dashing at high speed.

FOR FURTHER REFLECTION

Cosmology sometimes seems more like mysticism than hard science. That's because some of the concepts are so alien to everyday experience. For example, our everyday experience tells us that space is the nothingness through which things move; but modern cosmology tells us that space, not objects in space (like stars and galaxies), is what has been expanding. The only way we can imagine space expanding is to think of it as a dynamic substance, like a flowing stream, carrying objects along.

...................................TRY THIS....................................

In a poem, describe a cosmic phenomenon like gravity or cosmic background radiation, the expanding universe, or black holes. Use vivid sensory imagery that will help root the concept in everyday human experience.

The Song of the Dodo: Island Biogeography in an Age of Extinction
by David Quammen

Biogeography is the study of the facts and the patterns of species distribution. It's the science concerned with where animals are, where plants are, and where they are not. On the island of Madagascar, for instance, there once lived an ostrich-like creature that stood ten feet tall, weighed half a ton, and thumped across the landscape on a pair of elephantine legs. Yes, it was a bird. One thousand pounds of bone, flesh, feathers. This is no hypothetical monster, no implausible fantasy of Herodotus or Marco Polo. In a remarkable museum in Antananarivo, I've seen its skeleton: I've seen its two-gallon egg. Paleontologists know it as *Aepyornis maximus*. The species survived until Europeans reached Madagascar in the sixteenth century and began hunting it, harrying it, transforming the ecosystem it was part of, scrambling those bounteous eggs. A millennium ago, *Aepyornis maximus* existed only on that single island; now it exists nowhere. To say that is the business of biogeography.

As practiced by thoughtful scientists, biogeography does more than ask *Which species?* And *Where?* It also asks *Why?* And, what is sometimes even more crucial, *Why not?*

FOR FURTHER REFLECTION

It is important to understand species in their geographical context—the nature of their habitat and how vulnerable that habitat can be to external as well as internal factors. Before they can protect endangered species from disease or habitat deterioration as well as from hunters and poachers, environmentalists must acquire in-depth knowledge of those habitats and determine the species' patterns of distribution.

...................................TRY THIS....................................

Select an endangered species from the list posted by the Environmental Protection Agency (EPA), and write an essay describing the factors contributing to that species' endangerment, and what must be done to keep that species from extinction.

NOVEMBER 5
Ex Libris:
Confessions of a Common Reader
by Anne Fadiman

When my son was eight months old, it could truthfully be said that he devoured literature. Presented with a book, he chewed it. A bit of Henry's DNA has been permanently incorporated into the warped pages of *Goodnight Moon*, and the missing corners of pages 3 and 8 suggest that a bit of *Goodnight Moon* has been permanently incorporated into Henry. He was, of course, not the first child to indulge in bibliophagy. The great Philadelphia book dealer A.S.W. Rosenbach deduced that one reason first editions of *Alice in Wonderland* were so scarce was that so many of them had been eaten.

Henry and his word-swallowing colleagues—they include a *Wall Street Journal* editor who absentmindedly tears off morsels from the newsroom dictionary, rolls them in little balls, and pops them in his mouth—are merely taking literally the metaphorical similarity between reading and eating, which makes us say, for instance, that we have browsed through a newspaper or had a hard time digesting an overlong biography. When we call people bookworms, we are likening them to the larvae of insects chiefly members of the orders *Thysanura* and *Psocoptera*, whose entire diet may consist of paper and glue. "Books are food," wrote the English critic Holbrook Jackson*, "libraries so many dishes of meat, served out for several palates."

FOR FURTHER REFLECTION

Whimsical as it sounds, eating and reading are intimately connected. It isn't simply that books feed the mind the way food feeds the body; reading feels like whole-body nourishment. An avid reader can experience the sensation of physically ingesting a book's content, of becoming satiated with the multi-sensory stimuli that a good novel or biography provides.

. . . . .TRY THIS. . . . .

The next time you begin reading a work of fiction or narrative nonfiction, record your experience with the book—how it pulls you into the story, how certain passages seem to satisfy various cravings—for sensory imagery, for suspense, for being immersed in a different world.

---

* See the entry for September 5.

NOVEMBER 6
"Enjoying Your Food"
by Edward Espe Brown

from *Tomato Blessings and Radish Teachings:*
Recipes and Reflections

At my Saturday meditation retreats, when we break for lunch, I often tell people, "Please enjoy your food." All morning I have been offering various instructions in sitting and walking meditation, and by lunchtime we have also had an hour of yoga with further directives, so I may leave it at that. I don't want eating to be another chore, or yet another place to worry about whether or not you are doing it "right." We do enough of that already, so I want to invite people to simply "please enjoy your food." ... I explain that enjoying your food is very important, because by enjoying something we connect to the world, to one another, to our inner being. When you enjoy your food you will be happy and well nourished by what you eat.

Sometimes I also explain to people that by enjoying their food, they will naturally find themselves practicing meditation. They will be paying attention to what they are eating, noticing flavors and textures and nuances of taste, because to enjoy something you need to experience it. ... Most of the problems that arise in the pursuit of pleasure are due to lack of devotion—not being fully enough committed to pleasure. Which bite of chocolate cake is no longer pleasurable? Which swallow of wine brings you down instead of up? Sure, restraint is needed, but it comes after pleasure or along with pleasure, not before and in place of pleasure.

FOR FURTHER REFLECTION
We need to distinguish between pleasure and gluttony. This means being better able to monitor the psychological changes that take place while we're eating a meal or savoring a glass of wine. "Enjoying your food" does not mean mindlessly indulging in it; on the contrary, it means slowing down and paying attention to the subtle flavors, aromas, and textures. That way we can better discern when the pleasure starts to fade. One might think of this as a Zen approach to eating; indeed, Edward Espe Brown is an ordained Zen priest.

...................................TRY THIS....................................

Prepare a list of suggestions for making fine dining a more pleasurable experience, and at the same time a healthier one. Things to consider: ambiance, pacing, presentation, table conversation. Afterwards, weave your suggestions into an essay on the subject.

NOVEMBER 7

"The Archaeological Revolution"

by William Foxwell Albright

from *From the Stone Age to Christianity:
Monotheism and the Historical Process*

Modern archaeological excavation may be said to have begun with the first organized work at Herculaneum (1738) and Pompeii (1748), and modern comparative
archaeology may be dated from the epoch-making researches of J.J. Winckelmann
(1717–68) in the history of Graeco-Roman art. It is interesting to note that the
serious collection and interpretation of pre-Christian literature and inscriptions
from the Near East began about the same time, with the remarkable expedition of
the Dane, Carsten Niebuhr, in 1761–67 and the recovery of the principal works of
Avestan literature by Anquetil-Duperron during the years 1755–71.

The systematic surface exploration of the Near East did not begin until the turn
of the century. In 1798 Napoleon's scientific expedition began an elaborate exploration of the Nile Valley which was promptly made available to scholars in the stately
volumes of the *Description de l'Egypte* (1809–13). The discovery of the Rosetta
Stone in 1799 was followed by its decipherment through the combined efforts of
Akerblad, Thomas Young, and especially of Champollion, who published his first
correct results in 1822. Mesopotamia was systematically explored and described,
with particular attention to its antiquities, by [C.J.] Rich and [Sir Robert K.] Porter
from 1811 to 1836, when Rich's posthumous work appeared.

FOR FURTHER REFLECTION

The ancient past comes to us through the painstaking work of archaeologists
over the course of centuries. Much of what is unearthed needs to be pieced
together (quite literally) and compared with similar artifacts from other sites
and then interpreted. The conclusions of one archaeologist will often clash
with those of another working with the same materials but interpreting the
findings in a different way.

...................................TRY THIS....................................

Select a famous archaeological site and compare the archaeological findings
with the historical or biblical accounts. Write a short story in which you dramatize
an incident suggested by the archaeological or the historical record.

The Greek Experience
by C.M. Bowra

Democracy, which reached its most advanced and most active form in Athens, arose from a series of extensions of power to a bigger and bigger class, until in the end this included all free male citizens. It soon developed a market character which distinguishes it from modern democracies in more than one way. It had, at least in its early days, an undeniably aristocratic tone. A tradition of taste and elegance was maintained by noble families like the Alcmaeonids, who, despite their wealth and lineage, welcomed the new system and took a leading part in establishing it. From them a sense of style spread to a wider circle and was enriched with a new strength and scope. Artists and writers, conscious that their public was no longer a few select families but a whole people, gave a new meaning to traditional forms and spared no effort to be worthy of their wider horizons. So too in civil and domestic life, as we see it painted on vases, there is nothing vulgar or mean. Style and taste are always dominant and have an aristocratic distinction, as if they belonged to men who knew instinctively how to infuse any occasion with charm and dignity.

This aristocratic quality was made possible by the existence of slavery. By it the common people of Athens had a degree of leisure which is almost unknown in a modern proletariat. It is easy to condemn this system, but its defects were not perhaps so grave as we might think. Athens differed from many slave-owning societies in its large proportion of free men to slaves, which has been calculated as about two to one. This is nothing like the scale of slavery in imperial Rome.

FOR FURTHER REFLECTION

We think of democracy and aristocracy as antithetical, but in ancient Athens, aristocratic values became the values of the populace. This situation was made possible by the fact that a much larger percentage of the people had the leisure to cultivate taste in the arts, thanks to slavery. Despite the fact that, as Bowra points out, there were far fewer slaves in proportion to the general population than in imperial Rome, we cannot regard Athens as a true democracy because of the existence of slavery.

.... TRY THIS ....

Write an essay comparing and contrasting Athenian democracy to pre–Civil War American democracy, keeping in mind that before 1865, slavery had been a part of American democracy also.

NOVEMBER 9

St. Francis of Assisi

by G.K. Chesterton

The whole point about St. Francis of Assisi is that he certainly was ascetical and he certainly was not gloomy. As soon as ever he had been unhorsed by the glorious humiliation of his vision of dependence on the divine love, he flung himself into fasting and vigil exactly as he had flung himself furiously into battle. ... It was not self-denial merely in the sense of self-control. It was as positive as a passion; it had the air of being as positive as a pleasure. He devoured fasting as a man devours food. He plunged after poverty as men have dug madly for gold. And it is precisely the positive and passionate quality of this part of his personality that is a challenge to the modern mind in the whole problem of the pursuit of pleasure. There undeniably is the historical fact; and there attached to it is another moral fact almost as undeniable. It is certain that he held on this heroic or unnatural course from the moment when he went forth in his hairshirt into the winter woods to the moment when he desired even in his death agony to lie bare upon the bare ground, to prove that he had and that he was nothing. And we can say, with almost as deep a certainty, that the stars which passed above that gaunt and wasted corpse stark upon the rocky floor had for once, in all their shining cycles round the world of laboring humanity, looked down upon a happy man.

FOR FURTHER REFLECTION

Surely one major way in which saints differ from ordinary spiritual folks is in their *desire* to renounce material goods, in the *pleasure* they derive from fasting and devoting their lives to the service of others. St. Francis seemed to have possessed the capacity for total altruism. His example reminds us of the enormous capacity human beings possess for spreading good in the world.

......................................TRY THIS...................................

1. Write a biographical profile of St. Francis, emphasizing the positive outcome of his life of poverty.
2. Do some in-depth reading in the life and works of a well-known saint and write a short story that dramatizes one incident in that saint's life.

NOVEMBER 10
"Oliver Wendell Holmes"
by Louis Menand
from *The Metaphysical Club*

The lesson [Oliver Wendell] Holmes took from the [Civil War] can be put in a sentence: It is that certitude leads to violence. This is a proposition that has an easy application and a difficult one. The easy application is to ideologues, dogmatists, and bullies—people who think that their rightness justifies them in imposing on anyone who does not happen to subscribe to their particular ideology, dogma, or notion of turf. If the conviction of rightness is powerful enough, resistance to it will be met, sooner or later, by force. There are people like this in every sphere of life, and it is natural to feel that the world would be a better place without them.

But this is not quite what Holmes felt. He did have an intense dislike of people who presented themselves as instruments of some higher power. "I detest a man who knows that he knows," as he wrote, late in life. ... And he had a knee-jerk suspicion of causes. He regarded them as attempts to compel one group of human beings to conform to some other group's idea of the good. ...

His standard example in criticizing the reformist mentality was the abolitionists. "[They] had a stock phrase that a man was either a knave or a fool who did not act as they (the abolitionists) knew to be right," he wrote. ..." When you know that you know persecution comes easy."

FOR FURTHER REFLECTION

When the Civil War swept away slavery, it also swept away the worldview that permitted slavery to exist. A new way of thinking about knowledge and morality began to take hold in America, and Oliver Wendell Holmes was one of its finest representatives. For Holmes, as Louis Menand points out, liberty is threatened by politicians and lawyers whose notions of right and wrong are inflexible and disconnected from the human condition.

....................................TRY THIS....................................

List several of the greatest defenders of human rights from the time of the Civil War to the beginning of the civil rights era a century later. Write a comparative biographical profile of three or four of them.

"Oenone to Paris" by Ovid

from *Heroides*. Translated by Harold Isbell

Will you read? Does your new wife
  [Helen] forbid? Read on,
  no Mycenaean has written this.
Rather, Oenone the fountain-
  nymph, well known
  in the Phrygian woods,
  writes these words
and complains of the way
  you—my very own,
  if only you will permit—treat her.
What god opposes my desires?
  Is there some
guilt that will not let me be
  your own?
If one must suffer, one should
  suffer calmly;
  but undeserved pain is much
  more sad.
You were a nobody when you
  married me;
  I was the daughter of a great stream.

You are one of the sons
  of Priam now, but
  then—with all respect—
  you were a slave;
you were held a captive and I
  was a nymph,
  but I was content to marry you.
With our flocks we took our rest
  beneath the trees
  on couches of fallen leaves and grass.
Often we lay together on hay or straw
  in a hut that kept the frost away.

...

  You carved my name on beech
  trees and I
can read there "Oenone,"
  product of your hand.
  As those trees grow the words
  likewise grow.
Grow high and straight so that
  everyone will know
  my name and the honor that
  is mine.

FOR FURTHER REFLECTION

Ovid's collection of verse letters is remarkable for at least two reasons: First, these verse letters, from the women as well as from the men to their respective absent lovers, skillfully capture the trials and tribulations of love and emotional commitment. And second, they skillfully blend psychological realism with the enchantment of these larger-than-life mythological heroes and heroines.

.................................TRY THIS....................................

Transform the contents of one of Ovid's imaginary verse letters in his *Heroides* (Penelope to Ulysses, Medea to Jason, Helen to Paris, Paris to Helen, in addition to Oenone to Paris) into a one-act play or short story.

NOVEMBER 12

The Courtier [Il Cortegiano]
by Baldassare Castiglione

from *The Renaissance in England*. Translated by Sir Thomas Hoby

When an amiable countenance of a beautiful woman cometh in [the courtier's] sight, that is accompanied with noble conditions and honest behaviors, so that, as one practiced in love, he wotteth [knows] well that his hue hath an agreement with hers, as soon as he is aware that his eyes snatch that image and carry it to the heart, and that the soul beginneth to behold it with pleasure, and feeleth within herself the influence that stirreth her and by little and little setteth her in heat, and that those lively spirits that twinkle out through the eyes put continually fresh nourishment to the fire, he ought in this beginning to seek a speedy remedy and to raise up reason, and with her to fence the fortress of his heart, and to shut in such wise the passages against sense and appetites that they may enter neither with force nor subtil practice. Thus, if the flame be quenched, the jeopardy is also quenched. But in case it continue or increase, then must the courtier determine, when he perceiveth he is taken, to shun thoroughly all filthiness of commune love, and so enter into the holy way of love with the guide of reason, and first consider that the body where that beauty shineth is not the fountain from whence beauty springeth, but rather because beauty is bodiless and … an heavenly shining beam, she loseth much of her honor when she is coupled with that vile subject and full of corruption, because the less she is partner thereof, the more perfect she is, and, clean sund'red from it, is most perfect.

FOR FURTHER REFLECTION

In *The Courtier*, that compendium of courtly morality and behavior that had influenced European high society in the high Renaissance, Castiglione recognized the baser (we would say libidinal) source of love and beauty; but the cultivated man and woman was urged to pay homage to its transcendent, spiritual flowering; for only then can civility and culture prevail. Without a code of courtly behavior, society would rapidly degrade.

..................................TRY THIS..................................

Compare today's courtship rituals with those advocated by Castiglione more than 400 years ago. Explain which directives you would like to see reinstated.

"Emblem VII"

by Francis Quarles

*Wherefore hidest thou thy face, and holdest me
for thine enemy?*

—Job 13:24

Why dost Thou shade Thy
   lovely face? Oh why
Does that eclipsing hand so long deny
The sunshine of Thy soul-enlivening eye?

Without that light, what light
   remains in me?
Thou art my life, my way, my light; in Thee
I live, I move, and by Thy beams I see.

Thou art my life: if Thou but turn away,
My life's a thousand deaths;
   Thou art my way:
Without thee, Lord, I travel not, but stray.

My light Thou art: Without
   Thy glorious sight,
My eyes are darkened with perpetual night.
My God, Thou art my way, my
   life, and light....

My path is lost, my wandering steps do stray;

I cannot safely go, nor safely stay;
Whom should I seek but Thee,
   my path, my way? …

And yet Thou turn'st away Thy
   face, and fly'st me;
And yet I sue for grace, and
   Thou deny'st me;
Speak, art Thou angry, Lord,
   or only try'st me?…

Disclose Thy sunbeams, close
   Thy wings and stay;
See, see how I am blind and
   dead, and stray,
O Thou that art my light, my life, my way.

Epigram 7

If heaven's all-quickening eyes
   vouchsafe to shine
Upon our souls, we slight; if not, we whine:
Our equinoctial hearts can never lie
   Secure beneath the tropics of that eye.

FOR FURTHER REFLECTION

The emblem was a popular literary form that consisted of a passage from
Scripture, a visual representation of that passage, followed by an original poem
reflecting on the passage, and concluding with an epigram. Quarles effectively
captures Job's anguished struggle to make sense of the seeming paradox of a
God who hides the very light that must lead mankind to salvation—a struggle
that becomes the means by which his faith is deepened.

....TRY THIS....................................

Compose an emblem of your own based upon a passage from Scripture that
you find baffling or paradoxical.

"Désirée's Baby"
by Kate Chopin

When the baby was about three months old, Désirée awoke one day to the conviction that there was something in the air menacing her peace. It was at first too subtle to grasp. It had only been a disquieting suggestion; an air of mystery among the blacks; unsuspected visits from far-off neighbors who could hardly account for their coming. Then a strange, an awful change in her husband's manner, which she dared not ask him to explain. When he spoke to her, it was with averted eyes, from which the old love-light seemed to have gone out. He absented himself from home; and when there, avoided her presence and that of her child, without excuse. And the very spirit of Satan seemed suddenly to take hold of him in his dealings with the slaves. Désirée was miserable enough to die.

She sat in her room, one hot afternoon, in her peignoir, listlessly drawing through her fingers the strands of her long, silky brown hair that hung about her shoulders. The baby, half-naked, lay asleep upon her own great mahogany bed, that was like a sumptuous throne, with its satin-lined half-canopy. One of La Blanche's little quadroon boys—half naked too—stood fanning the child slowly with a fan of peacock feathers. Désirée's eyes had been fixed absently and sadly upon the baby, while she was striving to penetrate the threatening mist that she felt closing about her. She looked from her child to the boy who stood beside him, and back again; over and over. "Ah!" It was a cry that she could not help; which she was not conscious of having uttered. The blood turned like ice in her veins, and a clammy moisture gathered upon her face.

FOR FURTHER REFLECTION

In this moving story we learn what it was like for a mother to discover that her newborn child manifested the mixed-race traits of her presumed all-white husband. Désirée's shock came not from the fact that her child was a "quadroon"—one fourth black—but that her husband had either deliberately hidden the truth of his mixed-race background or was unaware of it himself.

...............................TRY THIS................................

If you discovered that your child, who you'd presumed to be of only one race, was of mixed blood, how would you react? How would your spouse? Write an essay about the way attitudes toward interracial marriage and miscegenation have changed over the past century—if you think they've changed at all.

NOVEMBER 15
Caligula
by Albert Camus
Translated by Stuart Gilbert

SCIPIO: How I loathe you! And how I pity you!

CALIGULA (Angrily): Enough, I tell you.

SCIPIO: And how horrible a loneliness like yours must be!

CALIGULA (In a rush of anger, gripping the boy by the collar, and shaking him): Loneliness! What do you know of it? Only the loneliness of poets and weaklings. You prate of loneliness, but you don't realize that one is *never* alone. Always we are attended by the same load of the future and the past. Those we have killed are always with us. But they are no great trouble. It's those we have loved, those who loved us and whom we did not love; regrets, desires, bitterness and sweetness, whores and gods, the celestial gang! Always, always with us! (He releases SCIPIO and moves back to his former place) Alone! Ah, if only in this loneliness, this ghoul-haunted wilderness of mine, I could know, but for a moment, real solitude, real silence, the throbbing stillness of a tree! …

SCIPIO: All men have a secret solace. It helps them to endure, and they turn to it when life has wearied them beyond enduring.

CALIGULA: Yes, Scipio.

SCIPIO: Have you nothing of the kind in your life, no refuge, no mood that makes the tears well up, no consolation?

CALIGULA: Yes, I have something of the kind.

SCIPIO: What is it?

CALIGULA (Very quietly): Scorn.

FOR FURTHER REFLECTION

Camus' Caligula is ravaged by the existential reality of conscience: His deeds, he discovers to his horror, remain with him, an eternal present. All he can do is to rage against the inevitable and the irreversible. Was the real Caligula so torn by conscience? We can never know, but through the lens of post-Freudian understanding of the human mind, we can make an educated guess.

· TRY THIS ·

After reading the lives of some of the ancient rulers, choose one and create a one-act drama in which the pharaoh, emperor, or king wrestles with his conscience over past misdeeds.

The Mysteries Within:
A Surgeon Reflects on Medical Myths
by Sherwin B. Nuland

When in the fifth century B.C.E. Greek physicians began to create what has come to be called the medicine of Hippocrates—a method of healing based on direct observation and the exclusion of the supernatural—they nevertheless remained heir to formulations whose origins are discoverable in the very theurgy they were determined to expunge. As accurate as were their observations of natural phenomena, these later Greeks not infrequently explained what they saw by attributing fanciful characteristics to body parts and fluids, just as had the superstitious healers before them. Paramount in their ideas of physiology was the principle that the action of the fluids known as humors determines not only one's state of health, but even one's temperament. As was true of the vestiges of their continuing belief in the specific personalities of the organs themselves, they adapted these notions from similar beliefs of earlier civilizations and even from certain traits they continued to attribute to the organs in which the fluids were said to originate.

There are lessons in contemplating the Greek absorptions of non-rational ideas into a system of medicine that historians are fond of hailing as rational. No matter the insistence of philosophers that objectivity and reason can replace emotionalism and tradition; no matter the homage we pay to the scientific method, new paradigms of detached fact-gathering, and a resolute rejection of a long tradition of magical thinking—no matter any of these determined seekings for a civilization guided by reason, there are inherent currents within the mind of *Homo sapiens* that will not be denied.

FOR FURTHER REFLECTION

The history of science and medicine is a history of struggle to distinguish between the rational and the irrational, objective truth from subjective belief—and as Sherwin Nuland, a professor of surgery, explains, the older belief systems will assert themselves to some degree, under the guise of "folk medicine," "folk wisdom," "faith healing," and the like.

......................................TRY THIS...................................

Describe your own or a friend's or family member's experience (positive or negative) with faith healing, folk medicine, or some other method of healing outside the paradigm of contemporary Western medical practices.

NOVEMBER 17
Simone Weil
by Francine du Plessix Gray

[Simone Weil] believed that work is the truest road to self-knowledge, and that it supplies the only valid form of social cohesion. For in her view, most other bonds—family ties, the affection of lovers, even the religion that links fellow worshipers—are nourished by destructive emotions, by "the same seductive accord that engenders all wars." Work, however, unifies in the purest way: "Religion makes love manifest, but work ... creates respect for the human person, and equality; that is why collaboration [in work] creates enduring friendships for which there is no substitute." [Simone Pétrement, *Simone Weil: A Life.* Trans. Raymond Rosenthal. (Pantheon, 1976): 45] This proto-Marxist view of work hinged on an admittedly naïve idealization—if not canonization—of the proletariat, which she saw as a form of contemporary sainthood. On the basis of having taught Plato and Descartes to railroad workers at evening school, Simone earnestly believed that a member of the working class, if given the proper study guidance, could reach the truth far better than the average intellectual. Sitting on the subway next to [her close friend] Simone Pétrement one day, she pointed to a man in his factory overalls, and said, "You see, it's not just in a spirit of justice that I love them. I love them naturally, because I find them far more beautiful than the bourgeois." [Gabriella Fiori, *Simone Weil: An Intellectual Biography.* Trans. Joseph R. Berrigan. (University of Georgia Press, 1989): 58]

FOR FURTHER REFLECTION

The social bonds created by labor are among the most enduring, according to the social activist and philosopher Simone Weil, who died from anorexia in her thirties. It is the working class that counteracts the impulse to dominate, to control—and for that reason holds the greatest promise for social justice.

..................................TRY THIS..................................

In an essay or short story, explore the virtues as well as the drawbacks of organized labor and the working classes. Focus on a particular labor-related issue, such as unions, workplace ethics, opportunities for advancement, or job variety.

NOVEMBER 18

Booked to Die

by John Dunning

You wouldn't believe the crap that accumulates in a bookscout's den. Book after book came down from the pile and went into another pile that I had labeled "Junk" in my mind. I thumbed each piece carefully, I went page by page to make sure a $50,000 pamphlet wasn't hidden inside a $2 book. It wasn't. There were some real heartbreakers—a fine little Faulkner poem, original 1932 issue, paper wraps, a $250 piece that Bobby [the bookscout] could've sold to me on the spot except that someone had lost his supper on the title page ... an early Steinbeck, nice, except that somebody had ripped out the title page ... Robert Frost's first book inscribed by Frost on the half title, very quaint except that a kid had been at the book with crayons. ...

I was resigned by then to coming up zero. I took a break at ten-thirty and let my eyes skim over the books as a lot. If there was anything worthwhile in that mess, I couldn't see it. ... Nothing anybody would kill for. Slowly the one natural motive—that Bobby had found something valuable—was dwindling before my eyes. Of course, the killer might have taken it away with him: I was going on the slim, bare hope that he had killed Bobby and had failed to find what he had killed for. But I was beginning to believe it was something as simple, and insane, as an old grudge, for a sudden fight between rivals.

Then I found the good books.

FOR FURTHER REFLECTION

The world of antiquarian books can be an ideal milieu for a murder mystery. An ardent book collector and dealer as well as a homicide detective, John Dunning's protagonist Cliff Janeway fascinates us with his knowledge of antiquarian books as well as of criminal investigation. Why, Janeway wonders, would anyone brutally murder a bookscout—someone who finds valuable books at cheap prices and resells them to dealers at a profit?

...................................TRY THIS...............................

Outline a mystery story in which a sophisticated book thief finds a way to steal priceless rarities from the Library of Congress, and then demands an extraordinary ransom for them.

NOVEMBER 19

Arctic Dreams: Imagination and Desire in a Northern Landscape
by Barry Lopez

The edges of any landscape—horizons, the lip of a valley, the bend of a river around a canyon wall—quicken an observer's expectations. That attraction to borders, to the earth's twilit places, is part of the shape of human curiosity. And the edges that cause excitement are like these where I now walk, sensing the birds toying with gravity; or like those in quantum mechanics, where what is critical straddles a border between being a wave and being a particle, between being what is and becoming something else, occupying an edge of time that defeats our geometries. In biology these transitional areas between two different communities are called ecotones.

The ecotone at the Admiralty Inlet floe edge extends in two planes. In order to pass under the ice from the open sea, an animal must be free of a need for atmospheric oxygen; the floe edge, therefore, is a barrier to the horizontal migration of whales. In the vertical plane, no bird can penetrate the ice and birds like gulls can't go below water with guillemots to feed on schools of fish. Sunlight, too, is halted at these borders.

To stand at the edge of this four-foot-thick ice platform, however, is to find yourself in a rich biological crease. Species of alga grow on the bottom of the sea ice, turning it golden brown with a patchwork of life. These tiny diatoms feed zooplankton moving through the upper layers of water in vast clouds—underwater galaxies of copepods, amphipods, and mysids. These in turn feed the streaming schools of cod. The cod feed the birds. And the narwhals. And also the ringed seal, which feeds the polar bear, and eventually the fox.

FOR FURTHER REFLECTION

The boundaries (ecotones) of landforms are of great scientific interest because they represent intersections of different communities of organisms. These ecotones shed light on the dynamics of the food chain, species behavior, and patterns of migrations, as well as on different weather systems.

. . . . TRY THIS . . . .

The next time you visit a beach keep an eye out for tidepools and estuaries, and write an essay describing the different kinds of organisms you find. Other unique ecotones to explore are edges of mountain ranges, forests, and riverbanks.

The Unity of Philosophical Experience
by Etienne Gilson

Himself a theologian, St. Thomas [Aquinas] had asked the professors of theology never to prove an article of faith by rational demonstration, for faith is not based on reason, but on the word of God, and if you try to prove it, you destroy it. He had likewise asked the professors of philosophy never to prove a philosophical truth by resorting to the words of God, for philosophy is not based on Revelation, but on reason, and if you try to base it on authority, you destroy it. In other words, theology is the science of those things which are received by faith from divine revelation, and philosophy is the knowledge of those things which flow from the principles of natural reason. Since their common source is God, the creator of both reason and revelation, these two sciences are bound ultimately to agree; but if you really want them to agree, you must first be careful not to forget their essential differences. Only distinct things can be united; if you attempt to blend them, you inevitably lose them in what is not union, but confusion.

FOR FURTHER REFLECTION

The paradox inherent in the effort to find unity between reason and divine revelation is that it is first necessary to accept the essential difference between them, and (following Aquinas's directive) never try to probe a matter in one domain with the tools of the other domain. The only way to resolve the paradox is to acknowledge that both emanate from God. Rationalists, however, cannot accept that resolution, however, because once you say that something emanates from God, it is part of revelation, not part of reason.

..............................TRY THIS..............................

1. In a meditative essay, suggest a way in which nature as phenomena can be reconciled with nature as a manifestation of the divine.
2. Write a story in which your protagonist, a scientist, experiences a divine revelation as he or she probes a mysterious natural phenomenon.

"Taking Off"

by Elizabeth A. Wood

from *Science From Your Airplane Window*

The important thing in getting an airplane off the ground is not its speed relative to the ground, but its speed relative to the air. If it can get up to 100 mph with a 25 mph head wind, its speed relative to the air is 125 mph. It could go faster, relative to the ground, down wind—perhaps 110 mph. But then its speed relative to the air would be only 85 mph.

If the speed of the plane relative to the air makes it rise, it must be that the forward motion causes more up-push than down-push, a net force upward. The air must somehow be pressing harder against the underside of the wings than against the top side, so much harder that it lifts the airplane. One way in which this difference in pressure is achieved is by shaping the wing so that the air that goes over the top has to go farther than the air that goes under the bottom. ... The molecules of air passing over the top of the wing spread farther apart and exert less pressure than those under the wing where they are packed more closely together. At the trailing edge of the wing the top air must come together again with the bottom air. The greater velocity of the air going over the top has resulted in a lifting force.

FOR FURTHER REFLECTION

How is it possible for anything so massive as an airplane to fly? Sometimes even basic principles of physics seem to contradict common sense until we investigate more closely. A wing is shaped in such a way that greater pressure is exerted against the bottom of the wing than against the top.

. . . . TRY THIS . . . .

Write a feature for children in which you explain how an airplane flies. For an analogy, you might adapt the one Elizabeth Wood uses: Hold the short edge of a rectangular sheet of paper just underneath your lower lip and blow across the top of the sheet. "The greater velocity of the air above the paper makes it rise. It is just this that helps to lift the plane off the ground and keep it in the air."

NOVEMBER 22

The Beauty Myth: How Images of Beauty Are Used Against Women
by Naomi Wolf

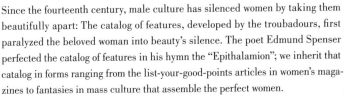

Since the fourteenth century, male culture has silenced women by taking them beautifully apart: The catalog of features, developed by the troubadours, first paralyzed the beloved woman into beauty's silence. The poet Edmund Spenser perfected the catalog of features in his hymn the "Epithalamion"; we inherit that catalog in forms ranging from the list-your-good-points articles in women's magazines to fantasies in mass culture that assemble the perfect women.

Culture stereotypes women to fit the myth by flattening the feminine into beauty-without-intelligence or intelligence-without-beauty; women are allowed a mind or a body but not both. A common allegory that teaches women this lesson is the pretty-plain pairing: of Leah and Rachel in the Old Testament and Mary and Martha in the New; Helena and Hermia in *A Midsummer Night's Dream*; Anya and Dunyasha in Chekhov's *The Cherry Orchard*; Daisy Mae and Sadie Hawkins in Dogpatch; Glinda and the Wicked Witch of the West in Oz. ...

Women's writing, on the other hand, turns the myth on its head. Female culture's greatest writers share the search for radiance, a beauty that has meaning. The battle between the over-valued beauty and the undervalued, unglamorous but animated heroine forms the spine of the women's novel. It extends from Jane Eyre to today's paperback romances, in which the gorgeous nasty rival has a mane of curls and a prodigious cleavage, but the heroine only her spirited eyes. The hero's capacity to see the true beauty of the heroine is his central test.

FOR FURTHER REFLECTION

We expect female stereotypes in which intelligence and physical beauty are antithetical to have been perpetuated by the mass media, but the problem is rooted even in the Old and New Testaments and in literary classics. But women novelists like Jane Austen, the Brontës, and George Eliot (Mary Ann Evans) have defused this unrealistic view of womanhood.

..................................TRY THIS..................................

Keats famously proclaimed that "beauty is truth, truth beauty." Write a story in which this ideal of beauty is made manifest through temperament, actions, intelligence, and grace.

The History of Sexuality
by Michel Foucault

Translated by Robert Hurley

Sexuality must not be described as a stubborn drive, by nature alien and of necessity disobedient to a power which exhausts itself trying to subdue it and often fails to control it entirely. It appears rather as an especially dense transfer point for relations of power: between men and women, young people and old people, parents and offspring, teachers and students, priests and laity, an administration and a population. Sexuality is not the most intractable element in power relations, but rather one of those endowed with the greatest instrumentality: useful for the greatest number of maneuvers and capable of serving as a point of support, as a linchpin, for the most varied strategies.

There is no single, all-encompassing strategy, valid for all of society and uniformly bearing on all the manifestations of sex. For example, the idea that there have been repeated attempts, by various means, to reduce all of sex to its reproductive function, its heterosexual and adult form, and its matrimonial legitimacy fails to take into account the manifold objectives aimed for, the manifold means employed in the different sexual politics concerned with the two sexes, the different age groups and social classes.

FOR FURTHER REFLECTION

For the French historian and philosopher Foucault (1926–1984), sexuality cannot be separated from the full spectrum of social interaction, particularly interactions in which individuals vie for power—and that includes a great many interactions indeed: the family, the classroom, the workplace. The reason is that the energies associated with literal sex are rechanneled into other endeavors with the same driving force.

· TRY THIS ·

Compose an essay in which you reflect on different ways sexuality gets rechanneled in the workplace or elsewhere. Consider age, gender, workplace hierarchy, and reputation.

NOVEMBER 24
"The Lake District"
by John Michell

from *The Traveler's Key to Sacred England: A Guide to
the Legends, Lore, and Landscapes of England's Sacred Places*

The landscape of the Lake District in the southwest part of Cumbria is considered by those who like dramatic, elemental scenery to be the most beautiful in England. Every summer its roads are jammed with cars, and the local farmers and shepherds are outnumbered many times over by visitors. Yet away from its main roads and public attractions is an endless paradise for ramblers, artists, and lovers of the wild spirit in nature. The spirit of the place gave voice to the nineteenth-century Lake poets who opened the eyes of their Victorian contemporaries to the glory of the English countryside and it sacred places. The house of William and Dorothy Wordsworth can be seen at Rydal by the beautiful lake, Rydal Water; Samuel Taylor Coleridge, Thomas De Quincey, and other friends lived nearby. ... The most ancient of Wordsworth's haunts were the two great Cumbrian stone circles which have inspired poets and scholars ever since. Castle Rigg, near Keswick, and Long Meg and her Daughters, near Penrith, 20 miles to the northeast.

"A dismal cirque of Druid stones upon a forlorn moor" was John Keats's description of this circle. On a gloomy, wet evening it is very appropriate, but at other times the stones seem vibrant with life and spirit. Their site is perhaps the most beautiful of any stone circle. It is on the flat crown of a low, green hill, almost surrounded by mountain ridges.

FOR FURTHER REFLECTION

England's Lake District is not only famous for its natural beauty but for its Druidic ruins and medieval castles. An inspiration to the Romantic writers, especially Wordsworth, his sister Dorothy, and Samuel Taylor Coleridge, the region continues to draw writers and artists from all over the world, for it is in places like this that one's creative imagination is nurtured by the spirit of nature and the sacred or fabled voices of centuries past.

...................................TRY THIS...................................

Visit a special place—a lake, a marine preserve, a park or scenic lookout—and let the spirit of the place move your pen. Write down feelings, observations, recollections (recalling one of Wordsworth's famous definitions of poetry as emotion recollected in tranquility).

"Three Zen Koans"

by Gyomay M. Kubose

from *Zen Koans*

I. One day Banzan was walking through a market. He overheard
a customer say to the butcher, "Give me the best piece of
meat you have." "Everything in my shop is the best," replied
the butcher. "You cannot find any piece of meat that is not
the best." At these words, Banzan was enlightened.

This koan illustrates the core of Zen teachings. Zen speaks of absolute value, not
relative values. The rose is best as a rose. ... Each individual is the best in the
whole world. The only obligation one has in life is to bring out one's best.

II. Emperor Taishu of the Sung dynasty dreamed one night of a god who
appeared and advised him to arouse his yearning for enlightenment. In
the morning the Emperor summoned the official priest and asked, "How
can I arouse yearning for enlightenment?" The priest made no reply.

Emperor Taishu already yearns for enlightenment; his dream is proof of it. To begin
with, enlightenment is not "there" to look for. And the Emperor's very question
reveals his dichotomous thinking. The priest knows that the Emperor's whole way
of thinking must be destroyed.

III. A monk told Joshu: "I have just entered the monastery. Please
teach me." Joshu asked, "Have you eaten?" The monk replied,
"Yes, I have eaten." Joshu said: "Then you had better wash
your bowl." At that moment the monk was enlightened.

Zen is everyday life: natural, orderly. Things are done one at a time. The truth is
simple and direct. Trouble comes from conceptualization and speculation.

FOR FURTHER REFLECTION

Zen koans are not designed merely to challenge one's puzzle-solving skills;
they are designed to teach spiritual wisdom. Our thinking, like our behavior,
can acquire bad habits, and intensive mental self-discipline may be necessary to get rid of them. The koan serves as a kind of catalyst for bringing poor
habits of mind such as dichotomous thinking and misplaced priorities to the
forefront, where they can be scrutinized and relinquished.

. . . . TRY THIS. . . . .

Create a few Zen koans of your own, each accompanied by an explanation.

"Ten Adages"

by Milton Berle

from *Milton Berle's Private Joke File*

1. If at first you don't succeed, your sky-diving days are over.

2. The only argument for marriage is that it remains the best way of getting acquainted.

3. Hard work never killed anybody. But then, relaxing is responsible for very few casualties.

4. Just when you're about to make both ends meet, somebody comes along and moves the ends.

5. Most people who fall in love with themselves have no rivals.

6. You can lead a man to Congress but you can't make him think.

7. Most of us aren't young enough to know everything.

8. Nothing lasts forever except a bad play.

9. Be moderate in all things, especially moderation.

10. A cocktail party is a get-together where olives are speared and acquaintances stabbed.

FOR FURTHER REFLECTION

With the adage—usually no more than a single sentence—wisdom and wit combine forces to generate an insight that is livelier than a flat philosophical reflection and more memorable than a mere joke. Milton Berle (1908–2002) was a master of the one-liner with staying power.

.................................TRY THIS....................................

Maintain a list of your own adages. To create an adage, think of a cliché expression or a traditional bit of wisdom and put a humorous spin on it. Milton Berle created adage number six by recasting "You can lead a horse to water but you can't make him drink."

NOVEMBER 27

Blood Music

by Greg Bear

Since each bacterium in the cultures had the potential intellectual capacity of a mouse, it was quite possible the cultures had turned into simple societies and the societies had developed functional divisions. [Vergil] hadn't been keeping track lately, involved as he had been with altered B-cell lymphocytes.

They were like his children, all of them. And they had turned out to be exceptional.

He felt a rush of guilt and nausea as he turned on a gas burner and applied each dish of altered *E. coli* to the flame with a pair of tongs.

He returned to his lab and dropped the culture dishes into a sterilizing bath. That was the limit. He could not destroy anything more. He felt a hatred for Harrison that went beyond any emotion he had ever felt toward another human being. Tears of frustration blurred his vision.

Vergil opened the lab Kelvinator and removed a spinner bottle and a while plastic pallet containing twenty-two test tubes. The spinner bottle was filled with a straw-colored fluid, lymphocytes in a serum medium. He had constructed a custom impellor to stir the medium more effectively, with less cell damage. ... The test tubes contained saline solution and special concentrated serum nutrients to support the cells while they were examined under a microscope.

... After warming to room temperature—a process he usually aided with a small fan to gently blow warmed air over the pallet—the lymphocytes in the tubes would become active, resuming their development after being subdued by the refrigerator's chill.

... They would continue learning, adding new segments to the revised portions of their DNA.

FOR FURTHER REFLECTION

The Frankenstein story can be told in many different ways. What are the consequences of creating new life, whether it be a human creature assembled out of dead body parts or a microscopic organism imbued with intelligence? Greg Bear's Vergil is the new Victor Frankenstein for the biotech age.

..................................TRY THIS................................

Write about a genetic engineer who creates an organism that can, say, transform greenhouse gases into breathable air. What happens if that organism proves to have certain undesirable side effects?

NOVEMBER 28

Brimstone

by Douglas Preston and Lincoln Child

The priest [Fr. Bernard Cappi] removed a microcassette recorder from his pocket. "I made a copy [of Grove's message] before turning it over to the police."

Holding it up in one hand, he pressed the play button. There was a beep. Then:

Bernard? Bernard! It's Jeremy Grove. Are you there? Pick up the phone, for God's sake!

The voice was high, strained, tinny.

Listen, Bernard, I need you here, now. You've got to come. ... Come immediately. It's ... horrible. Bring a cross, Bible, holy water. My God, Bernard, he's coming for me. Do you hear? He's coming for me! I need to confess, I need forgiveness, absolution. ... For the love of God, Bernard, pick up the phone—

His voice was cut off by the message machine using up its allotted time. The harsh voice echoed into silence in the bare, whitewashed room. [Sergeant Vincent] D'Agosta felt a shiver of horror.

"Well," said [FBI agent] Pendergast after a moment, "I'd be curious to hear your thoughts on that, Father."

Father Cappi's face was grim. "I believe he felt damnation was upon him."

FOR FURTHER REFLECTION

In a skillfully told horror story, the supernatural feels *natural*, a part of the real world. This feeling is enforced by the fact that agent Pendergast and police sergeant D'Agosta conduct a gritty murder investigation, making the creepy supernatural horror elements seem that much creepier.

................................TRY THIS................................

Work up a tale of supernatural horror, but make the supernatural elements seem as much a part of the real world as possible. One way to achieve verisimilitude is to describe actions and settings in familiar detail, while at the same time introducing something that doesn't quite fit: a wound on a murder victim's body, for example, that the medical examiner cannot identify.

NOVEMBER 29

Philosophy of Technology
by Frederick Ferré

The technology of clocks, and machines in general, provided an immensely influential model for modern thinking about reality in general. Long before Newton's scientific depiction of the astronomical and physical order as a great machine, the regular motions of the moon and planets had been modeled in clockworks. Great European cathedrals, like Strasbourg, combined the display of religious and astronomical regularities in their awe-inspiring clocks, some of which still function for the admiration of tourists today. The image of the clock could capture the metaphysical imagination. Its parts were exquisitely adjusted to one another, without redundant or conflicting elements, embodying cooperation, regularity, reliability, numerability, and intelligibility. One could see, with enough patience, what "made them tick." With Galileo and the stress on the language of mathematics as the key to "reading the book of nature," with Descartes and the integration of the geometry of space with the algebra of thought, and with Newton's triumphant equations, the model of the clock-machine could be articulated in detail by the powerful mechanistic theory of the world.

This "mechanical world picture" has obvious significance for human nature. If everything, at bottom, runs like clockwork, then it must follow that we, too, are complex and wonderful machines. Consistent with William Harvey's (1578–1657) contemporary discovery that the heart is a pump circulating blood through our bodies in a fluid-mechanical system of valves and pipes, Thomas Hobbes (1588–1679) drew the full implications of the mechanical world model even before Newton (1642–1727). Everything about us, Hobbes theorized, would turn out to be matter following the laws of motion.

FOR FURTHER REFLECTION

Organisms, humans included, have long been regarded as machines of varying degrees of complexity. Philosophers and scientists from the seventeenth century onward thought so; Kepler's laws of planetary motion and Newton's laws of motion suggest that the universe itself is one great machine.

....TRY THIS................................

To what extent is the machine a satisfactory analog for living beings? Does a single plant or animal cell function like a machine? What about a mouse or a dog? A human being? In a meditative essay, suggest where you think the machine analogy breaks down, if at all.

NOVEMBER 30
Monster: Living Off the Big Screen
by John Gregory Dunne

Once known mainly for its animated features and the cartoon shorts of Mickey Mouse and Donald Duck, [Walt Disney Pictures] had become a Hollywood powerhouse. After a string of tightly budgeted commercial hits, Disney was on a roll, and believed it had found a formula, sure-fire as long as that formula—family entertainment that did not too rigorously tax the imagination—was controlled by its own executives. …

Toward those members of the creative community not covered by other studios, Disney's attitude was to take no prisoners. Late one evening, at … a Sunset Strip restaurant much favored by the Industry, a producer and a writer we knew were arguing vigorously against the changes the studio was demanding in a picture already in production. The president of the Disney division overseeing the picture suddenly demanded silence. He was, he said, forced by the writer's intransigence to take the monster out of its cage.

In the silence that ensured, the division president reached under the table, pretended to grab a small predatory animal from its lair, and then, as if clutching the creature by the neck in his fist, exhibited his empty, clawlike hand to the people around the table. He asked the screenwriter if he saw the monster, and the writer, not knowing what else to do, nodded yes.

I'm going to put it back in its cage now, the executive said … and I never want you to force me to bring it out again. Then he mimed putting the monster back into its cage under the table. When he was done, the executive asked the writer, Do you know what the monster is?

The writer shook his head.

The executive said, "It's *our money.*"

FOR FURTHER REFLECTION

The movie industry is full of paradoxes, like the executive of a studio famous for family-values entertainment characterizing their money as a monster in a cage, never to be let out under any circumstances.

......................................TRY THIS................................

Plan a story about a company whose wholesome public image radically contradicts its ruthless private one.

DECEMBER 1

Literature and the Irrational:
A Study in Anthropological Backgrounds
by Wayne Shumaker

Is the animizing tendency active in literature to such an extent that literary speech, like primitive thought, endows dead matter with living energy? …

It is not only that the animism in nonliterary language is often unconscious and nonperceptual ("Morning has come"), whereas that in literature tends to be vigorously sensory ("Jocund morn / Stands tiptoe on the misty mountaintop"), or that personification has been recognized for at least two thousand years as a peculiarly literary "ornament." The point is that good writers, in energizing their materials, instinctively endow them with life.

> All day I hear the noise of waters / Making moan, / Sad as the
> sea-bird is, when going / Forth alone, / He hears the winds
> cry to the waters' / Monotone.*

Not even for the twentieth-century poet is the ocean mere salt water, heaving or pounding because of meteorological pressures such as the moon's pull and the failure of the earth's gravity to hold the atmosphere motionless. It has moods, feelings, consciousness; and the winds which produce its movements do not simply blow (a verb which itself implies personification) but, more actively, "cry."

FOR FURTHER REFLECTION

Even for modern writers, inanimate objects from oceans to storms to mountains are imbued with a life force that goes beyond the mere conventions of figurative language. Perhaps this has something to do with the nature of literature itself, which often searches for links between human beings and their environment, or seeks to capture the animating forces that imbue the world with meaning.

························TRY THIS····················

Write a survival story in which you subtly personify an inanimate object like a lake or river or mountain, making it either the ally or an adversary of your protagonist.

---

* James Joyce, from "All Day I Hear," in *Collected Poems*

DECEMBER 2
Frank Lloyd Wright
by Ada Louise Huxtable

The horizontal flow of the plan [for Wright's Studio] gave continuous, changing vistas through open passageways. Constructed around a large willow tree, the Studio became known as the house with the tree growing through it, adding to Wright's local reputation for eccentricity.

The ambience was pure then and future Wright—oak leaves and wild and dried flowers in handcrafted pottery and copper containers; tall, slatted wood benches and chairs, softened with cushions, before huge brick fireplaces; Japanese prints displayed on Wright-designed easels; and an eclectic range of statuary from reproductions of the Winged Victory of Samothrace and the Venus de Milo (both of which appeared and reappeared strategically in Wright interiors) to Beaux Arts nymphs.

His style was a balancing act between romantic naturalism and geometric abstraction. He never left the natural world out of the design equation, but decorative details derived from nature were increasingly rendered in simplified, geometric terms. He was not an admirer of the fin de siècle sinuosities of art nouveau. The straightedge, the triangle, and the compass were his tools; the intriguingly complex patterns of circles, squares, triangles, and hexagons that these tools produced made up his preferred design vocabulary. The passage of a century and the advent of minimalism and computer-aided geometry have dimmed the radical edge of Wright's work; seen in context, and by his contemporaries, it was shockingly unconventional.

FOR FURTHER REFLECTION

Frank Lloyd Wright found a way to synthesize the natural with the modern, to establish an aesthetic harmony between the geometrical designs that represent the architect's (and the draftsperson's) basic tools and the contours of a given landscape. As Huxtable suggests, Wright found no aesthetic appeal in the "sinuosities" of trendy art.

...................................TRY THIS................................

What appeals to you most in architectural design—the traditional arches and spires of medieval cathedrals, the angular structures of modern skyscrapers? Write an essay on the structures (churches, office buildings, stadiums, memorials, in the United States or abroad) that you find most aesthetically appealing.

DECEMBER 3

The Stars of Heaven
by Clifford A. Pickover

Humans have always looked to the stars as a source of inspiration and transcendence to lift them beyond the boundaries of ordinary intuition. The ancient Sumerians, Egyptians, Chinese, and Mexicans were very aware of the locations and motions of visible stars and perhaps thought that the visible stars were all the stars that existed. On the other hand, the Old Testament writers theorized that there were many more stars than humans could see. According to Genesis 22:17, the stars were as great in number as the sands of the seashore and simply could not be numbered. The vast reaches of the cosmos were utterly incomprehensible to humans. ...

In the Bible, stars are a sign of God's power and majesty. In Job 38:31–32, God reminds Job of His omnipotence and names several constellations of stars: "Can you bind the beautiful Pleiades? Can you loose the cords of Orion? Can you bring forth the constellations in their seasons or lead out the Bear with his cubs? Do you know the laws of the heavens? ...

Probably the most famous star in the Bible occurs in Matthew 2:1–2, which describes a group of travelers, called Magi, heading toward Bethlehem from somewhere in the east. These Magi are most likely astrologers. They had seen a special star and were bringing gifts for "the one who has been born king of the Jews."

FOR FURTHER REFLECTION

It isn't surprising to learn that in ancient times the stars evoked mystery and majesty, representing God's infinite power. Nor is it surprising that astrology evolved out of the sense that the stars in their fixed positions and constellations represented God's control over human destiny.

······························TRY THIS····························

1. Research the history of astrology, and, in an essay, reflect upon the relationship between religious views of the heavens and the tenets of astrology. Where do you draw the line, if at all, between religious faith and superstition?

2. Several astronomical theories accounting for the Star of Bethlehem have been proposed; research these and write a feature in which you compare them, and perhaps decide which one seems the most plausible.

DECEMBER 4
The Periodic Kingdom: A Journey into the Land of the Chemical Elements
by P.W. Atkins

A particularly important product of the region of magnesium [in the periodic kingdom] is an organic molecule called chlorophyll, which contains a single magnesium atom at its eye. Without chlorophyll, the world would be a damp warm rock instead of the softly green haven of life that we know, for chlorophyll holds its magnesium eye to the sun and captures the energy of sunlight, in the first step of photosynthesis. ... Magnesium has exactly the right features to make this process possible. Had the kingdom lacked this element, chlorophyll's eye would have been blind, photosynthesis would not take place, and life as we know it would not exist.

At the southern end of this family are the metals strontium, barium, and radium. The kingdom's patterns are beginning to be established, and since patterns are the foundation of prediction we are able to predict that these regions will be much more reactive than those to the north. Indeed, they are too aggressive to their environment to be of much use, and nature has found no use for them. Nature's child, humanity, though, has put them to use. Radium [for example] is highly radioactive (a nuclear, not a chemical, property), and is used to kill unwanted proliferating cells.

FOR FURTHER REFLECTION
The periodic table tells many stories about the behavior of atoms in molecular structures—the role of the carbon atom in a carbon dioxide or methane molecule, or the role of the magnesium atom in the chlorophyll molecule, as Atkins explains. It is startling to learn we owe our existence to chlorophyll's magnesium "eye."

................................TRY THIS...................................

Write a parable or skit in which the characters are atoms in the context of their molecular configurations or lack of them. For example, sodium and chlorine in the context of sodium chloride (table salt); or one of the noble gas elements (e.g., xenon, neon), none of which are able to combine with other elements.

DECEMBER 5

The Gutenberg Elegies: The Fate of Reading in an Electronic Age
by Sven Birkerts

We tend to think of reading as a means to an end. Like driving, it gets us from here to there. We do it, often, in order to have done it; the act is considered a sponge for contents. When we ask someone "Have you read *Bleak House*?" we are not so much inquiring whether the person has had the experience of reading Dickens's novel as asking whether they know the plot and the basic reference points of character and theme. Ours is a checklist sort of culture and our approach to artistic expression cannot be expected to diverge much from our general approach to the business of living.

But such an attitude greatly diminishes the scope and importance of reading. For beyond the obvious instrumentality of the act, the immersing of the self in a text has certain fundamental metaphysical implications. To read, when one does so of one's own free will, is to make a volitional statement, to cast a vote; it is to posit an elsewhere and to set off toward it. And like any traveling, reading is at once a movement and a comment of sorts about the place one has left. To open a book voluntarily is at some level to remark the insufficiency either of one's life or of one's orientation toward it. The distinction must be recognized, for when we read we not only transplant ourselves to the place of the text, but we modify our natural angle of regard upon all things; we reposition the self in order to *see* differently.

FOR FURTHER REFLECTION

We read for different reasons, many of them purely practical, such as reading the weather forecast to determine how to dress or reading a recipe in order to prepare a meal. But the type of reading Sven Birkerts describes we might call experiential or immersion reading—reading a work of literature to enlarge our perception of human nature or our insight into the way the world works. Such reading requires immersion into the world the author has created. In our high-tech age of sound bites and Internet surfing, experiential reading is at risk.

......................................TRY THIS....................................

How would you defend experiential or immersion reading to an audience whose reading habits have deteriorated as a result of spending most leisure time watching television or surfing the Internet? Present your views in a spirited essay.

DECEMBER 6

"The Romance of Chestnuts"

by James Villas

from Villas at Table: A Passion for Food and Drink

Roasted over an open fire, braised with fresh vegetables, added to stuffings for poultry and game, ground into flour, and puréed for any number of garnishes and elegant desserts, the versatile chestnut has played a very special role in world gastronomy throughout modern history. Who could imagine, for example, Christmas in France without those rich, luxurious *marrons glacés*, or the banquet table in England without a sumptuous chestnut pudding, or, as a matter of fact, the American Thanksgiving or Yuletide season without a golden bird bursting with chestnut stuffing? So universal is the association of this unique palate-pleasing nugget with the year-end festivities that there's hardly a country where it doesn't enhance the various gustatory rituals.

In Italy, "drunken chestnuts" (roasted nuts soaked in wine) are an integral part of cold-weather feasts, and it is not unusual for Japanese connoisseurs to send to distant cities for the exact type of chestnut they prefer on their New Year's menus. The Greeks would hardly invite friends over to celebrate the season without serving plenty of boiled chestnuts kept warm under a heavy cloth cover. And even New Yorkers seem to find temporary respite from their misanthropy when the chill in the air is perfumed by the aroma emanating from Fifth Avenue's chestnut carts.

FOR FURTHER REFLECTION

During these late-autumn to early-winter days we become attuned to the sights and smells and tastes of the holidays. Roasted chestnuts, like hot cider and gingerbread, are high on the list of cozy, nestle-beside-the-fireplace food. Chestnuts are also favored because they can be served in many different ways, as James Villas notes.

· TRY THIS ·

What are some of your favorite foods and beverages of the holiday season? Write an essay about one of them, describing why it's your favorite and the different ways it is prepared in other cultures.

DECEMBER 7

Supercontinent: Ten Billion Years in the Life of Our Planet

by Ted Nield

The deep ocean trench that skirts the Indonesian Archipelago ... marks the contact between two of the tectonic plates making up the cracked eggshell of the Earth's crust. One is the Australian Plate, consisting of Australia and the floor of the Indian Ocean, and the other, to the north, carries Europe and Asia and is called the Eurasian Plate. At this trench the floor of the Indian Ocean is subducting, sinking down into the mantle, beneath the island arc of Indonesia. This is but one small part of the long process of building the next supercontinent, piece by piece, each fragment edging into place, just as India has already been annealed to Asia in the collision that is today creating the Himalayas and the Tibetan Plateau.

In many ways the earthquake that caused the 26 December [2004] tsunami should have taken nobody by surprise. There are known to have been two great earthquakes of over magnitude 8 along this part of the Indonesian Arc: in 1833 and 1861. The zones of rupture that caused these two events sit along adjoining, non-overlapping parts of the same plate boundary, adjoining the Batu Islands. No quake of similar size happened during the twentieth century, until June 2000, when a 7.9 quake struck near Enggano at the extreme south-eastern end of the 1833 rupture zone. The 26 December event extended movement along the plate boundary from the island of Simeulue, at the other end of the chain, almost to the coast of Myanmar (Burma).

FOR FURTHER REFLECTION

The earth's crustal plates are constantly shifting because they rest upon a mantle of high-pressure molten rock. Over the vast span of geologic time, continents have broken apart, fused back together, then broken apart again, in different configurations. The powerful earthquakes in Indonesia suggest that a new supercontinent is slowly forming: The arc of islands is being pushed toward the mainland and eventually will collide with it.

.................................TRY THIS...................................

In a feature for young readers, describe the processes of plate tectonics and continental drift. Along the way you may also want to explain why earthquakes occur and describe the difference between the earth's mantle and the relatively thin crust that in effect floats on top of it.

DECEMBER 8

Hypatia of Alexandria

by Maria Dzielska

Translated by F. Lyra

From the beginning of his [Theophilus's] pontificate, in 385 [C.E.], he had conducted a campaign against paganism in the city, expunging through various methods the religious cults still in existence. With the outbreak of riots sparked by the church's appropriation of pagan temples, Theophilus seized the opportunity to strike a blow at the Serapeum, once the cult center in Alexandria. The action against the shrine took place in either 391 or 392. ...

A body of Alexandrian pagans, whose numbers were still substantial, barricaded themselves in the temple, making sallies on the besieging Christians. This gave Theophilus a pretext to turn to the civil and military authorities for help. The matter was terminated by an edict from the emperor ordering the pagans to leave the temple, proclaiming the killed Christians martyrs, and handing the Serapeum over to the church. The magnificent statue of the god Serapis ... was shattered into pieces by a soldier's ax. ...

Given the support of the Alexandrian intellectual elite for the defenders of the old faith, the question inevitably arises how Hypatia stood on the issue. After all, in the early 390s she was already a famed and esteemed philosopher. Why did she not join Olympius in defending the threatened sacred objects of the Serapeum? Why did she not, along with her students, give moral aid to the defenders?

FOR FURTHER REFLECTION

Ancient Alexandria was the site of the fabled Alexandrian Library and the lesser-known Serapeum serving as sanctuaries for thousands of scrolls covering the full spectrum of literature, philosophy, science, mathematics, politics, and history of the ancient world. But to the religious zealots of the day, such pagan learning represented a threat. Not enough is known about Hypatia's efforts to establish a harmonious relationship with the early Christian church—but we do know that she was brutally murdered, and the libraries destroyed.

.....................................TRY THIS.....................................

The story of Hypatia has been told many times, most notably by the British author Charles Kingsley in his highly romanticized novel, *Hypatia*. Write your own story about this legendary woman, focusing on how she might have striven to establish a peaceful relationship with the Christians.

Medieval and Early Modern Science
by A.C. Crombie

The object of Greek science had been understanding, and under the influence of later classical philosophers such as the Stoics, Epicureans and Neoplatonists natural curiosity had given way almost entirely to the desire for the untroubled peace which could only be won by a mind lifted above dependence on matter and the flesh. These pagan philosophers had asked the question: What is worth knowing and doing? To this Christian teachers also had an answer: That is worth knowing and doing which conduces to the love of God. The early questions continued their neglect of natural curiosity and at first also tended to disparage the study of philosophy itself as likely to distract men from a life pleasing to God. St. Clement of Alexandria in the 3rd century poked fun at this fear of pagan philosophy, which he compared to a child's fear of goblins. Both he and his pupil Origen claimed that all knowledge was good since it was a perfection of mind and that the study of philosophy and of natural science was in no way incompatible with a Christian life. St. Augustine himself in his searching and comprehensive philosophical inquiries had invited men to examine the rational basis of their faith. But in spite of these writers natural knowledge continued to be considered of very secondary importance during the early Middle Ages. The primary interest in natural facts was to find illustrations for the truths of morality and religion.

FOR FURTHER REFLECTION

In the Middle Ages the Church exerted profound influence on everyday life. Knowledge was regarded as important insofar as it served one's love of God. Gradually, however, thanks to philosophers like Origen, knowledge began to be regarded as having intrinsic value because it led to perfection of mind, which in turn had the potential to lead people to experience a heightened love of the divine.

. . . . TRY THIS. . . . .

Research the life of Origen and write a biographical essay on his contribution to the reconciliation between knowledge and faith.

DECEMBER 10
"Acton's 'Madonna of the Future'"
by Daniel J. Boorstin

from *The Seekers: The Story of Man's*
Continuing Quest to Understand His World

The eloquent prophet of the modern liberal spirit, Lord Acton (1834–1902), would poignantly refer to his unfinished lifework—a history of liberty—as "The Madonna of the Future." This was the title of Henry James's story of an artist who devoted his life to a single great painting, but at the artist's death the easel in his studio showed only a blank canvas. ... His history of liberty has been described as "the greatest book never written." Yet Acton became one of the most influential and most often quoted of the historians of his age.

Acton's life and work (and nonwork) included numerous lectures, essays, and reviews on historical subjects, but he never wrote a book. It was significant, too, that while he authored unforgettable aphorisms (for example, "Power tends to corrupt, and absolute power corrupts absolutely"), which have attained the authority of cliché, he is not famous for his theories of history. ... There was no more strenuous, nor more frustrated effort to reconcile the ancient doctrines of Christianity with the modern doctrines of liberalism. ...

Born into an age that was dissolving the certitudes of Christianity, Acton still dared not abandon them. His life, he once said, was "the story of a man who started in life believing himself a sincere Catholic and a sincere Liberal; who therefore renounced everything in Catholicism which was not compatible with Liberty and everything in Politics not compatible with Catholicism." He was the perfect embodiment of the Seeker—too Catholic to renounce the wisdom of the past and too searching not to follow the inquiring spirit of his age.

FOR FURTHER REFLECTION

Lord Acton sought to preserve the Catholic Church's spiritual legacy and the great experiments in human liberty. The common denominator for the great traditions and cutting-edge progress is the dynamic human spirit.

. . . . TRY THIS . . . .

Write an essay in which you highlight the commonalities between a traditional institution and a progressive one.

The Iliad

by Homer

Translated by W.H.D. Rouse

The Trojans raised a loud din and clamour, like a huge flock of birds. ... But the Achaians marched in silence, breathing fury, shoulder to shoulder, with grim determination. The dust rose in clouds under their feet as they marched apace over the plain, as thick as the mist which a south wind spreads over the mountains. Shepherds hate it, the robber likes it better than night; a man can see a stone's throw and no farther.

No sooner had the two armies come near than a champion stept out of the Trojan ranks, the noble prince Alexandros [Paris]. A leopard-skin hung over his shoulders with bow and sword; he shook his two sharp spears, and challenged all comers to fight him man to man. So he strode out with long steps. Menelaos saw him with joy, as a lion spies a victim, when he is hungry, and finds a horned stag or a wild goat: greedily he devours his prey, even if dogs and lusty lads set upon him. So Menelaos was glad when he set eyes on Alexandros, for he thought he was sure to punish the traitor; at once he leapt down from his chariot in his armour.

But as soon as Alexandros saw him come out in front, his heart sank and he slunk back into the ranks to save himself. He might have been someone walking through the woods who suddenly sees a snake, and jumps back all of a tremble pale with fear. ...

Then Hector rated him with scorn: "Damn you, Paris, you handsome woman-hunter, you seducer! I wish you had never been born, I wish you had died unwedded!"

FOR FURTHER REFLECTION

In the Iliad Homer brilliantly parallels the rage between individuals and the rage between armies. In fact in the case of the Trojan War, the latter is precipitated by the former—Helen, King Menelaos's incomparably beautiful wife (she was, after all, the daughter of Zeus), becoming "the face that launched a thousand ships" after Paris abducted her.

.................................TRY THIS....................................

Write your own modernized version of one incident from the epic poem. For example: Your Paris might be a modern-day playboy who lures the wife of a governor or senator onto his yacht and absconds with her.

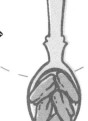

DECEMBER 12

"Loving in Truth, and Fain in Verse My Love to Show"

by Sir Philip Sidney

from *Astrophel and Stella*

Loving in truth, and fain** in verse my love to show,
That she, dear she, might take some pleasure of my pain,
Pleasure might cause her read, reading might make her know,
Knowledge might pity win, and pity grace obtain,
I sought fit words to paint the blackest face of woe,
Studying inventions fine, her wits to entertain,
Oft turning others' leaves, to see if thence would flow
Some fresh and fruitful showers upon my sunburnt brain.
But words came halting forth, wanting Invention's stay;
Invention, Nature's child, fled step-dame Study's blows;
And others' feet still seemed but strangers in my way.
Thus great with child to speak, and helpless in my throes,
Biting my truant pen, beating myself for spite;
"Fool," said my Muse to me, "look in thy heart and write."

FOR FURTHER REFLECTION

"Loving in Truth" is the first of 108 sonnets and songs comprising *Astrophel and Stella*, which marks the zenith of Elizabethan love poetry. As the title suggests, Sidney sought to combine the power of poetic expression of love with utter candor—a combination that inevitably generates internal conflict in the lover—as he struggles to balance grace with anguish.

.....................................TRY THIS....................................
Compose a love song or sonnet in which the speaker wishes to praise his or her beloved while at the same time feeling the need to share the psychological stress of weathering the ups and downs of a tempestuous love relationship.

** gladly, willingly
....

DECEMBER 13
"Of Dreams"
by Owen Felltham
from *Resolves: Divine, Moral, and Political*

Dreams are notable means of discovering our own inclinations. The wise man learns to know himself as well by the night's black mantle as the searching beams of day. In sleep we have the naked and natural thoughts of our souls; outward objects interpose not, either to shuffle in occasional cogitations, or hale out the included fancy. The mind is then shut up in the borough of the body; none of the *Cinque Ports* of the *Isle of Man* are then open, to in-let any strange disturbers. Surely, how we fall to vice or rise to virtue we may by observation find in our dreams. It was the wise Zeno that said, he could collect a man by his dreams, for then the soul, stated in a deep repose, bewrayed [exposed] her true affections, which, in the busy day, she would either not show nor not note. ... Certainly the wise man is the wiser for his sleeping, if he can order well in the day what the eyeless night presenteth him. Every dream is not to be counted of; nor yet are all to be cast away with contempt. I would neither be a Stoic, superstitious in all, nor yet an Epicure, considerate of none. If the physician may by them judge of the disease of the body, I see not but the divine may do so concerning the soul. I doubt not but the genius of the soul is waking and motive even in the fastest closures of the imprisoning eyelids. ... The best use we can make of dreams is observation, and by that, our own correction or encouragement. For 'tis not doubtable but that the mind is working in the dullest depth of sleep. ... Dreams do sometimes call us to a recognition of our inclinations, which print the deeper in so undisturbed times.

FOR FURTHER REFLECTION
The phenomenon of dreaming has fascinated us for millennia. In ancient times, dreams were regarded as forms of divination, prophecy. Although it wasn't until the beginning of the twentieth century that Sigmund Freud presented a detailed explanation of dream processes (see the entry for January 23), the obscure but brilliant English essayist Owen Felltham offers a startlingly modern insight into the nature of dreams, while at the same time regarding dreams as a manifestation of the soul, not just the mind or the body.

...............................TRY THIS...............................

In a short story or novel create a world in which people can enter dreamscapes at will, where one's dreams are optional realities.

DECEMBER 14

An Enemy of the People
by Henrik Ibsen

MAYOR STOCKMANN: As usual, in your report you let your language get out of hand. You say ... that what we're offering our summer visitors is guaranteed poison.

DR. STOCKMANN: But, Peter, how else can you describe it? You've got to realize— this water is poison for internal or external use! And it's foisted on poor, suffering creatures who turn to us in good faith and pay us exorbitant fees to gain their health back again!

MAYOR STOCKMANN: And then you arrive at the conclusion, by your line of reasoning, that we have to build a sewer to drain off these so-called impurities from Mølledal, and that all the water mains have to be relaid.

DR. STOCKMANN: Well, do you see any other way out? I don't.

MAYOR STOCKMANN: ... I brought up these proposals as something we perhaps ought to take under advisement at some time in the future.

DR. STOCKMANN: Some time in the future!

MAYOR STOCKMANN: He [the town engineer] smiled at my whimsical extravagance—naturally. Have you gone to the trouble of estimating just what these proposed changes would cost? From the information I received, the expenditure would probably run up into several hundred thousand crowns.

DR. STOCKMANN: As high as that?

MAYOR STOCKMANN: Yes. But that's not the worst. The work would extend over at least two years.

FOR FURTHER REFLECTION

At the dawn of microbiology and the understanding of the relationship between bacteria and disease, the great Norwegian dramatist Henrik Ibsen conceived this bitter conflict between an overzealous but competent scientist and his politician brother who is not about to let what seems like an irrational scare tactic involving invisible organisms sabotage the new health spa, a major municipal investment. The conflict resonates with us today as we argue over whether to invest billions in alternative energy sources to counteract global warming—something many politicians refuse to take seriously.

...................................TRY THIS....................................

Create an updated version of Ibsen's play by having the two family members clashing over opposing values (preserving the status quo vs. affecting change).

DECEMBER 15

The Time Traveler's Wife

by Audrey Niffenegger

"Henry!" I can barely refrain from throwing my arms around him. It is obvious that he has never seen me before in his life.

"Have we met? I'm sorry, I don't. …" Henry is glancing around us, worrying that readers, co-workers are noticing us, searching his memory and realizing that some future self of his has met this radiantly happy girl standing in front of him. The last time I saw him he was sucking my toes in the Meadow.

I try to explain. "I'm Claire Abshire. I knew you when I was a little girl …" I'm at a loss because I am in love with a man who is standing before me with no memories of me at all. Everything is in the future for him. I want to laugh at the weirdness of the whole thing. I'm flooded with years of knowledge of Henry, while he's looking at me perplexed and fearful. Henry wearing my dad's old fishing trousers, patiently quizzing me on multiplication tables, French verbs, all the state capitals; Henry laughing at some peculiar lunch my seven-year-old self has brought to the Meadow; Henry wearing a tuxedo, undoing the studs of his shirt with shaking hand on my eighteenth birthday. Here! Now! "Come and have coffee with me, or dinner or something. …" Surely he has to say yes, this Henry who loves me in the past and the future must love me now in some bat-squeak echo of other time.

FOR FURTHER REFLECTION

Love transcends time—on this we can all agree; but in Audrey Niffenegger's novel, Claire travels through time to encounter her lover Henry before he even met her. And elsewhere in this magical novel, the adult Henry meets up with the child Claire. Of course this sort of slipping back and forth through time can result in all sorts of even stranger consequences. Fantasy, yes, but then again being in love is itself a fantasy.

. . . . TRY THIS . . . .

1. Write a fantasy romance about a twenty-first century actor who travels back to ancient Egypt and so enchants Queen Cleopatra that she falls in love with him. You might complicate things by having her current lover, Julius Caesar, seek revenge.

2. In a reverse scenario to the preceding, have Cleopatra accidentally step through a portal and find herself, let us say, in twenty-first century Las Vegas, where she meets an entertainer who pretends to be Julius Caesar.

DECEMBER 16

Beyond Appearance: Reflections of a Plastic Surgeon

by Robert M. Goldwyn, M.D.

Sara W, a twenty-one-year-old black aspiring model … wants her nose less negroid. After much deliberation and a few visits with me, she has decided to let me narrow her nasal bones, decrease the flare of her nostrils, and build up the dorsum of her nose, the part that most people would call the top. … We both agreed that males, mostly white, dominated the modeling business, and they decided what blacks should look like. …

Patients often tell me in the office before operation that they want "enough anesthesia so I can't hear the hammer when you break my nose." The fact is that, even though a patient may hear the mallet striking the chisel, he or she is so obtunded and tranquilized that the sound arouses no anxiety, and sometimes it is even forgotten. Sara does not seem to mind the sound and never mentioned it as a worry.

With the nasal bones now narrower, I insert the silicone without any difficulty and close the incision with fine nylon stitches. To reduce the nostrils' flare, I remove a small piece of skin and cartilage from the floor of her nostril. …

The new profile of the nose is what Sara wanted. The tip is higher, and so is the bridge of the nose; thus far the silicone has done its job. Nevertheless, a good operation does not necessarily mean a good result. Complications such as infection and shifting of the implant can happen.

FOR FURTHER REFLECTION

The term "plastic surgery" is a euphemism that does not convey the virtual mutilation of a person's natural physical appearance in order to have that appearance remolded into something more "acceptable"—but acceptable to whom, or to what? When considering the credentials of those who judge appearance—white men deciding on what constitutes attractiveness in black females or Hollywood producers deciding that actresses older than forty need to look younger—it is not surprising to feel resentful of the fact that we collectively possess such a narrow-minded, racially biased, media-conditioned notion of beauty.

................................TRY THIS....................................

Watch a fashion show or peruse a current issue of a magazine that features fashion models. What do the appearances of the models—male and female—tell you about our current notions of attractiveness?

DECEMBER 17

Emily Dickinson Face to Face

by Martha Dickinson Bianchi

[Emily Dickinson] loved to fence in words with an able adversary. Circumlocution she despised. Her conclusions hit the mark and suggested only an arrow in directness, cutting the hesitancies of the less rapid thinker. She arrived at the heart of the matter with a velocity which made the ordinary processes of thought seem sluggish. She loved a metaphor, a paradox, a riddle; and she was both shy and enormously self-confident. Her imagination knew no hindrance, and the mystic in her gained immeasurably from her power to project herself into an abstraction, beyond the hindering visible limitations surrounding her. ...

She had a way of alluding to and talking about the characters in books familiar to us both, as if they were people living right about us—the three Brontë girls were nearer to her than most such.

> Oh, what an afternoon for Heaven,
> When Brontë entered there!

she once wrote, reversing the accepted terms to suit her own conviction. But of all her adopted spiritual kin she identified herself closest with the Brownings. Robert Browning was in her eyes all a brave man and a poet might be to a frail, shy poet-woman like Elizabeth Barrett—or herself.

FOR FURTHER REFLECTION

An unmarried recluse, Emily Dickinson devoted her life to poetry; and because her poems were so innovative only a handful of them appeared in her lifetime—and these without her permission. Her notion of "publication" was to share her poems with friends and relatives, especially her sister-in-law Susan Gilbert Dickinson. Emily's niece Martha Dickinson Bianchi (Susan's daughter) published several volumes of Emily Dickinson's poetry and letters, as well as this 1932 biography.

. . . . TRY THIS . . . .

Read a few of Emily Dickinson's poems. Based on those poems and Martha's impressions of her Aunt Emily, what connections would you make between the poet's personal life and her poems?

DECEMBER 18
In the Woods
by Tana French

I rang Missing Persons, and they came up with a possible ID almost immediately. Katharine Devlin, aged twelve, four foot nine, slim build, long dark hair, hazel eyes, reported missing ... at 10:15 the previous morning, when her mother went to wake her and found her gone. Twelve and up is considered old enough to be a runaway, and she had apparently left the house of her own accord, so Missing Persons had been giving her a day to come home before sending in the troops. ...

I was disproportionately relieved to have an ID, even a tentative one. Obviously I had known that a little girl—especially a healthy well-groomed little girl, in a place as small as Ireland—can't turn up dead without someone coming forward to claim her; but a number of things about this case were giving me the willies, and I think a superstitious part of me had believed that this child would remain as nameless as if she had dropped from thin air and that her DNA would turn out to match the blood from my shoes and a variety of other *X-File*-type stuff. We got an ID shot ... a Polaroid, taken from the least disturbing angle, to show to the family.

FOR FURTHER REFLECTION

With a few masterful brushstrokes, Tana French combines scientific verisimilitude with creepiness, the familiar with the bizarre. Past and present traumas collide as the detective narrator of this story comes upon a murder that is frighteningly similar to the one he had witnessed twenty years earlier.

. . . . TRY THIS . . . .

Plot a mystery story in which your narrator—a police detective or private investigator—has been assigned to investigate a crime that he or she finds deeply disturbing because of its similarity to a traumatic childhood experience. What measures will your protagonist take to prevent the memories from overwhelming him or her—and will your protagonist perhaps even draw from those memories to help solve the present crime?

Imagining the Earth:
Poetry and the Vision of Nature
by John Elder

The clarity of winter's usual snowy dream is a quality our writers of nature have known how to appreciate. Aldo Leopold tells us, at the beginning of *Sand County Almanac*, that "the months of the year, from January up to June, are a geometric progression in the abundance of distraction. ..." Much is stripped down; much that is left is removed from sight by the covering snow. A person standing in this field of sleep can feel a new attentiveness awaking in himself. It is not that those natural phenomena left out to view are inherently more interesting from a human perspective than those we lose sight of, but that, as Leopold suggests, the movement and variety of summer distract our attention from any one thing. Winter holds up objects in high relief—tree, boulder, bird—for our most careful regard. It invites us to be still and cool, to let one curve, one color truly enter the mind. ...

A winter landscape is like a Zen garden. One reacts first to a refreshing simplicity of setting, but soon the sparseness of the garden's obvious "features" and the superficial randomness of their arrangement engage the eye and the mind: the few things that *are* there gather significance until they become a configuration at the center of meaning.

FOR FURTHER REFLECTION

As we cross the threshold into winter and regard the landscape, we might follow John Elder's suggestion and see that landscape not as bleak or barren but as a Zen garden, beautiful in its stark simplicity, lulling us to stillness and calm. Winter is a time for inwardness, reflection; a time to give undivided attention to our writing.

......................................TRY THIS......................................

Study the late December landscape outside your window and empty your mind of all distractions, concentrating only on the shapes of the trees, the grayness of the sky, the relatively weak light from the sun, the long shadows. Then capture the mood in a poem about the beginning of winter.

Fuzzy Thinking: The New Science of Fuzzy Logic
by Bart Kosko

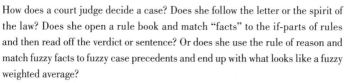

How does a court judge decide a case? Does she follow the letter or the spirit of the law? Does she open a rule book and match "facts" to the if-parts of rules and then read off the verdict or sentence? Or does she use the rule of reason and match fuzzy facts to fuzzy case precedents and end up with what looks like a fuzzy weighted average?

The letter and spirit of the law arise from the split between rules and principles. Rules are precise, black and white, all or none. They have no exceptions. You get kicked out or fired or fined or jailed if you break them. We post rules on signs or send them in memos or print them on contest forms and drivers' licenses: No one under 17 admitted without parent or guardian. Must be at least 35 years old to run for President of the United States. $1000 fine for littering. ... Right turn only.

Principles are vague and abstract and full of exceptions. They change slowly with time as culture evolves. The U.S. legal system got most of its principles from medieval British common law and the Magna Charta: Innocent until proven guilty. ... Equality before the law. Full disclosure. Buyer beware. You cannot profit from a crime. You cannot challenge a contract if you act on it. ...

Law as rules. That view still holds sway in legal theory. And it's what lawyers mean when they tell you that "the court gives law not justice."

FOR FURTHER REFLECTION

Rules and laws manage society on a daily basis; principles, ethical directives, ensure that our lives have dignity, that our rights are honored as well as protected, that we respect those whose views differ from our own. Good rules evolve out of good principles, and vice versa. If one of the principles of a society is that certain kinds of people are inferior to others, then unjust laws will be spawned: Blacks must use separate restrooms, must sit in the back of the bus, and so on. When laws are considered unjust, the principles that had brought them into being must be changed.

..................................TRY THIS....................................

We can easily spot the unjust laws of the past, but what about unjust laws that exist today? Write an essay in which you identify laws you consider to be unjust, and argue for their abolition by interrogating their underlying principles.

The Physics of Christmas: From the Aerodynamics of Reindeer to the Thermodynamics of Turkey

by Roger Highfield

The first Christmas card was designed by the artist John Horsley, an exponent of what the Victorians called the narrative style. The side panels of the card depict acts of charity toward the less fortunate, a familiar theme of the day. However, the subject of the centerpiece, surrounded by leafy trelliswork, is not the traditional Dickensian quest to right social wrongs, but a scene with a great deal of resonance today: a large family enjoying Christmas dinner.

Whether roast turkey, latkes, or stollen, seasonal cooking is nothing more than a branch of applied chemistry, and here science can provide many insights. The color of turkey meat, for example, offers a glimpse of the bird's lifestyle. Scanners … can be turned on food to reveal pockets of fat or a sixpence hidden in a plum pudding. Thermodynamics can help us cook that same pudding to perfection. Indeed, scientists have demonstrated that even the brandy sauce owes its consistency to a unique arrangement of molecules, in structures measuring up to fifty-millionths of a meter across.

For all those who worry that these materialist insights somehow jar with the romance of Christmas tradition, don't forget that this tradition has already been subject to very diverse influences. When English-speaking countries settle down for their traditional fare, they eat an Aztec bird by a German tree, followed by a pudding spiced with subtropical preserves.

FOR FURTHER REFLECTION

We tend to set thick boundaries between material and emotional or spiritual aspects of life, forgetting that the two always intertwine. Roger Highfield demonstrates in his book that a material perspective on the holiday season can enhance our pleasure. In the kitchen, an understanding of the chemical changes that take place during cooking can be valuable in protecting or enhancing a meal's nutrients, flavors, and appearance.

······································TRY THIS····································

Study the properties of the foods and spices for a meal, along with the different methods of cooking each dish. Describe your innovations in an article.

The Politics of Experience
by R.D. Laing

Only when something has become problematic do we start to ask questions. Disagreement shakes us out of our slumbers and forces us to see our own point of view through contrast with another person who does not share it. But we resist such confrontations. The history of heresies of all kinds testifies to more than the tendency to break off communication (excommunication) with those who hold different dogmas or opinions; it bears witness to our intolerance of different *fundamental structures of experience*. We seem to need to share a communal meaning to human existence, to give with others a common sense to the world, to maintain a *consensus*.

But it seems that once certain fundamental structures of experience are shared, they come to be experienced as objective entities. These reified projections of our own freedom are then introjected. By the time the sociologists study these projected-introjected reifications, they have taken on the appearance of things, they are not things ontologically. But they are pseudo-things.

… Collective representations come to be experienced as things, exterior to anyone. They take on the force and character of partially autonomous realities, with their own way of life. A social norm may come to impose an oppressive obligation of everyone, although few people feel it as their own.

FOR FURTHER REFLECTION

Why is it sometimes so difficult for some persons to tolerate ways of life, beliefs, or behaviors that differ markedly from their own—a devout Christian feeling intense resentment toward non-Christians or atheists; a heterosexual person's intolerance of homosexuality; a liberal's refusal to consider the views of a conservative, and so on? A part of us perhaps wishes that our way of experiencing reality be the only way; life would be so much more harmonious, we think, if that were the case.

...................................TRY THIS...................................

In a short story, create a conflict situation between two persons (perhaps from the same family), whose views regarding sexuality, religion, politics, or child-rearing are radically different. How, if at all, will they resolve their differences?

DECEMBER 23
"The Improvement of Memory"
by Dale Carnegie
from *How to Develop Self-Confidence and
Influence People by Public Speaking*

"The average man," said the noted psychologist, Professor Carl Seashore, "does not use above ten per cent of his actual inherited capacity for memory. He wastes the ninety per cent by violating the natural laws of remembering."

Are you one of these average persons? If so, you are struggling under a handicap both socially and commercially. ... These "natural laws of remembering" are very simple. There are only three. Every so-called "memory system" has been funded upon them. Briefly, they are impression, repetition, and association.

The first mandate of memory is this: get a deep, vivid and lasting *impression* of the thing you wish to retain. And to do that, you must concentrate. Theodore Roosevelt's remarkable memory impressed everyone he met. And no little amount of his extraordinary facility was due to this: his impressions were scratched on steel, not written in water. He had, by persistence and practice, trained himself to concentrate under the most adverse conditions. ...

Five minutes of vivid, energetic concentration will produce greater results than days of mooning about in a mental haze.

FOR FURTHER REFLECTION
Memory is key to so many things in life—to achieving excellence in school and in the workplace, to interacting effectively with others, to communicating through speech—and for writing. Yes, you can always look things up, but when you're in the middle of drafting a story, you want to maintain a steady word-flow. Looking things up disrupts your flow of thought, ruins your momentum. As Dale Carnegie points out, you cultivate good memory skills by enhancing your ability to concentrate.

..................................TRY THIS....................................

Begin a month of intensive memory training, focusing on Carnegie's three laws of concentration, repetition, and association. Maintain a record of your progress in a memory journal.

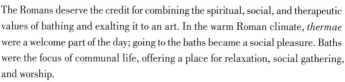

DECEMBER 24
"Roman Baths"
by Alev Lytle Croutier
from *Taking the Waters: Spirit, Art, Sensuality*

The Romans deserve the credit for combining the spiritual, social, and therapeutic values of bathing and exalting it to an art. In the warm Roman climate, *thermae* were a welcome part of the day; going to the baths became a social pleasure. Baths were the focus of communal life, offering a place for relaxation, social gathering, and worship.

Historians explain the growth of public bathing as a function of mounting prosperity in the Roman Empire. By the third century B.C. wealthy Romans had bathing chambers in their town houses and country villas, but bathing was still a private act and a great deal of modesty was attached to it. Gradually, however, the Roman obsession for cleanliness led to public bathing. In 33 B.C. the Roman soldier and statesman Agrippa built the Julia aqueduct at Rome and introduced free public bathhouses that included hot baths, tepid baths, cold baths, and massage rooms. The bathhouses were separated into two parts, the *balneae*, or communal part, and the *balneum*, or private bath.

The way water was supplied to the city of Rome is one of the marvels of ancient times. In 312 B.C., Appius Claudius Caecus built the first aqueduct on the Appian Way; it was eleven miles long and partly subterranean. This caused such a sensation that an aqueduct craze spread throughout the country. The ducts bringing water to Rome from the surrounding hills soon totaled 381 miles in length. Suddenly there was enough water not only for utilitarian purposes but for pleasure as well.

FOR FURTHER REFLECTION

Bathing was the great luxury of the Roman Empire. Thanks to that marvel of engineering, the aqueduct, which transported great quantities of water across from the highlands, all Roman citizens, not just the wealthiest, were able to experience the pleasures of baths.

.... TRY THIS ....

Today we take bathing (or showering) for granted thanks to indoor plumbing and hot-water heaters; but before 1890, water had to pumped from wells and heated in kettles over a fire. Write an essay about everyday hygiene in the 1800s (or before), focusing on bathing customs before plumbing.

Miracles: A Preliminary Study
by C.S. Lewis

When St. Joseph discovered that his fiancée was going to have a baby, he not unnaturally decided to repudiate her. Why? Because he knew just as well as any modern gynecologist that in the ordinary course of nature women do not have babies unless they have lain with men. No doubt the modern gynecologist knows several things about birth and begetting which St. Joseph did not know. But those things do not concern the main point—that a virgin birth is contrary to the course of nature. And St. Joseph obviously knew *that.* In any sense in which it is true to say now, "The thing is scientifically impossible," he would have said the same: the thing always was, and was always known to be, impossible *unless* the regular processes of nature were, in this particular case, being over-ruled or supplemented by something from beyond nature. When St. Joseph finally accepted the view that his fiancée's pregnancy was due not to unchastity but to a miracle, he accepted the miracle as something contrary to the known order of nature. All records of miracles teach the same thing. In such stories the miracles excite fear and wonder (that is what the very word *miracle* implies) among the spectators, and are taken as evidence of supernatural power. If they were not known to be contrary to the laws of nature, how could they suggest the presence of the supernatural? How could they be surprising unless they were seen to be exceptions to the rules?

FOR FURTHER REFLECTION

Miracles are intended to violate the laws of nature in order to show that there is more to existence than natural law. No more miraculous than life itself, the virgin birth marks the point at which God enters the world to reopen the path to salvation for humanity.

................................TRY THIS....................................

1. Take a moment from the Christmas festivities to draft a poem, a song, or a meditation on the miracle of Christ's birth, what it means for humanity.
2. If you do not celebrate Christmas, reflect on the significance of the story of Christ's birth—of the need for God to incarnate himself to redeem humanity.

The Loved One
by Evelyn Waugh

The pickled oak, the chintz, the spongey carpet and the Georgian staircase all ended sharply on the second floor [of the mortuary]. Above that lay a quarter where no layman penetrated. It was approached by elevator, an open functional cage eight feet square. On this top floor everything was tile and porcelain, lino-leum and chromium. Here there were the embalming rooms with their rows of inclined china slabs, their taps and tubes and pressure pumps, their deep gutters and the heavy smell of formaldehyde. Beyond lay the cosmetic rooms with their smell of shampoo and hot hair and acetone and lavender.

An orderly wheeled the stretcher into Aimée's cubicle. It bore a figure under a sheet. Mr. Joyboy walked beside it.

"Good morning, Miss Thanatogenos."

"Good morning, Mr. Joyboy."

"Here is the strangulated Loved One for the Orchid Room."

Mr. Joyboy was the perfection of high professional manners. Before he came there had been some decline of gentility in the ascent from show-room to workshop. There had been talk of "bodies" and "cadavers"; one jaunty young embalmer from Texas had even spoken of "the meat." That young man had gone within a week of Mr. Joyboy's appointment as Senior Mortician.

FOR FURTHER REFLECTION

Love and death are sometimes said to be two sides of the same coin. The British novelist Evelyn Waugh takes this adage to an extreme by making death the very occasion for love. As if this is not satire enough, the setting is a mortuary adjacent to a Hollywood motion picture studio. The deceased "waiting ones" (i.e., loved ones waiting to be embalmed and dressed for their respective funerals), indeed, become, in the hands of Mr. Joyboy and Miss Thanatogenos, made over just as one would expect any movie star to be. Who would have guessed that the rituals of love, death, and movie-making had so much in common?

. . . . .TRY THIS. . . . .

People often resort to clichés and euphemisms when the reality seems too harsh or painful or embarrassing. Write a satire on the way some people over-rely on such "cosmetic" language in certain contexts.

DECEMBER 27

Dimension of Miracles

by Robert Sheckley

"Congratulations, Carmody, and here is your prize."

[The clerk] handed the gaily wrapped box to Carmody, who muttered his thanks and began eagerly to unwrap it. He didn't get far, though; there was a sudden, violent interruption. A short, hairless man in glittering clothes burst into the room.

"Hah!" he cried. "I've caught you in the act, by Klootens! Did you really think you could get away with it?"

The man rushed up to him and grabbed at the Prize. Carmody held it out of arms' reach.

"What do you think you're doing?" he asked.

"Doing? I'm here to claim my rightful Prize, what else? I am Carmody!"

"No, you aren't," Carmody said. "I am Carmody."

The little man paused and looked at him with curiosity. "You claim to be Carmody?"

"I don't claim, I *am* Carmody."

"Carmody of Planet 73C?"

"I don't know what that means," Carmody said. "We call the place Earth."

The shorter Carmody stared at him, his expression of rage changing to one of disbelief.

"Earth?" he asked. "I don't believe I've heard of it. Is it a member of the Chlzerian League?"

FOR FURTHER REFLECTION

If parallel universes exist, imagine the chaos that might result if one were able to move from one universe to another. For Robert Sheckley, such movements are not only potentially chaotic but comic as well, as Carmody meets an alternate version of himself as he strives to find his way back to Earth after winning a very special prize. But which Earth is his home? There are countless parallel universes, each with its own Earth. In trying to figure out his dilemma (with the help of his prize, which happens to be sentient), Carmody learns a great deal about the elusive nature of reality.

......................................TRY THIS......................................

Write a science fiction story, serious or comic, in which your protagonist stumbles through a portal that connects his universe to a parallel one and encounters another version of himself, very similar, but with some strange differences.

Coldheart Canyon: A Hollywood Ghost Story
by Clive Barker

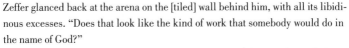

Zeffer glanced back at the arena on the [tiled] wall behind him, with all its libidinous excesses. "Does that look like the kind of work that somebody would do in the name of God?"

As I said," [Father] Sandru replied, "I no longer know where God is and where He isn't."

There was a long silence, during which Zeffer continued to survey the walls. Finally he said, "How much do you want for it?"

"How much do I want for what?"

"For the room?"

Sandru barked out a laugh.

"I mean it," Zeffer said. "How much do you want for it?"

"It's a room, Mister Zeffer," Sandru said. "You can't buy a room."

"Then it's not for sale?"

"That's not my point—"

"Just tell me: is it for sale or not?"

Again, laughter. But this time there was less humor; more bemusement. "I don't see that it's worth talking about," Sandru said, putting the brandy bottle to his lips and drinking.

"Let's say a hundred thousand dollars. What would that be in lei? What's the lei worth right now? A hundred and thirty-two-and-a-half to the dollar?"

FOR FURTHER REFLECTION

Good horror fiction generates strangeness on any number of levels: strange characters who make strange requests; incidents that defy rational explanation; appearances that don't conform to real-world expectations. Clive Barker is a master of strangeness. In his Hollywood—a place that's plenty strange enough!—the supernatural and the natural come face to face.

..................................TRY THIS....................................

Try your hand at a Hollywood ghost story. You might tell the story of an up-and-coming actor who is haunted by the ghost of the actor he or she most admires, with bizarre consequences.

DECEMBER 29

Failure Is Not an Option: Mission Control From Mercury to Apollo 13 and Beyond
by Gene Kranz

In the early afternoon of December 23 [1968], after a brief countdown, a Mission Control wall clock clicked over to 00:00:000—"all balls" in the controllers' idiom—and civilization crossed another boundary. Now only 30,000 miles from the Moon the Apollo 8 crew [Frank Borman, Jim Lovell, William Anders] had left Earth's gravity field. At 2:29 P.M. Central Standard Time, mankind for the first time was captured by the Moon's gravity. The celebration was brief; the pressure mounting, the controllers were already computing the critical lunar orbit insertion maneuver to be executed in fourteen hours. ... Borman had maneuvered Apollo to the burn attitude [engine firing position]. In the control room, the computers had been rechecked and the pregnant waiting continued ... As the final minutes counted down, cigarette smoke hovered above the consoles, the room silent.

"Apollo 8 you're looking good ... ten seconds to loss of signal."

After a quick "atta boy" from Bill Anders, the final words came from Jim Lovell: "We'll see you on the other side." To the split second, a burst of static marked the expected signal loss. The first humans to see the "far side" of the Moon were now on their own. It would be thirty-two minutes until we saw the crew again and we would know the maneuver result.

FOR FURTHER REFLECTION

Gene Kranz, the flight director for Mission Control, here tells the behind-the-scenes story of NASA's Mercury, Gemini, and Apollo launches, and elucidates the complex technology involved. One of the most memorable of these launches prior to the first landing on the moon (Apollo 11) or the extraordinary accident-recovery saga of Apollo 13, was Apollo 8's first manned mission to orbit the moon during Christmas 1968. Once the crew entered lunar orbit, Bill Anders read from the book of Genesis: "In the beginning God created the heaven and the earth. ..."

......................................TRY THIS....................................

Anders's reading from Genesis transfixed not only Mission Control, but the whole world. It was a coming together of scientific discovery, technological triumph, and spiritual epiphany. Write an essay in which you explore the connections between these concepts.

His Way: The Unauthorized Biography of Frank Sinatra

by Kitty Kelley

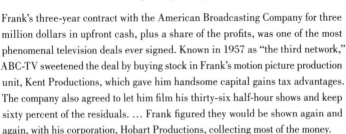

Frank's three-year contract with the American Broadcasting Company for three million dollars in upfront cash, plus a share of the profits, was one of the most phenomenal television deals ever signed. Known in 1957 as "the third network," ABC-TV sweetened the deal by buying stock in Frank's motion picture production unit, Kent Productions, which gave him handsome capital gains tax advantages. The company also agreed to let him film his thirty-six half-hour shows and keep sixty percent of the residuals. ... Frank figured they would be shown again and again, with his corporation, Hobart Productions, collecting most of the money.

"This guarantees me seven million dollars, and most of that will go into a trust fund for the children. For years I've been looking to get into a position to set aside money for them, and this is the one way I can do it."

The network gave Frank complete artistic control, allowing him to develop each show in his own way, a degree of freedom that was unheard of in television. ... With his records selling in the millions and his movies (*Johnny Concho, Meet Me in Las Vegas, High Society, Around the World in 80 Days*) box office successes, he was the number one star in Hollywood. ...

Yet, loathe to rehearse, Frank dashed off eleven shows in fifteen days, sailing through them with little attention to detail. At CBS [five years earlier] one show would have taken seven days to film, and the star would have been required to rehearse. At ABC Frank made his stand-in ... do the rehearsing while he simply jumped in at the last minute to do the filming.

FOR FURTHER REFLECTION

Frank Sinatra was a legend in his own time. His success is easily accounted for: He was a superbly gifted singer, actor, and all-around entertainer. His colorful and controversial involvement in politics, and with the mob, reinforced his iconic status. Sinatra, whose romantic music and engrossing screen presence captured the heart of what it meant to be alive, was himself larger than life.

......................................TRY THIS....................................

Research one of the many facets of Frank Sinatra for a magazine feature. Possible topics: Sinatra and his Rat Pack; Sinatra's influence on JFK's election; Sinatra the actor; Sinatra's singing style.

The Writer's Journey: Mythic Structure for Writers
by Christopher Vogler

At heart, despite its infinite variety, the hero's story is always a journey. A hero leaves her comfortable, ordinary surroundings to venture into a challenging, unfamiliar world. It may be an outward journey to an actual place: a labyrinth, forest or cave, a strange city or country, a new locale that becomes the arena for her conflict with antagonistic, challenging forces.

But there are as many stories that take the hero on an inward journey, one of the mind, the heart, the spirit. In any good story the hero grows and changes, making a journey from one way of being to the next: from despair to hope, weakness to strength, folly to wisdom, love to hate, and back again. It's these emotional journeys that hook an audience and make a story worth watching [or reading].

The stages of the Hero's Journey can be traced in all kinds of stories, not just those that feature "heroic" physical action and adventure. The protagonist of every story is the hero of a journey, even if the path leads only into his own mind or into the realm of relationships.

The way stations of the Hero's Journey emerge naturally even when the writer is unaware of them, but some knowledge of this most ancient guide to storytelling is useful in identifying problems and telling better stories.

FOR FURTHER REFLECTION

Writers, especially novelists and screenwriters, often assimilate the stages of the hero's journey into their novel or screenplay. Drawing from the archetypal story pattern of ancient myths as described by Joseph Campbell in *The Hero With a Thousand Faces*, the distinguished Hollywood story consultant Christopher Vogler shows writers how to construct a story using the twelve stages of the hero's journey, including the call to adventure, crossing the first threshold, facing enemies, suffering ordeals and setbacks, and the return home.

...................................TRY THIS....................................

Compose a synopsis of your novel using the twelve stages of the hero's journey Vogler lays out in *The Writer's Journey*. For example, in the first stage, the call to adventure, explain how and why your protagonist is called upon to embark on a difficult (perhaps seemingly impossible) journey, and the nature of his or her immediate response.

subject index

15 **Literature, 20th and 21st Centuries**

16 **Medicine and Health**

about the author

Fred White, a professor of English at Santa Clara University in Northern California, received his Ph.D. in English (emphasis on rhetoric and the teaching of writing) from the University of Iowa. In 1997, he received Santa Clara University's Louis and Dorina Brutocao Award for Teaching Excellence. He is the author of four textbooks on writing, the latest of which, *The Well-Crafted Argument*, co-authored with Simone Billings, will print its fourth edition in 2010 (Wadsworth/Cengage Learning). Other recent books include *The Daily Writer: 366 Meditations to Cultivate a Productive and Meaningful Writing Life* (Writer's Digest Books 2008); *LifeWriting: Drawing from Personal Experience to Create Features You Can Publish* (Quill Driver Books, 2004; a Writer's Digest Book Club Selection); *Essential Muir: A Selection of John Muir's Best Writings* (Heyday Books, 2006); and *Approaching Emily Dickinson: Critical Currents and Crosscurrents Since 1960* (Camden House, 2008). He has also published numerous shorter works—most recently a one-act children's play, *Beowulf & Grendel*—an adaptation of the great Anglo-Saxon epic (Big Dog Plays, 2007); a full-length play, *Bones*, based on the life of the poet John Berryman (Oregon Literary Review, 2005); plus essays, short fiction, and poetry in *The Cambridge Companion to Emily Dickinson*, edited by Wendy Martin (Cambridge University Press, 2002); *The Chronicle of Higher Education*; *College Literature*; *Confrontation*; *Pleiades*; *Rattle*; *The San Jose Mercury News*; and *South Carolina Review*. He lives in San Mateo, California, with his wife, Therese (an attorney), and their insubordinate cat, Cordelia.